MOVING TOWARD JUSTICE

Moving Toward Justice

Legal Traditions and Aboriginal Justice

Edited by

John D. Whyte

Published by
PURICH PUBLISHING LIMITED
Saskatoon, Saskatchewan, in association with the
SASKATCHEWAN INSTITUTE OF PUBLIC POLICY
University of Regina, Regina, Saskatchewan.

Purich Publishing Ltd.
Box 23032, Market Mall Post Office, Saskatoon, SK, Canada, S7J 5H3
Phone: (306) 373-5311 Fax: (306) 373-5315 Email: purich@sasktel.net
Website: www.purichpublishing.com

Library and Archives Canada Cataloguing in Publication

Moving toward justice : legal traditions and Aboriginal justice / edited by John D. Whyte.

(Purich's aboriginal issues series)
Proceedings of a conference held in Regina, SK, Mar. 1-3, 2006.
Includes index.
ISBN 978-1-895830-33-0

1. Native peoples – Legal status, laws, etc. – Canada. 2. Justice, Administration of – Canada. I. Whyte, John D., 1940- II. Series.

KE7708.M68 2008   342.7108'72   C2008-900430-2

Published in association with the Saskatchewan Institute of Public Policy (SIPP), University of Regina, Regina, Sask., Canada

Edited and indexed by Ursula Acton.
Designed and typeset by Donald Ward.
Cover design by Duncan Campbell.
Printed and bound in Canada.

Purich Publishing gratefully acknowledges the assistance of the Government of Canada through the Book Publishing Industry Development Program and the Government of Saskatchewan through the Cultural Industries Development Fund for its publishing program.

This book is printed on 100 per cent post-consumer, recycled, ancient-forest-friendly paper.

CONTENTS

PART II: CHALLENGES OF FIRST NATIONS AND MÉTIS JUSTICE

Foreword

Tony Penikett

This book is a collection of essays on Aboriginal justice, a phrase that represents more than one concept. It may refer to the experience of Aboriginal people and Aboriginal communities in the Canadian justice system. It may describe systems of justice and accountability that are rooted in Aboriginal societies and could be reconstructed and reinstituted. It sometimes refers to the collective rights of Aboriginal peoples in the Canadian constitutional and legal system. Most challengingly, it might mean the justice – or injustice – of the social conditions experienced on a daily basis by Aboriginal people in Canada. All of these perspectives on Aboriginal justice are reflected in this book, where they are subjected to a variety of analyses – legal, social, developmental, political, administrative, and comparative.

For a non-academic, what is notable about these essays is their veiled passion, evident in two forms. For the most part, these pieces argue for a radical – or at least transformative – change in the ways that Aboriginal people experience justice and view the justice system. Frequently, their authors argue for recognition of an Aboriginal entitlement to be self-determining with respect to the instruments of Aboriginal social health. Second, the majority of the essays recognize the unbearable injustice that Canada's Aboriginal people and communities face. These writers argue for legal rights, social rights, administrative rights, equality rights, and political rights that would begin to create a path away from acute social injury and past cruel indifference.

I want to underscore the hidden passion of these essays by stating clearly the enormity of the justice challenge in this country. Aboriginal people are not the only group to face daily systemic oppression, but they are disproportionately represented among the other marginalized groups who do. Often, this kind of injustice is undeniably a matter of life and death.

In 1988 there were fewer than 20 drug overdose deaths in Vancouver, British Columbia. By 1993 there were ten times that many. During the same period, the incidence of HIV infection among injection drug users in Vancouver's Downtown Eastside climbed to alarming levels. Neither the drug deaths nor the HIV data provoked any governmental action.

In the mid-nineties, an employee of a Vancouver juice bar was diagnosed with Hepatitis A, a highly communicable disease. Overnight, the health care system responded. Ads appeared in local papers advising any at-risk customer to report immediately for tests and, if necessary, treatment. In Vancouver's Downtown Eastside, six blocks away, people were dropping dead on the sidewalks, in coffee shop washrooms, and in back alleys. Yet the authorities were silent. No newspaper advertisements appeared, and no emergency facilities emerged to deal with this public health crisis. Instead, it took years for the political and health systems to respond with initiatives such as a supervised drug injection site.

With federal and provincial support, Vancouver's safe injection site has saved numerous lives. But rumours abound that Canada's Conservative government will close the site in favour of a "law and order" approach to drugs. If the Conservatives continue to treat addiction as a crime, not a health issue, many more sick people will die. This is not justice.

The 14 November 2007 edition of the *Globe and Mail* carried two stories about individuals who had died at the hands of Canadian police officers. One story described how four RCMP officers with a taser gun killed a unilingual Polish immigrant, Robert Dziekanski, at the Vancouver International Airport – the eighteenth taser-related fatality in Canada. After the media broadcast a video of the incident around the world, the public outcry led the province to order an independent inquiry. The second death covered in the newspaper that day was that of a 47-year-old Mi'kmaq alcoholic, Frank Joseph Paul. Paul had been dragged out of the city jail in Vancouver and dumped in a back alley on a cold December night. Nine years passed before an independent inquiry into Paul's death began. A Vancouver police department representative conceded at the inquiry that Frank Paul had been "ill-served."

In this volume, Thomas Isaac writes compellingly about the Supreme Court of Canada's balancing of the rule of law and the rights of Aboriginal peoples. However, as these *Globe and Mail* stories suggest, a tragic imbalance persists in the way our institutions deal with death. Some deaths are presented as catastrophic. The November 14 edition of the *Globe and Mail* also covered the funeral of RCMP Constable Doug Scott. Constable Scott was shot while on duty in Kimmirut on Baffin Island. Thousands, including mounted police officers, motorcycle escorts, and local dignitaries, attended the constable's funeral in Brockville, Ontario.

Other deaths – those of the poor, the powerless, and the Aboriginal – are business as usual. The world knows about the Aboriginal women from the Downtown Eastside who were murdered and whose mutilated bodies were buried on a suburban pig farm. Yet, those whom the BC Government seeks to lure to the province for the 2010 Winter Olympics know almost nothing of the world of hurt that exists here. That police ignored information about the plight of women taken from the streets of Vancouver for years is shameful enough. But members of other groups – addicts, mental patients, working-class people, and the poor, among all of them many Aboriginals – have suffered violent death at the hands of the police.

On average, police kill three people a year in British Columbia. Vancouver police officers shot 17 people to death between 1980 and 2005. Perhaps half of the victims were mentally ill, yet the force does not require officers to learn alternative or non-violent conflict resolution techniques.[1] Truly independent investigations never follow such events. Police officers investigate police officers, and, evidently, police officers are never held criminally responsible for taking life.

The police justify their multiple roles as judge, jury, and executioner through resort to the murky authority of section 25 of the *Criminal Code*, which sanctions deadly force to protect officers from "death or grievous bodily harm." A non-lawyer like me wonders how these killings can ever be, in the ordinary sense of the word, constitutional.

Canada abolished capital punishment in 1976. Our laws grant no power over life and death to the prime minister or to the Cabinet or, indeed, to the country's highest court. Yet the Canadian record shows that we permit police officers to take the lives of mental patients, addicts, and Aboriginals. There is no appeal after a police bullet to the brain. Restorative justice cannot reach out to a victim's family or friends. And, it seems, political leaders will not join the lament for these dead. This is not justice.

Merrilee Rasmussen and other contributors to *Moving Toward Justice* discuss how much has been done, albeit slowly, to address the issues of rights and title, treaty needs, and self-government deficits on tribal homelands. Since 1982, the courts have been defining the boundaries of section 35, and federal, territorial, provincial, and First Nation governments have negotiated agreements to reconcile their competing views about the governance of tribal lands. But, in truth, little has been achieved where most native peoples now live – in the ghettos of six western Canadian cities. The federal government spends $8 billion annually on Aboriginal programs, but only a small fraction of that goes to urban Aboriginal populations.

At the heart of this injustice is the politically induced poverty of Aboriginal people. Thousands of them live in Vancouver, yet the Aboriginal population has no Aboriginal MP, MLA, or city councillor. In Vancouver's Eastside, one observes many acts of kindness among individuals in the neighbourhood, but these individuals exercise no governance over their community. Recently, as chair of a meeting on homelessness with Miloon Kothari, United Nations Special Rapporteur on Adequate Housing, I heard numerous powerful, passionate, even poetic pitches for housing as a basic human right. That it took Kothari, an architect from India, to bring out these voices, and a local community-based organization to create a safe space for the hearing, seems rather remarkable, and somewhat unjust.

Of course, self-government by and for urban Aboriginal communities is easier said than done. The struggles for land and governance of the First Nations, whose territory Vancouver straddles, are largely unresolved. Competing provincial and municipal claims for jurisdiction frustrate negotiations on these questions. Unless and until urban reserves are created in Vancouver's Eastside – or in any of our country's other large urban Aboriginal communities – the best that might be achieved are co-operative management regimes, delegated administrative arrangements, or perhaps even multi-party Aboriginal social service agencies.

No inner-city organization can yet claim legitimacy as the sole political representative of urban Aboriginal populations in discussions around these political options. However, nothing prevents the federal government or the provincial government from funding facilitators to initiate community dialogues that will lead to the creation of basic institutions of urban Aboriginal governance. And nothing stops governments from recognizing and declaring that greater self-governance powers for urban Aboriginal populations are the best hope for healthier communities. That would be justice.

Building a just society on Vancouver's Hastings Street, in Winnipeg's North End, or in the Aboriginal majority areas of Prince Albert, Regina, and Saskatoon will demand more than this, including real political authority and generous transfers. But acknowledgement of the need to recognize governance over, for instance, schools, housing, police, and social care, would be the right place to start.

The essays collected in *Moving Toward Justice* include commendable and considered analyses of the challenges of legal pluralism, restorative justice, gender and race in sentencing, generative conceptions of Aboriginal rights, notions of community, and reconciliation in Aboriginal justice. These issues, too, are a good place to start the social reformation that is needed. But justice, as ordinary folk see it, requires that political actors, not just lawyers, judges, and academics, press against the existing injustice in public debates and push onto governmental agendas the changes that will build actual, politically enabled communities. Only when we overcome our willful blindness to injustice and our resistance to change can we claim to be moving toward justice.

INTRODUCTION

John D. Whyte

The theme of moving toward justice that informs the chapters of this book is double-faceted. It suggests both the idea of creating a just situation for Aboriginal people and communities of Canada and the idea that legal processes that bear on Aboriginal Canadians must be developed and applied in light of the unique and special circumstances of Aboriginal peoples. These two ideas – the ideas of justice for Aboriginal people and the need for instruments of justice that are responsive to Aboriginal people – are seemingly rooted in two discrete realms of public policy: constitutional law and the administration of justice. They are, however, closely linked through both the overarching concepts of self-determination and intersocietal respect and the practices of social development. The opposites of self-determination and respect are subjugation and exclusion, and the resultant loss of social capacity, dignity, purpose, identity, and self-respect. The infliction of these losses on a discrete people is an injustice that must be challenged again and again until cries for justice create a political imperative and calls for reform through which recovery will flow forms our common policy.

The essays that comprise the chapters of this book are not themselves these cries for justice, nor for the most part do they chart specific reforms. What they do offer are considered critical analyses of how we can cast, through constitutionalism, law, and public administration, the kind of the intersocietal relationship between Aboriginal and non-Aboriginal peoples that will lead to social development. They explore developments that, it is believed, will facilitate an improved relationship and they criticize structures that have impeded development. There is an undoubtedly normative political perspective to be found in these essays: at the heart of the ineffectiveness of current Aboriginal policies in establishing respectful relations between Aboriginal and non-Aboriginal communities and in developing communities marked by confidence and social well-being is the failure to recognize that positive public policy for

Aboriginal peoples must be based on Aboriginal initiatives developed through Aboriginal governments. Nations, of course, prefer not to conceive of themselves as mere aggregates of sub-state groups, each one of which fashions for itself crucial channels of social and economic redemption. Yet, that is a central condition of Canada. While Canada is not without its national pride, national symbols, and national projects, its most pressing challenge is to recognize the essential value of community autonomy for those peoples for whom the promise of continuing distinctiveness has become a national undertaking.

It is not just promises, however, that are being spoken of. There is also a justice claim. When there is a serious social need, the nation must respond in ways that are effective. This may not be the application of common remedies but the development of policies that meet the needs of safety, self governance, dignity, and well-being. These goals cannot be successfully pursued through apathy – the apathy of state actors who do not feel responsible for social failures or the apathy of communities which do not recognize their voices and values in programs of social development. Thomas Gordon, a community development writer, has said: "No-one is apathetic except in pursuit of someone else's goals."[1] This claim has profound implications for the course of Aboriginal policy in Canada. It is a claim that lurks in the analyses of many essays in this book.

With respect to the specific matters of legal process and the administration of justice which are the focus of the second half of this book, there is, perhaps, a less overt claim for political self-determination, but there can be no mistaking the theme in these essays that distinct peoples need clear recognition, special powers, and unique instruments in order to sustain their integrity and to engage in governance that will lead to strong and respected communities. Naturally, in the matter of justice innovation, it is the dramatic challenge of sustaining social order – the business of criminal justice – that most commands the attention of both analysts and innovators, and this is reflected in these essays. While rate of offending is only one of the manifestations of poverty, despair and exclusion, it is the one that commands a lion's share of attention. To the credit of many within Canada's criminal justice community, that disorder is widely recognized as not simply a function of the lack of, for instance, culturally aware policing, or of restorative responses to offending. It is seen as a function of a host of other, more complex, social causes. The one that seems most to compel criminal justice reform is the deep alienation between Aboriginal people and the state instruments of criminal justice. This condition includes the uncertain legacy and, hence, the uncertain legitimacy of the institutions by which in Canada we promote social order.

The implication of this for criminal justice policy is the pressing need to construct responses to social harming that attract broad-based community trust and confidence. This may include improving relations between police and communities, creating culturally sensitive courts, establishing sentencing regimes that recognize difference, developing tribal correctional institutions, adopting Aboriginal precepts of healing and community restoration, conducting community-based processes of truth and reconciliation, or creating First Nation police services and Aboriginal police commissions. But, perhaps, what is required is more than this – self-governing communities with full capacity to develop mechanisms to promote social order and respond to social disorder. The essays in this book do not attempt to cover the broad array of reform mechanisms. Nor do they insist on innovations that must be adopted or political accommodations that must be made. Instead, they represent a tentative evaluation of the innovations that are now emerging and of the spirit that lies behind them. Their aim is not to fix justice in and for Aboriginal communities but to explore the conditions under which communities will grow safer and healthier and in this they reflect the agenda of political recognition as the condition by which self-respecting communities can live in mutually supportive ways.

The essays in Part I of this volume examine the broader context for Aboriginal development – that is, political development and, consequently, the development of self-administered justice mechanisms. All of these essays make the case that Canada in its jurisprudence, actual governance practices, and scholarly understanding of Aboriginal rights is unquestionably moving toward recognition of Aboriginal communities as rights-bearing entities, entitled to act collectively and destined, through their own governance institutions, to form intergovernmental relationships. Brian Slattery provides a comprehensive survey of how the Supreme Court of Canada is now articulating and vindicating First Nations and Métis constitutional rights. It is evident that the Supreme Court has a dynamic understanding of the content of Aboriginal rights, and has also engendered dynamism in the relationship between the Aboriginal polity and the jurisdictions of the Canadian state. What is also clear in this work – and in almost every essay in this part – is that the basic concept of Aboriginal self-determination exists within the current Canadian constitutional regime, and its effective realization requires neither major constitutional reform nor bold claims of sovereignty and secession.

Merrilee Rasmussen's essay argues bluntly for Aboriginal self-determination as a development that will assist in preventing social dysfunction. She bases her claim for self-government on already-established instruments of our constitutional order and on mechanisms of group empowerment that have already been fully developed in our legal system.

Martin Blanchard, pursuing a similarly pragmatic approach, argues that recent treaty negotiations – although often analyzed in the high concepts of autonomy for distinct societies and the right of minorities to preserve cultural identity – in fact create new operational relationships under which devolution to new governance institutions, resource sharing, land co-management, powers for sustaining cultural integrity, and responsibility for economic development are all accepted. In the end, new treaties are less an expression of political philosophy and more a practical manifestation of intersocietal equality. He concludes by arguing that their success depends on good-faith implementation.

Dwight Newman's eloquent recognition of the multi-faceted and challenging task of realizing justice in intersocietal arrangements begins with an exploration of the ubiquitous concept (in Aboriginal rights cases) of reconciliation. That idea has been used both to require accommodation of Aboriginal entitlements and to limit Aboriginal rights. It has been used in the process of judicial definition of entitlements and as the basis for the requirement of political negotiation. Notwithstanding its exigent role, Newman defends the concept as reaching toward something that is vital to our accommodation of the complexities that lie within the Constitution's commitments to justice.

Thomas Isaac explores the tension between the rule of law and its attendant idea of a single source of valid legal rules, and legal pluralism or the idea that laws in a nation can flow from diverse communities and diverse regimes of ordering. The former view establishes too rigid a rule for the recognition of laws, while the latter view is sometimes seen to threaten the authority of the state. Isaac, however, maintains that a stark choice between these paradigms is not essential. Drawing on the Supreme Court's concept of merged sovereignty, he describes the convergence of these concepts that flows from incorporating Aboriginal peoples' normative regimes within the broad context of the Canadian legal framework.

John Whyte weaves together a myriad of historical and legal considerations, and social development theories, to show why Aboriginal claims for more extensive recognition of political autonomy are compelling. He argues for a bold approach to self-government.

More specific challenges that are faced in developing justice systems that meet the needs of First Nations and Métis communities are explored in Part II. Stephanie Irlbacher-Fox's critical essay focusses on the lessons to be learned from the *Inuvialuit and Gwich'in Self-Government Agreement in Principle* and its implementation. She concludes that the elements of forced reliance on public government to make self-government effective and the fragmentation of Aboriginal authority, both of which are present in the administration of justice provisions of the self-government agreement, have largely defeated its underlying purposes. Since there was no actual shared conception of the self-government right, the result is embedded restrictions and controls that undermine that right and prevent realization of the goals of decreasing state interference in the lives of Aboriginal peoples and restoring their dignity.

Two essays look explicitly at criminal justice and Aboriginal peoples. Margot Hurlbert and John McKenzie, after providing a theoretical background, examine the practical changes that have been made to policing and court practices. They evaluate changes from the perspective of crime reduction, removing systemic discrimination and government responses to notorious cases of justice mismanagement. While they are sceptical of claims for significant improvements, including scepticism over the sufficiency of restorative justice to effect major improvement, they acknowledge the positive reality of the state's justice system working hard at adapting its methods in order to move toward the goals of social order and fairness. Angela Cameron's paper looks at Canada's special sentencing standard for Aboriginal people and at the experience of women under it. Her assessment is unequivocal; the consequences, for women, of sentencing under the *Criminal Code* are inappropriately harsh. Judges and defence counsel do not often enough take account of the gendered impact of colonialism on Aboriginal women, and this failure defeats the specific requirements of the *Gladue* decision and the *Code*. It is time, she argues, that the progress made in applying cultural and social awareness to the sentencing of Aboriginal offenders be extended to understanding the different historical experience and present condition of Aboriginal women.

Barbara Tomporowski takes as her starting point what is perhaps the single most promising element of justice reform as it affects Aboriginal peoples: the extensive development of community justice mechanisms in Aboriginal communities through which to respond to offending according to restorative justice goals and with processes designed to heal ruptured trust between offenders and victims. These innovations are designed to pick up on, and validate, Indigenous peoples' values and methods for nurturing social health and order. But, as this essay points out, these positive intentions can be undermined by state funding mechanisms and structures of accountability that fail to take account of communities' complexities and needs. This sensitive paper is careful not to condemn either side of what can be an Aboriginal/non-Aboriginal gulf, but urges better understandings of each other's needs.

INTRODUCTION

Bill Rafoss's essay tackles the challenging question of whether governmental action (legislative or executive) taken by First Nations' governments should be subject to the constitutional constraints of the *Canadian Charter of Rights and Freedoms*. This issue arises both as a matter of interpreting the constitutional text and as a matter of giving appropriate respect to cultural and legal pluralism. Rafoss, however, claims that the real question is what rights-respecting limitations should First Nations' governments accept for themselves. His recommendation is against a definite and imposed application of the *Charter*, but urges First Nations to adopt human rights regimes that match national and international norms and reflect the values and wishes of their own people.

Winifred Kamau lifts the discussion of Aboriginal justice to the international plane by examining the experience with legal pluralism in independent African states, particularly Kenya. Her conclusions are startlingly pertinent to Canada. First, the goal behind legal pluralism is not primarily regime integrity but real justice for all. Second, the persistence of Indigenous ordering norms represents a compelling case for recognition because it matches law to actual social expectations. Third, justice administration and law are part and parcel of community development, and, if they are forcefully held apart, social development is very likely to be undermined. Finally, state law and Indigenous systems cannot be treated as competitors; they need to work through mutually supportive interaction so that cultural values and justice values merge.

These essays neither exhaust the topic of Aboriginal justice nor even capture all – or most – of its salient issues. They suggest themes: themes for discussion and debate; themes that suggest channels of transformation; themes that promote the political visions of diversity, cultural recognition, and pluralism; and, most important of all, themes that promote real justice for Aboriginal peoples.

The provenance of three quarters of the essays in this volume was a lively and successful conference held in Regina, Saskatchewan, in March 2006, "Moving Towards Justice: Legal Traditions and Aboriginal and Canadian Justice." The conference was organized by the Saskatchewan Institute of Public Policy (SIPP) and the First Nations University of Canada.

The conference's success was due to the high quality of speakers and participants, the extensive planning assistance provided by Professor Lorena Fontaine of the First Nations University of Canada, the fine organizational work of the staff at the Saskatchewan Institute of Public Policy, and generous grants from the Department of Justice Canada; Saskatchewan Justice (now Ministry of Justice and Attorney General); Saskatchewan First Nations and Métis

Relations; the University of Regina; the Law Foundation of Saskatchewan; the Law Foundation of Ontario; Harvard Developments Inc.; SaskTel; Sask Learning (now Ministry of Education); Sask Community Resources (now Ministry of Social Services); Gerrand Rath Johnson; MacPherson, Leslie & Tyerman LLP; Blake, Cassels & Graydon; The Information Institute; The Canada Research Chair in Social Justice at the University of Regina; and the Indigenous People's Fund at the University of Regina.

This publication has been partially funded by a further generous grant from the Law Foundation of Saskatchewan. Preparation of the book has been in the tremendously able hands of Elsa Johnston and Sharri Dewey of the SIPP publication team.

Three papers have been added to the conference papers to make this collection. They are by Brian Slattery, John Whyte, and Angela Cameron. Brian Slattery delivered a paper at the conference; what is included here is a considerably elaborated version of his conference paper. This version was originally published in Volume 38 of the Supreme Court Law Review and we acknowledge the graciousness of LexisNexis Canada, Inc. in giving permission to include it in this collection.

There were many fine sessions at the conference that did not result in papers for publication. These included talks by Chief Justice Emeritus Robert G. Yazzie of the Navajo Nation, Professor John Borrows of the University of Victoria, and Professor J. Edward Chamberlin of the University of Toronto. Their wonderful presentations gave to the conference its spirit of hope and optimism.

The conference was chaired by Judge Mary Ellen Turpel-Lafond, then of the Saskatchewan Provincial Court, and the Honourable Roy Romanow, former Premier of Saskatchewan. By virtue of their sure and gracious management and their inspiring contributions the conference was also marked by the spirit of resolution and reconciliation.

Perhaps the most significant conference session in terms of galvanizing concern, outrage, and resolve with respect to the justice experience of many Aboriginal people in Canada was a panel on the victimization of Aboriginal women. This moving session was led by Chief Marie-Ann Day Walker Pelletier of the Okanese First Nation. This book is dedicated to the memory of those Aboriginal women of Canada who have been insufficiently protected by our system of justice, and, in particular, to "missing women" – women who have been abducted, violated, and murdered.

PART ONE

THE LEGAL AND POLITICAL CONTEXT
FOR ABORIGINAL JUSTICE

1

THE GENERATIVE STRUCTURE
OF ABORIGINAL RIGHTS[*]

Brian Slattery[†]

I. INTRODUCTION

Are Aboriginal rights historical rights – rights that gained their basic form in the distant past? Or are they generative rights – rights that, although rooted in the past, have the capacity to renew themselves, as organic entities that grow and change? Section 35(1) of the *Constitution Act, 1982*,[1] provides little guidance on the point, referring ambiguously to "existing aboriginal and treaty rights."[2] In the *Van der Peet* case,[3] decided in 1996, the Supreme Court of Canada characterized Aboriginal rights primarily as historical rights, moulded by the customs and practices of Aboriginal groups at the time of European contact, with only a modest ability to evolve. However, as a brief review of the Court's reasoning reveals, this approach left much to be desired.

In his majority opinion, Antonio Lamer C.J. holds that section 35(1) is animated by two main purposes: recognition and reconciliation.[4] With respect to the first, he argues that the doctrine of Aboriginal rights exists because of one simple fact: when Europeans arrived in North America, Aboriginal peoples were already here, living in communities on the land, and participating in distinctive cultures, as they had done for centuries. It is this fact that distinguishes Aboriginal peoples from all other groups in Canadian society and mandates their special legal and constitutional status.

[*]   Reprinted with permission of the publisher from Volume 38, *Supreme Court Law Review* (Second Series) (LexisNexis Canada Inc., 2007).

[†]   I am indebted to John Borrows, Willy Fournier, Shin Imai, Kent McNeil, Tom Marshall, and Jeremy Webber for their generous comments on earlier versions of this chapter.

So a major purpose of section 35(1) is to recognize the prior occupation of Aboriginal peoples.[5]

However, recognition is not the sole purpose of the section, which also aims to secure reconciliation between Indigenous peoples and the Crown. Chief Justice Lamer notes that the essence of Aboriginal rights lies in their bridging of Aboriginal and non-Aboriginal cultures, so that the law of Aboriginal rights is neither entirely English nor entirely Aboriginal in origin: it is a form of intersocietal law that evolved from long-standing practices linking the various communities together.[6]

In light of these two fundamental goals, Lamer C.J. proceeds to craft the following test for Aboriginal rights. In order for an activity to qualify as an Aboriginal right, it must be an element of a practice, custom, or tradition that was integral to the distinctive culture of a particular Aboriginal group in the period prior to European contact.[7] If a practice only arose after the critical date of contact, it cannot be an Aboriginal right. Although pre-contact practices are capable of evolving and adapting somewhat to modern conditions, they must maintain continuity with their ancient roots.[8] Applying this test to the case at hand, Lamer C.J. holds that the pre-contact practice of fishing for food and ceremonial purposes, with limited exchanges of fish in the familial and kinship context, cannot evolve into a modern Aboriginal right to exchange fish for money or other goods.[9]

Several features of this approach merit comment. First, the *Van der Peet* test assumes that Aboriginal rights are shaped entirely by factors particular to each Indigenous group – that they are specific rights rather than generic rights. Chief Justice Lamer rejects the notion that Aboriginal rights make up a range of abstract legal categories with normative underpinnings, opting instead for the view that Aboriginal rights assume a myriad of particular forms, as moulded by the distinctive customs of the specific groups in question.[10] In effect, the test suggests that identifying Aboriginal rights is a largely descriptive matter – an exercise in historical ethnography. The judge plays the role of ethnohistorian, attempting to discern the distinctive features of Aboriginal societies in the distant reaches of Canadian history. He need not trouble himself with normative questions – such as whether these features merit recognition as constitutional rights and, if so, what basic purposes they serve.

Second, the *Van der Peet* test looks exclusively to conditions prevailing in the remote past – the era prior to the critical date of European contact – which may be as much as 500 years ago.[11] The test excludes many activities that became central to the lives of Aboriginal peoples in the post-contact period and that linked them socially and economically to neighbouring settler communities.

Not surprisingly, it tends to yield rights that have a limited ability to serve the modern needs of Aboriginal peoples and may also fit uneasily with third-party and broader societal interests.

Third, the test makes no reference whatever to the extensive relations that developed between the Indigenous peoples and incoming Europeans in the post-contact period, or to the legal principles that informed those relations. While the Court pays lip service to the view that Aboriginal rights are grounded in an intersocietal law that bridges Aboriginal and non-Aboriginal cultures, it does not assign this idea any real role in the *Van der Peet* test, which looks entirely to the period before settlers arrived and intersocietal relationships were formed.

So, while Lamer C.J. identifies both recognition and reconciliation as the underlying goals of section 35(1), in practice he focusses mainly on the goal of recognition – that is, the identification of the central attributes of Aboriginal societies in the period before European contact. He does not take into account the historical modes of reconciliation that occurred when the Crown established relations with Indigenous peoples, nor does he consider the need for new modes of reconciliation today. The result is that Aboriginal rights are identified in an almost mechanical manner, without regard to the contemporary needs of Aboriginal peoples, the rights and interests of other affected groups, or the welfare of the body politic as a whole.

Nevertheless, in the decade since the *Van der Peet* case was decided, the Supreme Court has shown mounting signs of discomfort with the test laid down there. In a series of important decisions, it has quietly initiated the process of reshaping the test's basic tenets. This process has taken place on three fronts. First, the Court has relaxed its exclusive focus on specific rights – rights distinctive to particular Aboriginal groups – and allowed for the existence of generic rights – uniform rights that operate at an abstract level and reflect broader normative considerations. Second, the Court has recognized that the date of European contact is not an appropriate reference point in all contexts and looked increasingly to the period when the Crown gained sovereignty and effective control. Finally, the Court has placed ever-greater emphasis on the need for Aboriginal rights to be defined by negotiations between the parties, tacitly signalling that Aboriginal rights are flexible and future-oriented, rather than mere relics of the past. Here I take stock of the matter and argue that these trends presage the birth of a new constitutional paradigm, in which Aboriginal rights are viewed as generative and not merely historical rights.[12]

II. Specific and Generic Rights

As just noted, in *Van der Peet* the Supreme Court expressed the view that all Aboriginal rights are specific rights – rights whose nature and scope are determined by the particular circumstances of each individual Aboriginal group.[13] However, this generalization proved to be premature. No more than a year was to pass before it was quietly discarded by the Court. The occasion was the *Delgamuukw* case,[14] in which the Gitksan and Wet'suwet'en peoples claimed Aboriginal title over their traditional homelands in northern British Columbia. In contesting the claim, the governmental parties maintained that there was no such thing as Aboriginal title in the sense of a uniform legal estate with fixed attributes. Rather, Aboriginal title was just a bundle of specific rights, whose contents varied from group to group. Each component in a group's bundle had to be proven independently. In effect, the group had to show that the particular activity in question was an element of a practice, custom, or tradition integral to its culture at the time of European contact. This argument was a logical extension of the approach taken in *Van der Peet*. Nevertheless, the Supreme Court rejected the argument and held that Aboriginal title gives an Indigenous group the exclusive right to use and occupy its ancestral lands for a broad range of purposes, which do not need to be rooted in the group's historical practices.[15] So, a group that originally lived by hunting, fishing, and gathering would be free to farm the land, raise cattle on it, exploit its natural resources, or use it for residential, commercial, or industrial purposes, subject to the limitation that the group cannot ruin the land or render it unusable for its original purposes.

The crucial point to note is that *Delgamuukw* treats Aboriginal title as a uniform right, whose dimensions do not vary significantly from group to group according to their historic patterns of life. Aboriginal title is not a specific right of the kind envisaged in *Van der Peet*, or even a bundle of specific rights. It is a generic right – a right of a standardized character that takes the same basic form wherever it occurs. The fundamental contours of the right are determined by the common law rather than the distinctive circumstances of each group.

How can this discrepancy in approach between *Delgamuukw* and *Van der Peet* be explained? As we will now see, the conflict is more apparent than real.

III. THE PANOPLY OF GENERIC RIGHTS

Recall that in *Van der Peet* the Court holds that Aboriginal groups have the right to engage in practices, customs, and traditions that are integral to their distinctive historical cultures. To be "integral" to a particular culture, a practice must be a central and significant part of the culture, one of the things that make the society what it is. If we consider this holding in the light of *Delgamuukw*, we can see that *Van der Peet* also recognizes a generic right – namely the right of Aboriginal peoples to maintain and develop the central and significant elements of their ancestral cultures.

In the abstract, this right has a fixed and uniform character, which does not change from one Aboriginal group to another. Each and every group has the same right – to maintain and develop the central elements of its ancestral culture. Of course, what is "central and significant" varies from society to society in accordance with its particular circumstances, so that at the concrete level the abstract right blossoms into a range of distinctive rights – a matter to be discussed later. The point to grasp here is that the abstract right itself is uniform. Like Aboriginal title, it constitutes a generic right – what we may call the right of cultural integrity.[16]

So now we have two generic rights: Aboriginal title and the right of cultural integrity. Are there still others? A little reflection shows that the answer is yes.[17] Here is a tentative list of generic Aboriginal rights, which includes the two just considered:

- the right to an ancestral territory (Aboriginal title);

- the right of cultural integrity;

- the right to conclude treaties;

- the right to customary law;

- the right to honourable treatment by the Crown; and

- the right of self-government.

While this list is not necessarily definitive or complete, it represents a fair estimate of the current state of the jurisprudence. I will say a few words about the last four rights, not yet discussed.

It has long been recognized that Aboriginal peoples have the right to conclude binding treaties with the Crown, a right reflected in the wording of section 35 itself.[18] Under Canadian common law, the treaty-making capacity of Aboriginal groups has a uniform character, which does not vary from group to group. The capacity of the Saanich Nation is the same as that of the Huron Nation. As such, the right to conclude treaties qualifies as a generic Aboriginal right.

Aboriginal peoples also have the right to maintain and develop their systems of customary law.[19] The introduction of French and English laws did not supersede Indigenous laws, which continued to operate within their respective spheres. As McLachlin J. observed in *Van der Peet*:

> The history of the interface of Europeans and the common law with aboriginal peoples is a long one. . . . Yet running through this history, from its earliest beginnings to the present time is a golden thread – the recognition by the common law of the ancestral laws and customs [of] the aboriginal peoples who occupied the land prior to European settlement.[20]

The right of Aboriginal peoples to maintain their own laws is a generic right, whose basic scope is determined by the common law doctrine of Aboriginal rights. The abstract right does not differ from group to group, even though the particular legal systems protected by the right obviously differ in content.

Aboriginal peoples also have the right to honourable treatment by the Crown. As the Supreme Court stated in the *Sparrow* case:

> . . . the Government has the responsibility to act in a fiduciary capacity with respect to aboriginal peoples. The relationship between the Government and aboriginals is trust-like, rather than adversarial, and contemporary recognition and affirmation of aboriginal rights must be defined in light of this historic relationship.[21]

Although the Court was referring here to section 35(1) of the *Constitution Act, 1982*, subsequent Supreme Court decisions have confirmed that the Crown's responsibility is not confined to this context but accompanies and controls the discretionary powers that the Crown historically has assumed over the lives of Aboriginal peoples.[22]

At the most abstract level, the right to honourable treatment by the Crown is a generic right, which vests uniformly in Aboriginal peoples across Canada. The point was underlined in the *Haida Nation* case,[23] where McLachlin C.J. held that the honour of the Crown is always at stake in its dealings with Aboriginal peoples. The Court explained that the Crown has the general duty to determine, recognize, and respect the rights of Aboriginal peoples over whom it has asserted sovereignty. This binds the Crown to enter into treaty negotiations in order to reconcile Aboriginal rights and achieve a just settlement. Pending the conclusion of such treaties, the Crown is obliged to consult with Aboriginal peoples before doing things that may affect their asserted rights, and to accommodate these rights where necessary. In situations where the Crown has assumed discretionary control over specific Aboriginal interests, the honour of the Crown gives rise to fiduciary duties, which require the Crown to act with reference to the Aboriginal group's best interests in exercising its discretion.[24] In effect, then, the abstract right to honourable treatment gives rise to a range of more precise rights and duties that attach to specific subject matters in particular contexts.

Finally, Aboriginal peoples have the right to govern themselves as a third order of government within the federal constitutional framework of Canada.[25] This right finds its source in the Crown's recognition that it could not secure the amity of Indigenous nations without acknowledging their right to manage their own affairs. As Lamer J. noted in the *Sioui* case,[26] the Crown treated Indian nations with generosity and respect out of the fear that the safety and development of British colonies would otherwise be compromised:

> The British Crown recognized that the Indians had certain ownership rights over their land, it sought to establish trade with them which would rise above the level of exploitation and give them a fair return. It also allowed them autonomy in their internal affairs, intervening in this area as little as possible.[27]

It is submitted that the right of self-government is a generic right, which recognizes a uniform set of governmental powers held by Aboriginal peoples as a distinct order of government within the Canadian federal system. At the same time, it allows Aboriginal groups to establish and maintain their own constitutions, which take a variety of forms. There are parallels here with the provinces, which are vested with a uniform set of governmental powers, but also have distinctive constitutions, which they have the power to amend.[28]

It might be argued that the Aboriginal right of self-government is not a generic right but a collection of specific rights, each of which has to be proven separately under the *Van der Peet* test.[29] In the *Pamajewon* case,[30] the Supreme Court viewed the question through the lens of *Van der Peet* and held that the right of self-government would have to be proven as an element of specific practices, customs, and traditions integral to the particular Aboriginal society in question. According to this approach, the right of self-government would be a collection of specific rights to govern particular activities rather than a generic right to deal with a range of abstract subject matters. However, the *Pamajewon* case was decided prior to the Court's decision in *Delgamuukw*, which expanded the horizons of Aboriginal rights and recognized the category of generic rights. In light of *Delgamuukw*, it seems more sensible to treat the right of self-government as a generic Aboriginal right, on the model of Aboriginal title, rather than as a bundle of specific rights. On this view, the right of self-government is governed by uniform principles laid down by Canadian common law. The basic scope of the right does not vary from group to group; however, its concrete application differs depending on the circumstances.

IV. THE UNIVERSALITY OF GENERIC RIGHTS

Generic rights are not only uniform in character; they are also universal in distribution. They make up a set of fundamental rights held by all Aboriginal groups in Canada. There is no need to prove in each case that an Aboriginal group has the right to occupy its ancestral territory, to maintain the central attributes of its way of life, to conclude treaties with the Crown, to enjoy its customary legal system, to benefit from the honour of the Crown, or to govern its own affairs. It is presumed that every Aboriginal group in Canada has these fundamental rights, in the absence of treaties or valid legislation to the contrary. This situation is hardly surprising, given the fact that the doctrine of Aboriginal rights applies uniformly throughout the various territories making up Canada, regardless of their precise historical origins or their former status as French or English colonies.[31]

The generic rights held by Aboriginal peoples resemble the set of constitutional rights vested in the provinces under the general provisions of the *Constitution Act, 1867*. Just as every province presumptively enjoys the same array of rights and powers regardless of its size, population, wealth, resources, or historical circumstances, so also every Aboriginal group, large or small, presumptively enjoys the same range of generic Aboriginal rights.

However this conclusion could be disputed. For example, it could be argued that the generic right of Aboriginal title is not a universal right. Some Aboriginal peoples, it is said, never had sufficiently strong or stable connections with a definite territory to hold Aboriginal title, as opposed to specific rights of hunting, fishing, and gathering. Certain musings of the Supreme Court seem to entertain such a possibility.[32] However, the better view is that every Aboriginal group holds Aboriginal title to an ancestral territory, the only question being its location and scope.

v. A Hierarchy of Rights

What is the relationship between generic and specific rights? The answer should now be clear. Specific rights are concrete instances of generic rights. So, for example, the generic right to honourable treatment by the Crown operates at a high level of abstraction and harbours a range of intermediate generic rights relating to various subject matters, such as the creation of new Indian reserves, or the protection of existing ones. These intermediate generic rights, in turn, engender myriad specific fiduciary rights, whose precise scope is determined by the concrete circumstances. Similarly, the abstract right of cultural integrity fosters a range of intermediate generic rights relating to such matters as language, religion, and livelihood. These intermediate rights give birth to specific rights, whose character is shaped by the practices, customs, and traditions of particular Aboriginal groups.

The interplay between generic and specific rights is reflected in the terms of treaties concluded by Aboriginal peoples with the Crown. Consider, for example, the following document signed by Brigadier General James Murray in 1760, which provides:

> THESE are to certify that the CHIEF of the HURON tribe of Indians, having come to me in the name of His Nation, to submit to His BRITANNICK MAJESTY, and make Peace, has been received under my Protection, with his whole Tribe; and henceforth no English Officer or party is to molest, or interrupt them in returning to their Settlement at LORETTE; and they are received upon the same terms with the Canadians, being allowed the free Exercise of their Religion, their Customs, and Liberty of trading with the English: – recommending it to the Officers commanding the Posts, to treat them kindly.[33]

In the *Sioui* case,[34] Lamer J. held that the document constituted a treaty and that it gave the Hurons the freedom to carry on their customs and religious rites over the entire territory that they frequented in 1760, so long as this freedom was not incompatible with the particular uses of the territory made by the Crown.

What is interesting about this brief treaty is its reference to a large array of generic and specific rights. It opens by recognizing the Hurons as an autonomous people under the protection of the British Crown. So doing, it endorses their right to honourable treatment by the Crown, and perhaps also by implication recognizes their right to govern themselves under the Crown's aegis.

The treaty allows the Hurons the free exercise of their religion, which, as just noted, is an intermediate generic right falling under the right of cultural integrity. The treaty also guarantees Huron customs, thus reflecting the generic right to a distinct legal system. The document further promises the liberty of trading with the English, which is a specific application of the intermediate generic right to gain a livelihood, which, as we will see shortly, falls under the right of cultural integrity. Finally, of course, the very existence of the document bears witness to the generic right to conclude treaties.

The precise nature of the relationship between generic and specific rights varies with the generic right in question. Consider, for example, the generic right of self-government. This right arguably confers the same set of governmental powers on all Aboriginal peoples in Canada. Nevertheless, this abstract homogeneity does not mean that Aboriginal peoples possess the same internal constitutions or that they exercise their governmental powers up to their full theoretical limits. The generic right of self-government gives an Aboriginal group the power to establish and amend its own constitution within the overarching framework of the Canadian federation. So, the abstract right engenders a range of specific governmental powers detailed in particular Aboriginal constitutions.

Likewise, the generic right to conclude treaties empowers Aboriginal groups to enter into binding agreements with the Crown. As such, the right spawns an array of particular agreements differing in subject matter and scope. Of course, it does not follow that each such treaty is a "specific right" or that the rights embodied in the treaty are "specific rights." Rather, the generic right gives the Aboriginal parties to a treaty a specific right to its performance, and the nature and scope of that right and the remedies it engenders are shaped by the overarching generic right. Similarly, the generic right to customary law harbours a host of distinct legal systems enjoyed by particular Aboriginal groups. Although these systems are concrete manifestations of the overarching generic right, it would seem an excess of legal logic to characterize them as "specific rights." Rather, we may say that an Aboriginal group has a specific right to possess its own legal system to the extent determined by the generic right that governs it.

Just as all generic rights give birth to specific rights, all specific rights are the offspring of generic rights. There are no "orphan" specific rights. In effect, generic rights provide the fundamental normative structure governing specific rights. This structure determines the existence of specific rights, their basic scope, and their potential for evolution. The significance of these points is illustrated by the right of cultural integrity, which we will now consider in detail.

VI. THE RIGHT OF CULTURAL INTEGRITY

As noted earlier, the right of cultural integrity shelters a host of specific rights that differ from group to group in accordance with their particular ways of life, such as the right to hunt in a certain area, the right to fish in certain waters, the right to harvest certain natural resources, the right to conduct certain religious rites, the right to speak a certain language, and so on. Despite their differences, these specific rights fall into a number of broad categories relating to such subjects as religion, language, and livelihood. These categories constitute cultural rights of intermediate generality – for short, intermediate generic rights.

For example, the right to practice a religion arguably qualifies as an intermediate generic right because spirituality and the performance of religious rites have always been central to Indigenous societies, a matter acknowledged in relations between the Crown and Aboriginal peoples, notably in the ceremonies attending diplomacy and treaty-making. As Professor Oren Lyons, a Peace-Keeper with the Six Nations, has written:

> The primary law of Indian government is the spiritual law. Spirituality is the highest form of politics, and our spirituality is directly involved in government. As chiefs we are told that our first and most important duty is to see that the spiritual ceremonies are carried out. Without the ceremonies, one does not have a basis on which to conduct government for the welfare of the people. This is not only for our people but for the good of all living things in general. So we are told first to conduct the ceremonies on time, in the proper manner, and then to sit in council for the welfare of our people and of all life.[35]

Viewed in the abstract, the right to practice a religion has a uniform scope, which does not vary from one Aboriginal people to another. However, the particular activities, rites, and institutions protected by the right differ from group to group, depending on their specific religious outlook. In effect, then, the generic right of cultural integrity harbours an intermediate generic right to religion, which in turn shelters a range of specific religious rights vested in particular Aboriginal groups.

Consider another example. Aboriginal peoples arguably have the right to use and develop their ancestral languages and to enjoy the educational and cultural institutions needed to maintain them. Language is normally an integral feature of a group's ancestral culture and an important means by which that culture is manifested, nurtured, and transmitted. As Elder Eli Taylor from the Sioux Valley First Nation explained:

> The Aboriginal languages were given by the Creator as an integral part of life. Embodied in Aboriginal languages is our unique relationship to the Creator, our attitudes, beliefs, values and the fundamental notion of what is truth. Aboriginal language is an asset to one's own education, formal and informal. Aboriginal language contributes to greater pride in the history and culture of the community: greater involvement and interest of parents in the education of their children, and greater respect for Elders. Language is the principal means by which culture is accumulated, shared and transmitted from generation to generation. The key to identity and retention of culture is one's ancestral language.[36]

So the right to use and develop an Aboriginal language has a strong claim to qualify as an intermediate generic right. The abstract dimensions of this right are identical in all Aboriginal groups; however, it gives rise to a spectrum of specific rights relating to particular languages and linguistic institutions.

Another important intermediate right is what may be called the right of livelihood. A fundamental principle informing the Crown's assumption of sovereignty was that Aboriginal peoples could continue to gain their living in their accustomed ways. Justice McLachlin identified this right in her dissenting opinion in the *Van der Peet* case.[37] Citing the terms of treaties and the *Royal Proclamation of 1763*,[38] she observed:

> These arrangements bear testimony to the acceptance by the colonizers of the principle that the aboriginal peoples who occupied what is now Canada were regarded as possessing the aboriginal right to live off their lands and the resources found in their forests and streams to the extent they had traditionally done so. The fundamental understanding – the *Grundnorm* of settlement in Canada – was that the aboriginal people could only be deprived of the sustenance they traditionally drew from the land and adjacent waters by solemn treaty with the Crown, on terms that would ensure to them and to their successors a replacement for the livelihood that their lands, forests and streams had since ancestral times provided them.[39]

A similar viewpoint subsequently attracted the Supreme Court's support in the *Marshall* case.[40] In the course of interpreting a Mi'kmaq treaty of 1760,

Binnie J. referred to the objectives of the British and Mi'kmaq in their negotiations, which were aimed at reconciliation and mutual advantage.[41]

It is apparent that the British saw the Mi'kmaq trade issue in terms of peace, as the Crown expert Dr. Stephen Patterson testified, "people who trade together do not fight, that was the theory." Peace was bound up with the ability of the Mi'kmaq people to sustain themselves economically. Starvation breeds discontent. The British certainly did not want the Mi'kmaq to become an unnecessary drain on the public purse of the colony of Nova Scotia or of the Imperial purse in London, as the trial judge found. To avoid such a result, it became necessary to protect the traditional Mi'kmaq economy, including hunting, gathering and fishing.[42]

In light of this policy, Binnie J. interpreted the treaty as recognizing the right of the Mi'kmaq parties to continue to obtain necessaries through hunting and fishing and by trading the products of those traditional activities. What the treaty contemplated, he emphasized, was not a right to trade generally for economic gain, but rather a right to trade for "necessaries." The concept of "necessaries" was equivalent to what may be described as a "moderate livelihood." which extends to such day-to-day needs as food, clothing and housing, supplemented by a few amenities, but not the accumulation of wealth.[43]

To recapitulate, the generic right of cultural integrity forms a pyramid with three levels. At the top is the abstract right itself, which takes the same form in all Aboriginal groups. Beneath this summit lies a tier of intermediate generic rights that relate to distinct subject matters such as religion, language, and livelihood. At the bottom rests a broad range of specific rights that differ from group to group in accordance with their particular cultures and ways of life.

In many respects, the middle tier of the pyramid is the most important of the three. Intermediate generic rights serve several crucial functions. First, they determine which concrete aspects of Aboriginal societies rise to the level of constitutional significance and merit recognition as specific cultural rights. In other words, they speak to the identity of Aboriginal rights. Second, intermediate rights determine the way in which specific practices are characterized for constitutional purposes, speaking to the scope of Aboriginal rights. So doing, intermediate rights also determine the generative potential of these rights. We will consider these points in turn.

A. The Identity of Rights

One of the shortcomings of the *Van der Peet* test is that it does not provide a reliable basis for distinguishing between Indigenous practices that are constitutionally significant and those that are not.[44] In its ethnohistorical bias, the test obscures the fact that identifying Aboriginal rights cannot simply be a descriptive exercise, that it has deep normative dimensions. The court's role is not to reconstruct the internal dynamics of long-vanished Aboriginal lifestyles. Rather it is to determine what general constitutional norms underpin section 35, and the kind of modern rights these norms support.

Recall that, in *Van der Peet*, Lamer C.J. says that Aboriginal rights represent practices that are truly "integral" to an Aboriginal society, in the sense of being "central and significant." However, "integrality" is an unsure guide to constitutional import. There are certain practices that obviously cannot qualify as Aboriginal rights no matter how "integral" they may be from a purely anthropological perspective. Otherwise there might be Aboriginal rights to sleep, to flirt, to tell jokes, to gamble, to make love, and so on. Chief Justice Lamer struggles with this fact in observing that "eating to survive" does not qualify as an Aboriginal right because it is "true of every human society" and so is not sufficiently "distinctive."[45] However, with respect, this puts the emphasis in the wrong place. The question is not what is distinctive but what is constitutionally significant. And indeed, later in his opinion, Lamer C.J. obliquely concedes the point in recognizing that "fishing for food" can constitute an Aboriginal right, notwithstanding the fact that it is practised by most societies around the world.[46] So, near-universal prevalence is no bar to recognition as an Aboriginal right.

The reason why such practices as eating, joking, and gambling fail to qualify as Aboriginal rights is not because they are not integral features of Aboriginal societies (they may well be) but because they do not rise to the level of constitutional significance. How do we know that? The answer, in part, lies in the historical relations between Aboriginal societies and the Crown and the principles that underpin those relations – what we have called intersocietal law.[47] There is little evidence that intersocietal law ever supported a right to sleep or joke, but much that attests to a right to gain a livelihood. Take another example. From a purely ethnographic point of view, the practice of bearing arms was a central feature of most Aboriginal societies in early times, because it was essential to their ability to defend themselves and ultimately to survive. However, that fact does not support a modern Aboriginal right to bear arms. The reason does not lie in any paucity of ethnohistorical evidence but in the fact that fundamental constitutional norms do not support such a right.

B. The Scope and Generative Potential of Rights

Intermediate generic rights play another function, closely related to the first. Not only do they determine the range of practices capable of constituting Aboriginal rights, they also shape the way those practices are characterized. This in turn influences the extent to which the concrete rights are capable of evolving and adapting to modern conditions without breaking the link to their historical progenitors – in effect determining the extent to which these rights are generative.

The *Van der Peet* test assumes that the character and scope of Aboriginal rights are matters determined simply by the historical and anthropological evidence. However, such evidence does not speak for itself. Social practices may be characterized in any number of different ways and at varying levels of abstraction. Ultimately, the question of characterization is normative as well as factual. The trick is to strike the right balance between the two.

The point is illustrated by the argument advanced by McLachlin J., in her dissenting opinion in *Van der Peet*. She maintains that, under section 35(1), Aboriginal peoples have the right to sustain themselves from the land or waters upon which they have traditionally relied for sustenance. In her view, this includes the right to trade in the resource to the extent necessary to maintain traditional levels of sustenance.[48] So, where an Aboriginal group can show that traditionally it sustained itself by fishing in the river or sea, then it has the right to continue to do so today. And if it further demonstrates that the modern trade in fish is the only way to gain the equivalent of what it traditionally took, it has the right to trade in the resource to the extent necessary to provide replacement goods and amenities. In this context, she says, "trade is but the mode or practice by which the more fundamental right of drawing sustenance from the resource is exercised."[49]

Nevertheless, McLachlin J. argues that such a right to trade is not unlimited. It does not extend beyond what is required to provide reasonable substitutes for what was traditionally obtained from the resource – in most cases, basic housing, transportation, clothing, and amenities, in addition to what is needed for food and ceremonial purposes. In effect, where the Aboriginal group historically drew a moderate livelihood from the fishery, it would have an Aboriginal right to obtain a moderate livelihood from the fishery today. However, there is no automatic entitlement to a moderate or any other livelihood from a particular resource. The right exists only to the extent that the Aboriginal group can show historical reliance on the resource. For example, if the evidence indicates the group used the fishery only for occasional food and sport fishing, it would not have a right to fish for the purposes of sale, much less to provide a moderate livelihood.

> There is, on this view, no generic right of commercial fishing, large-scale or small. There is only the right of a particular aboriginal people to take from the resource the modern equivalent of what by aboriginal law and custom it historically took.[50]

In McLachlin J.'s view, the Aboriginal right of traditional sustenance is subject to two limitations. First, it must be exercised in a manner that respects the need for conservation, because use of the resource cannot be sustained over the long term unless the product of the lands and adjacent waters is maintained. Second, any right by its nature carries with it the obligation to use it responsibly. So, for example, the right cannot be used in a way that harms people, Aboriginal or non-Aboriginal.[51]

In effect, then, McLachlin J. holds that Aboriginal peoples have an intermediate generic right to sustain themselves from the land or waters upon which they traditionally relied for sustenance, subject to the requirements of conservation and responsible use. The existence and basic scope of this intermediate generic right are matters of law. However, the specific resources to which the right attaches and the level to which the right rises are determined, not by general norms governing the generic right, but by the particular historical practices of each group. So, for example, there is no generic right of commercial fishing as such; the matter turns on the evidence relating to the specific group in question. Nevertheless, where a group can show that traditionally it drew a moderate livelihood from the fishery, it has a specific Aboriginal right to do so today, and this right includes the right to trade in fish in order to obtain the equivalent of what it traditionally got, even where there is no evidence of significant trade at the critical historical date. Justice McLachlin's approach, then, represents an effort to strike the balance between normative and historical considerations in a way that favours the generative potential of livelihood rights, so as to support the modern welfare and prosperity of Aboriginal peoples.

Compare this approach with that taken by the Supreme Court in the recent *Sappier/Gray* decision.[52] The case concerns a claim by members of the Maliseet and Mi'kmaq peoples of New Brunswick to an Aboriginal right to harvest timber for personal uses. In a seminal judgment, the Court unanimously adopts the view that section 35(1) protects the means by which an Aboriginal society traditionally sustained itself.[53] In so doing, the Court effectively accepts the existence of an intermediate generic right of livelihood. Speaking for the majority, Bastarache J. holds that section 35 seeks to protect the integral elements of the way of life of Aboriginal societies, including their traditional means of survival.[54] He cautions, nevertheless, that there is no such thing as an Aboriginal right to sustenance as such, the right being confined to traditional means of sustenance, to wit the pre-contact practices relied upon for survival.[55]

As for the precise characterization of the right, Bastarache J. holds that the respondents' claim of "a right to harvest timber for personal uses" is too general. The practice should be characterized as the "harvesting of wood for domestic uses," including such things as shelter, transportation, tools, and fuel.[56] He notes that, so characterized, the right has no commercial dimension. The harvested wood cannot be sold, traded, or bartered to produce assets or raise money, even if the purpose is to finance the building of a dwelling. In other words, although the right permits the harvesting of timber to be used in the construction of a dwelling, the wood cannot be sold to raise money to purchase or build a dwelling.[57]

Turning to the generative potential of the right, Bastarache J. holds that "[l]ogical evolution means the same sort of activity, carried on in the modern economy by modern means."[58] So, the right to harvest wood for the construction of temporary shelters may evolve into a right to harvest wood by modern means for the construction of a modern dwelling. Any other conclusion would freeze the right in its pre-contact form. Justice Bastarache notes the Crown's argument that the construction of large permanent dwellings from multi-dimensional wood, obtained by modern methods of extraction and milling, could not constitute an Aboriginal right or a proper application of the "logical evolution" principle. However, he rejects this argument in strong terms, noting that under the established jurisprudence Aboriginal rights must be interpreted flexibly so as to permit their evolution over time.[59] In a striking passage, he explains:

> In *Mitchell*, McLachlin C.J. drew a distinction between the particular aboriginal right, which is established at the moment of contact, and its expression, which evolves over time (para. 13). L'Heureux-Dubé J. in dissent in *Van der Peet* emphasized that "aboriginal rights must be permitted to maintain contemporary relevance in relation to the needs of the natives as their practices, traditions and customs change and evolve with the overall society in which they live" (para. 172). If aboriginal rights are not permitted to evolve and take modern forms, then they will become utterly useless. Surely the Crown cannot be suggesting that the re-

spondents, all of whom live on a reserve, would be limited to building wigwams. If such were the case, the doctrine of aboriginal rights would truly be limited to recognizing and affirming a narrow subset of "anthropological curiosities", and our notion of aboriginality would be reduced to a small number of outdated stereotypes.[60]

In summary, then, in *Sappier/Gray*, the Supreme Court effectively recognizes what we have described as an intermediate generic right of livelihood. The existence and basic scope of the right are established by general legal norms – so that, for example, the Court construes the right as extending to traditional means of sustenance, rather than to sustenance generally. However, in other respects, the character of the right is governed by the evidence relating to the particular group in question – such as, for example, the question whether a resource can be sold in order to raise money. The specific right at issue in the case is characterized at a fairly high level of generality, which in turn allows considerable scope for its evolution over time. However, the Court does not explore in any depth the normative underpinnings of the generic right of livelihood. Had it done so, it might have adopted a position closer to that of McLachlin J. in *Van der Peet*.

The point to be drawn from this analysis is simple. The assessment of claims to Aboriginal rights has two complementary dimensions: historical and normative. A court has to consider not only the historical evidence mounted to support the specific claim, but also the underlying rationale of the generic right invoked. While the Supreme Court has finally acknowledged the normative dimensions of the question, it still has some distance to go.

VII. THE CRITICAL DATE

As a matter of Anglo-Canadian law, Aboriginal rights came into existence when the Crown gained sovereignty over an Indigenous people. Before that time, the relations between an Indigenous people and the Crown were governed by international law and the terms of any treaties. Although Aboriginal peoples held rights under international law prior to the change of sovereignty (and continue to hold such rights today), it was only upon the advent of the Crown that Aboriginal rights arose in Anglo-Canadian law.[61]

Consider for a moment the generic right of honourable treatment by the Crown. This right clearly did not come into existence at the point of European contact, for mere physical interaction could not vest an Aboriginal group with rights under Anglo-Canadian law, any more than it could burden the Crown with duties. The Crown's honour was engaged only when the Crown assumed sovereignty over the Aboriginal group in question. As McLachlin C.J. says in *Haida Nation*:

> The historical roots of the principle of the honour of the Crown sug-gest that it must be understood generously in order to reflect the un-derlying realities from which it stems. In all its dealings with Aboriginal peoples, from the assertion of sovereignty to the resolution of claims and the implementation of treaties, the Crown must act honourably. Nothing less is required if we are to achieve "the reconciliation of the pre-existence of aboriginal societies with the sovereignty of the Crown"....[62]

In other words, under Anglo-Canadian law (as distinct from international law), the Crown has no legal responsibilities for Indigenous peoples until such time as it assumes sovereignty over them. At that point, the principle of the honour of the Crown takes hold and imposes basic standards governing the Crown's conduct. However, the same observation holds true of the other generic Aboriginal rights. It seems implausible that any one of them could come into force simply at the point of contact. As a matter of Anglo-Canadian law, they all accompany and control the Crown's assumption of governmental respon-sibility over Indigenous peoples. So, it seems natural to think that the critical historical date for establishing the existence of Aboriginal rights is the time of sovereignty. However, the matter is not so straightforward. We have to distin-guish between generic and specific rights.

As seen earlier, when an Aboriginal people passes under the Crown's sov-ereignty, it automatically gains a basic set of generic rights – the right to an ancestral territory, the right of cultural integrity, and so on – as well as a range of intermediate generic rights arising under their auspices. These rights come into existence at the time of sovereignty and possess a uniform character. Nev-ertheless, generic rights have specific aspects or applications, many of which originate at later dates and change over time. For instance, the principle of the honour of the Crown takes effect at the date of sovereignty, however specific fiduciary rights and duties generally arise from events occurring well after sovereignty, for example upon the conclusion of treaties sharing Aboriginal lands with the Crown, or the creation of particular reserves. In such cases, the critical date for proving the specific fiduciary right is clearly the date of the event that triggered it, not the date of sovereignty.

Likewise, the generic right to customary law arises at the time of sovereignty; however, the particular bodies of customary law protected by the right are not static but continue to evolve and adapt to keep pace with societal changes. It follows that the relevant date for determining the existence of a particular rule of customary law is not the date of sovereignty but the date of the activity or transaction whose legality is in question. So, for example, the validity of a customary adoption that took place in southern Québec in 1980 would be governed by the customary rules prevailing at that date, rather than in the year 1763, when New France was ceded to the British Crown. Of course, while the customary rules must have existed for an appreciable period of time before they can gain the status of law, there is no need to show they existed at the time of sovereignty.

The right of cultural integrity poses more difficult and complex questions. As with other generic rights, the abstract right comes into existence at the time of sovereignty, and the same holds true of the intermediate generic rights that shelter under its auspices, relating to such subjects as language, religion, and livelihood. What, then, of the specific rights that occupy the bottom tier in the pyramid? In principle these cannot date from a period earlier than the time of sovereignty, because Anglo-Canadian law (as distinct from international law or Indigenous law) did not apply prior to that date. So, presumably they must arise at the time of sovereignty or at some later period, depending on the precise nature of the right in question.

The question is bedevilled by the fact that Indigenous cultures (like all cultures) are organic entities that change constantly over time. After Europeans arrived in North America, Aboriginal societies responded in dynamic and creative ways to the new opportunities, circumstances, and influences that presented themselves.[63] Just as European cultures quickly adopted many products of American origin, such as tomatoes, corn, and potatoes (to say nothing of tobacco), so also native American cultures swiftly absorbed many items of European origin, such as horses, metal artefacts, and firearms. Trade in furs, skins, and fish transformed the economies of Aboriginal societies and helped sustain the economies of settler colonies. Religious ideas born in the crucible of the Middle East had a notable impact on Aboriginal spirituality, as did Aboriginal conceptions of personal freedom and federalism on European political thought. On the negative side, European-borne diseases such as smallpox decimated many Aboriginal societies and caused important changes in lifestyle, political organization, and outlook, while venereal syphilis (often thought to be of American origin) took a lesser toll in Europe.[64]

So the question arises: given the dynamic nature of Aboriginal cultures and the fact that they underwent significant changes both before and after sovereignty, what date is "critical" for determining the existence and content of specific cultural rights? The answer has two facets. First, the critical date cannot normally be *earlier* than the date of Crown sovereignty, because, except in unusual situations, it does not make sense for the content of a right to be fixed by reference to a period prior to the time that the right itself came into existence. Second, it seems possible that the critical date may vary depending on the kind of cultural right at issue and the underlying purposes it serves. The date appropriate for language rights may not serve well for livelihood rights. It follows that the matter should be determined on a category-by-category basis, so that the considerations appropriate to each context may be thoroughly assessed.

Nevertheless, as seen earlier, the Supreme Court held in *Van der Peet*[65] that the critical date for determining the content of specific cultural rights was the time of initial European contact – normally well before Crown sovereignty – and that this date held true for Aboriginal rights across the board. The Court apparently thought that the right of cultural integrity was designed to preserve the central aspects of Aboriginal cultures as these existed in their "pristine" form, prior to the advent of European influence. So, while Aboriginal rights themselves only came into existence at the time of sovereignty (for they could not arise earlier under Anglo-Canadian law), the concrete content of these rights was determined by social conditions prevailing at a much earlier period, when Europeans first arrived. This means, for example, that, when the Indigenous nations of New France fell under British rule in 1763, they gained the right to maintain their antique way of life as it existed as much as three centuries previous, when French adventurers sailed up the St. Lawrence River. The result is somewhat puzzling, since it is not clear why the Crown or Indigenous nations would have any interest in reviving or protecting long-vanished modes of life.

Van der Peet was not to be the last word on the matter. When the question of Aboriginal title came up in the *Delgamuukw* case, the Supreme Court beat a partial retreat. It held that the critical date for establishing the existence of Aboriginal title (as distinct from other Aboriginal rights) was the time the Crown asserted sovereignty rather than the date of first contact.[66] The Court said that this difference was justified for three reasons.

First, Aboriginal title represented a burden on the Crown's underlying title. However the Crown did not gain this underlying title until it asserted sovereignty over the lands in question. It did not make sense, argues the Court, to speak of a burden on the underlying title before that title existed. So Aboriginal title only crystallized at the time sovereignty was asserted.[67] The Court's reasoning, with respect, is impeccable. However, the underlying logic is not limited to Aboriginal title but extends to other generic Aboriginal rights. Like Aboriginal title, they all pose legal limitations or burdens on the Crown's sovereign rights under Anglo-Canadian law – limits that only arose at the time of sovereignty. Consider the right of cultural integrity, which binds the Crown to respect the integral elements of an Indigenous culture. In the Court's words, it does not make sense to speak of such a limit on the Crown's sovereignty before sovereignty itself existed.

The Court mounts a second argument. Aboriginal title "does not raise the problem of distinguishing between distinctive, integral Aboriginal practices, customs and traditions and those influenced or introduced by European contact." Under common law, it says, the act of occupation or possession is sufficient to ground Aboriginal title, and it is not necessary to prove that the land was an integral part of the Aboriginal society before the arrival of Europeans.[68] With respect, this reasoning is somewhat self-serving. Aboriginal title does not raise the problem of distinguishing between pre-European Aboriginal practices and those introduced by European contact because the Court has (correctly) defined Aboriginal title as a generic right, whose character and scope are not determined by the practices of specific Aboriginal groups, either before or after contact. However, the same observation holds true of all the other generic rights. For example, the right of cultural integrity does not itself arise from Aboriginal cultures, nor is the scope of the abstract right shaped by traditional Aboriginal practices. The right arises from an intersocietal body of law governing relations between the Crown and Aboriginal peoples. As such, it comes into existence at the point of sovereignty, just like Aboriginal title.

The Court gives a third reason for choosing a distinctive critical date for Aboriginal title. From a practical standpoint, it says, the date of sovereignty is more certain than the date of first contact. It is often very difficult to determine "the precise moment that each aboriginal group had first contact with European culture."[69] However, once again, the Court's logic has a broader application. The difficulty of determining the date of contact is no greater or less for Aboriginal title than for Aboriginal rights generally. What is sauce for the Aboriginal goose is sauce for the Aboriginal gander.

Carried to its natural conclusions, then, *Delgamuukw* makes a convincing case for rejecting the time of European contact as the critical date for Aboriginal rights and for choosing a date no earlier than the time of sovereignty. However, this conclusion does not take us much further than the position arrived at earlier. As we have seen, generic Aboriginal rights arise at the time of Crown sovereignty, and specific rights often come into existence at later dates or have aspects that change over time. So, the critical date for determining the existence and scope of a specific right varies depending on the kind of generic right at issue and its underlying rationale. In effect, as suggested earlier, the courts ought to deal with each generic right separately, so that the appropriate considerations may be weighed in their context.

The need for an incremental approach is shown by the *Powley* decision,[70] where the Supreme Court determined the critical date governing the Aboriginal rights of the Métis people.[71] As entities of mixed European and Indigenous descent, Métis groups only came into existence in the post-contact period, so a critical date of European contact is clearly problematic for determining their rights. Realizing this difficulty, Lamer C.J. in *Van der Peet* explicitly postponed the question to a later day.[72] In *Powley*, the Court finally grasped the nettle and held that the critical date for the Métis is the time when Europeans established effective political and legal control in a particular area – what we may call the date of effective control. The Court rejected the argument that the rights of Métis groups must be grounded in the pre-contact practices of their Aboriginal ancestors, arguing that this approach would deny to Métis their full status as distinctive rights-bearing peoples.[73]

Once again, the Court's logic is persuasive, and once again it undermines the approach taken in *Van der Peet*. Take the case of two modern Aboriginal groups – one Métis, the other Indian – that live side by side in a certain area. The groups have common ancestors on the Indigenous side; they are both the descendants of an Indian nation that occupied the area when Europeans first arrived. By the time the Crown gained effective control over the area, a Métis community had grown up alongside the Indian one, and both groups had become heavily involved in the commercial fur trade – something absent from the culture of their Indian forefathers at the time of contact. Under the *Powley* test, the Métis group would gain an Aboriginal right to trade in furs, while under the *Van der Peet* test the Indian group would not. The rights of the Métis would be ascertained by reference to their practices at the time of effective control, while the rights of their Indian neighbours would be determined by their practices at the time of contact. The result, needless to say, is paradoxical. The group of mixed Aboriginal-European descent is credited with an Aboriginal right that is denied to their Indian neighbours, despite the fact that both groups were engaged in the fur trade at the time of effective control, and both are the descendants of an Indian nation that did not trade in furs at the time of contact. A similar problem arises in dealing with claims to Aboriginal title advanced by the two groups, because, at the time of sovereignty, the Indian group may well have occupied lands that, by the time of effective control, were occupied by the Métis. What these conundrums show is the need for uniform critical dates for all Aboriginal peoples, at least in the context of livelihood rights and Aboriginal title.

VIII. FROM RECOGNITION TO RECONCILIATION

At the start of this chapter, we noted that in the *Van der Peet* case Lamer C.J. held that section 35(1) was animated by the twin goals of recognition and reconciliation. However, in practice, the test he enunciated gave almost exclusive priority to the goal of recognition: it mandated that Aboriginal rights should be identified on a purely descriptive basis, by reference to Indigenous customs and practices existing in remote historical periods. No thought was given to the question of how far these primordial practices, reified as rights, might serve the cause of reconciliation at the present day. The doctrine of generic rights goes a long way toward resolving this deficiency. In focussing attention on the underlying rationales of various categories of Aboriginal rights, it provides a bridge between the historical groundings of Aboriginal rights and their modern-day incarnations, as living rights that serve the ongoing needs of Indigenous peoples.

Reconciliation is a complex and multi-faceted objective. While the doctrine of generic rights gives Aboriginal peoples a strong legal basis for achieving reconciliation with the larger society, it may in certain cases be insufficient to attain that goal. In focussing (necessarily) on the rights of Aboriginal groups, the doctrine has difficulty taking proper account of the competing interests of third parties and indeed the body politic as a whole. So, for example, while the new approach supports a broader interpretation of Aboriginal livelihood rights regarding resources such as fish, game, and timber, it does not provide an adequate basis for determining how these limited resources should be shared with other user groups, whose welfare may be gravely affected. Again, the straightforward application of the legal criteria governing recognition of Aboriginal title may have far-reaching effects on the interests of innocent third parties and indeed society as a whole – interests that the law may have trouble accommodating.

In certain cases, of course, the resolution of such problems may safely be left to legislation, which in turn is subject to judicial review under section 35(1).[74] In other instances, the external interests affected by Aboriginal claims may be so important or deep-seated that the mere fact of judicial recognition may risk precipitating a crisis in relations between Aboriginal and non-Aboriginal peoples, thus setting back the cause of reconciliation. On the other hand, for a court to give routine priority to third-party interests would be to ignore the promise of section 35(1) and the demands of historical justice. What is the way out of this dilemma?

The answer, interestingly enough, is suggested by the wording of section 35(1) itself. The provision states that the existing Aboriginal and treaty rights of the Aboriginal peoples of Canada are hereby "recognized and affirmed." The use of two terms – "recognized" and "affirmed" – is an obvious but little-discussed feature of the section. Indeed, at first blush, the two words may seem to say more or less the same thing. Yet closer examination suggests that their orientation is actually somewhat different. In saying that Aboriginal rights are "recognized," the section seems to focus on rights in their original, historically-based forms. The word "affirmed," by contrast, seems more concerned with the way these rights are to be treated in contemporary times – as living rights that serve the modern interests of Aboriginal peoples and at the same time promote reconciliation with the larger society.

What this suggests, then, is that the process of identifying Aboriginal rights under section 35(1) is governed by two distinct but complementary sets of constitutional principles, which we may call Principles of Recognition and Principles of Reconciliation.[75] Principles of Recognition govern the identification of generic Aboriginal rights and the specific rights that arise under their auspices, based on a mix of historical and normative considerations. In a word, they encompass the set of basic principles discussed in earlier sections of this chapter. These principles provide the point of departure for any modern inquiry into the existence of Aboriginal rights and a benchmark for assessing the historical scope of Indigenous dispossession and deprivation. By contrast, Principles of Reconciliation govern the legal effects of Aboriginal rights in modern times. They take as their starting point the historically-based rights of the Aboriginal group concerned, as determined by Principles of Recognition, but they also take into account a range of other factors, such as the modern condition of the lands or resources affected, the Aboriginal group's contemporary needs and interests, and the interests of third parties and society at large. So doing, Principles of Reconciliation posit that certain Aboriginal rights cannot be implemented in their entirety by the courts but require the negotiation of modern treaties.

Unless we distinguish between these two sets of principles, we may fall into the trap of assuming that historical Aboriginal rights automatically give rise to modern rights, without regard to societal changes that have occurred in the interim. Such an assumption fosters twin judicial tendencies. The courts may be led to identify historical Aboriginal rights in a highly restrictive way – as by imposing an artificially early critical date – in the effort to minimize conflicts with third-party interests. Alternately, a restrictive view may be taken of the ability of an Aboriginal right to evolve and adapt, so as to curtail its modern effects. These tendencies, if left to operate unchecked, will diminish the possibility of reconciliation ever occurring. The successful settlement of Aboriginal claims must involve the full and unstinting recognition of the historical reality of Aboriginal rights, the true scope and effects of Indigenous dispossession and exclusion, and the continuing links between an Aboriginal people and its traditional culture, lands, and resources. By the same token, the recognition of historical rights, while a necessary precondition for modern reconciliation, is not always in itself a sufficient basis for reconciliation, which may have to take into account a range of other factors. So, for example, to suggest that historical Aboriginal rights give rise to modern rights that automatically trump third-party interests represents the attempt to remedy one injustice by committing another.

The point is nicely captured in the *Mikisew* case, where Binnie J. affirms that the "fundamental objective of the modern law of aboriginal and treaty rights is the reconciliation of aboriginal peoples and non-aboriginal peoples and their respective claims, interests and ambitions."[76] Nevertheless, he observes, the management of these relationships takes place in the shadow of a long history of grievances and misunderstanding. The process of reconciliation requires the courts to take account of the claims and interests of both Aboriginal and non-Aboriginal peoples. Neither side can be left out of the equation. However, the process takes place in the wake of historical injustices and grievances that cannot be minimized or ignored. In effect, reconciliation must strike a balance between the need to remedy past injustices and the need to accommodate the full range of contemporary interests. On the one hand, unless the modern law provides appropriate standards (in the form of Principles of Recognition) for understanding the true nature and scope of historical Aboriginal rights, there can be no proper basis for modern reconciliation. On the other hand, if historical rights are taken to give rise to modern rights *tout court*, without regard to their effects in present-day society, the cause of reconciliation will be equally ill-served.

What form do Principles of Reconciliation take? It would be a mistake to attempt an answer on the basis of *a priori* reasoning. The matter can only be settled by detailed discussion in the context of actual cases. Indeed, it seems likely that these principles take a variety of forms, depending on the kind of Aboriginal right in question. Subject to this caution, nevertheless, I suggest that Principles of Reconciliation must have the following basic features:

- They should acknowledge the historical rights of Aboriginal peoples, as determined by Principles of Recognition, as the essential starting point for any modern settlement.

- They should take account of how historical Aboriginal rights have been affected by changes in the circumstances of Indigenous peoples and the rise of third-party and other societal interests.

- Where appropriate, they should distinguish between the "inner core" of Aboriginal rights, which may be implemented by the courts without need for negotiation, and a "penumbra" or "outer range" that needs to be defined in treaties negotiated between the Aboriginal people concerned and the Crown.[77]

- They should provide guidelines governing the accommodation of rights and interests held by other affected groups, both Aboriginal and non-Aboriginal.

- Where appropriate, they should create strong incentives for negotiated settlements to be reached within a reasonable period of time.[78]

- They should provide for judicial remedies where negotiations fail to yield a settlement.

The constitutional basis for this approach has already been identified by the Supreme Court in the path-breaking *Haida Nation* and *Taku River* decisions.[79] The Court effectively portrays section 35 as the basis of a generative constitutional order – one that mandates the Crown to negotiate with Indigenous peoples for the recognition of their rights in a form that balances their contemporary needs and interests with those of the broader society.

According to these decisions, when the Crown claimed sovereignty over Canadian territories, it did so in the face of pre-existing Indigenous sovereignty and territorial rights. The tension between these conflicting claims gave rise to a special relationship that requires the Crown to deal honourably with Aboriginal peoples. The fundamental principle of the "honour of the Crown" obliges the Crown to respect Aboriginal rights, which in turn requires it to negotiate with Aboriginal peoples with a view to identifying those rights. It also obliges the Crown to consult with Aboriginal peoples in all cases where its activities affect their asserted rights and, where appropriate, to accommodate these rights by adjusting the activities.[80] Chief Justice McLachlin sums up the matter as follows:

Put simply, Canada's Aboriginal peoples were here when Europeans came, and were never conquered. Many bands reconciled their claims with the sovereignty of the Crown through negotiated treaties. Others, notably in British Columbia, have yet to do so. The potential rights embedded in these claims are protected by s. 35 of the *Constitution Act, 1982*. The honour of the Crown requires that these rights be determined, recognized and respected. This, in turn, requires the Crown, acting honourably, to participate in processes of negotiation. While this process continues, the honour of the Crown may require it to consult and, where indicated, accommodate Aboriginal interests.[81]

The Chief Justice emphasizes that the Crown has the legal duty to achieve a just settlement of Aboriginal claims by negotiation and treaty. So doing, she attributes a generative role to section 35. In effect, she holds that the Crown, with judicial assistance, has the duty to foster a new legal order for Aboriginal rights, through negotiation and agreement with the Aboriginal peoples affected. This approach views section 35 as serving a dynamic function – one that does not come to an end even when treaties are successfully concluded. As she states:

> The jurisprudence of this Court supports the view that the duty to consult and accommodate is part of a process of fair dealing and reconciliation that begins with the assertion of sovereignty and continues beyond formal claims resolution. Reconciliation is not a final legal remedy in the usual sense. Rather, it is a *process* flowing from rights guaranteed by s. 35(1) of the *Constitution Act, 1982*.[82]

In other words, section 35 does not simply recognize a body of historical rights whose contours are ascertained by the application of general legal criteria to particular historical circumstances. Rather, the section envisages Aboriginal rights as flexible and future-oriented rights that need to be adjusted and refurbished from time to time through negotiations with the Indigenous peoples concerned.

IX. CONCLUSION

Over the past decade, the Supreme Court has reshaped the *Van der Peet* test in several important respects. First, the Court has moved toward accepting the fact that Aboriginal rights are not just specific rights, particular to each individual group, but rather are grounded in a range of generic rights recognized by the common law of Aboriginal rights. Second, in certain contexts, the Court has adopted critical dates that effectively undermine the view that Aboriginal rights crystallized at the time of European contact, pointing rather to the time of Crown sovereignty and effective control. Third, the Court has increasingly emphasized the fact that Aboriginal rights are not just historical in nature; they are also generative rights that need to accommodate the full range of modern interests, both Aboriginal and non-Aboriginal, and as such may require articulation in agreements with the Crown.

This evolution in the jurisprudence should come as no surprise. It is a distinctive feature of common law systems to shun absolute principles conceived *a priori* in favour of flexible principles fleshed out in concrete cases. The *Van der Peet* decision was handed down at a time when there was a dearth of judicial authority on the Aboriginal rights recognized in section 35(1). The Supreme Court set out a comprehensive approach to the matter, with the aim, no doubt, of providing guidance to lower courts that were struggling to apply the section's somewhat enigmatic terms. While the test served its purpose at the time, inevitably it has needed revision and amendment. As McLachlin J. observed in *Van der Peet*, there is much to commend the pragmatic approach adopted by the common law – reasoning from the experience of decided cases and recognized rights – all the more so given the complexity and sensitivity of the task of defining Aboriginal rights.[83] The Court's jurisprudence in the decade since *Van der Peet* shows the wisdom of this approach.

2

HONOURING THE TREATY

ACKNOWLEDGEMENT OF

FIRST NATIONS SELF-GOVERNMENT

ACHIEVING JUSTICE THROUGH SELF-DETERMINATION

Merrilee Rasmussen

1. INTRODUCTION

The idea of "justice" can be viewed broadly or narrowly. Narrowly, it is generally intended to refer to the machinery of the criminal justice system. Broadly conceived, "justice" is the ability of all individuals to participate fairly in the benefits of society. Once justice is conceived of in this way, it is important to emphasize the conditions that will secure the prevention of crime, rather than to emphasize the efficient processing of those who commit crimes. It is trite to observe that, as all our grandmothers have told us in their various ways, an ounce of prevention is worth a pound of cure. But it is only trite because it is true.

The research conducted by the Harvard Project[1] over almost 20 years has demonstrated that people, individually and collectively, take responsibility for their actions and for the actions of those around them when they have a measure of control over the decisions that affect their lives. As the Harvard Project concludes, sovereignty, institutions, and culture "matter." Thus, it follows that the implementation of Aboriginal self-government is a means by which to establish and nurture the relationships that will ultimately secure justice, in the broad sense, for Aboriginal peoples in Canada.

This chapter proceeds from the premise that if there is a rabbit that can be pulled out of a hat to address the multi-faceted challenges that face Aboriginal peoples, it is self-determination. This chapter does not presume that anyone has to be convinced that recognition and implementation of Aboriginal government makes sense legally, constitutionally, politically, and humanly; it starts from this point as a given.

It must be acknowledged, of course, that there are many people who do not accept this premise, for a variety of reasons.[2] Some of these critics will have reasonable arguments. Some of them will not. Many will believe that non-Aboriginal governments and institutions merely have to become more sensitive to Aboriginal concerns, and that will be enough. This argument is essentially about power and control and premised on a claim that Aboriginal peoples can trust non-Aboriginal governments to make good decisions for them. The experience of Aboriginal peoples contradicts that claim. In addition, those who ask Aboriginal peoples just to trust non-Aboriginal society should be prepared just to trust them in return.

Professor Brian Slattery characterizes the Supreme Court's decision in *R. v. Van der Peet*[3] as one that establishes a right to what he has termed "cultural integrity."[4] It seems eminently sensible that if Aboriginal rights are to mean anything, they must include the ability to preserve the very existence of the rights-bearing group. Building from that base, Slattery discusses generative rights, including a generative right to negotiate treaties with the Crown and the right to customary law.[5] It is arguable that these latter two generative rights are really one: the right to self-government (although the Supreme Court has not exactly dealt with that issue in any direct way yet). But a right to self-government, conceived of as a generative right in the sense that Professor Slattery intended, leads to the conclusion, which he describes as coming from the Court's decision in *Haida Nation* v. *British Columbia (Minister of Forests)*,[6] that Aboriginal peoples are entitled to recognition and respect, and there is therefore an obligation on the Crown to consult and negotiate with them with respect to their self-governing jurisdiction.[7]

II. THE NEED TO DEFINE

Critics of Aboriginal self-government typically point to a perceived lack of definition around Aboriginal jurisdiction to justify their failure to recognize that such jurisdiction exists. Interestingly, the complete jurisdiction of the federal and provincial governments in Canada is set out in a handful of reasonably short provisions in the Canadian Constitution,[8] and is described by such vague phrases as "criminal law" and "property and civil rights." Perhaps in 1867 there were those who criticized the confederation project on the basis that these descriptions of jurisdiction were also too vague, too open-ended.

Of course, these concepts have been examined by the courts countless times since 1867, and no doubt will be examined countless more. This is necessarily so. The project of defining jurisdiction of any government, Aboriginal or non-Aboriginal alike, is iterative and organic; its many facets are revealed over time and circumstance. Each time a court considers the meaning of phrases such as "property and civil rights" in the context of a specific dispute about the limits of provincial jurisdiction, a greater understanding of the specific contours of that jurisdiction is articulated. Putting off recognizing Aboriginal jurisdiction until a definition agreeable to all parties in the jurisdictional debate can be secured is to set a standard that is not only unattainable but is also a chimaera. In effect, it is not a postponement of Aboriginal claims to self-government; it is a denial of them.

Thus, it is necessary to look at definition in a more pragmatic and realistic sense. The first step might be to find an understanding of what the specific content of Aboriginal jurisdiction could entail, recognizing that this is only a place to begin to understand its scope and, like the jurisdiction of other governments, it too will change. It is also necessary to suspend concern, for a time and for the sake of discussion, about where things might lead. This is not to suggest that no attention should be paid to consequences. Rather, it is to acknowledge that we cannot be hamstrung in the here and now by our inability to predict the future.

III. SECTION 91(24)

A useful starting point, therefore, is the constitutional statement of federal jurisdiction in relation to "Indians, and Lands reserved for the Indians" contained in section 91(24) of the *Constitution Act, 1867*. Examining the scope of jurisdiction contained within the grant to Parliament in section 91(24) provides a jumping off point for developing a definition of jurisdiction of Aboriginal governments. If the federal jurisdiction under section 91(24) applies to "Indians *qua* Indians," as the courts have often stated, then legislation relating to the establishment and structures of First Nation governments, the continued existence of the community, whose rights are protected by section 35 of the *Constitution Act, 1982*,[9] and the regulation of relationships within that community and between that community and others, is, at the very least, legislation that First Nation governments could enact.

Of course, this is not to suggest that Aboriginal jurisdiction is derived from the Canadian Constitution. The exercise of federal jurisdiction under section 91(24) fills a legal vacuum resulting from the practical dearth of Aboriginal legislation. Aboriginal jurisdiction is recognized by the Canadian Constitution, not granted by it, through the protection of Aboriginal and treaty rights and the grounding of the fiduciary relationship in the Constitution by virtue of the requirement for federal and provincial governments to reconcile their "power" with their "duty" (as directed by the Supreme Court of Canada in *R. v. Sparrow*[10]).

Because the federal government is the primary bearer of jurisdiction in relation to "Indians and their lands," it is primarily this scope of federal power that indicates where Aboriginal governments can begin to act unilaterally. In the terms used by the Royal Commission on Aboriginal Peoples, the scope of the federal jurisdiction under section 91(24) approximates the scope of the "core" of Aboriginal jurisdiction.[11]

IV. SECTION 88

It is difficult to form a very clear understanding of the scope of section 91(24) because of the existence of section 88 of the *Indian Act*.[12] Section 88 provides that provincial laws of general application apply, with some exceptions,[13] to Indians in the province. As a result, provincial law will apply in most cases, although it may not be clear if it applies because of section 88 or because it relates to a matter that falls outside the scope of section 91(24). Thus, it is not often necessary for a court to determine whether the provincial law applies of its own force, because it relates to a matter of provincial competence and does not strike at the core of "Indianness," as the courts have described it, or because it would not otherwise apply but section 88 provides that it does. Either way, provincial law applies, and it has not usually been necessary for courts to figure out why. But the difference is significant in a consideration of the scope of Aboriginal jurisdiction.

V. SECTION 91(24) AND JURISDICTION

There are two important features of what is apparently federal policy as applied to self-government negotiations. The first is the idea that federal responsibility stops at the reserve boundary. This cannot be a correct view of the law. Section 91(24) sets out jurisdiction in relation to both Indians and to their reserve lands. And, as the Supreme Court said in *Four B Manufacturing v. United Garment Workers of America*, an Indian is not any less an Indian because he or she is off the reserve or any more an Indian because he or she is on one.[14]

The second feature is the idea that if a matter would otherwise fall under provincial jurisdiction, then it will fall under provincial jurisdiction when applicable to Indians as well. This cannot be correct either. If the only things that section 91(24) authorizes Parliament to do are the things that it was already capable of doing, section 91(24) would obviously not have been necessary. Section 91(24) must therefore authorize Parliament to make laws in relation to subjects that it would not have been able to deal with if section 91(24) did not exist. Since the only things that Parliament is unable to do otherwise are the things that are granted by the Constitution to the provinces – or that are acknowledged to be within the body of Aboriginal and treaty rights protected by section 35 of the *Constitution Act, 1982*[15] – then these are the very things that section 91(24) enables.

Professor Peter Hogg suggests that section 91(24) authorizes Parliament to make laws that are rationally connected to intelligible Indian policies, even if the laws would ordinarily be outside federal competence.[16] This is a rather broad scope for law-making, and if the federal government can make laws that are rationally connected to intelligible policies, it seems only reasonable that First Nation governments could do the same. Indeed, as has already been argued, the only things that section 91(24) can authorize are the things that other governments, including Aboriginal governments, are able to do.

VI. TREATIES

Because we are in Saskatchewan, it is also necessary to look at self-government from a treaty perspective. The treaties are significant for a variety of reasons, but perhaps most importantly, because they establish an intergovernmental process based on a nation-to-nation agreement that acknowledges that First Nations, who were self-governing at the time the treaties were signed, would continue to be self-governing in this new context. As Slattery has observed, the courts never suggest that Indian peoples did not have the capacity to enter into treaties; the treaties are always assumed to be valid, and the only question is what they provide for.[17] This is an extremely important point. Although the specific language of the treaty is not itself enough to determine its meaning (since it does not contain within it any of the understandings of the First Nations that are found in their oral history), nevertheless, the text of Treaty 4 is typical in this regard. It reveals, even from the perspective of the non-Aboriginal signatory, these hopes for the future:

[the Indian signatories] will maintain peace and good order between each other, and between themselves and other tribes of Indians and between themselves and others of Her Majesty's subjects, whether Indians, Half-breeds, or whites.[18]

The conclusions to be drawn from the treaty text, coupled with the Indian understanding, are inescapable. Through their existence, the treaties themselves acknowledge the Aboriginal signatories as nations. By their continued existence, and indeed by their constitutional protection, Canada continues to acknowledge them as nations. It follows, therefore, that, at a minimum, First Nation governments have authority to enact laws constituting themselves, determining who their members are, regulating their internal relationships, and adjudicating disputes arising under their laws. First Nations also have authority to work out the intergovernmental relationships with their federal and provincial "neighbours." It falls to Canada and the provinces to acknowledge and respect their existence as nations and the laws they enact, and to work together with First Nations to find the practical arrangements between and among neighbours that in the federal-provincial context are described as intergovernmental affairs.

VII. Giving Effect to Self-Government

This chapter addresses three concrete examples for First Nation jurisdiction, which are based on this model of respect and honour the acknowledgement of jurisdiction contained in the treaties through their text and through the fact of their existence, as well as the First Nation understanding of them. These are not necessarily large ideas. They do not try to pull together a comprehensive regime of Aboriginal self-government. What these ideas do try to accomplish is to suggest areas in which Aboriginal and non-Aboriginal governments could move forward and test the self-government waters in an atmosphere of mutual trust and respect and with less fear.

A. Governance

Self-government can only be implemented by peoples when they organize themselves for those purposes through institutions and systems of governance. These generally develop in a society over time, evolving and changing to meet the needs of the day. Non-Aboriginal peoples in Canada and Saskatchewan, who established a political and governance system by Acts of Parliament[19] sometimes forget this process. As David Smith, a Saskatchewan political scientist, has described it, Saskatchewan was created "*de novo*, within invisible, geometrically determined boundaries" in which "state preceded society"[20] (non-Aboriginal society that is).

When First Nations say they are societies that have been living in Canada for thousands of years with institutions, systems, and laws, the non-Aboriginal reaction is to look for documents. The Canadian Parliament and the Saskatchewan Legislature enact laws that are written down, and they therefore comprise a fixed text or formulation of words that does not change, except through an elaborate and specific process of amendment. These written texts provide a comforting notion that in some sense the law is immutable.

However, even though the words of the law may not change, societal understandings of laws change with time and circumstance. Fixed texts are interpreted in different ways depending on what they are being applied to and when. So, for example, it was not difficult for courts to conclude that the *Copyright Act* applied to protect computer software programs as literary works, even though that legislation was written in the 1920s, long before computers were invented and software programs existed.[21] The words of the law had not changed, but they had been adapted to accommodate new understandings of the world.

It is also sometimes forgotten that a great deal of non-Aboriginal law is not written down in the form of a legal text comprising a statute. Non-Aboriginal law also exists in the form of decisions of judges applying normative principles to situations, sometimes in which no statutes are involved at all. So, for example, the law of negligence, which is largely ungoverned by statute,[22] allows courts to hold individuals responsible for the reasonably foreseeable harm they may cause to others. Although this law can be described as "written," in the sense that it emanates from the written judgments of many courts over a lengthy period of time, it is not fundamentally different in concept from the common law of Aboriginal societies.

In Saskatchewan and Canada, the laws made by legislatures and Parliament are honoured because the systems that produce those laws have been put in place for this purpose, and we respect them because that is the agreement we have struck as a society.

First Nations in Saskatchewan have organized themselves in a variety of ways. There has been much interference in the manner of their organization via the Government of Canada and the *Indian Act*. But as a result of those primary, generative rights Slattery describes, Aboriginal peoples have the right to organize themselves and to determine who their members are, both as an incident of their right to self-government and also as an incident of their right to cultural integrity. These laws help to preserve the very existence of the group in whom the rights inhere.

Non-Aboriginal governments can acknowledge these basic rights by simply acknowledging the manner in which Aboriginal peoples have constituted themselves. Since these are laws internal to the rights-bearing group, it is difficult to understand why non-Aboriginal governments would be threatened by this manifestation of self-determination. Constitutions of Aboriginal governments, just like constitutions of other governments, generally provide for key elements in a governmental structure: the establishment of governmental bodies for the purpose of making, administering, and enforcing Aboriginal laws; the selection processes for, and terms of office of, members of the governmental bodies; the democratic accountability of the government to the people; the procedures to be followed by the government in making, amending, and repealing laws; and the procedure by which the Constitution can be amended. These are the basic means by which a constitution seeks to establish governmental structures that have the legitimacy to enhance public confidence in, and support for, the government; accountability, transparency, and responsibility to enhance responsiveness to and operation for the benefit of members; and flexibility to adapt over time in an orderly process, while providing equilibrium, reliability, and predictability.

Other key constituents of basic governance include membership and election codes. In the federal and provincial context in Canada, the *Constitution Acts* and, in Saskatchewan, the *Saskatchewan Act*, provide the basic governance framework. Citizenship and election legislation not only address the process of selecting governmental representatives within this framework, but also identify who is permitted to participate. Provinces obtain legitimacy internally through the shared features of the constitution and externally through recognition and acknowledgement of other governments. Non-Aboriginal governments should be prepared to recognize the ways in which Aboriginal peoples choose to organize themselves, in the same way that they expect that recognition to be provided to them by others, including Aboriginal peoples.

B. Access to Laws

Many people have had occasion to ponder the classic philosophical conundrum: if a tree falls in the forest and there is no one there to hear it, does it make a sound? There is a parallel question that can be asked about law: if a lawmaker makes a law and no one knows, is it a law? Aboriginal governments must appreciate that if their laws are not heard, they might just as well not exist. This means that Aboriginal laws must be ultimately captured in some written or crystallized form and must be easily accessible. In the age of the internet, this generally means having the full text available online, but it could also include oral explanations or descriptions of the law that might approximate the teachings of the Elders. As technology continues to improve, this method of the keeping and recording Aboriginal laws is more possible.

There is already a significant body of Aboriginal law, but it is not widely known. This body of law not only includes laws about Aboriginal peoples, but also laws by Aboriginal peoples. Perhaps these laws exist on some websites, but they cannot easily be found. Saskatchewan's Queen's Printer has developed a certain skill with respect to managing the on-line database of provincial legislation. It would not be difficult to use that expertise to assist Aboriginal governments in establishing and maintaining a similar website. The mechanism to achieve this goal is not law but intergovernmental agreement. However, it would require the Province of Saskatchewan to acknowledge the existence of Aboriginal laws.

C. Corporate Organization

Both Saskatchewan and Canada enact statutes that incorporate specific entities or that provide for a general means of incorporation. Saskatchewan, for example, has a large number of private Acts that establish various corporate entities. These include bodies such as religious organizations,[23] exhibition associations,[24] educational institutions,[25] and health services organizations.[26] In each case, the statute creates these organizations as legal entities, provides for their mandate or objects, authorizes them to perform certain types of activities in pursuit of those objects, and regulates the relationships between owners or shareholders and directors.

General legislation, such as *The Business Corporations Act*,[27] provides a mechanism whereby private individuals can file documents containing information in a corporate registry that is run by government. In return, they receive legal status as a body corporate. The information that must be provided is minimal: they must indicate who the shareholders are and how many shares they have, who the directors are, where the registered office is located, and any restrictions on the activities the corporation can carry on. This information must be updated at least annually or when changes occur in directors or the location of the registered office.

Legal status as a body corporate includes two critical features: legal personality, which provides for the right to sue or be sued in the corporation's name and for the continuation of the corporate entity after the death of the individuals who establish it; and limited liability. Incorporation also puts in place a structure of corporate governance, and the corporations legislation provides a framework within which the corporation must function. Legislation in Canada and in each of the provinces is all very similar. However, each provincial jurisdiction must enact corporations legislation in order to provide for incorporation in the province. The legislation also provides for recognition and registration of extra-provincial corporations doing business within the jurisdiction.

Federal and provincial legislation also establishes what are called "Crown corporations." These are corporate entities set up as instruments of government action. The first *Crown Corporations Act* in Saskatchewan was enacted in 1945.[28] It creates a mechanism for government to use corporate structures to advance government objectives.

Aboriginal governments are frequently required to incorporate corporate entities under provincial or federal law in order to comply with the funding requirements of other government or in order to achieve their own objectives and to have the advantages that corporate structures provide: legal personality and limited liability.

Why then can First Nations' governments not enact corporations legislation to provide for the incorporation of First Nation corporations? What does incorporation involve? It simply involves the creation and maintenance of a list that contains basic information. These entities are corporations because they have provided basic information to the province and they have paid a fee. It is not obvious what problems will be created by Aboriginal governments creating their own corporations. What is obvious are the positive consequences that would result: respect, acknowledgement, and a small measure of self-determination.

All that is required for these positive consequences is a small amount of co-operation. This is also an area in which it is possible to start with a small step: acknowledging the right of Aboriginal governments to create the equivalent of Crown corporations for economic and social development. The public will know that these corporations exist in the same way that Saskatchewan or Canada lets the public know – by passing a law that creates the entity. The federal and provincial governments can also assist by providing for Aboriginal corporations in the same or a similar way that they provide for corporations incorporated in other provinces – through "extra-provincial" registration.

Thus, an Aboriginal corporation would be on the same footing as an Alberta or Manitoba corporation doing business in Saskatchewan. It would also be possible to enter into intergovernmental agreements to provide for integrated online corporate registry systems.

There is a whole range of related legislation that could be dealt with in a similar way. In particular, the Uniform Law Conference of Canada has pursued for several years what it describes as a Commercial Law Strategy, which aims to provide a degree of seamlessness among the legislation of provinces in the commercial law area.[29] This is an important matter for the conduct of business in a globalized world. If it is a matter of importance to provinces, it is likely also a matter of importance to Aboriginal governments. Recognition of Aboriginal laws in relation to these subjects would assist provinces in their pursuit of economic objectives, and would be another example of the ease with which Aboriginal jurisdiction can be recognized and implemented in a manner that is not threatening to non-Aboriginal governments and institutions.

Of course, this is not to suggest that the only Aboriginal jurisdiction that could or should be recognized is jurisdiction that does not rock the boat.

D. Constitutional Questions

Although there are many other matters that could be pursued in a similar manner, the last area this chapter will discuss the matter of *The Constitutional Questions Act*.[30] Under the Saskatchewan legislation, whenever someone wishes to call into question the validity of a provincial law or if a constitutional question is at stake, the Attorney-General must be notified and is given the right to intervene. The court is directed that it may not reach a conclusion on such issues unless this notice is given. The Attorney-General is then entitled as of right to appear in court and to be heard on the issue, or to choose not to participate in the proceeding. In practical terms, the Attorney-General will only intervene in those matters where there is a matter of significant concern and the court should have all arguments available to it before making its decision.

This legislation is viewed as being good public policy. Fundamental questions about the validity of legislation or the application of the *Canadian Charter of Rights and Freedoms*[31] should not be decided without the Crown being heard in support of its legislation. The same public policy applies to Aboriginal governments. The rights of Aboriginal peoples, which are constitutionally protected rights, after all, should not be determined by courts in the absence of representations from the very peoples whose rights are under scrutiny. Many of the important issues of Aboriginal rights have been determined without any input from Aboriginal peoples, and this is a matter of sensitivity and concern as a result. Indeed, *St. Catherine's Milling and Lumber Co. v. R.*,[32] a seminal case relating to Aboriginal title, was ultimately decided by the Judicial Committee of the Privy Council in just this way.

There are some apparently difficult logistical issues concerning this legislation, however. For example, would all 72 individual First Nation governments in Saskatchewan be entitled to intervene? This sounds somewhat overwhelming. However, there is no need to worry about the floodgates opening because the practicalities of the situation will produce a pragmatic result. Simply stated, litigation is expensive. Aboriginal governments will intervene only when they have assessed the situation as one so important that intervention is required. In addition, Aboriginal governments will be able to work together to intervene, since in many cases they will have similar interests at stake and co-operating will be a viable approach. But those are questions for Aboriginal governments to decide in individual cases. They do not need to be answered at the outset and in a factual vacuum. However, it would be necessary to streamline the notification process for litigants, who will need to know who to contact and how. Again, this is an issue that can be dealt with through administrative or intergovernmental arrangements, as long as it is clear that the outcome is agreed upon: Aboriginal governments will have notice of cases in which issues of Aboriginal or treaty rights are being raised and they will have an opportunity to intervene.

Achieving this objective will require legislation to be enacted by Aboriginal governments, but it will also require legislation to be enacted by the Province of Saskatchewan to recognize that legislation and to direct Saskatchewan courts to act upon it.

VIII. CONCLUSION

In conclusion, it must be said that the implementation Aboriginal self-government is essential to a positive future for Saskatchewan. Aboriginal and non-Aboriginal governments alike must work toward establishing and maintaining a relationship that is truly built on mutual respect and equality. The suggestions in this chapter are intended as illustrations of areas in which it is possible to implement self-government incrementally so that all of us are able to see that self-government is not just possible but is also pragmatic. Those of us who are non-Aboriginal peoples in Saskatchewan must also recognize that the work to be done to implement self-government is work that will assist us in future, when the demographic pendulum has swung and we are the minority that is asking for recognition.

3

LOOKING AHEAD

A PRAGMATIC OUTLOOK ON ABORIGINAL SELF-RULE

Martin Blanchard[*]

1. INTRODUCTION

Many philosophers and political theorists have explored the accommodation of claims made by Aboriginal people in Canada.[1] The majority of these works are about the theoretical problems surrounding these accommodations. While public officials on both sides are negotiating territorial, political, social, and cultural matters, philosophers and political theorists have concentrated their efforts on debating conceptual issues, and they have rarely stepped out of academic circles to discuss public policies. The major goal of this chapter will be to explore the actual public policy of the Canadian federal and provincial governments, a policy that tries to answer Aboriginal self-rule claims in the form of treaty negotiations. Much has been written on Aboriginal court cases, while few have investigated the actual treaties and agreements negotiated between Aboriginal people and non-Aboriginal people. Yet, there is much that can be learned from studying the public policy mechanisms used in treaty negotiations in order to understand contemporary conflicts.

A pragmatic framework – deemed by some to be the only philosophical approach that originated in North America – is needed to illuminate potential lessons from the study of treaty negotiations. Popularized at the end of the nineteenth century in the works of Charles Sanders Peirce, William James,

* A first version of this chapter was presented at the SIPP conference, "Moving Towards Justice," held in Regina in March 2006. I would like to thank the conference organizers for their wonderful work. I would also like to thank all persons who have commented on this paper, especially the research team at the Centre de recherche en éthique de l'Université de Montréal.

and, principally, John Dewey, the pragmatic approach is characterized by a methodology which evaluates the reasonableness of actions and concepts, through their usefulness or practicality.[2] It strongly criticizes abstract ideas that idealize singular experiences and have limited or no useful application in the real world. Instead, pragmatists recommend a problem-solving approach that carefully balances empirical observation and rigorous normative thinking in order to adapt ideas to an ever-changing experience. In the last few decades, pragmatism has taken on numerous forms that are not reducible to the classical model described here, although the spirit is still the same.

This chapter endeavours to steer clear of difficult methodological questions concerning the value of pragmatism as compared to other philosophical positions.[3] Instead, and in keeping with the pragmatist spirit, this chapter will directly assess the value of the pragmatic approach by considering the contribution it can make to the debate over Aboriginal claims. In this respect, this chapter will investigate if recent agreements signed in Quebec have any chance of meeting the claims made by Aboriginal people, and how one must understand these claims and the agreements recently signed, in order to evaluate the likelihood that these claims will be met.

Finally, it is necessary to clarify an important philosophical concern. In most of its modern expressions, political philosophy has been silently complacent with the "powers that be" in regard to Aboriginal issues, and has, on some occasions, even encouraged the means and goals of colonization. Post-colonialist philosophical theory must break with this tradition. This chapter has no intention to encourage what is believed to be, at the present time, procrastination over Aboriginal claims in government offices. Instead, this chapter will evaluate the ability of modern treaties to bring about justice and, thus, halt the enervation in treaty negotiations as a means to postpone justice. Many Aboriginal persons are becoming increasingly impatient with the procrastination over the application of the treaties that are already signed. This chapter is a public plea to act quickly to bring about justice. Consequently, if treaties should prove to be an impediment to justice, then in a true pragmatic spirit, treaty apologists will have to end their pleadings in favour of the treaties.

This chapter will provide an outline of a model of justice that would satisfy the most developed positions of claims made by Aboriginal peoples, followed by a pragmatic interpretation of this model of justice, and a discussion of the most important aspects of the recent agreements signed in Quebec. In a pragmatic fashion, the final section will show how different viewpoints on the treaties can be made to work together toward common goals, which can be described using three fundamental objectives: individual self-development, balance of power between groups, and the protection of cultural diversity.

II. A Model of Justice

Political philosophers devote considerable time to supporting reasoning that justifies common goals. While it is a good thing to insist on justification, such an activity artificially creates philosophical oppositions that are rarely overcome. Moreover, public policies are evaluated in light of these oppositions and become themselves entangled in theoretical clashes.[4] In order to answer many urgent problems that Aboriginal communities are now facing,[5] philosophers must learn to propose sound advice concerning public policies in Aboriginal matters and rise above the opposition that characterizes debates over justifications. With its focus on the commonalities that foster acceptable results, a pragmatic approach can answer this need by insisting on the connection that links attainable goals and actual institutions.[6] In this respect, it is important to depict a model of justice that best captures the common goals of all the parties involved in the reconciliation of Aboriginal and non-Aboriginal people.

What is needed is a model of justice that presents attainable goals through the examples of actual institutions. To simplify this model, it will be limited to the major social institutions that form the "basic structure of a society," a move inspired by the seminal work of John Rawls in his *Theory of Justice*.[7] Rawls is right to point out that "justice is the first virtue of social institutions";[8] a society moving toward justice must, as its starting point, consider the design of social institutions as supporting much of the fabric of a society, even if there may be more to justice than merely benefiting from just social institutions.

The second simplification is to define justice as fairness, another idea taken from Rawls.[9] Social institutions are characterized as "just" if every member of the society is better off as a whole in a given institutional scheme. In other words, if each and every citizen's primary needs are met in a balanced set of institutions where giving preferential treatment to any one member of the society would not be possible without unfairly disadvantaging another, then we have an equitable distribution of resources that accounts for the relative position of each and every member of society. That is what fairness is about, and justice is defined here as primarily addressing fairness.

Third, it is necessary to develop a preliminary sketch of fair institutions that will respond to a number of claims made by non-urban Aboriginal people in Canada. Combined with the two preceding remarks, this means that the goal of a model of justice geared toward Aboriginal people can be characterized by "the reconciliation of aboriginal prior occupation with the assertion of the sovereignty of the Crown."[10] In our contemporary era – that is, since 1973 when a strong dissenting opinion in *Calder* v. *A.G.(B.C.)*[11] recognized the existence of Aboriginal title, despite colonial proclamations – Aboriginal people have consistently demanded that they be treated as equal peoples. Additionally, public policy officials have rejected the strategy of assimilating Aboriginal persons in the cultural majority of the Canadian society.[12] Therefore, distributing resources in a fair way will involve treating many Aboriginal claims as claims originating from peoples that were prior occupants of Canada. Thus, equality will involve fairness of treatment between different peoples inhabiting Canada.

Keeping these three limitations in mind, the following six social institutions would be constitutive of a fair model of justice balancing the interests of Aboriginal and non-Aboriginal people:

(i)   Territories: Aboriginal people would have recovered what they deem to be a fair share of the territories over which they are now claiming their right. A portion of this territory, one much larger than the surface of their actual reserves, would be for their exclusive use: on this territory, they could fish, hunt, and exploit resources as they wish, and they would enjoy exclusive juridical control. A second and much larger portion would be administered in co-operation with the provincial and federal governments.

(ii)   Political representation: Something akin to a First Nations' parliament would represent the Aboriginal people. It would elect representatives who are accountable to the people, vote statutes, audit the bureaucratic structure, etc. This political representation would be characterized by a mixture of Aboriginal and modern models of governance. It would form part of a three-level structure with the federal and provincial governments without being absolutely superseded by either of these two levels; in some fields, it would have more power than the federal or provincial levels, and in other fields, it would defer its competences to the other levels.

(iii)   Economy: A substantial amount of money would be raised by the federal and provincial governments in order to enable the administration of territorial, political, social, economic, and other institutions by the autonomous First Nations. As the Aboriginal people would gain sovereignty, they would learn to take control of their own resources. They would gain control over natural resources, but also over services and goods: ecotourism could be a great development path, for instance, as well as specialized services such as IT niches, etc. Tribal decision-making would have many ways of expressing itself, which would respect and encourage a linking of sustainable economic development with self-rule.

(iv) Education: With increased confidence, Aboriginal people would enjoy an education system of their own which would continue to grow. They would develop a system adapted to the small size of their population, a system admired by non-Aboriginal people to the point that more than a few would send their own children to Aboriginal schools in exchange programs. Universities would develop partnerships that allow students to acquire education and training in different communities.

(v)   Justice: Aboriginal people would possess their own tribunals, with their own procedures and jurisprudence. They would sentence non-Aboriginal people if the offence was committed on Aboriginal territory. Their expertise with reconciliation and community healing would attract many specialists from all over the world.

(vi) Health: Aboriginal people would treat traditional health problems in a holistic way, which would require a general plan directed at healing socio-psychological problems. By channelling their resources toward a more holistic health care plan, they would produce promising results, which could lead to profitable research activities. In return, these resources could help to develop a comprehensive and more effective social and medical care system.

III. The Potential of Pragmatism

Most philosophers and political theorists who have an awareness of Aboriginal claims can agree with this model of justice, in part because it meets many of their moral intuitions, but also because it is attainable. To be sure, one can imagine that such an outcome would necessitate many struggles. Also, since the exact nature of an institution depends on the reasons that justify its existence, there would be additional struggles over the defining features of these institutions. While this argument does not rely on some kind of magical thinking that would pretend to erase these difficulties, it is still important to stress the fact that our society is deeply pluralistic: many members of our society possess reasonable but competing worldviews. In such a pluralistic society, moving toward justice requires a goal that can be adopted by many different points of view, which creates the difficult task of justifying proposals without being able to rely on a single worldview shared by all citizens.

Since the beginning of our modern era, many philosophical strategies have been developed to downplay this problem. Among these, there is the strategy of limiting justifications to the evaluation of the costs and benefits of a given scenario, insisting on the usefulness or practicality of a proposed model and claiming that any plurality accepting a given proposal is, in itself, a sufficient justification. Finally, one could claim that even if a "thick" worldview is unavailable, a "thin" or "public" worldview is all that we would need to justify institutional proposals.

There is no single answer to the difficult problem of justifying policy proposals in a pluralistic society. Some particular problems require the use of shared reasons, especially where crucial decisions relating to the human body are involved (for instance, prohibiting or permitting the death penalty). Other problems are so complex that they mix cost/benefit schemes, reflexive acceptance from all parties, usefulness, public reason-giving, and other justifications (the signature and implementation of international conventions is one case in mind). The only way out of this murky reality is to adopt a pluralistic version of the problem of justification, which would contend that depending on the situation at hand, some strategies are better than others. However, in order to choose one strategy over the other, a pragmatic outlook on justifications is needed. With its focus on practicality, pragmatism can make the case that the model of justice this chapter outlines is (at least partly) justified on the grounds that it is acceptable from many reasonable viewpoints; a further proviso is that this model, which is anchored in the institutional fabric of our society, would be an attainable model of justice that could stand out as the best outcome of a debate involving every reasonable position.

The potential of pragmatism is found in demonstrating how it can transform the proposed model of justice in a reasonable consensus over fair social institutions that would give Aboriginal and non-Aboriginal people all the necessary tools to work together on equal footing. A starting point is the assumption that the expression of Aboriginal claims and their resolution involves irreducible points of view. This situation arises because the parties have reputedly put forth many competing worldviews. In such a complex society, there is no single view that could legitimately cover all the necessary ground to render a model of justice that is acceptable to all citizens. Too many complex justifications are involved over a very wide range of problems and competing worldviews. Accepting this starting point is based on the observation of important facts in our society. Yet, being pluralistic about this model of justice is not just a question of observing facts. A pluralistic and pragmatic philosophical stance can show us that a multi-faceted and problem-solving model is the best way to answer Aboriginal claims. In fact, it represents the best hope to move toward the model of justice that this chapter proposes.

Instead of illustrating the potential of pragmatism in an abstract way, examination of the recent agreements signed in Quebec will establish that the content of these agreements represents a promising means to approach a fair set of social institutions. Pragmatic reading of these agreements can be adopted from many points of view, since their content can be viewed by concerned parties as justified means in the aim of moving toward justice. A pragmatic approach can show that the model of justice previously outlined represents a common goal in the form of the recent agreements signed in Quebec that most informed actors would support.

IV. JUSTICE NOW: THE RECENT AGREEMENTS SIGNED IN QUEBEC

In Quebec, two major agreements with Aboriginal people have been signed in the last few years. Many observers have said that these agreements mark the beginning of a new era. While this has yet to be shown, it has been repeated so many times that it deserves a certain amount of scrutiny.

Signed in February of 2002 by, among others, Ted Moses, Grand Chief of the Cree Council and Bernard Landry, Prime Minister of Quebec at the time, the first agreement discussed is the *Agreement Concerning A New Relationship between le Gouvernement du Québec and the Crees Of Québec*, which both parties have called the *Paix des Braves*.[13] This agreement has the concrete effect of withdrawing a great number of court litigations intended by Cree people against the government of Quebec and Hydro-Québec, in exchange for a financial compensation of 4.5 billion dollars spread over 50 years.

In a nutshell, the *Paix des Braves* stands as the implementation of the *James Bay and Northern Quebec Convention* of 1975,[14] pompously presented at the time as a modern treaty, but subsequently and disgracefully only half-implemented. In this perspective, the *Paix des Braves* is an avowal that the 1975 promises were, in the least, half-void. This is not the whole story, however. What really drew attention when the *Paix des Braves* was revealed is the "new relationship" hinted at in the title:

> This Agreement marks an important stage in a new nation-to-nation relationship, one that is open, respectful of the other community and that promotes a greater responsibility on the part of the Cree Nation for its own development within the context of greater autonomy.[15]

The "nation-to-nation" phrase was coined again during the signing ceremony and was so prominent in the media that it has certainly marked Quebec's recent history. Among other things, it has drawn attention to nation builders of the Cree nation. While many Cree people, including the Grand Council, are claiming that they are not deferring to the "white people" to empower them – a call for self-development that is perfectly understandable – being a nation still implies being recognized as such. A true and sincere recognition that is really mutual implies at least two conditions:[16] first, the recognition must take place between peoples who consider each other as equals, and second, the subsequent actions of each must respect this equality. As for the *Paix des Braves*, it is too early to assess whether or not this agreement is truly mutual recognition. Starting with the political and academic elites, relationships improved between the communities as a result of the agreement. Inside the Cree communities themselves, the financial compensations and the confidence gained have also caused a great leap in the Cree business community (examples include Air Creebec, Cree Construction and Development Company, Cree Regional Economic Enterprises Co. [CREECO], and CREEADGA Limited Partnership, etc.).[17]

The economic development of the Cree nation therefore seems to be on the rise, and part of the reason can be attributed to the *Paix des Braves*. Much more, however, needs to be achieved in order to attain justice as defined earlier, a model of justice that includes six institutional domains: territorial sovereignty, political representation, education, economic development, justice, and health. Except for economic development and territorial sovereignty, none of the other four domains have received any attention in the "new relationship" agreement of the *Paix des Braves*.

This could simply be a matter of time. A second treaty, this time negotiated with Innu nations, indicates that some progress may be underway.[18] The content of this treaty can be foreseen by looking at a pre-treaty agreement that was signed in March of 2004, called the *Approche Commune*, which outlined the principles to be contained in the future treaty.[19] Though it is important to remain prudent in analyzing this *Agreement-in-Principle* (AIP), principles do justify one's actions; principles are thus acted upon and are powerful tools to criticize incompatibilities between justified norms, public acceptance of principles, and observed acts. For instance, the more a society solemnly adopts the principles of sustainable development, the less it can act in derogation of these principles. Leaving aside the hypocritical use of public declarations of principles, to which this chapter will return shortly, it is possible to predict if and how the treaties are moving toward justice by examining the AIP's underlying principles.

First, it is necessary to enumerate and qualify what are the most important principles at work in the AIP, and then attempt to demonstrate that not only can these principles be justified from many perspectives, but they can also lead to implementation of the model of justice previously described. Five important principles are at work in the AIP.

A. The Move from a Politics of Extinction to a Politics of Recognition

In a "Whereas" clause, the AIP states that the parties are committed not to the extinction but to the "recognition, confirmation and continuation"[20] of the ancestral rights of First Nations, including the Aboriginal title. Moreover, this recognition is said to be preferably assured by political negotiations rather than by judiciary fights. Section 3.3 of the AIP is devoted to the question of negotiation: it states, among other things, that self-government, as an inherent right, is an ancestral right of First Nations peoples.[21] To attain political stability, the extinction of Aboriginal rights would be replaced by "suspending" other rights than those defined in the treaty. This clause is qualified by other clauses compelling the parties to renegotiate the treaty in the event that a court has granted ancestral rights that infringe on the Treaty.

B. Empowerment

To be empowered is to possess the means to enjoy one's own autonomy. Section 11.2.1 of the AIP qualifies this empowerment principle: it states that the parties agree to finance Aboriginal self-government as a joint responsibility, and the common aim is to gradually move toward autonomous funding of the Aboriginal self-government. This implies a good control over territorial resources, among other things, as well as exploitation royalties from non-Aboriginal firms and governments. Another important qualification of the empowerment principle is that its stated aim is to ensure that "First Nations catch up, when required, with the level of economic self-development enjoyed by neighboring communities."[22] These two qualifications of the principle of empowerment are also explicitly referred to in the *Paix des Braves*.[23]

C. Self-Government

The AIP refers to *Innu tshishe utshimau* as the autonomous governing authority of Innu First Nations (each First Nation having its own authority).[24] For instance, they would be consulted for territorial exploitation by the provincial and federal governments. A more constructed reference is to the future legislative assemblies of First Nations, which would possess legislative powers over a great number of domains for which they would have legal preponderance:

> [I]nternal organization and administration of *Innu tshishe utshimau*; administration of treaty rights; protection and promotion of language, culture, heritage, identity and traditional life; hunting, fishing, trapping and cherry-picking matters; control and administration of Innu Assi; environmental concerns; education; family law; peace, security and public order; health and social services; traditional medicine; welfare; labour formation and development; quality control of traditional arts; and "Any other matter that has a meaningful link with the identity of First Nations or that aims to protect Innu aboriginality ("indianité") or a dominant characteristic of its society."[25]

Clearly, laws that First Nations would be empowered to enact, by virtue of these treaties, are not backed by what some call cultural rights, since a "dominant characteristic" is not necessarily cultural (for instance, business laws are seldom if ever understood as cultural laws). With this explicit reference to First Nations as societies, the treaties grant to First Nations a collective right to govern themselves in all relevant domains, with the important qualification of not infringing on the rights of other communities. This interpretation clarifies the above quote, where the legislative powers of First Nations extend to any dominant characteristic of its society.[26]

The recognition of the collective rights of First Nations goes much further than the recognition of their cultural rights. The latter is totally compatible with a unitary state that strongly asserts exclusive control over important political matters, while the former implies a multinational state which balances power issues between different societies or nations. One may question the capacity of a multinational state to meet Aboriginal claims concerning self-government, but cultural rights are far from meeting these claims, even if they offer a convenient resolution to language and cultural identity claims. In other words, effective political pluralism is better served by the sort of collective rights referred to in the AIP than it would be by cultural rights granting minorities some control over identity matters, while retaining effective political power in the hands of the unitary state. This view may be assessed through weighing the different reasoning patterns that justify the treaties.

The recent treaties refer to the devolution of power, and there are all sorts of mechanisms designed to resolve incompatibilities resulting from the legal pluralism that will entail. All the above domains[27] have Innu preponderance, while a number of domains are excluded from Innu legislative powers.[28] These are matters pertaining to section 91 of the Constitution:[29] immigration, registration of vehicles, and no-fault regimes. In domains other than AIP subsection 8.4.4.1, Canadian and Québécois laws would continue to apply, except in a few cases.[30] An important planned mechanism is one that would adapt interpretative principles to Innu, Québécois, and Canadian laws.[31] Finally, while Innu First Nations possess the duty to elaborate their own Constitution in section 8.1, the Canadian Constitution, including the *Charter*,[32] continues to apply to Innus, to their territories, and to *Innu tshishe utshimaut*, as stated in the preamble and in other parts of the AIP.[33]

D. Justice Administration

The AIP plans the creation of an Innu tribunal that will effectively be responsible for the administration of Innu laws.[34] This tribunal is to be gradually implemented, extending its jurisdiction as far as penal and criminal law. It will have the legitimate power to initiate alternative justice mechanisms, such as restorative justice, justice circles, and other forms of mediation. Finally, the jurisdiction of the Innu tribunal will extend to non-Innu people on Innu territory and to Innu people on non-Innu territory, though the wording of this clause is quite vague.

E. Negotiation and Reconciliation

This principle is not defined at all in the AIP. Moreover, it has been inserted only in a "Whereas" clause and in the general dispositions clauses of the arbitration chapter. It could thus be said to be ineffective, but one might wonder why both the *Paix des Braves* and the AIP refer at all to these principles. Two general answers can be provided.

The first and more optimistic answer would attempt to demonstrate that reconciliation is the most important principle upon which this new relationship is being built. The challenge facing Aboriginal people and non-Aboriginal people is not just one of mutually recognizing each other on a piece of paper; the core issue is about acting in accordance with this mutual recognition. Therefore, if the recognition is mutual and sincere, values like conciliation, co-operation, harmony, negotiation, and the like will have to act as effective principles. The fact that the two agreements exist is a first and important sign of the existence of a new relationship that replaces the extinction of rights policy with a politics of recognition. Another fact pointing to the effectiveness of the new relationship is the Quebec parliamentary commission held in 2003, which had the mandate of inquiring about the ratification of the AIP.[35] This commission received 80 mémoires from all sorts of public organisms, the majority of which were favourable to the ratification, but also to the negotiation and the reconciliation pattern. Although a motion was voted in 2003 at the National Assembly of Quebec compelling the government to introduce a non-Aboriginal regional representative in the negotiation, this move has been denounced as politically suspect by many non-Aboriginal people, another hint of a shift in negotiation patterns. Finally, the economic development of Aboriginal communities is in better shape since the agreements were signed,[36] although it is clear that Aboriginal peoples have not waited for the recent treaties to take control of their own collective matters. These facts thus seem to indicate that the treaties are part of a general movement of Aboriginal emancipation.

A second and more pessimistic answer would argue that the treaties are so imprecise and vague on the deeper question of reconciliation that they can be suspected of not addressing the issues at hand. Objectives are not really stated, stakes are not pointed at, aims are not refined, and nuances are largely absent. What exactly are the objectives of these agreements, then? Are they just a way of buying time? While ancestral and collective rights are recognized in the treaties, are there any signs that they will be respected? The facts outlined in the preceding paragraph do not easily prove that the treaties themselves are responsible for some kind of rebirth in the Aboriginal communities. It could be more appropriate to say that, tired of waiting for some positive response from the government, Aboriginal people have taken matters in their own hands. It seems, therefore, that one must stop praising the treaties and develop community-based projects if the goal is to move toward Aboriginal justice here and now.

At present, it is difficult to determine which of these two interpretations is more relevant. Each has some compelling justification. However, what is instructive, at least from a pragmatic and pluralistic point of view, is that both positions are implicitly based on the idea that anchoring the treaties and other modes of political mobilization in a model of justice resembling the one proposed earlier is the best way to proceed.

v. A Pragmatic and Pluralistic Interpretation of the Treaties

The previous sections defend two important ideas. The first idea is that despite the profound pluralism of views that characterize our society, it could be possible to secure quite a large consensus around a set of fair social institutions that would express what justice toward Aboriginal people is primarily about. While this fair set of institutions in the model of justice proposed may not be sufficient to speak about a true and full-blown model of justice, it must be viewed as a necessary starting point in the context of our society. Moving toward justice would imply this minimum stage.

In order to show that such a model is attainable, a pragmatic viewpoint insists not only on its anchoring in actual institutions, but also on its acceptability from many reasonable viewpoints. It is with this idea in mind that one can look at the recent agreements signed in Quebec. In many ways, their content comes within reach of the model of justice this chapter proposes. Concerning territorial dispositions and economic development, they grant to Aboriginal communities co-management with non-Aboriginal people of a large territory over which the Cree and the Innu people would enjoy full autonomy in many domains;[37] they offer a compensation plan that appears to be strong enough to build a development path. As for the other domains, these agreements grant a full devolution of powers in education and health services, and they propose what appears to be a balanced devolution of the administration of justice. Further, these agreements embrace executive and legislative assembly powers which include a great number of claims made by First Nations. Finally, they clearly express a will to recognize ancestral rights while disavowing the disgraceful politics of extinction.

These recent agreements are, in my view, about moving toward justice. Most philosophical positions supporting or rejecting the agreements are not only convergent over the content of these agreements, but they are also complementary in their interpretations of the best means to attain justice, at least as far as the agreements are concerned. They are complementary in two ways: the "minority rights" approach stresses individual empowerment and would be mostly optimistic in its interpretation of the agreements, while the "difference" approach insists on collective empowerment and would have more pessimistic comments, as far as the agreements are concerned. Possible interpretations of the treaties will be limited in this chapter to these two mainstream approaches.

While this is a simplification, it must be viewed as a heuristic device designed to cover all possible cases in a synthetic perspective.

The minority rights position has been well developed and popularized by Will Kymlicka.[38] This position aims to transform the Canadian state through a cultural rights approach centered on the individual. This view would grant Aboriginal peoples the right to create special institutions and laws in order to protect their culture (language laws, for instance) as long as these laws did not infringe on the rights of individuals. In order to guarantee this protection, most proponents of this view proscribe any collective rights and assertions of self-determination that would be suspected of infringement on the individual.

The rationale of this position is to argue that we face identity claims because individuals wish to protect their culture, and therefore, we should limit these claims to the protection of the individual's cultural environment. Yet, this defence of Aboriginal claims and other minority rights creates many problems. Concerning the agreements studied in this chapter, the problem is that all self-government clauses are interpreted under the minority rights view as clauses devoted to preserving individuals' preferences over cultural settings of their choice. Even before criticizing this reading of self-government as culture preservation, one should resist the interpretation of culture as a matter of individual preferences; this interpretation violates our intuition that preserving culture is a matter of collective action voiced as a duty for the individual.[39] For instance, the preservation of language does not gain efficiency simply by maximizing benefits. To be sure, preservation measures do account for costs in a certain way, but no one would think to discard language protection as soon as the costs and benefits involved are unbalanced. People continue to speak their language because they feel it is a duty to do so, not because it involves lower costs than speaking another language.

There are other normative problems, such as the difficulty in precisely determining an individual's preferences over culture. Concerning the Quebec agreements, two comments are noteworthy. The first one is that the whole point of the minority rights position is to promote a diversity of social institutions so that all individuals, including those belonging to minorities, benefit from a full spectrum of choice in which they can develop their capacities. Even if this position has difficulties with, among other things, defining culture as a preference scheme, it is important to stress that Kymlicka would view the proposed model of justice as a reasonable goal of the minority rights approach, since it would realize something akin to an Aboriginal context of choice that the minority rights position advocates.

Kymlicka would certainly qualify his acceptance of this model of justice by insisting on the protection of individuals' rights. This qualification would not however prohibit an endorsement of the Quebec agreements, since they insist on the application of the *Canadian Charter of Rights and Freedoms* on Innu and Cree territories. This clause makes the minority rights approach a potentially strong supporter of the agreements through claims that are directed at enabling Aboriginal institutions to be on par with what the majority of Canadians are enjoying. Yet, Kymlicka's individualist bias would make it difficult to identify which group may benefit from these contexts of choice. This support is, nonetheless, a strong indicator of the normative weight that can be attached to the treaties, as well as the attainability of justice through the promotion of the treaties.

The second approach, the difference approach, is congruent with many nationalist theories. Supporters of this approach, such as Patrick Macklem, argue that Aboriginal claims are grounded in the cultural differences of Aboriginal ways of life.[40] These differences do not in themselves justify adopting the social institutions outlined in this chapter's model of justice; these social institutions are justified through the acknowledgement of the individual's benefits. The fact that Aboriginal peoples have a right to their social institutions is attributed to the fact that they are different. What is at stake here is a fair distribution of sovereignty between groups identified by their internal differences in cultural, social, political, and other areas. Any group providing a "shared intelligibility"[41] to its members would be recognized as worthy of taking part in the distribution of sovereignty.

A first objection to this position concerns the awkwardness of defining distinct group rights by reference to their differences from other groups. If a group starts to appear similar to other groups, is it any less a group that can enjoy its autonomy? If an Aboriginal group builds its development path in a similar vein as the Canadian majority, would it lose its claim to recognition as a group that deserves its fair share of self-government? Defining autonomy on the grounds of cultural differences would then lead to the reification of group identities. Another problem related to the reification menace is that relating group rights to their internal constitution jeopardizes the task of balancing equal rights. Any group not satisfied with its share of resources could invoke the misrecognition of its differential rights, a move which would surely spark inflated claims from other groups.

This is not to say that the difference paradigm – and in fact, the related nationalist paradigm – is completely flawed. It seems reasonable to think that the best way to attain stability and peace in multinational states is to fairly distribute state power within internal groups, and this intuition is supported by at least one important study.[42] One can also see the moral point of insisting on recognizing distinct societies; while any majority in a given state enjoys full protection and promotion of its particular way of life, why should minority groups not be able to benefit from the same institutions, if a meaningful life is one "lived within," as according to Kymlicka[43] (*i.e.*, where one's own individual path is genuinely linked to its social and natural environment)? Why should the plight of social environment always fall on the shoulders of individuals belonging to a minority? Is it fair that members of the mainstream society remain silent on these issues? These questions all point to the recognition of the diversity of groups as an important feature of modern political communities.

The insistence on the recognition of cultural diversity gives supporters of the difference paradigms strong reasons to support the model of justice this chapter is defending. In the same vein, if these supporters are serious about the argument of equality between groups, they should see that the "new relationship" agreements are the strongest assertions of equality that have been made in the modern history of Canada. However, if these agreements lead to a dead end, and if their promises are broken, then the fact that government representatives have nonetheless signed the agreements and proclaimed a new era would constitute a powerful moral argument for the continuation of the legal and political struggles. In other words, to assert difference through the implementation of the treaties seems to be the best solution, since either these treaties would create an important starting point for the deployment of Aboriginal peoples' distinct rights or the failure in their implementation would shift the burden to the provincial and federal governments and create strong moral arguments for First Nations peoples in their struggle for recognition.

The two approaches outlined demonstrate diametrically opposed difficulties. The minority rights approach focusses on the individual for many good reasons, but its difficulty lies in identifying groups that are worthy of recognition. Limiting claims to individuals' rights could damage the legitimate empowerment of groups and could therefore degenerate in a frustrating status quo where only feeble claims are satisfied. On the other side, the difference approach too readily identifies a group's internal constitution with the recognition of its rights. The result could be an escalation of conflict through a multiplied assertion of claims.

A third path is possible, which would explore the challenge posed by Aboriginal claims and would not oppose, but would complement, these two approaches: It is known in philosophy as pragmatism.[44] An important move in pragmatist theories is to reject what is called *a priori* thinking. In regard to the recognition of Aboriginal claims, the idea is to abandon any way of grounding political rights in *a priori* abstract thinking. What is at stake is not so much the direct translation of moral intuitions in the political domain, but is instead a fair balance of power between groups that uses moral intuitions as goals that motivate persons to attain equality. One of these moral intuitions concerns the value of social institutions for self-development. Avigail Eisenberg has demonstrated how a pluralist balance of power serves both the goals of group equality and of individual self-development:

> First, with regards to aggregative power, pluralists argue that groups provide the resources through which individuals can vindicate their interests. Second, this power is abused when a single group monopolizes all the resources. Pluralism protects against this sort of monopolization. Third, with regards to developmental power, pluralism recognizes that groups facilitate individual development. And fourth, this power is abused when a single group dominates all others. Without pluralism, the individual's personality is cut off from diversity, and the possibility of autonomy is extinguished.[45]

This argument owes much to Kymlicka's minority rights approach, but it departs from Kymlicka's continued insistence on individual rights and prefers to examine the link between self-development and group autonomy in a pluralist setting. Note that if self-development is not so much a moral law as a goal to be realized in the balance of power between groups, then it becomes possible to understand the balance of power as serving many ends, provided that the idea is to relate the personality of individuals with diversity, while minimally respecting individual autonomy and fairness between groups. This may sound trivial at first, but it carries a potentially convincing method of arguing in a pluralistic context. The task of convincing non-individualists could then be limited to finding good reasons to support a given institutional balancing of power without referring to a strong version of individual autonomy.

Something that is missing in this picture, however, is an argument for the protection of diversity that would be independent from self-development. For even if pluralists argue for recognizing diversity for the sake of individual development, one could always reply that enough diversity has already been recognized and that self-development would instead require a commonality of resources. For instance, one could insist that, for the sake of individual self-development, the implementation of the treaties should be conservative, since granting too many powers of self-government to Aboriginal peoples would scatter valuable resources. In order to respond to this objection, one would need an independent argument for diversity. This argument is supported by pluralists who assert that good distinct societies benefit particular individuals' self-development, but they also benefit the human species in general. As Michel Seymour's work argues, "Just as a diversified economy can be a necessary condition for prosperity, the protection of cultural diversity is an insurance policy against the disappearance of the human species."[46] This way of asserting the value of diversity preserves the plurality of the internal constitution of groups. It is, however, a powerful argument to promote cultural diversity without directly relating the recognition of diversity to the internal differences between groups.

VI. CONCLUSION

A pragmatic and pluralist interpretation of Aboriginal claims represents a very promising approach to evaluating the modern "new relationship" treaties as a means of attaining justice. As a philosophical methodology that concentrates on the practical output of concepts, pragmatism addresses issues and problems to be solved in the very language in which they are raised. In other words, one way to build a common language is to build common goals, and the outlined model of justice identifies six institutional domains: territorial autonomy, political autonomy, economic development, education, justice, and health.

Even in the broad analysis given here, one can see that the recent Quebec agreements signed with Cree and Innu people are within reach of this model of justice. These agreements can also be viewed as means to attain justice from many viewpoints. In particular, using a pragmatist interpretation, one can bring together the two mainstream and opposed approaches on Aboriginal justice, since they share the same goals. Minority rights insist on the individual's right to take advantage of a context of choice that respects his or her cultural upbringing. The treaties respond to this claim. The difference approach argues that distinct societies should be able to enjoy their collective autonomy because they are culturally different. The treaties also answer this claim. Moreover, in the event that the treaties would not be implemented, the difference approach would benefit from a powerful moral argument to advance its claims, and this would complement the minority rights approach.

However, a pragmatic and pluralistic understanding of the goals of the agreements is necessary. One needs to understand the balance of power instituted by the agreements as a means to implement multiple goals: individual self-development and fairness between groups both need to be accounted for. Finally, an independent argument for cultural diversity is also needed, since a conservative interpretation of the agreements would probably not be convinced that needs associated with individual self-development mean that important self-government measures have to be implemented. Thus, although the "new relationship" agreements certainly need refining, a pragmatic analysis of their content demonstrates how they can represent a path to justice that is supported by multiple perspectives.

4

RECONCILIATION

LEGAL CONCEPTION(S) AND FACES OF JUSTICE

Dwight G. Newman[*]

The aim of this chapter is to examine and engage with the concept of reconciliation as it arises in the Canadian legal discourse on Aboriginal rights. More specifically, there is actually a set of conceptions, in the plural, of "reconciliation" being applied in case law on section 35, the Aboriginal rights provision of the *Constitution Act, 1982*.[1] However, there are ways to work toward synthesizing these conceptions.

The plurality of conceptions of reconciliation arises at both a macro level and a micro level. The macro stream of conceptions consists of those within the main trend line of Supreme Court of Canada case law on reconciliation. There has been a major shift in the Supreme Court of Canada's conception of reconciliation from, first, a restraint on the Crown to, and second, a factor limiting Aboriginal rights claims to, most recently, a description of a process flowing from section 35. However, matters are more complicated yet. Turning to the micro level, lower courts have used the term "reconciliation" in a number of ways seemingly not fitting with this main trend line of cases and potentially creating further confusion through the sheer variety of ways in which these lower courts have used the concept. However, our task in this area must be to try to move from confusion to coherence, and indeed, there are ways to reinterpret the concept of reconciliation so as to synthesize the plural conceptions in past jurisprudence.

At the outset, though, I must add two notes about the nature of this

[*] The author would like to thank Kelly Gould and Brian Pfefferle for helpful research assistance. I also thank the organizers of the "Moving Towards Justice" conference for the opportunity to present the paper that was the foundation of this chapter. I thank Nicole O'Byrne, Judge Mary Ellen Turpel-Lafond, and John Whyte for comments.

project. First, one common concern, and one that has no application to the claims I make in this chapter, arises from the notion that reconciliation between Aboriginal and non-Aboriginal Canadians will not be achieved until a whole series of reforms are in place outside the legal process.[2] Such criticism is a true and very important reminder of the limits of what law alone can achieve. However, it is no reason for not carefully examining the relevant legal doctrine for what it is or is not achieving and what it could potentially achieve. Second, some might express concerns about the synthesizing nature of this project. Attempting to synthesize from the set of plural conceptions of reconciliation is not an attack on "legal pluralism" per se (in the sense of the body of theory examining and developing the significance of the existence of multiple normative orders that are applicable within a certain territory).[3] Indeed, the very notion of reconciliation presupposes a plurality of normative systems, but what we cannot meaningfully have is a plurality of simultaneously valid approaches to the interaction of any such plurality of systems. We must develop shared principles on the intersystemic interaction of systems, if those systems are to operate viably. These preliminary concerns to the side, then, let us turn to how the concept of reconciliation has, or has not, functioned as an intersystemic concept, within the corpus of Canadian law.

Claims concerning reconciliation, as a purpose of section 35, first appeared in the Supreme Court of Canada's jurisprudence in *Sparrow*.[4] There, the Supreme Court, offering its first extended interpretation of section 35 and lacking prior jurisprudence on which to ground this interpretation, drew heavily on academic theory concerning section 35,[5] with various academic theorists having attempted to show how section 35 could offer pathways to a "just settlement"[6] between Canada and Aboriginal peoples. Most pertinently to the holding in the case, the Court claimed to draw, from a seminal article by Brian Slattery,[7] the concept of a justificatory scheme that the Court would impose on section 35 rights somewhat analogously to the way it applies a section 1 analysis of limits to rights contained in the *Canadian Charter of Rights and Freedoms*.[8] The term "justification" does not appear on the cited page of Slattery's article,[9] nor anywhere else in the article, but the notion may appropriately arise as an implication of Slattery's argument on what constitutes a sensible reading of section 35.[10]

However, apart from Slattery's argument, the concept of reconciliation serves as a grounding in the case for a demand of justification on government action that infringes on Aboriginal rights; as Dickson C.J. phrases it, "federal power must be reconciled with federal duty and the best way to achieve that reconciliation is to demand the justification of any government regulation that infringes upon or denies aboriginal rights."[11] Here, then, appears reconciliation of power and duty as a basis for limitation on government action; reconciliation functions as a restraint on governmental action.

Compare this conception with that propounded in more recent cases, such as *R. v. Van der Peet*[12] and *Delgamuukw v. British Columbia*.[13] The terminology now becomes one of section 35 being directed toward "the reconciliation of the pre-existence of aboriginal societies with the sovereignty of the Crown," as expressed in Lamer C.J.'s majority judgment in *Van der Peet*.[14] In that case, McLachlin J. dissented, and her dissent adhered more closely to the *Sparrow* conception of reconciliation.[15] However, Lamer C.J.'s modified conception of reconciliation won out, as he reaffirmed it in very similar language in *Delgamuukw*[16] without further objection from the other judges.[17] As he stated there, reconciliation is as he described it in *Van der Peet*: "I explained in *Van der Peet* that those [section 35] rights are aimed at the reconciliation of the prior occupation of North America by distinctive aboriginal societies with the assertion of Crown sovereignty over Canadian territory."[18]

This conceptualization was broad in its terms. However, it also supported a particular conclusion in the area of evidence law. A major issue in these cases was the adaptation of the rules of evidence to better accommodate Aboriginal rights claims, and one of the themes flowing out of them was that the courts must find ways to put weight on both Crown and Aboriginal "perspectives."[19] Chief Justice Lamer's judgment in *Delgamuukw*, in particular, did speak of adapting the rules of evidence to better accommodate Aboriginal oral history evidence, although it did so at such a sufficiently abstract level that later cases dealing with the matter more practically have ended up somewhat in retreat from it (not entirely without justification, as I argue elsewhere).[20]

However, these conclusions for evidence in Aboriginal rights cases notwithstanding, the *Van der Peet* reconceptualization of reconciliation actually places significantly more pressure on the claims of Aboriginal societies, the scope of Aboriginal rights, and the weight of evidence from Aboriginal traditions; reconciliation now becomes a concept for balancing each of these with competing Crown objectives. Instead of reconciliation functioning as a concept that calls for limits on federal powers in light of federal duties, it becomes a concept that limits the scope of section 35, based on the interpreted purpose of the section. As Patricia Monture has described it, we have an "inversion of the earlier discourse."[21]

Indeed, the sources of the *Van der Peet* concept of reconciliation are not immediately obvious. Russell Barsh and Sákéj Henderson discuss the *Van der Peet* analysis and note Lamer C.J.'s lack of reference to related concepts that were, by then, emerging in documents of the Royal Commission on Aboriginal Peoples (RCAP);[22] Barsh and Henderson go so far as to say that "'Reconciliation'... was pulled from thin air, in defiance of the main trends in contemporary constitutional thought."[23]

The claim that the modified form of the concept was plucked from thin air, however, is contestable. The judges were no doubt aware of the ongoing discussions on reconciliation in Australia, discussions that by this point were not concerned solely with the limitation of Australian governmental power.[24] They were certainly aware of the articles they cited, some of which, like those of André Émond,[25] cast a challenge as to how assertions of certain Aboriginal rights could be made consistently with the rule of law and the assertion of Crown sovereignty. As in *Sparrow* in the first place, and thus consistent with the Court's earlier methodological approach, the Court drew on academic theory to flesh out the meaning of section 35. The Court, however, seemingly turned in part to different theorists, notably some on the other side of a linguistic divide that bedevils the claims of those who attempt to characterize dominant Canadian constitutional thought in any monolithic or unilingual way. Indeed, the French-language writings of theorists like Émond manifest a different approach to Aboriginal rights that, in this instance, appears partly to have undergirded the Court's approach.[26] Although there might be further research on the point, it would seem that the Court did redevelop reconciliation in light of further intellectual influences on its jurisprudence.

One could, of course, wonder whether something more pragmatic motivated the Court's redevelopment and redeployment of the concept. Is the Court's adaptation of the concept of reconciliation motivated, rather, by something as simple as an aspiration of maintaining stability? Justice Binnie's judgment in *Mitchell* v. *Minister of National Revenue*[27] might be the sort of judgment to make one think along such lines. There, Binnie J.'s concurring opinion was, in a sense, at pains to constrain any notion of Aboriginal self-government or Aboriginal rights that would transcend Canada's national boundaries. Justice Binnie concluded against the respondent's claim in that case:

> Affirmation of the sovereign interest of Canadians as a whole, including aboriginal peoples, should not necessarily be seen as a loss of sufficient "constitutional space for aboriginal peoples to be aboriginal".... [T]he respondent's claim relates to national interests that all of us have in common rather than to distinctive interests that for some purposes differentiate an aboriginal community. In my view, reconciliation of these interests in this particular case favours an affirmation of our collective sovereignty.[28]

Here, reconciliation functions to buttress Binnie J.'s argument that the Mohawk of Akwesasne, the respondent in the case, had no Aboriginal right to trade across the Canada-US border. The case functions at once to show the pragmatic nature of reconceptualized reconciliation and also to make us wonder what conclusions should be drawn from a context that no doubt raised particularly unique concerns for the Court.

Reconciliation is by no means the sole operative concept in Aboriginal rights cases. Indeed, the concept makes only a brief and undeveloped appearance in the recent and controversial cases of *R. v. Marshall* and *Bernard*.[29] The new and very real constraints on Aboriginal title that developed in these cases flow, rather, from a renewed demand for evidence of prior occupation and an insistence on Aboriginal title claims being grounded in a proven, genuinely equivalent Aboriginal use of the land, prior to contact. So, the Court takes what it sees as pragmatic directions with Aboriginal rights jurisprudence, without relying on the concept of reconciliation and somewhat undermining any claim that reconciliation functioned fundamentally as a pragmatic check on Aboriginal rights claims.

As one further historical argument on the matter, we might note that not long after *Van der Peet*, the Court made a dramatic use of the concept of reconciliation – one not specifically in the Aboriginal rights area. In the *Secession Reference*,[30] the Court imbued the whole constitutional history of Canada with the purpose of "reconciling" diversity with unity,[31] and they went on to hold that "reconciliation" of various interests would be a necessary task in any move toward secession.[32] However, there is no genuine reason to think that the Court set up the concept of reconciliation in *Van der Peet* in preparation for the *Secession Reference* – as we might speculate about the Court's dramatic shift in interpretive methodology in the *Provincial Court Judges Reference*,[33] which cleared the way for similar reasoning in the *Secession Reference* a year later. Saying this much, of course, is not to deny the ongoing interplay in Canadian political discourse between how to respond to the collective rights claims of Aboriginal peoples and of the Québécois.[34] Indeed, we might speculate that the judicial conceptualization of negotiation from the *Secession Reference* has been infused into the latest section 35 reconciliation cases. None of this makes the *Van der Peet* concept of reconciliation into something created for a context other than section 35 itself.

If the reconceptualization of reconciliation has functioned to assist the law in maintaining stability over massive change, it is not necessarily at the expense of justice. Stability can also be a component of justice. Much of the turn in modern political theory has been, in one sense, toward the place of stability within the concept of justice.[35] There would be an interesting project in further investigating how the Supreme Court of Canada's concept of reconciliation would situate itself within this discourse, but we have now somewhat digressed from the main trend line of cases, which actually goes on to yet another conception of reconciliation.

Indeed, the Supreme Court has recently returned to the concept of reconciliation and emphasized it. The first words of Binnie J.'s judgment in the recent *Mikisew Cree First Nation* v. *Canada* ring out: "The fundamental objective of the modern law of aboriginal and treaty rights is the reconciliation of aboriginal peoples and non-aboriginal peoples and their respective claims, interests and ambitions."[36] This phrasing, of course, blurs what is to be reconciled, a matter to which we shall return. There is, even in this blurring, a sort of consensus between this judgment and the Court's recent judgments in *Haida Nation* v. *British Columbia (Minister of Forests)*[37] and *Taku River Tlingit First Nation* v. *British Columbia (Project Assessment Director)*.[38]

Reconciliation is now something that structures the processes of current interaction between the Crown and Aboriginal peoples, leading, for instance, to ongoing requirements of responsive consultation and accommodation where Aboriginal rights or title have potential application. The concept of reconciliation is not new in these cases, but the conception is. These cases, transforming section 35 from a static guarantee into a bulwark of a dynamic constitutional process,[39] also transform the conception of reconciliation from a description of an end state into a concept that simultaneously shapes a creationary constitutional process.[40] As McLachlin C.J. phrases it in the *Haida Nation* judgment, "To limit reconciliation to the post-proof sphere risks treating reconciliation as a distant legalistic goal,"[41] and the Court thus finds more in it to make it meaningful at a process level. As McLachlin C.J.'s judgment explains, the concept of reconciliation now grounds further requirements:

> Balance and compromise are inherent in the notion of reconciliation. Where accommodation is required in making decisions that may adversely affect as yet unproven Aboriginal rights and title claims, the Crown must balance Aboriginal concerns reasonably with the potential impact of the decision on the asserted right or title and with other societal interests.[42]

Thus, both the *Haida Nation* case and the *Taku River Tlingit First Nation* case find an obligation to negotiate, consult, and conceivably accommodate, even prior to final proof of Aboriginal rights claims. They ground this in the continually-renewed concept of reconciliation. The *Mikisew Cree First Nation* case sees reconciliation grounding an obligation of consultation, within the context of an ongoing treaty relationship. All these cases provide that reconciliation is a concept that guides dynamic, ongoing constitutional processes, creating a new era within the main trend line of cases we have been discussing.

If this chapter's task were to add further to confusion, it would not be difficult. We could also compile uses of the concept of reconciliation in the lower courts, where we find diversity on what is to be reconciled (including Aboriginal rights or interests with Crown sovereignty,[43] Aboriginal rights with those of non-Aboriginals,[44] Aboriginal title with rights of innocent purchasers of land,[45] different uses of the same land,[46] and exercise of Aboriginal rights with other interests[47]); how reconciliation is to occur (including the imposition of restraints on Crown power,[48] negotiation,[49] and accounting for different perspectives[50]); and a series of other issues. Some of these usages relate well to the main trend lines from the Supreme Court of Canada jurisprudence (although an interesting research project would explore the time gaps between the Supreme Court uses and the lower court uses), while other uses seem to go in different directions yet again, further manifesting the slippery nature of the concept.[51]

However, rather than adding to confusion, the aim of this chapter is further synthesis in this area. I would humbly suggest that behind the different conceptions of reconciliation and behind these different images of bringing together, resides still a uniting theme. Reconciling federal power with federal duty, pre-existing Aboriginal societies with Crown sovereignty, and claims of Aboriginal peoples and non-Aboriginal peoples are all concerned with bringing together different claims of justice.

Nothing assures us that all claims grounded in justice are necessarily compatible. Claims of historic justice, individual justice, and social justice will all present valid claims and share commonalities but may also be in tension, as may also retributive justice and restorative justice, corrective justice and present justice, and Aboriginal conceptions of justice and non-Aboriginal conceptions of justice. The legal doctrine of reconciliation asks us to find as much compatibility as possible between different justice claims.

We may be able to distinguish spheres in which such claims will be more compatible or less compatible. For instance, our discourse might be more zero-sum in nature if we are discussing the distribution of fixed resources such as property (although even there, we might be able to break up the bundle of property rights), and there might be areas in which there is genuine space for non-zero-sum compromise.

In his frustrating, yet tantalizing, words in *Mitchell*, Binnie J. writes: "I agree with Borrows . . . that accommodation of aboriginal rights should not be seen as 'a zero-sum relationship between minority rights and citizenship; as if every gain in the direction of accommodating diversity comes at the expense of promoting citizenship.'"[52] Justice Binnie, incidentally to his purposes in the case, has opened realms for further analysis with these comments; there is every reason to seek where to agree and where to disagree, and most importantly, why.

In the end, the unique word, "reconciliation," does not present a unique problem but the sort with which political and legal thought has always had to engage. To this task we must bring all of our careful thought and analysis. Reciting a particular word does not solve our problems, but it challenges us to the most careful analysis possible. In my recent work on finding compatibilities in cross-cultural moral claims,[53] on what negotiation theory says about the impacts of litigation versus negotiation for resolution of Aboriginal claims,[54] and other related areas,[55] I am forever humbled by the complexity of the analysis required. But that is no reason not to undertake it.

When read holistically, and with section 35 alongside other sections, the Constitution challenges us to make multiple faces of justice the different facets of a whole, so far as possible, and to undertake all of the necessary steps to do so. This task does not call us to something easy, but rather to something difficult. Still, it calls us.

5

STRIKING A BALANCE

THE RIGHTS OF ABORIGINAL PEOPLES
AND THE RULE OF LAW IN CANADA

Thomas Isaac*

"The *Constitution Act, 1982*, ushered in a new chapter, but it did not start a new book."[1]

I. INTRODUCTION

Since the Supreme Court of Canada first addressed Aboriginal and treaty rights under subsection 35(1) of the *Constitution Act, 1982*,[2] in *R. v. Sparrow*,[3] the Court has walked a narrow line in balancing the tension between pluralistic visions of law which include the "Aboriginal perspective" and the rule of law as generally understood when dealing with the rights of Aboriginal peoples. In resolving such tension, the Supreme Court has favoured the rule of law by affirming the Canadian legal framework on the basis of the reality of Canadian sovereignty. However, the Supreme Court has also recognized the plurality created through the continuing existence of incidents of Aboriginal sovereignty by incorporating Aboriginal perspectives within the existing Canadian legal framework.

This chapter examines the approach taken by the Supreme Court to create space for the Aboriginal perspective and to resolve the underlying tension between the pluralism, as represented by Aboriginal perspectives of the law

---

* The author wishes to thank Sam Adkins and Sean Rowell for their assistance in writing this chapter.

and the rule of law generally. Part II explores the meaning of the concepts "rule of law" and "pluralism" and considers the tension that exists between them. Part III briefly outlines the scope and development of section 35(1). Part IV considers a specific example of the incorporation of Aboriginal law and perspectives into the Canadian legal framework by examining the Supreme Court's approach to incorporating Aboriginal oral tradition into the law of evidence when considering Aboriginal claims. Finally, Part V evaluates the Supreme Court's approach to plurality within the Canadian legal framework, in the context of Aboriginal law.

II. THE RULE OF LAW AND PLURALISM IN CANADIAN LAW

A. Rule of Law

The phrase "rule of law" refers to the concept that legal authority must be exercised in accordance with the law. In the *Patriation Reference*, the Supreme Court described the rule of law as involving "a sense of orderliness, of subjection to known legal rules and of executive accountability to legal authority."[4] The Supreme Court elaborated on this description of the rule of law in *Re Manitoba Language Rights*:

> The rule of law, a fundamental principle of our Constitution, must mean at least two things. First, that the law is supreme over officials of the government as well as private individuals, and thereby preclusive of the influence of arbitrary power. . . . Second, the rule of law requires the creation and maintenance of an actual order of positive laws which preserves and embodies the more general principle of normative order. Law and order are indispensable elements of civilized life. "The rule of law in this sense implies . . . simply the existence of public order." (W.I. Jennings, *The Law and the Constitution* (5th ed. 1959), at p. 43)[5]

Thus, the rule of law lies at the heart of the modern concepts of democracy and civility. The rule of law is often equated with "constitutionalism," a concept focussed on governmental action being limited by the law.[6] Indeed, the preamble to the *Constitution Act, 1982*, confirms this relationship by pronouncing that Canada is founded upon principles that include the recognition of the rule of law. The interaction between the Constitution and rule of law is expressly stated in subsection 52(1) of the *Constitution Act, 1982*: "The Constitution of Canada is the supreme law of Canada, and any law that is inconsistent with the provisions of the Constitution is, to the extent of the inconsistency, of no force or effect."

The Supreme Court has addressed the relationship between the rule of law and the Constitution of Canada on numerous occasions. In *Re Manitoba* the Supreme Court stated:

> Additional to the inclusion of the rule of law in the preambles of the *Constitution Acts* of 1867 and 1982, the principle is clearly implicit in the very nature of a Constitution. The Constitution, as the Supreme Law, must be understood as a purposive ordering of social relations providing a basis upon which an actual order of positive laws can be brought into existence. The founders of this nation must have intended, as one of the basic principles of nation building, that Canada be a society of legal order and normative structure: one governed by rule of law. While this is not set out in a specific provision, the principle of the rule of law is clearly a principle of our Constitution.[7]

Clearly, the constitutional framework of Canada and the rule of law are closely related; the Constitution is the framework, and the rule of law is the means by which the framework is adhered. This fundamental understanding or basis of the Canadian legal framework is perceived by some as being at odds with the "Aboriginal perspective" of the law.

B. Legal Pluralism

Broadly defined, "legal pluralism" refers to the concept that law is not merely the result of positive actions by the state or courts, but rather, it emanates from numerous sources beyond the institutional setting. Pluralism is law, as expressed elsewhere, in which "nonstate actors within a domestic legal order participate in making the law in force."[8] From this perspective, law is a result of interactions between various actors, including, but not limited to, the state.

Pluralism poses a challenge to the normative ordering which the rule of law demands, thereby creating tension between pluralistic conceptions of the law and the rule of law. Potentially, pluralism could be seen to threaten or question the sovereign authority of the state to create and administer law and upon which the legal framework, and thus, the rule of law, is based. Despite such a tension, elements of plurality within an established, yet flexible, legal framework may exist without offending the principle of the rule of law. For example, the Supreme Court's response to plurality, in regard to the interaction of Aboriginal law with Canadian law has been to incorporate, in some circumstances, the Aboriginal perspective into the larger Canadian legal framework. The Supreme Court's approach is described in *Mitchell*:

> Accordingly, European settlement did not terminate the interests of Aboriginal peoples arising from their historic occupation and use of the land. To the contrary, Aboriginal interests and customary laws were presumed to survive the assertion of sovereignty, and were absorbed into the common law as rights, unless (1) they were incompatible with the Crown's assertion of sovereignty, (2) they were surrendered voluntarily via the treaty process, or (3) the government extinguished them.[9]

The exceptions to Aboriginal rights being absorbed into common-law also provide insight into the Supreme Court's reasoning on this issue. If such rights were surrendered by way of treaty, or if the Crown extinguished them, then they did not survive. Most notably, however, is the reason that if the rights were "incompatible" with Crown sovereignty, they also did not survive the assertion of Crown sovereignty. The Supreme Court has resisted questioning the legal framework or the sovereign assertions of the Canadian state by finding that Aboriginal rights do not exist because of their own inherent strength or validity, but because they are expressly recognized and affirmed in section 35(1). As Binnie J. stated in *Mitchell*:

> Counsel for the respondent does not challenge the reality of Canadian sovereignty, but he seeks for the Mohawk people of the Iroquois Confederacy the maximum degree of legal autonomy to which he believes they are entitled because of their long history at Akwesasne and elsewhere in eastern North America. This asserted autonomy, to be sure, does not presently flow from the ancient Iroquois legal order that is said to have created it, but from the *Constitution Act, 1982*. Section 35(1), adopted by the elected representatives of Canadians, recognizes and affirms existing Aboriginal and treaty rights. If the respondent's claimed Aboriginal right is to prevail, *it does so not because of its own inherent strength, but because the Constitution Act, 1982, brings about that result* [emphasis added].[10]

This acceptance of Canadian sovereignty as the starting point is fundamental to understanding why the rule of law figures so prominently in Canada's (and many other states') legal reality. The Supreme Court resolves the tension between the rule of law and the plurality created by Aboriginal perspectives of the law by favouring, in cases of ultimate conflict between the two, the rule of law, as it arises out of the legal framework based on Canadian sovereignty. However, while the rule of law remains the Supreme Court's guiding principle, space has been created within Canada's legal framework for plurality, including aspects that consider Aboriginal perspectives.[11]

The Supreme Court's approach to incorporating Aboriginal legal perspectives within Canada's legal framework has been the subject of criticism. It has been argued that the Supreme Court ought to go further in recognizing legal plurality by understanding Aboriginal law and perspective not as *contingent* on recognition under the existing Canadian legal framework and Canadian sovereignty, but rather, as a *separate* source of law arising out of Aboriginal sovereignty.[12] This chapter will examine the tension between the position taken by advocates of this wider form of pluralism and the Supreme Court's resistance in favouring a rule of law approach that is based on an acceptance of Canadian sovereignty as the starting point.

III. OVERVIEW OF THE SCOPE AND DEVELOPMENT OF ABORIGINAL AND TREATY RIGHTS UNDER SECTION 35[13]

Prior to 1982, and the express recognition and affirmation of existing Aboriginal and treaty rights in s. 35(1), the status of Aboriginal and treaty rights in Canada had been fluid and vulnerable. The Supreme Court summarized the state of Canadian law prior to 1982, respecting treaty rights and their vulnerability, in *R. v. Moosehunter*: "The Government of Canada can alter the rights of Indians granted under treaties. . . . Provinces cannot."[14] Although Aboriginal rights existed at common law prior to 1982, they were subject to extensive restriction by the Crown and could be unilaterally extinguished by the Crown if a clear and plain intention to extinguish them could be demonstrated.

Jurisprudence after 1982 has shown that key elements of Aboriginal law, while not examined much before 1982, nevertheless existed before section 35(1). Clearly, the concept of the "honour of the Crown," now a central component to understanding the Crown's duty to consult Aboriginal peoples, has existed from at least 1763.[15] Also, case law indicates that Aboriginal peoples have been recompensed for breaches of the Crown's fiduciary duty to them which occurred prior to 1982.

On 17 April 1982, the legal status of Aboriginal and treaty rights changed with the constitutional recognition and affirmation of "existing" Aboriginal and treaty rights under section 35(1).[16] Subsection 35(2) defines "aboriginal peoples of Canada" as including the Indian, Inuit, and Métis peoples of Canada.

Aboriginal rights are those rights held by Aboriginal peoples that relate to activities which are an element of a practice, custom, or tradition integral to the distinctive culture of the Aboriginal group claiming such rights. They may include rights related to activities which, of necessity, take place on land or relate to land such as hunting, fishing, and trapping, and Aboriginal title.[17] Aboriginal title is: (a) a sub-category of Aboriginal rights, (b) a right to the land itself, and (c) the special legal interest that some Aboriginal peoples may possess in specific lands not covered by treaties or not otherwise extinguished. Aboriginal title is an encumbrance on the Crown's underlying title to land.[18]

Treaty rights are those rights that are contained in written agreements, usually known as treaties, entered into between the Crown and Aboriginal peoples.[19] Some treaties date back to the seventeenth century and deal with specific rights, such as those related to hunting, fishing, and trapping in specified territories in return for peace, but they do not contemplate any cession of lands.[20] Other Canadian historic treaties entered into in the nineteenth to early twentieth centuries are brief documents that contain provisions for cession, release, and surrender of Aboriginal rights and title, in return for specified rights set out in the treaty, such as hunting, fishing, and trapping, and the reservation of lands to establish Indian reserves. Modern treaties, or land claim agreements, have been concluded during the past thirty years in areas not formerly subject to one of the historic treaties.

The Supreme Court set out the test to determine infringements of existing Aboriginal rights and treaty rights in *Sparrow*[21] (as applying to Aboriginal rights), *Badger*[22] (as applying to treaty rights), and *Delgamuukw*[23] (as applying to Aboriginal title). Once an Aboriginal right has been proven to exist by the group or person claiming the right,[24] the first question to be asked in determining whether an infringement has occurred under section 35(1) is "whether the governmental action in question has the effect of interfering with an existing Aboriginal right. If it does, . . . it represents a *prima facie* infringement of s. 35(1)."[25]

Other questions to be asked to determine whether interference and infringement has occurred are: (a) whether the limitation is unreasonable, (b) whether the infringing act imposes undue hardship on the Aboriginal group claiming the right, (c) whether the infringing act denies the holders of the right their preferred means of exercising that right, and (d) whether the infringing act unnecessarily infringes the interests protected by the right.[26]

If a *prima facie* infringement is found, the next step of the analysis is justification; that is, the Court will determine whether the governmental infringement of an existing Aboriginal or treaty right can be justified,[27] including whether the Crown's challenged action has a valid legislative objective. The Supreme Court has recognized that "the range of legislative objectives that can justify the infringement ... is fairly broad."[28] The legislation must advance "important general public objectives"[29] or be in furtherance of a "compelling and substantial"[30] objective, such as "where the objectives furthered . . . are of sufficient importance to the broader community as a whole."[31] The Supreme Court has recognized such specific valid objectives as conserving and managing a natural resource[32] and "the development of agriculture, forestry, mining, and hydroelectric power, . . . general economic development, . . . protection of the environment or endangered species, the building of infrastructure and the settlement of foreign populations."[33] The list is not closed.[34]

If a valid legislative objective is found to justify an infringement, the justification test proceeds to the second stage of analysis that deals with the "honour of the Crown."[35] The special trust relationship and, in appropriate circumstances, *sui generis* fiduciary duty owed by the Crown to Aboriginal people, "must be the first consideration" to determine whether infringing governmental action is justified.[36] The appropriate questions to be addressed in order to determine if an action of the Crown is compatible with the Crown's honour include "whether there has been as little infringement as possible in order to effect the desired result; whether, in a situation of expropriation, fair compensation is available; and, whether the Aboriginal group in question has been consulted."[37]

Although the Constitution protects existing Aboriginal and treaty rights, these rights are not absolute.[38] The Courts may hold legislation and administrative decisions that interfere with, or infringe on, Aboriginal and treaty rights to be of no effect. However, Parliament and the provincial legislatures may continue to enact legislation, and representatives of the Crown may continue to make decisions and act within their respective jurisdictional areas that infringe Aboriginal and treaty rights, if such infringements can be justified according to the test set out by the Supreme Court.

In *Haida Nation* v. *British Columbia (Minister of Forests)*,[39] the Supreme Court confirmed and elaborated upon the Crown's duty to consult with Aboriginal peoples. The duty to consult emanates from the concept of the "honour of the Crown." The duty arises where an Aboriginal interest, or unproven but *prima facie* claim for rights, exists: that is, the honour of the

Crown requires that the Crown acknowledge both proven and *bona fide* unproven claims, for the purpose of consultation. In some circumstances, the duty to consult may lead to a duty to accommodate Aboriginal interests; however, accommodation does not necessarily always accompany consultation. The duty to accommodate will arise on a case-by-case basis, and the extent of such accommodation will depend on the circumstances, taking into account all interests at stake.

The Crown's duty to consult, confirmed by *Haida*, represents the continuing theme first established by the Supreme Court in *Sparrow* that recognition and incorporation of Aboriginal rights within the Canadian legal framework requires a balancing of Aboriginal and non-Aboriginal interests. The Crown's duty to consult represents this balance by requiring the Crown to consider Aboriginal interests whenever such interests may be affected by governmental actions or decisions but, simultaneously, not necessarily allowing such interests to prevent the Crown from governing and making decisions in the face of Aboriginal opposition, when appropriate. This theme that Aboriginal rights are not absolute and must be balanced with the rights of other Canadians is consistent in the post-1982, section 35(1) jurisprudence.

IV. APPLICATION OF PLURALISM TO THE LAW OF EVIDENCE AND ABORIGINAL CLAIMS

The history of section 35(1) illustrates that the Supreme Court has endeavoured to incorporate the Aboriginal legal perspective into some aspects of Canadian common law, rather than to recognize an alternate form of Aboriginal jurisdiction. This approach is consistent with the fundamental principles of the Constitution of Canada. In the *Secession Reference*, the Supreme Court affirmed that the Constitution "embraces unwritten as well as written rules" and includes "the global system of rules and principles which govern the exercise of constitutional authority in the whole and in every part of the Canadian state."[40] The Supreme Court also noted that:

> our constitutional history demonstrates that our governing institutions have adapted and changed to reflect changing social and political values. This has generally been accomplished by methods that have ensured continuity, stability and legal order.[41]

The process of balancing between adaptation and continuity or between stability and legal order, respecting Aboriginal legal systems, can be illustrated through an examination of the laws of evidence as they relate to Aboriginal claims and the development of the test respecting infringements of Aboriginal rights.

In *Delgamuukw*, the Supreme Court adapted the law of hearsay in an attempt to "come to terms with the oral histories of Aboriginal societies, which for many Aboriginal nations, are the only record of their past."[42] However, this adaptation follows the commonly accepted common law rules now in place for hearsay generally: "Oral histories are admissible as evidence where they are both useful and reasonably reliable, subject always to the exclusionary discretion of the trial judge."[43]

In *Van der Peet*, Lamer C.J., for the majority, set out the principles to be followed in assessing a claim for the existence of an Aboriginal right:

> In assessing a claim for the existence of an aboriginal right, a court must take into account the perspective of the aboriginal people claiming the right. In *Sparrow, supra* Dickson C.J. and La Forest J. held at p. 1112 that it is "crucial to be sensitive to the aboriginal perspective itself on the meaning of the rights at stake." It must also be recognized, however, that that perspective must be framed in terms cognizable to the Canadian legal and constitutional structure. As has already been noted, one of the fundamental purposes of s. 35(1) is the reconciliation of the pre-existence of distinctive Aboriginal societies with the assertion of Crown sovereignty. Courts adjudicating Aboriginal rights claims must, therefore, be sensitive to the Aboriginal perspective, but they must also be aware that Aboriginal rights exist within the general legal system of Canada.[44]

The need for a flexible approach goes beyond the unique place of Aboriginal peoples in Canadian society, and it touches on the unique challenges of Aboriginal litigation. Arguably, there is no other area of the law where history, and specifically, cultural history, are as determinative of the outcome. For example, in the case of Aboriginal title, the need to prove occupation and practice, pre-contact or before the assertion of sovereignty, requires by definition an inquiry into the motivations and actions of people living in past centuries.[45] Such a unique inquiry necessitates an adaptation of evidence rules that developed in the context of civil and criminal litigation largely concerned with living individuals and present history. Still, this adaptation would have to be completed in such a way as to ensure "continuity, stability and legal order."[46] This adaptation has meant the inclusion of Aboriginal oral histories, laws, and traditions *within* the modern common law.

The approach adopted by the Supreme Court, respecting the admissibility of Aboriginal oral tradition as evidence, is flexible in accepting pluralistic elements; however, it is not a strictly pluralistic approach. For example, recent decisions such as *Badger, Canada* v. *Benoit,*[47] and *Mitchell* show that the courts have not applied a strictly pluralistic approach to the examination of oral history evidence, but instead, they have used principles of common law rules of evidence to provide for the expression of Aboriginal law.

In *Benoit*, the Federal Court of Appeal noted that, "Oral history evidence cannot be accepted, *per se,* as factual unless it has undergone the critical scrutiny that courts and experts, whether they be historians, archaeologists, or social scientists, apply to the various types of evidence which they have to deal with."[48] In *Mitchell*, the Supreme Court noted that, "In determining the usefulness and reliability of oral histories, judges must resist facile assumptions based on Eurocentric traditions of gathering and passing on historical facts and traditions."[49] The Court also noted that courts "render decisions on the basis of evidence," and this "fundamental principle applies to Aboriginal claims as much as to any other claim."[50]

Also in *Mitchell*, the Supreme Court, following *Van der Peet* and *Delgamuukw*, affirmed that the common law rules of evidence continue to apply. A flexible application of the rules of evidence is needed, both because of the inherent difficulties in adjudicating Aboriginal claims, and because of the necessity to fulfil the "promise of reconciliation embodied in s. 35(1)."[51] The Supreme Court noted that this flexible approach allowed courts to admit evidence of post-contact activities to prove continuity with pre-contact practices, customs, and traditions, as in *Van der Peet* and the consideration of oral history evidence in *Delgamuukw*.[52]

In *Mitchell*, the Supreme Court highlighted that this flexibility was an application of basic, fundamental principles of Canadian law and not necessarily some *sui generis* feature peculiar to Aboriginal law. Chief Justice McLachlin noted that the rules of evidence are "not cast in stone," but they are rather, flexible principles which should be applied "purposively to promote truth-finding and fairness."[53] Chief Justice McLachlin further stated that:

The rules of evidence should facilitate justice, not stand in its way. Underlying the diverse rules on the admissibility of evidence are three simple ideas. First, the evidence must be useful in the sense of tending to prove a fact relevant to the issues in the case. Second, the evidence must be reasonably reliable; unreliable evidence may hinder the search for the truth more than help it. Third, even useful and reasonably reliable evidence may be excluded in the discretion of the trial judge if its probative value is overshadowed by its potential for prejudice.[54]

Chief Justice McLachlin went on to note that while *Delgamuukw* allows for the accommodation of oral histories, this does not "mandate the blanket admissibility of such evidence or the weight it should be accorded by the trier of fact.... [O]ral histories are admissible as evidence where they are both useful and reasonably reliable, subject always to the exclusionary discretion of the trial judge."[55] The underlying theme is that while the Aboriginal perspective should be considered, it should not fundamentally alter the requirement of reliability and the ultimate discretion of the trial judge, on a case-by-case basis.

The principles set forth in *Delgamuukw* were echoed by the Supreme Court in *Mitchell*, in finding that while Aboriginal perspectives are critical to the special nature of Aboriginal claims, the incorporation of an Aboriginal perspective does not take away from the need to follow the general rules of evidentiary law:

> While evidence adduced in support of aboriginal claims must not be undervalued, neither should it be interpreted or weighed in a manner that fundamentally contravenes the principles of evidence law, which, as they relate to the valuing of evidence, are often synonymous with the "general principles of common sense" (Sopinka and Lederman, *supra*, at p. 524). As Lamer C.J. emphasized in *Delgamuukw*, *supra*, at para. 82:
>
> > [A]boriginal rights are truly *sui generis*, and demand a unique approach to the treatment of evidence which accords due weight to the perspective of aboriginal peoples. However, that accommodation must be done in a manner which does not strain "the Canadian legal and constitutional structure" [*Van der Peet* at para. 49]. Both the principles laid down in *Van der Peet* – first, that trial courts must approach the rules of evidence in light of the evidentiary difficulties inherent in adjudicating aboriginal claims, and second, that trial courts must interpret that evidence in the same spirit – must be understood against this background.[56]

This application of the Aboriginal perspective to the operation of Canadian evidentiary law generally must be carried out in a manner that does not fundamentally alter such evidentiary law, and it should be compatible with it.

Additionally, being conscious of both the special issues in litigating Aboriginal claims and the requirements of section 35(1) does not mean that such evidence produced should be accepted on a lesser standard:

> Evidence advanced in support of aboriginal claims, like the evidence offered in any case, can run the gamut of cogency from the highly compelling to the highly dubious. Claims must still be established on the basis of persuasive evidence demonstrating their validity on the balance of probabilities. Placing "due weight" on the aboriginal perspective, or ensuring its supporting evidence an "equal footing" with more familiar forms of evidence, means precisely what these phrases suggest: equal and due treatment. *While the evidence presented by aboriginal claimants should not be undervalued "simply because that evidence does not conform precisely with the evidentiary standards that would be applied in, for example, a private law torts case" (Van der Peet, supra, at para. 68), neither should it be artificially strained to carry more weight than it can reasonably support. If this is an obvious proposition, it must nonetheless be stated* [emphasis added].[57]

This flexible adaptation of the laws of evidence can also be seen in the context of expert witnesses and opinion evidence. Historically, the provision of opinion evidence by lay witnesses was not admissible in Canadian courts. A witness could only testify to facts within his or her knowledge and the trier of fact was left to make inferences from the facts proven. A more modern approach has posited that it may not be possible to differentiate between fact and opinion. Therefore, it is only where such evidence approaches the central issues that the courts must decide that the witness is required to limit his or her testimony to facts and refrain from opinion or inference.[58]

An exception to this rule is where an expert witness is allowed to give this testimony. The test to be applied on the admissibility of an expert witness is based on these factors: relevance, necessity in assisting the trier of fact, absence of an exclusionary rule, and a properly qualified expert. The test for admissibility as an expert is that the witness has knowledge "which is likely to be outside the experience and knowledge of a judge or jury."[59] Courts have been reluctant to rule against an Aboriginal expert giving testimony. For example, in *Tsilhqot'in* v. *British Columbia*, Vickers J. found that although Chief Roger William was not recognized as an elder and had not consistently led a traditional life, he could, nevertheless, provide oral history evidence[60] as his traditional knowledge and position of respect in the community was sufficient expertise.

The Supreme Court's approach in adapting the existing rules of evidence in order to accommodate Aboriginal oral tradition provides an example of how the Court has incorporated plurality, in the form of Aboriginal perspective, into the Canadian legal framework. Aboriginal perspective is not an external source of law outside the existing Canadian legal framework; rather, it exists and is incorporated within this framework.

v. COMMENTARY ON THE SUPREME COURT'S PERSPECTIVE AND ITS IMPLICATIONS

The Supreme Court has approached Aboriginal and treaty rights by incorporating and interpreting such rights within the context of the Constitution of Canada. The Supreme Court has not adopted a purely pluralistic view of the Aboriginal legal perspective as an external source of law, but rather, it has affirmed the rule of law and created space for the incorporation of plural elements *within* the existing framework.

There are two key elements to the approach taken by the Supreme Court in reconciling Aboriginal law within the Canadian legal framework. First, the Supreme Court has accepted the assertion of Canadian sovereignty. Second, the Supreme Court seeks to balance the interests of Aboriginal and non-Aboriginal Canadians in the development of the law under section 35(1). This section considers the appropriateness of the Supreme Court's perspective, in regard to its acceptance of Canadian sovereignty over Aboriginal peoples, and the balanced approach the Court has developed in respect of section 35(1).

A. Canadian Sovereignty and Aboriginal Rights

The Supreme Court's approach in resolving the tension between pluralism and the rule of law that is in favour of the existing legal framework and Canadian sovereignty may not have been inevitable, but it ought to not be surprising. The Supreme Court may be independent of the government, but it is not independent of the framework and assumptions upon which the Canadian state and the Constitution of Canada exist.

Despite the near-certainty of the Supreme Court's conclusion on Canadian sovereignty and its acceptance of the existing legal framework, such a conclusion ought to not to be dismissed as merely the result of institutional bias, or more appropriately, reliance on the status quo. Fundamentally, the assertion of sovereignty is a political phenomenon that is not explained by a simple reference to legal principles:

No one doubts that legal consequences may flow from political facts, and that "sovereignty is a political fact for which no purely legal authority can be constituted . . .", H. W. R. Wade, "The Basis of Legal Sovereignty", [1955] Camb. L.J. 172, at p. 196. . . . If the principle of "effectivity" is no more than that "successful revolution begets its own legality" (S. A. de Smith, "Constitutional Lawyers in Revolutionary Situations" (1968), 7 West. Ont. L. Rev. 93, at p. 96), it necessarily means that *legality follows and does not precede* the successful revolution. Ex hypothesi, the successful revolution took place outside the constitutional framework of the predecessor state, otherwise it would not be characterized as "a revolution" [emphasis added].[61]

While the mere assertion of sovereignty may be less satisfying than a legal justification for the Supreme Court's acceptance of Crown sovereignty, legitimacy may be gained over time through acceptance and reliance upon a political fact, even if the basis of the initial assertion was, in the view of some, fundamentally illegitimate. As Patrick Macklem concludes:

> Although the assertion of European sovereignty over indigenous peoples was clearly based on racist assumptions about indigenous difference, can it be said that the assertion of Canadian sovereignty over Aboriginal people today is based on racist principles? That is, the assertion of sovereignty by one nation over another nation is not per se normatively illegitimate; its legitimacy depends on the reasons that can be offered in its defence. One reason will no doubt be the actual historical reason for the initial assertion of sovereignty; however, other reasons, unrelated to the historical justification, may emerge over time to independently support the assertion of sovereignty. . . . [I]t may be that, regardless of the historical reasons behind its existence, there are pragmatic reasons to continue to respect Canadian sovereign authority over Aboriginal people.[62]

In this regard, the Supreme Court is in agreement. The political question of Canadian sovereignty is not a legal question for the courts to consider, it is rather a political fact from which legal consequences arise. In *Mitchell*, Binnie J. wrote:

> The respondent's 17th century ancestors were no doubt unaware that some of the Kings in distant Europe were laying claim to sovereignty over

Mohawk territory. As Marshall C.J. of the United States Supreme Court observed in *Worcester* v. *Georgia*, 31 U.S. (6 Pet.) 515 (1832), at p. 543:

> It is difficult to comprehend the proposition, that the inhabitants of either quarter of the globe could have rightful original claims of dominion over the inhabitants of the other, or over the lands they occupied. . . .

Nevertheless, this is what happened. From the aboriginal perspective, moreover, those early claims to European "dominion" grew to reality in the decades that followed. Counsel for the respondent does not dispute Canadian sovereignty. He seeks Mohawk autonomy within the broader framework of Canadian sovereignty.[63]

In terms of recognizing incidents of Aboriginal sovereignty, the Supreme Court has adopted a similar line of reasoning to that which is accepted at international law.[64] While it is accepting of Canadian sovereignty over Aboriginal peoples, the Supreme Court recognizes that such sovereignty is not automatically threatened by the sharing of sovereignty with Aboriginal peoples. For example, in *Mitchell*, the Crown argued that section 35(1) only protected those Aboriginal practices, customs, and traditions that are compatible with the "historic and modern exercise of Crown sovereignty."[65] Therefore, the Mohawk practice of cross-border trade could not be protected by section 35(1), as it was incompatible with the Crown's sovereign right to regulate its borders. While McLachlin C.J., for the majority in *Mitchell*, did not to address the issue in her reasons, Binnie J., in concurring reasons, did address the issue of sovereign incompatibility. After confirming that the mere assertion of sovereignty by the European powers in North America was not necessarily incompatible with the survival and continuation of Aboriginal rights, Binnie J. stated that, "Because not all customs and traditions of aboriginal First Nations are incompatible with Canadian sovereignty, however, does not mean that none of them can be in such conflict."[66]

Justice Binnie noted that Mitchell viewed his Aboriginal rights as "a shield against non-aboriginal laws,"[67] including the imposition of a border. According to Binnie J., Mitchell envisaged a constitutional framework such as that memorialized by the "two row" wampum, in which a ship representing the white people and their laws, customs, and traditions moves down the same river as a birch bark canoe, representing the First Nations people, their laws, and customs, with each group in their own boat and neither trying to steer the others' boat. This pluralistic vision is modified and updated by Binnie J. to the idea of a "shared" or "merged sovereignty."[68] With the passage of time and the patriation of the Constitution, all aspects of Canada's sovereignty are now firmly located within its borders. According to Binnie J.:

> If the principle of "merged sovereignty" articulated by the Royal Commission on Aboriginal Peoples is to have any true meaning, it must include at least the idea that aboriginal and non-aboriginal Canadians together form a sovereign entity with a measure of common purpose and united effort. It is this new entity, as inheritor of the historical attributes of sovereignty, with which existing aboriginal and treaty rights must be reconciled.[69]

Justice Binnie evoked a different metaphor to describe merged sovereignty:

> On this view, to return to the nautical metaphor of the "two-row" wampum, "merged" sovereignty is envisaged as a single vessel (or ship of state) composed of the historic elements of wood, iron and canvas. The vessel's components pull together as a harmonious whole, but the wood remains wood, the iron remains iron and the canvas remains canvas. Non-aboriginal leaders, including Sir Wilfrid Laurier, have used similar metaphors. It represents, in a phrase, partnership without assimilation.[70]

Further, Binnie J. noted that:

> It is unnecessary, for present purposes, to come to any conclusion about these assertions. What is significant is that the Royal Commission itself sees aboriginal peoples as full participants with non-aboriginal peoples in a shared Canadian sovereignty. Aboriginal peoples do not stand in opposition to, nor are they subjugated by, Canadian sovereignty. They are part of it.[71]

This final sentence in the above-noted quotation from Binnie J. is instructive. Aboriginal law and the Aboriginal perception are not separated from Canadian sovereignty: they are *part* of Canadian sovereignty. This statement is likely most definitively portrayed by section 35(1) itself and the fact that in certain circumstances, Aboriginal and treaty rights can displaced, or they fetter the applicability of federal and provincial laws. Law is ill-equipped to explain the source of Canadian sovereignty. The Supreme Court in *Mitchell* and elsewhere clearly accepts assertions of Canadian sovereignty as the basis of legal framework, although the Court has also maintained space for Aboriginal law within such sovereignty. Aboriginal peoples are not subjugated by Canadian sovereignty; they are part of it. Political events will continue to affect our understanding of the relationship between the Canadian state and Aboriginal peoples; however, the Supreme Court is an unlikely venue and likely an improper player in the renegotiation and revision of Canadian sovereignty itself.

B. Reconciliation

Once Canadian sovereignty is accepted as a political fact, the question of reconciliation of Aboriginal interests within the overall legal framework remains. Unlike questions of sovereignty, the Supreme Court is well-equipped to deal with the issue of reconciliation, particularly since the adoption of section 35(1). As outlined above, the law reconciling Aboriginal interests with Canadian sovereignty has developed rapidly in relation to section 35(1). The Supreme Court has pursued a balanced approach to reconciliation that considers both the rights of those with historical occupation and the rights of the society that has developed around the fact of Canadian sovereignty. In *R. v. Blais*, Scott C.J.M. stated:

> I am mindful of the fact that the underlying issues that have brought these proceedings before us are not only legal, but also political in nature; by definition *they involve a reconciliation and balancing between historic aboriginal rights and the claims and interests of others* [emphasis added].[72]

In *Haida*, the Supreme Court stated that:

> Balance and compromise are inherent in the notion of reconciliation. Where accommodation is required in making decisions that may adversely affect as yet unproven Aboriginal rights and title claims, *the Crown must balance Aboriginal concerns reasonably with the potential impact of the decision on the asserted right or title and with other societal interests* [emphasis added].[73]

In *Delgamuukw*, La Forest J. stated that:

> On a final note, I wish to emphasize that the best approach in these types of cases is a process of negotiation and reconciliation that properly

considers the complex and competing interests at stake. This point was made by Lambert J.A. in the Court of Appeal, [1993] 5 W.W.R. 97, at pp. 379-80:

> So, in the end, the legal rights of the Indian people will have to be accommodated within our total society by political compromises and accommodations based in the first instance on negotiation and agreement and ultimately in accordance with the sovereign will of the community as a whole.[74]

The Supreme Court's approach to interpreting the Constitution incrementally (which is the nature of the common law), in pursuit of the goal of reconciliation, is fundamental in serving the need for both the certainty provided by the legal framework and the rule of law, as well as for the flexibility required to respect the constitutionally recognized rights of Aboriginal peoples. As Aileen Kavanagh writes, balancing the competing forces of stability and flexibility is the purpose behind a "living constitution":

> Given that written Constitutions are normally entrenched to some degree and intended to last for a long time, constitutional interpretation becomes a means by which the Constitution provides for its own development. If its meaning could not be adapted and changed in this way, it would remain 'frozen' in the time it was written and too rigid to adapt to current circumstances. It would also be unable perform its function of providing a stable legal framework which, more or less, stays in place from one generation to the next.[75]

The Supreme Court's approach in regard to the development of Aboriginal law under section 35(1) is sensitive to the competing needs of certainty and flexibility within the legal framework. As Binnie J. stated in *Mitchell*, "The *Constitution Act, 1982*, ushered in a new chapter but it did not start a new book."[76] The incremental approach of the Supreme Court in reconciling Aboriginal law within the Canadian legal framework, through seeking to balance Aboriginal and non-Aboriginal interests, is an appropriate approach for providing flexibility, certainty, and continuity, and upholding the rule of law. Reconciliation is a process that will continue. The existing legal framework provides the space and flexibility for further development of the relationship between the Aboriginal perspective and the reality of Canadian sovereignty.

VI. CONCLUSION

The approach of the Supreme Court in recognizing Aboriginal law, as existing within the Canadian legal framework, demonstrates that the tension between pluralism and the rule of law may be resolved without mutual exclusion. The Supreme Court has favoured an approach that confirms the rule of law, but it also favoured an approach in which space exists for the incorporation of pluralistic elements, such as those presented by Aboriginal peoples. In its approach, the Supreme Court avoids the uncertainty of competing sources of law by affirming the Canadian legal framework; yet, it maintains the flexibility for further negotiation and political development in the relationship between Aboriginal and non-Aboriginal peoples in Canada.

The Supreme Court properly accepts Canadian sovereignty as a political fact beyond the scope of legal review but also from which legal consequences flow. Acceptance of Canadian sovereignty provides a starting point for the Court to develop the principles of reconciliation under section 35(1). As Lamer C.J. noted in *Van der Peet*:

> More specifically, what s. 35(1) does is provide the constitutional framework through which the fact that aboriginals lived on the land in distinctive societies, with their own practices, traditions and cultures, is acknowledged and reconciled with the sovereignty of the Crown. The substantive rights which fall within the provision must be defined in light of this purpose; the aboriginal rights recognized and affirmed by s. 35(1) must be directed towards the reconciliation of the pre-existence of aboriginal societies with the sovereignty of the Crown.[77]

From the Supreme Court's first decision under section 35(1) in *Sparrow* to its decisions in *Haida, R. v. Marshall; R. v. Bernard*[78] and *Mikisew Cree First Nation v. Canada (Minister of Canadian Heritage)*,[79] the judicial pendulum has gradually narrowed the path of its swing, incrementally describing and interpreting the relationship between the incidents of Aboriginal and Canadian sovereignty. Aboriginal law will continue to develop; however, the Supreme Court has provided an appropriate, and indeed, necessary legal framework to guide the relationship between the Crown and Aboriginal peoples into the future.

6

DEVELOPMENTAL AND LEGAL PERSPECTIVES ON ABORIGINAL JUSTICE ADMINISTRATION

John D. Whyte[*]

I. INTRODUCTION

This chapter is about the place of self-determination in constructing responses to social challenges – especially the challenge of crime – in Aboriginal communities and among Aboriginal populations. The developmental aim is to explore conditions for producing stronger social cohesion and better levels of social health and social order in Canadian Aboriginal communities. The chapter's underlying thesis is that community well-being rests most profoundly on self-respect and on respect from the other communities that are bound together with it in a common polity. Its corollary is that when a community's distinctiveness becomes the basis for social exclusion by dominant ethnic and social groups then strengthening community identity creates risks of further social harms. The consequence of these claims is that the development aims of First Nations and Métis communities depend on both the preservation of strong identities and the presence of genuine national pride in those communities and those identities. The surest route – perhaps the only route – to achieving these conditions is the promotion of greater self-determination for Aboriginal societies. What, in essence, this means is that communities need to possess the capacity to identify their social needs, choose the steps that will meet those needs, and possess the political and fiscal ability to implement those steps for themselves. Any program of development that is less respectful of the autonomy of Aboriginal peoples as distinct minority communities is

[*] This chapter is based on an unpublished report originally prepared for the Saskatchewan Law Reform Commission. The author is grateful to the Commission for permission to draw on this report.

likely to fail to produce the social reformation that is needed and yearned for.

All societies construct "otherness" and all groups have a sense of the ways that they are distinctive or exceptional. All societies construct an idea about which people are within them and which people are not and, as well, construct markers of inclusion and exclusion that often erode respect. In Saskatchewan, for instance, nearly a century ago, the different European points of origin for immigrant communities represented otherness for each other. Sometimes this structure of differences carried status and privilege (perhaps, for immigrants from the United Kingdom) and sometimes it carried denigration (perhaps, for immigrants from Ukraine). Today, it is difficult to see disabling or comprehensive constructions of otherness with respect to descendents of European immigrant communities. It may be the case that the harmful creation of otherness has also largely ended for the descendents of the earlier Chinese community, even though being Chinese in Saskatchewan once entailed being caught in that province's extremely harmful construction of otherness.[1]

A fortunate state is one that includes communities of others that, while fully retaining distinctiveness, become self-respectful of that distinctiveness and, through self-respect and pride, evoke from the rest of society respect for – and celebration of – the enriching otherness that is in their midst. This condition of mutual appreciation of difference is not the same as social integration or assimilation. It is an authentic form of recognition and inclusion and represents a completely positive form of intersocietal relations. The question that this situation poses for social theorists, especially those whose think about how to arrange political power so that political stability, equity, and inclusion are engendered, is whether a positive form of accommodating difference depends on the terms of the nation's formal political organization or if it is simply the result of social and political practices. For instance, when reflecting on the often positive face of ethnic diversity in Canada's major cities, one might conclude that the practice of sustaining distinct communities in conditions of self-respect – and mutual respect – has been established without the aid of constitutional imperatives.[2] Some might claim that the constitutional projects of formalizing political status and power for minority communities, entrenching recognition of distinctiveness, and conferring on them regulatory authority over their members are unnecessary measures, motivated by desire for political aggrandizement, and serving to defeat the central task of generating intercultural respect.

In truth, the history of intersocietal relations in Canada is both complex and formal; it goes beyond the aspiration to produce respect and tolerance through socialization processes. Canada's intersocietal history includes constitutionalizing political authority for minority communities in order to achieve the protection and preservation of those communities. At Confederation, while Canada became a new state, it did not become a new single nation, conceived under general political ideas that were assumed to be powerful enough to form a common political identity for all of its citizens. Its dominant political idea was, in fact, anti-assimilationist, and its history has certainly not been a narrative of overcoming difference and fashioning a single identity or a single idea of national belonging.[3] On the contrary, group identities have been given constitutional recognition, and certain historic communities have been granted constitutional powers to sustain their integrity. Canadian intercultural experience, then, has reflected two streams of accommodation: the social project of respecting otherness and the establishment of constitutional arrangements that are designed to preserve distinctive communities with distinctive identities. That Canada has successfully pursued both informal and formal forms of ethnic recognition suggests that it might be considered a model state in the structure and the practice of intersocietal relations. However, if Canadian political achievements with respect to its distinctive communities are truly something to celebrate, there are hard questions. Why does the actuality of Aboriginal/non-Aboriginal relations reflect a record of mutual distrust? Why is this particular instance of intersocietal relations marked by lack of respect, the exercise of harmful power, the experience of cultural despoliation, and most distressingly, the presence of a dramatically negative social condition for one of the societies? Canada, with respect to its most appealing political objectives (pursuing the grand projects of promoting distinctiveness, accommodating difference, and preserving the integrity of distinct cultures), has failed to meet the specific challenge of forming healthy relations with Aboriginal peoples.

II. HISTORICAL PERSPECTIVE

The source of Canada's failure to establish mutually enriching Aboriginal/non-Aboriginal relations is found in a history that might be labelled the history of European settlement but can be more accurately described as the history of European colonialism.[4]

We cannot act responsibly if we attempt to understand our current condition without examining the history that has brought us to it. If the abiding concerns of the good state are political stability and justice,[5] the part of history that it is most dangerous to deny are the stories of oppression, especially the oppression by one people against another, in which the vulnerable society has been stripped of its capacity for respect for itself and, hence, respect from others. When a society has had taken from it many of its cultural instruments, particularly the vital instruments of cultural transmission, social order, and governance, the shred of identity that is left to it (which is its continuing self-recognition as a special and distinct community[6]) must inevitably be expressed through emphatic rejection of the instruments and values of that society that has all but taken it over. In this way, the history of political and cultural delegitimation[7] constructs the very foundations of continuing intersocietal disrespect. Cultural degradation, designed to ease the process of taking land and authority from Indigenous peoples, leads instead to resistance, disruption, and loss for all.

Taking current responsibility for the oppression and degradation that took place in earlier times is not easy. Nevertheless, those who purport to act for the good of Canadian intersocietal relations, especially those who wish to act constructively in the state's relationship with Aboriginal peoples, should not claim that our moral responsibility is limited to addressing present social needs, or does not extend to taking actions that will set aside continuing structures of oppression and disempowerment. When we believe that the processes that produce political and cultural injury are found only in the past, we ignore the ways those harms continue to damage communities that are caught in the living legacy of oppression. This insensitivity is a further barrier to the construction of intersocietal respect. The current conditions of Aboriginal communities reflect specific historic injuries. It is our history that has constructed the conditions that have been unacceptably damaging to people and communities. We need to understand the continuing force of that historic oppression and work to disentangle ourselves from both these current conditions and the structures that have caused them. We need to abandon governmental practices that are grounded in the historic colonial relationship and that have produced serious social, political, and spiritual injuries.[8]

What is the nature of the harm that has been suffered by Aboriginal peoples? In Canadian colonial history, Aboriginal peoples have experienced extreme and destructive dislocation. The base of a subsistence economy harvesting plants and wildlife was impeded by severe restrictions on mobility, by intensive regulation of the activity, and by the radical depletion of wildlife, leading, in some instances, to starvation. A mature and well-functioning system of order was first denied and then displaced by settler communities and their criminal justice system. A spiritual understanding of creation, based on the interconnectedness of all human interests and the connectedness of human consciousness to all the elements of the world and over all of time, was replaced with the "better God" of Christianity, with its human bias and its insidious promise of God's personal love and personal redemption. An effective normative order, based on narratives of the physical and spiritual worlds, was displaced by the formalism of law and text. Rootedness – the role of place in forming one's identity, and the idea of knowing who you are by knowing where you are – was considered backward and rendered obsolete by European concepts of factor mobility and personal mobility. Hearth and family were displaced by enforced institutionalization in the form of residential schools and through the relentless power of Indian Agents, and, as a result, the transmission of the richness of Aboriginal cultures and important life skills were frustrated, and the very fabric of Indigenous identity was reduced to tatters. Indigenous language was denigrated and banished in favour of English, a language barely capable of sustaining the nuances of living effectively in the natural world. The practice of meeting basic needs through a usufructuary[9] relationship with land and property ran into the markedly less exigent European concept of exclusive possession. For administrative reasons, communities were moved from the island to the shore and from distant shores to near shores, as if the fit between culture and geography was meaningless. Livelihood sustained through the wise and careful use of resources was replaced with welfare transfers, and the universally valued social role of providing support to families was taken from many Aboriginal adults. All of these dislocations suggest that Aboriginal societies in Canada were subjected to acts of repression and cultural eradication that, cumulatively, have been as destructive as the effect of ethnic oppression at almost any time in world history. This destruction brought by colonialism to all elements of Aboriginal society produced a degradation of spirit and identity that now demands the momentous task of reconstruction.[10] The reconstruction that is required cannot be simply an attempt to meet acute social needs, re-establish traditional practices, validate spiritual understandings, or provide more economic opportunities. While all of these are appropriate objectives, the underlying condition of social failure has been the systemic dismantling of self-determining communities, as well as the injury to cultural, spiritual, and political structures that make self-government effective. Meeting these harms requires starting at the very foundation of social health – recognizing the historic integrity and· present validity of Aboriginal culture, Aboriginal identity, and Aboriginal political community. The political empowerment of Aboriginal communities is not claimed as reparation for former exploitation and injury as much as it is the need to create the central condition for social well-being. Aboriginal political rights represent a current strategy for defending culturally distinct communities against both the effects of past political colonialism and on-going exclusion.[11]

Our history of insufficient respect for Aboriginal communities lives on in the relationship between public government and Aboriginal political leaders. This is evident when governmental policy-makers, faced with Aboriginal policies that entail the political empowerment of Aboriginal communities, respond with new claims: the first is that Aboriginal capacity for governance is weak because basic instruments for ensuring that power is exercised democratically and accountably are poorly understood and poorly followed within Aboriginal communities. The second is that Aboriginal structures present an unacceptable political risk of poor government – the ineffective use of resources, negative external effects that lead to high social costs for everyone, and compromised core political values (with respect to, for example, gender equality, due process, victims' rights, workers' rights, human rights, and so forth). In these claims, colonialist dislocation and disempowerment are connected to an on-going deficit of respect, and that deficit serves as the basis of not accepting remedial responses that are based in self-determination and as the condition that warrants opposition to self-government.

iii. Social Condition through the Lens of Criminal Justice

The consequence of these cultural and political assaults – both the historic campaign of dislocation and the current campaign of distrust of Aboriginal government – has been a low quality of social health. The incidence for Aboriginal people of every form of social deprivation – the incidence of AIDS and diabetes, the rate of births to women under sixteen, the level of academic achievement, the levels of family disposable income, rates of unemployment, risk of assault and sexual assault, and standard of housing – is roughly five to fifteen times more disadvantageous than it is for the population as a whole.[12] As for the incidence of criminal offending by the Aboriginal population, Carol La Prairie, in her studies of Aboriginal over-representation in the criminal justice system,[13] has shown that there is nearly a nine times greater representation of Aboriginal people in provincial correctional institutions in the prairie provinces.[14] La Prairie also speaks to the problem of victimization among the Aboriginal population and concludes that "aboriginal people experienced violent crime at a rate that was nearly three times greater than for non-aboriginal people."[15] She points out that similar patterns of over-representation are present among Native Americans in the United States, Maori and Pacific Island people in New Zealand, and Aborigines in Australia.[16]

The data can be put in even starker terms. La Prairie cites one study that found that crime rate data (incidents reported to police) showed that in Regina, Saskatoon, and Prince Albert, the three largest cities in Saskatchewan, the rate of reported crime by Aboriginal people was eleven times higher than reported crime by non-Aboriginal people.[17] In a similar vein, Royal Canadian Mounted Police internal reports on crime reported to Saskatchewan detachments show that crime levels in smaller southern Saskatchewan detachments are typically 4 per cent to 8 per cent (which means that for every 100 people, there are four to eight reported crimes), while the crime levels in small northern First Nations-based detachments range from 30 per cent to 77 per cent (which means that in that year, there were 30 to 77 reported crimes in those communities for every 100 people).[18]

Notwithstanding the political effect of these disturbing indicators of social distress, it is certainly not a sound practice of social development to adopt blanket negative assessments of the social health of minority communities. This labeling can serve to deny the many positive and encouraging instances of personal and community development.[19] Certainly, it would be folly not to recognize the emerging political, social, and economic power that has flowed from a vibrant appreciation of cultural heritage and a determination to recapture the strength of every aspect of the Indigenous tradition, its epistemology, its spirituality, its traditions of governance, and its aesthetics.[20] Furthermore, there is always the horrible risk that focussing exclusively on the indicators of social failure carries the implication that widespread offending and victimization, as well as the other serious social problems, are an entrenched condition of Aboriginal communities. The instances of successful political and economic developments in those communities should forestall language that denies progress, defeats hope and precludes improvement. Yet, the social condition of many Canadian Aboriginal communities – those in the middle of cities and those in the remote corners of the country – is, without doubt, distressing. Too many Aboriginal communities do not enjoy social practices that produce in the people who live in them either hope for their future or strategies for escaping deprivation. Insofar as hope and resolution to develop social health are not experienced, the situation of marginalization and exclusion will continue.

There are many theories about what has caused such damaging levels of offending and victimization. None of them are irrelevant, and, as a result, there is no single strategy for developing safe and healthy communities. A list of causes, presented without detailed critical analysis, includes the following: a driver of Aboriginal crime is the comparative youth of the Aboriginal population. In all populations, the incidence of crime falls off sharply after people leave their twenties. Canadian demographic data shows a pyramidal structure for Aboriginal age distribution with the largest numbers of persons in the youngest age category and the smallest number in the oldest category. General population data in Canada roughly takes the shape of an inverse pyramid with the lowest number of persons in the younger age categories. It is hard to calculate the extent to which this incongruity in the distribution of the population among age categories accounts for the disproportionate level of Aboriginal offending, but it is undoubtedly significant.

Another recognized cause of social deviance is the criminogenic social condition of discrete populations. As has been noted, the social condition of Canada's Aboriginal population is markedly less advantageous than it is for the general population, and this difference shows up in housing conditions, levels of poverty, levels of educational attainment, and incidence of disease. A related compounding factor with respect to the social conditions of Aboriginal people is the scarcity of social support services, such as child protection, pre- and post-natal care, and mental health services, to meet the sometimes acute social needs in many Aboriginal communities, particularly remote communities.[21] In addition, the role of poverty in levels of criminal conduct is undoubtedly profound; the correlation between poverty and crime can be established throughout the world. Poverty is closely associated with poorer personal options, and communities of poverty are not successful in modelling a diverse and promising range of life choices. Poverty, therefore, is associated with the hard social fact of fewer opportunities for effective personal strategies and the hard emotional facts of hopelessness and despair. While these personal conditions hardly lead directly to the commission of crimes, they suggest that the usual incentives and disincentives that are in place with respect to discouraging offending do not have the same social power. However, it is likely that the condition of aboriginality compounds the experience of poverty in a way that exacerbates the sense that there are few effective strategies for personal development. The social motivators of affirmation and encouragement would seem to be harder to come by in those Aboriginal communities where processes of socialization and development are eroded by community disorder.[22]

There are social pathologies that are collateral to both deprivation and despair, as well as to life lived without a sense of positive possibilities, and these pathologies are also criminogenic. Included here are such behaviours as substance abuse, spousal abuse, child abuse, child neglect, and sexual abuse, especially the sexualization of children. It is vitally important not to ethnicize the incidence of these deeply destructive behaviours. What can be said, however, is that manifestations of low personal respect and inter-personal respect are frequently a product of systemic devaluation of persons and identities.[23] The cultural and ethnic identity of Aboriginal persons has been treated as having low value through being subjected to policies designed to eradicate identity. There are inevitable linkages between radically devalued ethnic identity and social pathologies and, then, between social pathologies and negative stereotyping and these linkages compound the condition of intersocietal disrespect.[24] Furthermore, when history and circumstance have left many Aboriginal adults – perhaps, especially, males – with no valued social role, then it is not the least bit unexpected that doubts over personal value arise – doubts over the value of one's own enterprises, and one's value to community and personal relationships. When it comes to a sense of worth, the historical political narrative, when destructive, shapes the personal sense. Possibly, this destructive progression will be reversed when communities openly challenge the legitimacy of that history and claim another history, one of traditions that deserve to be honoured, wrongs that need to be righted, capacities that need to be acknowledged, and powers that need to be claimed.

Another cause of offending may be the problem of living inside an epidemic of social harm. This can especially show itself through peer group pressure, or more accurately, from the perspective of those who are otherwise socially excluded, from peer group support. As Judith Rich Harris has shown, the social development of children is determined less by the nurturing practices of parents, no matter how positive these may be, and more by the influences of peers and the mores of the communities in which they circulate.[25] The point here is not simply that bad influences lead Aboriginal youth astray but that weak neighbourhoods with high levels of mobility and low levels of social solidarity do not permit the formation of relationships that can be relied on or development of the practices of looking out for and censuring harmful social actions. Furthermore, they may not contain community-based alternatives such as recreation programs and social centres. The absence of institutions that play a normative role, provide positive adult models, or construct supportive social membership means that peer group linkages can lead in any direction, including group-sponsored crime such as theft, prostitution, and drug dealing.

Group membership can serve as an effective sponsor of crime through offering young people a sense of belonging and worth that is otherwise not experienced. If it is the case that Aboriginal communities are often made to feel they are not well functioning or respectable, but rather troublesome and unwelcome, the ground is fertile for the recruitment of individuals based on the appeal of gaining a proud identity. While this appeal could be based on positive acts of community-building and on group and personal achievements (as, indeed, it often is), it can just as easily be based on defiance, non-compliance with the social order, and a sense of immunity from accountability to both the criminal justice system and one's community. In fact, we should recognize the extent to which offending can be transformed into something that has both a political virtue and is positive for the self-image of individuals. It seems entirely plausible that high rates of offending in Aboriginal communities are not solely attributable to poverty and social deprivation but, in some part, at least, are the result of politically rational and identity affirming acts – acts that defy visible manifestations of government, its police and courts – and that express the belief that the coercive power of the state lacks legitimacy. Those agencies, even when performing at the highest level of professionalism, are functionally connected to a history of oppression, and use enforcement processes that are not effective instruments of community development. Criminal justice is, in this way, an appropriate target of intersocietal frustration and can serve to sponsor crime. While criminal justice could certainly become an integral part of a community's strategy for developing social cohesion, this is most promising when it becomes a part of the self-determining apparatus of communities striving to develop their own social well-being.

It must be acknowledged that a final source of the high rate of criminal offending can be the bias (or racism) of the criminal justice system. This bias could be the result of laws that criminalize culturally appropriate practices, such as holding ceremonies (potlatches, for example) or harvesting wildlife. A sense of bias results from too rigorous an application of neutral legal rules under which the special cultural significance of some actions is ignored or the distinctive social experience of Aboriginal persons is not acknowledged.[26] The most common suspicion pertaining to the impact of racial bias is that police forces in policing Aboriginal communities are both too rigorous in charging and too casual in responding to situations of high risk.[27] In racially-mixed urban communities, the sense of police bias is expressed in the charge that police officers are much quicker to detain and charge Aboriginal persons whom they suspect of committing a crime than they are when dealing with non-Aboriginal suspects. Beyond the issue of the level of the formal police practices of detaining and charging, Aboriginal people complain about being treated disrespectfully and, at times, abusively; they complain about being under constant suspicion; and they complain that police do not conduct serious and thorough investigations of crimes committed against them.[28] As can be imagined, these are not the sorts of claims that one would, or could, categorically deny. Likewise, one could not speak with confidence about the extent of actual bias. In Saskatchewan, the issue of bias is of sufficient concern that all major police forces have created Aboriginal liaison officers to hear complaints from Aboriginal people and to try to create higher levels of confidence in Aboriginal communities in the professionalism and neutrality of police services. In addition, the Commission on First Nations and Métis People and Justice Reform, in its second report, addressed the question of complaints from Aboriginal people about police conduct. The Commission, without coming to a specific finding about bias or racism, noted that an earlier review of Aboriginal justice in Saskatchewan[29] had recommended that a citizens' complaint mechanism for First Nations and Métis communities be assessed but that the recommendation had not been addressed. The Commission, therefore, simply recommended that a citizens' complaint review mechanism be implemented.[30] It also recommended that the Federation of Saskatchewan Indian Nations' Special Investigation Unit, which since early 2000 had looked into a large number of complaints against the police (over 2000 complaints leading to the opening of 521 files[31]), continue to be funded by the government. It based this recommendation on the view that "[p]ersonal accounts will be forthcoming only if a safe environment such as an independent investigative body is available to have them heard."[32] These recommendations should not be read as an explicit Commission finding of bias or racism, but they do reflect recognition that the neutrality and professionalism of police services are not always trusted within Aboriginal communities.

A further instance of careful expression of the significance of race in the administration of justice, without supporting the claim of race hatred, is found in the Report of the Commission of Inquiry into Matters Relating to the Death of Neil Stonechild, in which the Commissioner, Justice David Wright, wrote:

> As I reviewed the evidence in this Inquiry, I was reminded, again and again, of the chasm that separates Aboriginal and non-Aboriginal people in this city and province. Our two communities do not know each other and do not seem to want to. The void is emphasized by the interaction of an essentially non-Aboriginal police force and the Aboriginal community. The justice system produces another set of difficulties.[33]

There is no doubt that all of the above factors have had some impact on Aboriginal offending and victimization. The dominant controversy over the causes of disorder is whether negative social conditions arising from the experience of colonization have led to over-representation in the criminal justice system and over-incarceration of Aboriginal people, or whether the specific features

of the experience of the colonization of Indigenous peoples – alienation, oppression, disempowerment, and delegitimation – have produced these levels
of offending through exacerbating the effects of social deprivation. If the
latter alternative is the more compelling – and it seems highly probable that
it is – then it follows that addressing the traditional social causes of crime in
response to the challenge of Aboriginal offending and victimization will not,
in itself, produce healthy communities. This is because the injury to social
solidarity and social capacity is rooted in the specific and damaging long-term
political project of colonization and the answer is not simply more extensive
social programming. The development idea that is called for is the specific
political notion of decolonization. In other words, social development must be
part of the deeper, more radical, more transformational project of Aboriginal
self-determination.

IV. The Perspective of Development

A widespread debate within the policy communities that deal with various
aspects of social and economic development is over the question of the
functional connections between that development and political development.
Claims that frequently give rise to controversy are, first, that it is economic
development that is both the *sine qua non* and the most effective engine of
social development and social improvement and, second, that it is the quest
for economic growth that spurs democratic development. This latter claim
seems based on the view that the creation of an open market which works well
enough to lead to increased production and wealth depends on the presence
of instruments of a sound democracy, such as rules to ensure fair and open
markets, impartial application of laws, transparency and accountability in
public administration, and democratic elections for choosing those who make
the laws.[34] The significance of this connection between economic development
and democratic practices is that since it may be the presence of the latter that
will create the conditions of community self-respect, as well as intersocietal
respect, it is important to give primacy to economic development because it
both contributes to well-being and compels the establishment of sound and
admirable political practices.

　　With respect to the first issue, the anecdotal evidence from Saskatchewan is
that small economic booms and income lifts in northern Aboriginal communities that are produced through new employment opportunities for northern
residents (sometimes produced by resources agreements, most notably forest
agreements, and sometimes produced by transportation and construction op-

portunities flowing from building resource-extraction infrastructure) do not lead to improved social indicators. Of course, such booms are generally not durable, while the indicators of social health reflect very deep social dysfunctions that are not likely to be remedied except through long-term projects. Clearly, rates of criminal charging, one short-term indicator, do not improve, and in some informal reports, actually go up, possibly because increased income facilitates substance abuse. In truth, nothing can be drawn from this sort of data, except, perhaps, the idea that harmful patterns of social life are not, in the short run, corrected through simple economic changes like increases in employment and income. On the other hand, the phenomenon of increased wages as described here should not be thought of as deep economic development – economic development that generates professional and management skills and broadens communities' perspectives. That requires that Indigenous populations become involved in economic planning, capital investment, developing value-added processes, assessing and opening markets, providing professional supports (law, accounting, promotion, etc), creating conditions for a strong workforce, and most vitally of all, becoming engaged in the on-going process of economic renewal. Economic development that has all of these elements in place would stand a good chance of generating social improvement, if only as a matter of definition, since these conditions could not be met without an established and strong political and social capacity. The real question, however, is whether these kinds of economic management capacities can possibly emerge through focussing exclusively on an Aboriginal community's economic condition and on economic strategies, or whether such development requires the coincident, or even prior, building of political capacity, social health, and high levels of community self-respect.

The development economist Albert O. Hirschman notes that although social scientists give preferential attention to sequences where economic events drive positive change in the field of politics, there are counter examples in which the important initial development is of democratic practices and is followed by economic improvements.[35] Hirschman concludes that it is impossible to prescribe a developmental flow-chart; no definitive pattern has emerged describing the connection between economic and political progress.[36] Other analysts are, perhaps, less cautious. Amartya Sen's prescription for effective development unambiguously includes political freedoms and democracy and, significantly, the social conditions for effectively exercising them.[37] Mancur Olson's project explores the conditions that make some economies perform well. His view is that an important determinant of economic vitality is the presence of market-enhancing governmental regulation that is reliably and consistently administered through strong government that is backed up by a strong rule of law tradition.[38] Of course, this conclusion does not necessarily value Aboriginal political authority above regulatory authority that is exercised by public government. In fact, if we were to believe that Aboriginal governments are likely to experience relative weakness and unevenness during early stages of their political development, this could produce disadvantageous conditions for strong economic development. On the other hand, public government's usurpation of economic development for Aboriginal communities would seem to do little for those communities' self-respect.

If establishing Aboriginal political authority over enterprise development were a developmental pre-condition, it would be essential that it be strong and effective. This would require solid political socialization as well as considerable governmental capacity. If good government is a prior condition to good economic development and if we also posit that a healthy and stable social context is a pre-condition to good government, we enter a vortex of developmental cause and effect. The sequencing of development strategies is not a simple matter, beyond the observations that each aspect of development bears on the others and that good political communities need to be formed in a context of appropriate and authentic political autonomy.

Apart from the work of theorists, the studies conducted by the Harvard Project on American Indian Economic Development at the John F. Kennedy School of Government of Harvard University show a striking connection between the success of tribal economies and the presence of mature tribal polities that reflect traditional tribal values with respect to political authority. This research has been summarized by Stephen Cornell and Joseph Kalt in this way:

> The lesson of the research is clear. It is increasingly evident that the best way to perpetuate reservation poverty is to undermine tribal sovereignty. The best way to overcome reservation poverty is to support tribal sovereignty. Furthermore, the evidence is mounting that successful tribes. . . can make important contributions to local, regional and national economies. . . . [T]he lesson is that those tribes that build governing institutions capable of the effective exercise of sovereignty are the ones that are most likely to achieve long-term, self-determined economic prosperity. They are the ones who will most effectively shape their own futures, instead of having those futures shaped by others.[39]

In the same vein as Olson's conclusions, the Harvard Project has also found that tribal economic success has depended on there being strong and capable institutions and independent and professional mechanisms of administration. The Project also emphasizes that economic success depends on governmental structures being culturally appropriate and enjoying legitimacy among tribal citizens.[40] Perhaps this conclusion is simply reductionist in the sense that no governmental apparatus will prove to be effective in constructing an economy (or a healthy society) if its power is seen as lacking legitimacy due to being based on values that do not come from or reflect that culture. This insight, after all, is what explains the entire project of seeking development through empowerment.

v. The Constitutional Context

A vital step in reconstructing relations between Aboriginal and non-Aboriginal people in Saskatchewan is, as I have argued, rolling back the hands of time to name and understand the practices and effects of colonization. This plunging into the darkness of history is driven by the sense of what might be achieved by the systematic unravelling of the fate of colonialism for Aboriginal people – the specific restoration of what was destroyed, both the content of distinctive cultural experience and the sweep of Aboriginal societal values of nurturing life, stewardship, accountability, and justice. With that effort at undoing colonialism, the essential underlying condition for the peaceable state – respect between cultures – is more likely to grow and is more likely to displace the current reality of exclusion and indifference to suffering. The harmed condition is, in essence, a relationship or intersocietal condition, and it is not as amenable to measures of social support as promoters of the welfare state might wish to believe. It must be addressed through reform of the terms of the intersocietal relationship. Fortunately, there is a happy coincidence between the scale of the reforms that are needed to achieve Aboriginal social health and the nature of the nation's constitutional commitments. In Canada, in addition to the colonial history of oppression and destruction, there is another history of Aboriginal/non-Aboriginal relating – one that presents a more positive view of European settlement and points us in the same direction as does our taking responsibility for the story of social harming. That better history is the story of imperialism at the level of its explicit statecraft aims with respect to Indigenous populations and other historic communities. As noted above, the claim can be made that Canadian constitutionalism has created a significant space for group rights and the protection of minority communities. There is, at least at the level of constitutional value, no resolute conviction that a common and uniform national citizenship is essential to preserving state stability and pursuing strong national purposes.[41]

In Canada, functional and conceptual claims for the monist, liberal democratic conception of the state have been countered through both a general recognition of multiculturalism[42] and the stronger specific recognition, without
qualification, of the "aboriginal and treaty rights of the aboriginal peoples of
Canada."[43] When constitutional recognition is given to rights of racially and
ethnically distinct minority communities, there is an undoubted constitutional
conferral of the capacity to sustain the integrity of that community, including, when it is functionally required, a political capacity that may be exercised
independently of the specific legislative authority of the state. This claim will,
of course, give rise to hard questions about what mechanisms and according
to which political norms the interests of the state must be represented in, and
protected from, exercises of political authority of constitutionally recognized
groups. However, for now, it is enough to recognize that there are bound to
be limits on sub-state political authorities and that such limits are likely to be
teased out of general constitutional arrangements and values.[44]

The positive inferences of self-governing authority drawn from general
constitutional recognition could possibly be more significant, and more rich in
content, than specific rights that are drawn from the language of First Nations
treaties, or rights that result from the cautious elevation of specific historical
practices to constitutionally protected activities through judicial interpretation
of Aboriginal rights. This general and inferred formulation of entitlement is
not the same as claiming that Aboriginal political societies are a third order
of government, if that claim implies complete parallelism between, say, the
structure and operation of provincial governments and First Nations, Métis,
and Inuit governments. On the other hand, a third order of government is
exactly what section 35(1) of the *Constitution Act, 1982*, seems to create, in the
more limited sense that it implies governance capacity and suggests what that
governance authority might consist of. While there is no list of authorities in
section 35(1) to correspond to the lists of authorities in sections 91, 92, 92A, 93,
94A, and 95 of the *Constitution Act, 1867*, the section does direct us to a purpose
for constitutional recognition and, hence, to a source of political competencies
for realizing that purpose. The most forceful source for interpreting section
35(1) is the concept of preserving Aboriginality, in terms of both its historic
entitlements and current requirements for sustaining its integrity. One reason
not to conflate the idea of a third order of government to the constitutional
position of Canada's public governments is that it is not clear that all of the
constitutional restraints and conditions on public governments should apply
with equal force to Aboriginal governments. This is an area of constitutional
analysis in which much of the detailed work lies ahead.[45]

SOVEREIGNTY AND DEVELOPMENT

Professor Brian Slattery has pointed out the evolution in the Supreme Court of Canada's approach in identifying Aboriginal rights from seeing Aboriginal rights as specific to a particular Aboriginal community to recognizing a range of generic rights that inhere in all, or most, Aboriginal peoples.[46] He argues that this range of rights flows from the constitutional recognition of the special place of the Aboriginal groups and the constitutional commitment to sustain the integrity of Aboriginal societies. Just as we are best able to understand the working of the federal principle in Canada through recognizing the generic constitutional rights of provinces to govern within their sphere of jurisdiction, we should also understand the range of entitlement of Aboriginal communities through drawing on general conceptions about capacities and instruments appropriate for ethnic-based political societies, especially Indigenous societies recognized in the Canadian Constitution.

As Professor Samuel LaSelva points out, however, Aboriginal claims in Canada do not represent a truly radical or sovereignist form of decolonization, in that they are moral claims against a polity in which they wish to continue as participants (albeit with a greater degree of autonomy and with enjoyment of a far higher level of respect) and from which they expect recognition and support.[47] The point of advancing a strong version of the implications of constitutional recognition is, therefore, not to separate Aboriginal communities from the Canadian state but to recognize exercises of self-determination over all of the societal functions that bear on preserving the integrity of Aboriginal peoples.

Moving from the perspective of the Canadian constitutional text to considerations of constitutional theory, it is important to note that the background purposes of group rights are to respect human rights and to preserve the stability of states that host communities with strong distinct cultural identities.[48] The underlying theme of the liberal democratic state is not individualism but self-determination, and the pursuit of self-determination depends on strong communitarian identities as much as on personal identities. This is true for all but it is especially so for Indigenous peoples whose historic way of life depended on powerful community attachments.[49]

Claims of self-determination are not exclusively claims of political morality (although their resonance or fit with the ways in which people actually acquire life's meaning and purposes means they can well stand as moral claims) as they are claims of sound state organization. The greatest threat to the well-being of persons within the state is the unreliability of the political order and the risk of radical upheavals,[50] and the goal of the good state is to remove the incentives for destabilization and overthrow. State well-being depends less on there being a single hegemonic regime than on there being space within the regime for the flourishing of the distinct identities of which states are invariably composed. Such things as legal pluralism, jurisgenerative constitutional provisions, and the validation of distinct communities are the traditional instruments for restraining assimilationist policies and forestalling destruction of identities.[51] We know few things in the world as well as we know of the durability and political power of cultural memory and historic experiences of distinct communities, especially the experiences of oppression, and destruction.[52] It is when the cultural memory is overwhelmingly negative that "the terrible burden of narrowly defined identities"[53] takes hold and all that becomes available for cultural expression is rage, resentment, and ultimately, destruction – most terribly, self-destruction. What is wanted in an open and pluralist society is honour for all of its communities and respect for all of its different cultures. If our practices of accommodation are simply an attempt to contain diversity through a simple combination of social control and social support then the project of state stability through minority recognition is at constant risk.

Likewise, the concepts of human rights embedded in the Canadian state through the *Universal Declaration of Human Rights*,[54] the *International Covenant of Civil and Political Rights*,[55] and emerging human rights norms in international customary law[56] have been transformed from mere words to authority with the inclusion of the *Charter* in the *Constitution Act, 1982*. This, too, has implicated the whole structure of our public governance with respect to political accommodation of minority communities.[57] Not only are the long-term goals of the good state achieved through recognition of group rights (which is the legal apparatus for accommodating multiculturalism), but the creation of the state all through the second millennium has recognized the need to capture social dynamism within the state through legitimating and enabling the role of groups and communities. In this way, liberalism (which is undoubtedly the core theoretical quality of the Canadian state) is not hostile to communitarianism but, through recognizing its legitimacy, has extended, enhanced, and enriched the goal of self-determination.[58]

With respect to specific legal recognition of an Aboriginal self-government right, the Supreme Court of Canada has not yet taken a definitive stand. In *R. v. Pamajewon*,[59] the Court, in deciding that there is no Aboriginal right to regulate gambling activity on a reserve, was willing to proceed on the basis that section 35(1) of the *Constitution Act, 1982*, encompasses a right to self-government, although not the precise governance authority that was claimed by the First Nations appellants in that case. This decisional strategy, however, should not be taken as clear Court support for a self-government right. It more likely represents the Court's exercise of the passive virtue of deciding the clearest issue when that decision leads to a disposition of the case. In this way, the Court avoided dealing with important issues of political authority until a later day. A more telling case is the British Columbia Supreme Court decision in *Campbell* v. *British Columbia (Attorney General)*.[60] It upheld the governance terms of the Nisga'a Treaty, which clearly contemplated a broad self-government capacity by the Nisga'a.[61] Based on the suggestion of the Supreme Court of Canada in *Delgamuukw* v. *British Columbia*[62] that Aboriginal title to community land entails both a collective right to the land and the community's right to make decisions with respect to that land, Williamson J. stated that section 35(1) includes "the right for the community to make decisions as to the use of the land and, therefore, the right to have a political structure for making those decisions."[63] The *Campbell* decision was not appealed, but if the matter were to arise again in a higher court in British Columbia or in another jurisdiction, it seems unlikely that it would be ignored or overruled. The whole process of modern land claim settlements is designed to specifically place First Nations on a more self-sufficient basis economically, socially, and politically. Of course, Aboriginal policy of this sort should never dictate the terms of constitutional law as it relates to Aboriginal peoples, but the consistent message from the Supreme Court of Canada has been that to close down the range of possibilities for Aboriginal political and social development through a narrow reading of the rights that are recognized in section 35(1) would undercut the pressure that section 35(1) has placed on governments to fashion a new, more respectful, and more equal relationship between First Nations and Métis communities and governments in Canada.

While there has been no clear Supreme Court of Canada majority decision explicitly recognizing a right of self-government, the case for its recognition is rooted in political commitments,[64] constitutional scholarship,[65] and history. The historical basis for self-government is found in the concept of treaty-making between the Imperial government and, after Confederation, the new national government of Canada. The Supreme Court of Canada has made it clear that the treaty-making process in Canada "indicates that the Indian nations were regarded in their relations with the European nations which occupied North America as independent nations."[66] A telling instance of an attempt to describe the nature of the relationship between the public government that represented the settler communities and the existing Aboriginal societies is found in the decision of the Federal Court Trial Division in *Benoit* v. *Canada*.[67] In that case, the applicants, members of Treaty 8 First Nations, sought not to have any taxes imposed on them, on the basis that they were promised exemption from all taxes during the 1899 treaty process that led to their ancestors entering into a treaty with the Canadian government.[68] The trial judge included in his judgment a part of the historical record of this process. In the report to the Minister of the Interior and Superintendent General of Indian Affairs from the government's Commissioners for Concluding Treaty 8, it is recorded that the First Nations leaders, although willing to fall under the protection and general authority of the Canadian government, especially with respect to obeying the law and living at peace with the settlers, were concerned to receive assurances that entering into a treaty did not imply curtailment of hunting and fishing privileges, suppression in the government's schools of their religious beliefs, enforced military service, or the imposition of any tax.[69] The Commissioners offered them assurances with respect to each of these matters: the only wildlife harvesting restrictions would be those that were for the interests of First Nations members, there would be no interference with "the religion of Indians," and "the treaty would not lead to any forced interference with their mode of life, that it did not open the way to the imposition of any tax, and there was no fear of enforced military service."[70] What is significant is not the specific guarantees asked for and received (nor, for present purposes, the uneven and unsatisfactory history of governmental compliance with the conditions that were accepted) but is instead the idea of the intersocietal relationship that both sides thought they were forging in making a treaty. Both parties accepted the concepts that the Indian nations[71] involved in Treaty 8 were well-functioning political communities, that behind the political identities of those nations were cultural identities, and that the treaty process was not designed to destroy either sort of identity; on the contrary, it was designed to ensure the continuation of those communities against the assimilating pressures of settlement. It is noteworthy that the spokespersons for the First Nations were very clear on two things: They knew that their political autonomy would be compromised on entering into a treaty with Canada, but they insisted that their political societies and structures continue.[72] This is exactly what the First Nations representatives wanted to make clear when they sought assurances that two basic needs of the settler government – the raising of revenues and the conscription of persons to engage in hostilities – would not be brought to bear on their communities and would not compel alteration of their priorities. Both the fact of the treaty-making process and the understandings under which it was conducted present strong evidence that Aboriginal political organization was fully recognized by the Imperial and Canadian governments and that it was expected to continue as an independent force within the Canadian political arrangement.[73]

Canada's record of treatment of Aboriginal people and Aboriginal peoples hardly suggests a strong grasp of, or commitment to, First Nations and Métis communities as capable and respected self-governing societies, yet that is our constitutional vision. That has been, and continues to be, our constitutional vision because at those moments of high political choice when basic arrangements, based on durable political principles have been constituted,[74] we have accepted the distinctive historical place of Aboriginal peoples in the Canadian state, and we have grasped what is owed to them both as a consequence of their accommodation of European settlement and as a matter of the legitimacy of their claim to preserve the integrity of their "indigenousness." Certainly, governments (and courts) have not "grasped the full implications of the fact that treaties, as constitutional accords, distribute constitutional power in Canada."[75] Canadian constitutionalism, however, is a rich tapestry and contains threads of history and value that cannot be suppressed by fear over altering our current practices or by despair over the extent of the political renovation needed. Through preserving continuity with our commitments, Canadian constitutionalism has constructed the channel through which we need to pass in meeting Canada's most pressing social and political challenge.

VI. CONCLUSION

Developing the nation-state was the political project of modernism; the challenge of the postmodern age is to manage intersocietal arrangements within states in a way that sustains the stability of states and offers real justice to all of the peoples that comprise a nation. Constitutionalism, particularly Canadian constitutionalism, has been inventive in devising mechanisms that will effectively protect vital historic interests from the tyranny of the national majority. It has adopted federalism, the concept of entrenched rights, the separation of powers, the rule of law, and constitutional recognition of historic language, as well as of religious and ethnic communities. Yet, as has been pointed out, notwithstanding these formal commitments to preserving the integrity of its minority communities, Canada must own the record of a destructive colonialist history. It must also, of course, own responsibility for the sad economic and social exclusion of many of its Aboriginal people together with the inevitable negative social consequences. Two questions face governments in Canada. The first question is: what are the key elements of an effective social and economic development policy? The second is: what is owed to Aboriginal communities as a matter of political and constitutional obligation? As has been argued, the answer to both of these questions is the same – recognition of the entitlement of Aboriginal communities to function as self-determining and self-governing political societies and, most pertinently from the perspective of crime and social disorder, recognition of Aboriginal jurisdiction over governmental response to offending. Behind this claim is the view that social needs and social priorities will be addressed best when they are self-identified and when the prescriptions for responding come from the communities that are experiencing the challenges. This claim represents nothing more complex than the idea that social health flows from autonomy and responsibility, not from being placed under the control and stewardship of another political authority and another population.[76]

What is not dealt with in this chapter are the questions of how self-government and Aboriginal justice systems should be structured. In recognizing Aboriginal political authority should we proceed nationally, provincially, through tribal councils, by First Nations and Métis villages, by status-blind urban Aboriginal authorities, or through provincial or regional service agencies? What is also not explored is how to construct principles for mediating policy conflicts and value conflicts. Many other questions have not been addressed, such as the role of rights and other constitutional protections in self-government and how policy conflicts between public governments and Aboriginal governments are to be worked out. Nor has the question of how to guarantee adequate political representation in the structures of Aboriginal government been confronted. All of these, and others, are serious matters,[77] but our reality is that there are not yet clear answers to these sorts of issues. This is no reason for not proceeding with Aboriginal empowerment initiatives that will lead to fashioning policies for social improvement, to early forms of First Nations and Métis public administration, and to economic promotion. Of course, in Canada, these steps are already being taken under the authority of land claims agreements, modern treaties, and the just-emerging comprehensive agreements-in-principle over taxation and governance. In this way, Aboriginal political development may be being driven as much by pragmatism as by constitutional theory. If so, we should know that our deepest commitments and our best long-term political aspirations give legitimacy and force to the important process of Aboriginal community empowerment.

PART TWO

CHALLENGES OF FIRST NATIONS
AND MÉTIS JUSTICE

7

JUSTICE AUTHORITIES IN SELF-GOVERNMENT AGREEMENTS

THE IMPORTANCE OF CONDITIONS AND MECHANISMS OF IMPLEMENTATION

Stephanie Irlbacher-Fox

1. INTRODUCTION

In Canada, negotiating self-government is an important element of federal attempts to renew the relationship between Indigenous peoples and the state, and it is a way to overcome a persisting colonial relationship. A self-government policy was issued during 1995, and self-government agreements are being negotiated and implemented, to varying degrees of success. The agreements are based on a notion of the inherent right, as conceived of by the state, and these agreements are meant to implement, rather than define, the content of the right. In many cases, negotiations will result in agreements that do not nearly approximate a notion of self-determination as understood by Indigenous peoples. Nevertheless, some Indigenous peoples have chosen to negotiate self-government, viewing it as a step toward decolonizing their relationship with the state.

This chapter examines how the administration of justice provisions of one self-government agreement will result in the exercise of the inherent right of self-government being compromised by two major factors: a forced reliance on the discretion of other governments to render self-government authorities effective, and the fragmentation of institutions that is necessary for implementing authorities. This chapter draws from the *Inuvialuit and Gwich'in Self-Government Agreement-in-Principle* (AIP), signed during 2003, to illustrate this point.[1] Further, the above factors mean that the AIP's justice provisions do not provide for: 1) conditions under which key aspects of the administration of justice are controlled by Inuvialuit, without relying on other governments and 2) mechanisms through which justice authorities can be implemented effectively. The result is that Inuvialuit administration of justice authorities are recognized, in part, by Canada, which merely confirms powers available to Indigenous organizations under current federal policy and reinforces federal control and discretion over the exercise of those powers. This case study supports the argument that rights can be made meaningful (or in some senses, meaningless) by the conditions and mechanisms of their implementation.

II. Implementation Conditions and Mechanisms and Meaningful Rights

The experience of land claims implementation among Northwest Territories (NWT) governments expanded the focus of subsequent self-government negotiations from rights recognition to including rights implementation.[2] Echoing the sentiment that real rights recognition relies on the extent to which these rights make a real difference in peoples' day-to-day lives, philosopher Raymond Geuss argues that rights are meaningless if they are not accompanied by meaningful implementation mechanisms.[3] Self-government negotiation is the process through which the "right of self-government" is described as a series of administrative and law-making authorities that are to be exercised by Indigenous peoples' governments and through co-operative arrangements with other governments. In effect, the inherent right is translated into concrete expressions of rights, often as "tools" for furthering specific interests or powers of Indigenous peoples, in specific areas of authority. For example, one such tool would be the ability to offer culturally-relevant approaches to deal with perpetrators of criminal offenses within alternative sentencing measures. However, such tools, and thus, aspects of a right, may be undermined if they are negotiated on their own merits and without equal attention given to creating conditions within which such tools may be used meaningfully or effectively. Therefore, it is the mechanisms used to implement a right, and the conditions within which mechanisms function, taken together, that give practical effect to a right.

Conditions and implementation mechanisms are constituted by both recognized forms and bases of authority (law-making power, administrative control) and the conditions through which these mechanisms are made meaningful (implementation and financing arrangements). Attention must be paid to the ways that mechanisms and conditions created through self-government may affect each other and, therefore, shape the nature, character, and extent of authority. Together, these factors determine whether an agreement establishes a basis for self-government that is both workable and politically – and practically – viable.

Effective implementation may be gauged by measuring the extent to which the discharge of an obligation that is contained in an agreement achieves the agreement's intention to animate rights. Arguing in the same vein through an analysis of the principles of legitimacy of constitutional democracy, philosopher James Tully critiques the tendency of studies on deliberative democracy to cease with agreements that have been reached between peoples and the states they inhabit.[4] He thus anticipates a critique offered by the Canadian Auditor General, in her 2003 review of the implementation of the *Gwich'in Comprehensive Land Claim* and the *Nunavut Land Claims* agreements.[5] The Auditor General found that implementation should be approached in a way that accounts for the spirit or broad objectives of the land claims, as opposed to an approach that interprets the agreements as requiring actions to implement specific provisions, without devoting attention to results.[6] This more desirable approach would view agreement implementation as an ongoing relationship, rather than as a legal contract between parties. Similarly, Tully argues:

> [The] traditional endpoint of normative analysis, even when it is related to practical case studies, leaves the entire field of implementation and review to empirical social sciences, often under the false assumption that implementation is different in kind from justification, simply a technical question of applying rigid rules correctly. There are many ways actors can agree to a settlement [a self-government agreement] and either avoid or subvert implementation while appearing to follow norms of legitimation.[7]

Tully hits upon precisely the issues that inspire great distrust among Indigenous communities on whose behalf such agreements are negotiated. Treaties made with Canada by Indigenous peoples have not been honoured in their entirety in any single case. This is as true for numbered treaties made over a century ago as it is of what are often referred to as "modern-day treaties."[8]

Within the administration of justice chapter of the *Inuvialuit and Gwich'in* AIP, implementation mechanisms are compromised by at least two key conditions.[9] These include:

(i)   Meaningful control: With respect to the administration of justice provisions, the scope and extent of self-government authorities are dependent on the discretion of other governments, instead of being clearly articulated within a transparent framework of power-sharing; and

(ii)   Fragmented institutional arrangements: Authorities are recognized through a "fragmented" set of institutions; these are institutions drawing their authority and legitimacy from different legal bases and political constituencies complicating self-governments' abilities to plan, prepare for, and execute measures that are necessary to implement their responsibilities and obligations under self-government agreements. For example, Inuvialuit governments appoint prosecutors, who must prosecute Inuvialuit laws within territorial government courts.

When meaningful control is exercised through cohesive institutional arrangements, it provides both certainty and stability to governments exercising authority.[10] As it stands, the absence of these conditions creates an environment within which self-government institutions cannot be expected to fully exercise authorities for which they have responsibility.

III. WHY ARE THERE DOUBTS ABOUT IMPLEMENTATION?

During 2004, the Canada-Aboriginal Peoples' Roundtable[11] was established by Canada as a discussion forum for Indigenous issues, partly in response to a growing consensus among land claim governments that the implementation of agreements was falling short of legal obligations. Implementation failures have resulted in re-negotiating aspects of agreements, such as the re-negotiations that occurred with the *James Bay and Northern Quebec Agreement* (JBNQA), where Canada and Cree people reached an agreement on a new relationship meant, in part, to address and improve implementation of the JBNQA.[12] In contrast, a court action was launched during 2006 over the state's failure to implement aspects of the *Nunavut Land Claims Agreement*.[13] The significance of implementation failures were underscored by the Auditor General in her February 2003 report, where she observed that the agency responsible for implementing land claim agreements, Indian and Northern Affairs Canada (INAC), approached implementation in ways that did not realize the spirit and intent of what land claims were meant to achieve; for example, when examining the implementation of the Gwich'in and Nunavut agreements, the report says:

> 8.1 Signing a land claim agreement is a major accomplishment. Managing it afterward is an ongoing challenge that requires collaboration by all parties to the agreement. That collaboration must begin with Indian and Northern Affairs Canada (INAC) taking a leadership role in making the claims work. It must also manage federal responsibilities set out under the agreements in a way that achieves results. We found that with respect to the two claims we looked at, the Gwich'in people of the Northwest Territories (NWT) and the Inuit of Nunavut, INAC's performance on both counts has left considerable room for improvement.
>
> 8.2 For example, INAC seems focused on fulfilling the letter of the land claims' implementation plans but not the spirit. Officials may believe that they have met their obligations, but in fact they have not worked to support the full intent of the land claims agreements.
>
> 8.3 Also, the various mechanisms for managing the claims are not effective in resolving all disputes. Land claims arbitration panels have not dealt with any of the long-standing disagreements since the claims were settled over 10 years ago.[14]

The cumulative effects of land claim organizations' common and ongoing dissatisfaction with the implementation of agreements culminated in the establishment of the Land Claim Agreement Coalition (LCAC), consisting of all land claim organizations in Canada. Its first major initiative was to convene a conference during 2003 in Ottawa to identify and discuss common land claims implementation issues.[15] The conference resulted in the LCAC focussing its subsequent efforts on lobbying for a new federal implementation approach. The coalition's efforts resulted in some early progress, with Canada establishing a policy group within INAC's implementation branch, to develop a new implementation policy.[16] The LCAC convened a second conference in June of 2006, where the new policy was expected to be announced.[17] However, political will to develop a national implementation policy waned with the change in government during 2006, and a new implementation policy has yet to materialize. These developments have occurred, despite mounting evidence from the Auditor General that implementation approaches continue to fail the NWT Land Claims,[18] as well as the 2006 Conciliator's Report on Nunavut implementation issues and potential solutions from Thomas Berger.[19] Berger's report, which found significant flaws in the Nunavut claim implementation process and called for educational reform in the territory aimed at addressing chronic social suffering, was met with indifference by the federal government. In sheer frustration, during 2006, Nunavut Tungavik launched a billion-dollar lawsuit against the federal government to press its concerns that Canada has failed to fulfill key land claim obligations. The case is currently before the Federal Court.[20]

Several self-government negotiations in the Northwest Territories stem from obligations in land claim agreements.[21] Often, Indigenous peoples' representatives are reluctant to "sign off" on the federal obligation to negotiate self-government after years of self-government discussions. This is due, in part, to the perception that current self-government policy does not permit federal officials to fully discharge the obligation to negotiate self-government in accordance with the prescribed provisions of land claims agreements. Essentially, the experience is that under the current federal self-government policy, self-government subjects listed in the land claims cannot be fully discussed.[22] The result is that in some cases, discussion over certain areas of authority may be postponed to future talks triggered by self-government agreement provisions. The reluctance to agree that Canada has fulfilled the land claim agreement obligation to negotiate self-government after a final agreement has been reached may also be due to situations where negotiated self-government powers are far less than what was initially expected. In such instances, jurisdiction or administrative authority may result in self-governments functioning, in part, according to the discretion of other governments with respect to funding, institutional arrangements, and the enforcement of laws.

Thus, a key lesson learned from land claims implementation has been that federal implementation approaches do not necessarily support the full realization of contractual obligations or the spirit and intent of agreements. This does not bode well for subsequent self-government agreements that may rely on the discretion and institutions of other governments to see their authorities rendered effective. To appreciate the extent to which the ongoing involvement and support of other governments will be required to animate self-government authorities, this chapter will turn to the example of administration of justice in the *Inuvialuit and Gwich'in AIP* to illustrate this last point, before engaging in an analysis of the implications of this situation for future Inuvialuit governments.

IV. THE CASE OF THE INUVIALUIT SELF-GOVERNMENT ADMINISTRATION OF JUSTICE AUTHORITIES[23]

The purpose of negotiating the self-government agreement with the Inuvi-aluit is to describe the "nature, character, and extent of self-government."[24] In Canada's 1995 policy, self-government is recognized as an existing right under section 35.1 of the *Constitution Act, 1982*.[25] While the agreement does not define the right of self-government, it implements aspects of that right, and thus, it has a status of something more than a contract.[26] It is, in that sense, a rights-based agreement.

Canada's approach to implementing the inherent right can be understood as having three main elements. These are:

(i)   recognizing authorities of self-governments, such as exercising ju-risdiction or having administrative powers;

(ii)   committing to implementation obligations through a plan or con-tract, where Canada commits to taking specific actions (such as pro-viding funding) to ensure authorities, programs, or governmental co-operation necessary to implement the inherent right; and

(iii)   permissive acknowledgement, where Canada recognizes that a self-government may enter into agreements with governments to deliver government programs and services for which the legal basis of au-thority lies with governments.[27]

With respect to justice, Inuvialuit self-government powers are described in chapter 18 of the *Inuvialuit and Gwich'in AIP*.[28] One of the major weaknesses of the chapter is that it consists mainly of the permissive acknowledgement approach noted above; justice powers are described by provisions in the agreement that confirm that the Inuvialuit may enter into agreements or take actions that are already allowable within federal policy. Such actions or agreements are possible for Inuvialuit in the absence of a self-government agreement. For example, subsection 18.7.1 discusses entering into agreements implementing community correction services for adult offenders; subsection 18.7.8, recognizes that Inuvialuit governments may enter into agreements with other governments for delivering programs relating to crime preven-tion, alternative measures, restorative justice, and legal aid. It should be noted that these provisions do not oblige other governments to negotiate with the Inuvialuit self-governments. Instead, the provisions merely recognize the self-governments as authorities with which agreements may be legitimately negotiated. This is also true for policing. Currently, the First Nations Policing Policy promotes the establishment of First Nation police forces in Canada; provision 18.6 recognizes that Inuvialuit governments may enter into agreements on policing.[29] However, the Government of the Northwest Territories (GNWT) has not yet adopted legislation that regulates policing. Instead, the GNWT simply contracts with the Royal Canadian Mounted Police to deliver all policing services. When pressed during self-government negotiations to recognize an Inuvialuit police force, Canada maintained that until the GNWT had policing legislation in place, it would be impossible for self-governments to create their own police forces.[30]

What powers do Inuvialuit governments have over the administration of justice, then? Similar to municipalities, they may appoint enforcement officers for their laws (equivalent to by-law officers), as per subsection 18.2.1; they may provide sentencing guidelines to the courts of other governments, as per subsection 18.2.5, similar to current practices where a court may exercise discretion in inviting Indigenous advisors to assist in sentencing; they are responsible for prosecutions of Inuvialuit laws, as per subsection 18.2.6, a function that will require prosecutors to operate within the courts of other governments; finally, as per subsection 18.2.8, Inuvialuit governments may provide for dispute resolution mechanisms outside of the courts, mechanisms which, unlike the courts of other governments, can only decide matters in a dispute with the consent of both parties. These powers are municipal in nature, to varying degrees, and they are predicated in some ways on the discretion of other governments' authority or optional mechanisms within a hierarchy in which other governments' institutions are paramount.

Notably, the inherent right policy has taken a rights-implementation approach over a rights-definition approach. Within such a context, rights can be understood to draw their currency and significance from the effectiveness of their implementation. This requires conditions where implementation mechanisms can work or be accessed. Without providing for conditions and mechanisms through which a right may be effectively and meaningfully realized, recognition of a right undercuts the content of the right. This is particularly true when the parties to an agreement, in this case, Canada and the Inuvialuit people, have agreed at the outset of negotiations not to define the inherent right of self-government but to instead reach an agreement that implements aspects of the right.[31] It is worth noting that in adapting an "implementation, not definition" approach to rights, Canada itself has necessitated an evaluation of self-government agreements that moves beyond agreement content to assessing the normative conditions within which agreements are implemented.

One of the major problems with taking an implementation approach is that without mutually agreed principles or criteria guiding how implementation will be evaluated, ensuring implementation's effectiveness is difficult. For example, in the *Inuvialuit and Gwich'in AIP*, we know that Inuvialuit governments may make laws and set penalties over minor criminal offences,[32] yet policing is under the sole authority of the GNWT (which contracts to the RCMP) and prosecutions can only be conducted in NWT courts.[33] Thus, while self-governments make laws (presumably infused with their cultural values), the laws are policed, prosecuted, and enforced within or by GNWT institutions predicated primarily on non-Indigenous cultures and values. At the same time, in retaining responsibility for bringing charges and sentencing, considerable discretion is exercised by the GNWT, not the Inuvialuit.[34] While it is true that with respect to prosecutions and enforcement officers, the Inuvialuit have significant control,[35] this will be largely determined by financing agreements that are yet to be negotiated.

Thus, the agreement constructs a situation where self-governments have the authority to make laws, but non-Indigenous governments have significant discretion over policing and enforcing the laws. This discretion is in no way bound or limited by any agreed-upon principles relating to how its exercise may or may not affect the inherent right's implementation. The exercise of discretion, coupled with the ongoing reliance of the self-governments on other governments' institutions to implement self-government laws, constitutes a moment of transformative significance and meaning for self-government rights. In the mundane day-to-day workings of the justice system, self-government rights will be strengthened or compromised; laws informed by Indigenous values and cultures will be animated by practices of non-Indigenous governments determining what resources, values, and priorities will shape Inuvialuit laws.

V. SELF-GOVERNMENT AND SELF-DETERMINATION

It is important to appreciate that there is a significant difference between self-government and self-determination. Self-government is broadly understood as a specific policy concept of the federal government. The right of self-government reflects the fundamental premise that its status is determined in reference to the Canadian Constitution, and it is therefore a right that is contingent on the state's political and legal recognition of it. Self-determination, on the other hand, reflects a universally-recognized human rights principle that peoples should determine their own collective futures, without reference or deference to other peoples or states, other than that demanded by common principles of coexistence. Recognizing Indigenous peoples' right of self-determination poses difficult challenges to Canadian sovereignty and to its legitimacy with respect to governing Indigenous peoples, and the state's ownership of lands and resources.

Clearly, self-government is an element of Canadian Aboriginal policy which, to a significant extent, ensures continuing federal influence and control over Indigenous peoples' governments. Given this, why would communities choose to negotiate self-government? Some communities reject self-government as a neo-colonial method of control and assimilation, and they will not negotiate. There is a view that self-government creates institutions that essentially mimic the band council system created by, and structured to serve, the needs and priorities of the *Indian Act*[36] and INAC, rather than the needs and priorities of Indigenous communities.

Communities that this author has worked with that have negotiated, or are negotiating, self-government view self-government as a step in an ongoing journey of decolonizing relations with the state and the pursuit of self-determination. Generally, these communities recognize that while implementation conditions and mechanisms are important elements that determine the meaningfulness of the right of self-government, recognition of a right has an intrinsic value independent of its exercise. Self-government agreements are imperfect and unlikely to achieve all of the results communities seek to gain; however, the existence and recognition of the right has a positive psychological effect on both Indigenous and non-Indigenous peoples, as well as being a benefit to governments. Recognition of the right marks a positive development in state-Indigenous relations; the negotiation of agreements engages parties in conversations and exchanges of ideas and perspectives, a process that is hoped to eventually result in yet more positive developments in state-Indigenous relations. At the same time, people are aware that achieving self-determination will require many different sources and resources of power. Thus, a critical concern is that self-government agreements should not result in decreasing the long-term potential for self-determination. Self-government agreements should not extinguish rights, and it is hoped that they establish a significant degree of flexibility with respect to the exercise of powers and relations with other governments.

VI. CONCLUSION

Canada's 1995 inherent right policy favours an implementation approach to the right of self-government, rather than a definitional approach.[37] The rationale for this approach was that the government wished to negotiate practical governing arrangements with Indigenous peoples that would allow immediate and expanded control of their own communities, rather than attempt to define the right of self-government and proceed on that basis. However, the effect is that the arrangements to implement aspects of the right negotiated define the right in a de facto sense: Canada's policy restricts discussion to areas unilaterally determined by Canada. Through negotiations, Canada, in important ways, determines the extent and nature of the right's exercise in practice, not only through restricting the areas and scope of authorities, but also by maintaining control of key elements of implementation. This is achieved through the administrative, legislative, and financial arrangements embedded within self-government and the associated financing and implementation agreements.

The result is that assessing the efficacy of self-government agreement implementation cannot be used as an index for determining whether a right of self-government is being fully and freely exercised. Rather, it is only possible to evaluate whether measures that are necessary to implement self-government authorities have been taken. This situation emphasizes a quantitative evaluative focus (one which asks whether Canada fulfilled specific implementation obligations), rather than a qualitative focus assessing whether arrangements, once implemented, allow for the robust exercise of the right to self-government. Canada is able to defend its quantitative approach to implementation by virtue of the fact that the agreements are about implementation arrangements and are not intended to fully describe or define all aspects of the inherent right of self-government. The result is that by not having a shared conception of what the right of self-government is, Canada and Indigenous peoples embark on agreements where Canada sees itself contractually bound to fulfill obligations of an agreed set of power-sharing arrangements, while Indigenous peoples may see the agreement as a starting point for an evolving relationship with Canada that is contingent, in part, on an evolving conception of a self-government right over time.

The administration of justice provisions examined in this chapter illustrate that the efficacy and meaningfulness of the inherent right of self-government relies, in part, on the political priorities of politicians and the discretion of bureaucrats who are accountable to non-Indigenous governments. The Inuvialuit self-government administration of justice provisions do not provide certainty and continuity in terms of a self-government's ability to establish and enforce laws and provide programs in keeping with Indigenous cultures and values.[38] This fact may be seen to undermine, in a fundamental sense, the implementation of the inherent right. The self-government agreement creates a situation where the control of the administration of justice promotes conditions that impair the meaningfulness of a right, as set out at the beginning of this chapter: lack of meaningful control, and fragmentation of institutions.

One essential purpose of negotiating self-government is to decrease state control and intervention in the lives of Indigenous peoples to the fullest extent possible. The administration of justice, including policing, prosecutions, and corrections, is a governmental function which has long been targeted for increased control by self-governments. Part of Canada's policy rationale for negotiating self-government is to "restore dignity to Aboriginal peoples."[39] This is, of course, an oblique reference to the social suffering created largely by the state through the colonial relationship between Canada and Indigenous peoples. To understand the restoration of dignity in this context can be taken to mean self-respect and respect or esteem of others. Translated into negotiated arrangements, this reasonably means that Indigenous peoples' self-governments should not be locked into arrangements that force them to rely on the dispositions of other governments or their agencies to gain meaningful involvement of key governance authorities.

If restoring dignity is a standard by which a self-government agreement may be measured, the section on justice in the *Inuvialuit and Gwich'in AIP* does not meet Canada's own standard. Self-government agreements, which are meant to implement aspects of the inherent right of self-government, must be evaluated with a view to how their implementation will affect overall governance in Indigenous communities. Authorities should not be dependent on the discretion of other governments, either in terms of their exercise of power and funding arrangements, or whether agreements and relationships between governments may develop and evolve. Placing self-governments in a position of practical and political supplication to federal and territorial governments reduces self-governments' practical and political efficacy, with implications for the content of the inherent right of self-government that reaches well beyond the discrete area of the administration of justice.

8

THE CRIMINAL JUSTICE SYSTEM
AND ABORIGINAL PEOPLE

Margot Hurlbert and John McKenzie

I. INTRODUCTION

The study and analysis of the criminal justice system over the last several decades, as well as its adaptation to competing cultural worldviews, provides optimism for positive change. In recent years, both literature and research have more frequently acknowledged the systemic failure of the criminal justice system to protect and reflect the needs of Aboriginal people;[1] as well, governments have increasingly responded to official inquiries arising from specific incidents where the criminal justice system has failed Aboriginal people. This chapter will review the genesis for structural change within the criminal justice system and areas of this change, specifically policing, the courts, and court practices.

This analysis of change in the criminal justice system illustrates the adaptive capacity of the Canadian criminal justice system and evidences a liberal pluralist change in response to shortcomings within the system. Although accommodation and change is slower and more painful than many would wish, the direction of change is nonetheless positive.

II. CRIMINAL JUSTICE SYSTEM ASSESSMENT: SYSTEMIC DEFECTS

Recently, three main areas have been used to assess the criminal justice system: the overall effectiveness of the criminal justice system in protecting society and reducing crime in general; assessing systemic discrimination in the criminal justice system; and the government's response to crisis events (horrific treatment of individual people within the criminal justice system; response to these horrific events has been the establishment of commissions of inquiry tasked with endeavouring to improve the justice system and prevent maltreatment in the future by making recommendations.) All of these critical assessments drive change within the criminal justice system, and each area will be discussed in turn.

The criminal justice system has changed significantly over the years. Decades ago, Canadians rejected capital punishment, and centuries ago, Canadian rejected debtor's prison. These types of changes were arguably due to changing social factors and critical analysis of the criminal justice system. Such critical assessment continues, and questions respecting traditional policing and its effectiveness have propagated the advent of community policing. Incarceration and its effectiveness have previously been, and are continually, questioned.[2] Critical analysis of the criminal justice system as a whole has resulted in the evolution of a different criminal justice system – one embracing principles of restorative justice. As a result, programs of mediation diversion and programs allowing impecunious people to work off their fines instead of going to jail have been implemented. Further change, appropriate for the recognition of Aboriginal culture is also now possible.

Systemic discrimination in the criminal justice system is not a new development nor is it something only recently recognized. As early as 1967, the Canadian Corrections Association recognized the police's role in the surveillance of Indian and Métis people, and acknowledged that drawing attention to conspicuous elements of Indian and Métis dress, personal hygiene, physical characteristics, and their prevalence in impoverished areas, lead the police into an open dislike for Indian and Métis people; this undoubtedly resulted in more arrests.[3] In the 1970s and 80s, systemic discrimination in the policing of Aboriginal people was acknowledged as an issue.[4] This is not startling as the police reflect the society within which they work and live and cannot help but bring to their jobs the same biases and prejudices that surround them in their daily lives.

High levels of crime in Aboriginal communities and justice system discrimination toward Aboriginal people are noted as causes of the over-representation of Aboriginal people in provincial and territorial prisons and federal penitentiaries. Crime and

other symptoms of social disorder, such as suicide and substance abuse, are linked to the historical and contemporary experience of colonialism, which has systematically undermined the social, cultural and economic foundations of Aboriginal peoples, including their distinctive forms of justice.[5]

The commissions and inquiries examining the justice system at the federal and provincial levels were implemented as a result of specific events and needs. The most notable of these was the Royal Commission on Aboriginal Peoples, which argued that the right of Aboriginal self-government was recognized by both federal constitutional common law and section 35 and thus, it did not need explicit constitutional recognition.[6] Other commissions include the Manitoba Aboriginal Justice Inquiry,[7] the Alberta Task Force,[8] the Saskatchewan Indian Justice Review Committee & Métis Justice Review Committee (the "Linn Reports"),[9] Saskatchewan's subsequent Commission on First Nation and Métis Peoples and Justice Reform,[10] the Law Commission of Canada,[11] and the Ontario Commission on Systemic Racism in the Criminal Justice System.[12]

These reports have relatively consistent conclusions and recommendations, and whether victims or offenders, on-reserve or off, Aboriginal people are significantly over-represented, as compared to the non-Aboriginal population.[13] When the term "failure of the justice system" is used in these reports, it references the fundamentally different worldviews of Aboriginal and non-Aboriginal people with respect to the substantive content of justice and the process of achieving justice.[14]

Common issues recognized in commission findings also included:

(i)   high incarceration rates among Aboriginal members;

(ii)   police intervention into matters felt to be purely private in nature;

(iii)   no community involvement in either diversion discussions or sentencing;

(iv)   a perception of harsh treatment for minor offences;

(v)   high incidence of police involvement in disputes;

(vi)   unwillingness of Crown and police to use diversion solutions;

(vii)   racist or inappropriate treatment of members of the community; and

(viii) ineffective or even non-existent programs.[15]

The Manitoba review, initiated in 1988, proposed the creation of a separate Aboriginal justice system, with its own criminal and civil laws and a separate system of courts.[16] It recommended the establishment of Aboriginal police forces for Aboriginal communities and greater numbers of Aboriginal officers on existing forces. More than a decade later, the Manitoba government established the Aboriginal Justice Implementation Commission,[17] working toward achieving Aboriginal rights, creating stronger links to the communities through improved Aboriginal relations, and establishing a focus on alternative and restorative justice.

Each successive review captured elements that targeted a more balanced and culturally-aware application of justice, recognizing Aboriginal cultural education as a key element for all individuals working within the justice system. A support system was needed that incorporated elders in the criminal justice system and established programs to address realities like drug and alcohol addiction.

The Saskatchewan review, otherwise known as the "Linn Reports,"[18] searched for ways to make practical changes to the criminal justice system, recognizing (as did the Manitoba review) that there was a lack of progress in implementing the many similar recommendations of past reviews. Key recommendations focussed on racism, family violence, and the need for cross-cultural education.[19] As a result, alternative-measures programs for youth and adults have been implemented in many communities across Saskatchewan. The Northern Cree Court has been established, as have healing lodges for youth, men, and women. For further discussion of the specific changes that resulted from these assessments, see section VI, below.

III. Differing Justice Paradigms

A cultural examination of the differences between the traditional Aboriginal approach to justice and the development of European traditions and legal frameworks are valuable for defining a suitable reference point when searching for appropriate solutions. Over the last several centuries, the opposing perspectives of the First Nations people and employees of what began as the Hudson Bay Company (who later became European settlers and now comprise Canadian society) have been reconciled in different ways. As an example, the "two row wampum" belt of the Haudenosaunee, which reflected their understanding of the Treaty of Niagara of 1764,[20] illustrated the partnership between First Nations people and the Hudson Bay Company that existed for many years.[21] The two row wampum belt reflected a diplomatic convention recognizing interaction yet separation of settler and First Nation societies. This symbolism is described by R.A. Williams:

When the Haudenosaunee first came into contact with the European nations, treaties of peace and friendship were made. Each was symbolized by the Gus-Wen-Tah, or Two Row Wampum. There is a bed of white wampum which symbolizes the purity of the agreement. There are two rows of purple and those two rows have the spirit of your ancestors and mine. There are three beads of wampum separating the two rows and they symbolize peace, friendship and respect. These two rows will symbolize two paths or two vessels, traveling down the same river together. One, a birch bark canoe, will be for the Indian people, their laws, their customs and their ways. The other, a ship, will be for the white people and their laws, their customs, and their ways. We shall each travel the river together, side by side, but in our own boat. Neither of us will try to steer the other's vessel.[22]

The two row wampum belt was the First Nation recording of their understanding of the Treaty and the relationship between the Crown and themselves. The First Nations' belief was this relationship was to be founded on peace, friendship, and respect, where neither Nation would interfere with the internal affairs of the other.

This reconciliation would later be replaced by a completely contradictory system that eventually became the segregation and assimilation policies of the early 1900s.[23] These policies fostered many unjust measures, including decades of imprisonment of First Nations people on reservations, the denial of First Nations people's ability to leave reserves unless their Indian agent issued them a permit, and First Nations people not being allowed to retain legal counsel or to vote. These policies were segregationist and are believed to have formed the blueprint for South African apartheid.[24] Aboriginal people were also subjected to assimilation policies through such vehicles as the residential school system, where native language and religion was prohibited.[25] It is only in the past few decades that these assimilation policies have been challenged and eroded. In today's legal environment, courts reconcile Aboriginal and non-Aboriginal claims, interests, and ambitions.[26]

Traditionally, Canadian justice was built on a Eurocentric model of justice adopted from Britain. Over hundreds of years, the British common law system developed the definition of a criminal action as one involving both a criminal act and the corresponding criminal intent to perform the act (*actus rea* and *mens rea*). What was or was not criminal was decided, ultimately, by the society constructing the definition of "criminal," and this definition was subject to change over time (*i.e.*, homosexuality was a crime until 1969). Dealing with lawbreakers was based on a trial with the presumption of innocence, an expectation that the accused would plead not guilty and require the state to prove guilt, and a combative, competitive court hearing with retributive punishment for deviance if guilt is proved. Traditional policing supported this model with the efficient response to complaints, charging and processing accused criminals through the court system.

Conversely, the Aboriginal values of justice were built on a different model of both crime and justice. An act may not be a criminal act if:

(i)   the act occurred (such as theft) and the offender intended to return the property or pay restitution at a later date;

(ii)   the act occurred and the offender apologized to the victim;

(iii)   the act occurred and it was committed for the purpose of gaining prestige; or

(iv)   the act was attempted (such as a break-and-enter) with the intent to steal an item that was then not taken. The actor did not complete the act as intended and, therefore, nothing was done wrong.[27]

In contrast to a traditional Canadian model of trial and policing, an Aboriginal society traditionally relied on elders to teach community values, issue warnings and provide counselling along with community leaders, mediate and negotiate and in the event of a criminal act, facilitate payment of compensation to the victim, and facilitate resolutions and the restoration of the entire community.[28] Aboriginal values of dignity, reluctance to plead not guilty and testify in court, conflict with the traditional Canadian combative court procedure and criminal sanction.

IV. Canadian Law for Diverse Institutions

The Supreme Court of Canada has recognized that Aboriginal governments were historically self-governing.[29] Some argue this is now an inherent right to self-government protected by section 35 of the *Constitution Act, 1982*.[30] This legal reasoning has not yet found favour in the Supreme Court of Canada,[31] but it is not yet completely precluded.[32] Although based on court decisions, a general right to Aboriginal self-government seems remote, though specific activities of governance are possible. The advent of consultation obligations are a form of involved governance. It is argued that Indigenous communities have a long-established and unextinguished traditional practice of settling disputes that arise from misconduct; this traditional practice is an Aboriginal right.[33] Although legislation such as the *Criminal Code* has been applied by the judiciary without question to Indian reserves since the beginning of the twentieth century, there has not been the clear and plain legislation that would be required to extinguish traditional First Nations models of justice.[34] To date, however, court cases that uphold such an Aboriginal right and would lead to a distinct and separate Aboriginal criminal justice system that reflects traditional First Nation justice have not occurred.

A parallel development to Aboriginal justice institutions that is consistent with the desire of Aboriginal communities to engage in strong internal community controls is the passage of band bylaws, or band council resolutions, banishing members involved in illegal drug activity.[35] While participation in the Aboriginal justice institutions discussed in this chapter is voluntary or appealable as court decisions, a First Nation bylaw, if objected to, will ultimately be challenged in a court of law and will not be appealed. This issue will raise questions of mobility, security of the person, and perhaps, equality rights in the *Canadian Charter of Rights and Freedoms*.[36] However, if challenged, this development may find favour for five reasons:

(i) the nature of reserve land is *sui generis*, which implies that community governance will predominate on the reserve because the Aboriginal title is held communally, and decisions are made by the community.[37] If a First Nation cannot decide who is in their community, it would imply a very narrow interpretation of the *sui generis* concept;

(ii) the Aboriginal justice practice reflected in the bylaw is a traditional practice that would arguably would pass the Eurocentric test established for similar Aboriginal rights in previous case law;[38]

(iii) section 25 of the *Charter* states that *Charter* rights will not abrogate Aboriginal rights.[39] The right of Aboriginal governance reflected in the band bylaw is perhaps just such right that should not be abrogated;

(iv) the decision of a First Nation to banish drug dealers from the reserve and allow the Canadian criminal justice system to deal with these offenders is something that Canadian society approve; and

(v) the courts have been able to balance competing *Charter* rights. An example is the delicate balancing of a sexual abuse victim's rights to privacy and the accused's right to full answer and defence.

Although the Supreme Court of Canada is committed to the resolution of Aboriginal and non-Aboriginal claims, interests, and ambitions,[40] many of the most significant projects empowering First Nation self-governance in the criminal justice field have been developed in the current constitutional framework. These initiatives have occurred either without the necessity of a formal self-government agreement or have been negotiated as self-government agreements in the current constitutional framework. Several of these initiatives in Saskatchewan and one in Alberta will be outlined in this chapter, below.

There have been many advances in recognizing these issues, but full resolution of this conflict has not yet occurred. It is clear that the Canadian justice system continues to fail Aboriginal people. Over-policing Aboriginal neighbourhoods in urban centers has been acknowledged for a number of years. Systemic discrimination within the criminal justice system and urban police forces is increasingly being recognized as a problem.[41] At the same time, by the mid-1980s, two decades of research confirmed that traditional policing (patrols and arrests) did not solve or reduce crime in Canadian society as a whole.[42] As a result, new police initiatives commenced such as the community policing model, wherein police officers focussed on connecting to the community and meeting citizens. Successful policing changed from solely being measured by the number of arrests and successful prosecutions an officer made to the number of contacts that were made with the community. Embracing a community model of policing has not only encouraged a police force reflective of the community in race and gender, but, in First Nation communities, it has encouraged a police force reflective of the First Nation community.

Overrepresentation of Aboriginal people within the inmate population and their reduced likelihood of eligibility for parole has been a chronic problem.[43] Given the difference in values between mainstream Canadian society and the Aboriginal peoples, it is understandable that many Aboriginal people perceive "the criminal justice system [a]s an alien one, imposed by the dominant white society."[44]

As a result of the failure of the Canadian criminal justice system to meet the needs of Aboriginal peoples, and its shortcomings in meeting the needs of the rest of Canadian society, a different Canadian justice system is evolving that endorses and adopts principles of restorative and community justice. Fortuitously, at the same time that First Nation projects are developing and advancing, Canadian society is embracing new principles of justice with the advent of restorative justice, alternative measures, and different models of policing. Canadian justice initiatives and Aboriginal justice initiatives both inform and advance each other's causes. These developments illustrate a changing model of Canadian justice that bodes well for a reconciliation of Aboriginal justice with Canadian justice. Much can still be learned, however.

V. Institutional Change

Over the past several decades, models of justice have evolved to reconcile Aboriginal and traditional Canadian views of justice. Self-government, policing, Aboriginal courts, sentencing circles, and alternative justice measures have each developed and contributed to changes in Aboriginal justice. Some of the lessons from these initiatives indicate that the vision of justice for restorative advocates and Aboriginal peoples may not be the same. Aboriginal justice may be much broader, and it is different from traditional Canadian justice in that it focusses on a collective responsibility instead of the restorative justice emphasis on individual accountability and responsibility. As well, it is difficult to go beyond general statements of Indigenous justice, as one risks overgeneralization and stereotyping. Aboriginal justice is a local institution, based on the community within which it is practiced; there is no universal blueprint for all Aboriginal peoples.[45]

Several important principles underlie the development of a justice approach in Aboriginal communities:

(i)   open negotiation with Aboriginal communities and their organizations;

(ii)   respect for Aboriginal people's rights, including that of self-determination;

(iii)   respect for Aboriginal peoples and their cultures;

(iv)   relinquishment of "assumed" governmental jurisdiction over Aboriginal people;

(v)   ongoing support for Aboriginal communities to assist in community problems (both socio-economic and crime related) and increasing community capital;[46] and

(vi)   allowing for trial and error, and permission to learn from mistakes.

A. Self-Government

Potentially, self-government has much to contribute to changes that reflect Aboriginal justice. The inherent right of Aboriginal self-government is arguably recognized under section 35 of the *Constitution Act, 1982*.[47] As David Newhouse and Yale Belanger assert, true modern treaties associated with Nunuvat, Nisga'a, and Nunatiavut each contain the ability to establish laws and control over policing, and justice oversight within their communities.[48] The establishment of these treaties represents a major step forward, and there will be much discussion as to how, in the self-government context, these issues move forward – including how the *Canadian Charter of Rights and Freedoms* is applied to all Aboriginal and non-Aboriginal people in Canada.

Today, there has not yet been a completely independent and autonomous First Nation self-government. However, partial First Nations justice and policing systems have been implemented. For instance, First Nations have negotiated and received jurisdiction over policing, child welfare, or criminal justice. This jurisdiction over governance is always subject to an overarching federal jurisdiction and, thus, is not full governance. However, initiatives such as the *Meadow Lake First Nations Comprehensive Agreement in Principle*[49] have yet to address, in detail, the principles associated with justice matters. Organizations such as the Federation of Saskatchewan Indian Nations (FSIN) have substantially invested in developing an understanding of Aboriginal governance, mechanisms, and a vision of self-administered policing, judiciary, and oversight. The vision of the FSIN secretariat is:

> healthy, safe, self-determined First Nations who have the capacity to govern themselves according to their ancestral laws, spiritual beliefs, values, customs and traditions in accordance with their inherent and Treaty rights.[50]

At the highest level, the outcome may ultimately include Aboriginal justice, self-determination in Aboriginal communities, and justice mechanisms that operate and recognize the unique needs of Aboriginal peoples. If one uses the justice vision of FSIN as a reference, and if one accepts the *Canadian Charter of Rights and Freedoms*, then challenges to this consideration include capability, independence, governance, and jurisdictional clarity in law-making (along with the potential for harmonization of laws, where appropriate, at the federal and provincial levels). Nevertheless, the challenges of establishing appropriate frameworks should not be underestimated.

B. Policing

The establishment of Aboriginal policing has the potential to address the deficiencies in the treatment of Aboriginal people within the Canadian criminal justice system. Some of the benefits of Aboriginal policing programs include:

(i)   decreased Aboriginal arrests;

(ii)   less tension when an Aboriginal police officer is involved; and

(iii)   better police response because of an officer's knowledge of, and commitment to, the community through his/her police training.[51]

The First Nations Policing Policy (FNPP) of the federal government in 1991,[52] proposed two approaches to policing: the first approach was a self-administered police service, which, prior to that date, had only been implemented in two communities[53] but currently involves 48 agreements with 197 communities – mostly in Ontario, Quebec, and Alberta.[54] In this model, the band council is responsible for policing and may delegate some of its powers over to a police commission.

The second approach envisioned in the FNPP is Community Police Service Framework between the Aboriginal community and the federal and provincial governments. The employer of the police is the Royal Canadian Mounted Police, and the officers hired are Aboriginal. A community consultant group provides a forum for the community; however, there is not a separate police commission. There are 78 such agreements covering 110 communities and, in Saskatchewan, the northern policing Framework Agreement is being reviewed in order to improve the police response to northern communities.[55] In Saskatchewan, there are 31 Community Tripartite Agreements (CTAs) with 45 First Nations that cover approximately 78 per cent of the on-reserve population of Saskatchewan.[56] Five new CTAs are anticipated in the next three years. File Hills First Nation is in the process of becoming a self-administered police force.[57] Neither the Aboriginal police forces nor the CTAs cover an urban community.

A study in First Nations policing[58] showed that at the time of the study, one governance challenge was conflict produced because police commissions or boards were created after key personnel were already in place and thus had no part in the hiring of this staff. The authors of the study suggested that the members of the police board receive training in order for them to better respect the police officers. They found training of police officers more consistent with "law enforcement" models of policing – not effective "peace-keeping and crime prevention" models – and discussed the need for culturally sensitive police training. The authors further noted that important traditions, such as the role and place of the elder, had not sufficiently been incorporated into Aboriginal policing.

Issues of community involvement and personal biases of First Nation constables, because of their community ties, have resulted in some recommendations for a separate Native provincial police force, to operate under the authority of the provincial attorney-general, with its own form of a police commission. This body could increase accountability, have power to investigate band council actions that are suspect, and prevent "sandbox politics."[59] Further issues have been noted, including funding uncertainties, the inability to plan in the long-term, and the inability to plan new programs and manage staff attrition and training because of the small size of the force.[60]

The evolution of Aboriginal justice has roots in colonial history, racism, cultural tradition, socio-economic conditions, and a harsh statistical reality of Aboriginal groups having high victim and offender rates. When one considers the view that Aboriginal groups, leadership, and community have, and when one contrasts that with the view (and the requirement for independence) that police and judiciary groups have, it is very clear that polarizations, stereotypes, and obscure role responsibility make it difficult for open dialogue, mutual trust, and constructive engagements to occur, even if they are well-meaning. The non-Aboriginal community at large and the many agencies that can become aware of or involved in the justice system are also to be considered.

An independent review, however, of the first five years of operation of the First Nations Policing Policy found the policy framework to be "relevant, sound and on-track."[61] The review also found that provincial, territorial, and most First Nations partners believe that the tripartite process is the most effective way to address First Nations policing at this time.

C. Courts

The creation of First Nation courts, through community involvement with the existing non-Indigenous justice system, has been successfully piloted in Saskatchewan as an alternative to separate First Nation courts established by a unilateral assertion of Aboriginal self-government rights in justice matters,[62] delegation of authority by federal and provincial governments, or creation by self-government agreements. This initiative has been a successful way of initially increasing Aboriginal influence in the court system.[63]

A. Cree Court

Saskatchewan has been a leader of innovation, possessing the first Cree Court, which is presided over by the Honourable Gerald Morin. This court was created as a result of collaboration between the Department of Justice, the judiciary, the communities, the Prince Albert Grand Council, and others.[64] All court members are Aboriginal and speak Cree. The Government of Saskatchewan has recently announced the expansion of this concept through the creation of an Aboriginal court system in the northwestern half of the province that offers services in the Dene and Cree languages.[65]

The use of traditional language in the Cree Court has been a critical step in ensuring that the facts of a case can be understood and that nothing is lost in translation. There are powerful words in the Cree and Dene languages for which there are no comparable words in English. Also, in northern Saskatchewan, Cree or Dene is frequently the first language to which youth have been exposed, and English is a second language.[66] Speaking Cree ensures that all participants understand one another and that they better understand the court process; it ultimately reduces wrongful convictions and guilty pleas by accused who are not guilty. The utilization of Cree symbolizes an important institutional endorsement of the First Nation culture.

The following illustrates how these courts operate. The Court will travel to a community on a given day, with many local residents wishing to observe. It is not unusual for 150 cases to be held per day, which can place a large strain on the personal, community, and diversionary alternatives to be implemented. These courts are structured slightly different than traditional Canadian criminal courts, with the judge in front, the prosecutor on one side, and the defendant on the other. Often the probation officer will be in attendance. Alternative justice options are evaluated prior to the court sessions, and recommendations are incorporated into the proceedings.[67]

The large number of cases is reflective of the challenges that a particular community faces, often the result of difficult socio-economic conditions, rampant alcohol and drug addiction, and domestic violence. The courts are at the tail end of these influences, and there is a desperate need to establish youth programs, counselling, and teachings that reflect balanced values within the Aboriginal cultural context. The spiritual, mental, physical, and emotional circles of influence must exist and remain balanced in order to truly have a chance at influencing outcomes in the Aboriginal communities.

B. Peacemaking

The Tsuu T'ina First Nation outside Calgary, Alberta, has successfully created a peacemaking court which sits on reserve lands. The impetus for the Tsuu T'ina Court started when the chief, council, and their advisors, having decided to pass a traffic bylaw to correct their traffic problem, started asking why their court should be limited to traffic issues, and decided to address all justice issues. Even with their own police and community corrections society, court worker, and probation supervision services, they found something lacking; their community was not becoming more peaceful.[68] The Tsuu T'ina elders advised that the traditional approach in dealing with conflict was to heal offenders to behave properly and restore offender and victim relationships.[69]

The Tsuu T'ina Court is the result of a successful investigation by the Tsuu T'ina First Nation into alternative criminal justice solutions, followed by successful lobbying and negotiations with both provincial and federal governments. The court is staffed by Aboriginal people. Judge Mandamin is Ojibway, not Tsuu T'ina, which prevents any conflicts of interests for personal and family connections within the community.[70]

The Tsuu T'ina Court has the full jurisdiction of a provincial court. However, Aboriginal traditions, including that of peacemaking, have been incorporated and merged into the traditional provincial court practices. The protocols of the court reflect the Tsuu T'ina tradition. Court is commenced with a smudging ceremony, which is a sacred pledge of truth to the Creator. In some diversions, healing ceremonies are held instead of the payment of fines. All peacemaking ceremonies end with an elders' panel, as the Tsuu T'ina people hold the elders in high regard and believe their directions to be mandatory. Many checks and balances exist within the peacemaking process: for peacemaking to be an option, the accused must choose peacemaking, and the process must be agreed to by the Crown who refers the matter, and the judge who adjourns the case to make way for this alternative solution. The Tsuu T'ina Court has many stories of success.[71]

C. Gladue Court[72]

In Toronto, a specialized Aboriginal court called the "Gladue" Court was established to ensure that the principles respecting Aboriginal sentencing contained in section 718.2 of the *Criminal Code*[73] and elaborated on by the Supreme Court of Canada in *R. v. Gladue*[74] can be applied to accused Aboriginal people in Toronto. The Gladue Court works closely with Aboriginal Legal

Services of Toronto (ALST or the "Community Council"), who have operated
a criminal diversion program since 1992. It is not an Aboriginal court, but a
court where Aboriginal people appear and cases can be dealt with in a cultur-
ally-appropriate fashion. The Community Council handles approximately
200-250 cases per year. The most important addition is the Gladue caseworker
who is responsible for writing "Gladue reports" on clients. There is also a
court worker assisting accused Aboriginal people through the processes of the
criminal justice system. The Gladue Court has a dedicated Crown, usually a
duty counsel, and dedicated Aboriginal bail program supervisors. People from
all different Aboriginal traditions appear in the Gladue Court.[75]

D. Circles of Justice

Four possibilities exist to utilize the circles-of-justice concept modelled on
Aboriginal traditions to resolve community issue.[76] First, the parties or community may utilize a circle of justice for the resolution of a dispute, prior to
the involvement of the police or courts. Second, after the criminal justice system is accessed, a criminal charge may be diverted and the charge withdrawn
through the use of mediation diversion. Third, once a guilty plea is entered, the
circle can be accessed for sentencing purposes.[77] The circle may be in the form
of a sentence advisory committee, an elders' or community sentencing panel,
or a sentencing circle.[78] The fourth main use of a circle is to assist an individual
seeking reintegration into the community after a period of incarceration.

The criterion for a sentencing circle that is largely accepted in courts includes:

(i)   voluntary agreement by accused to have recommendations as part of
        the judge's consideration;

(ii)   willingness of victim to participate;

(iii)   resolution of disputed facts;

(iv)   acceptance of responsibility by offender for his or her actions;

(v)   guilty plea;

(vi)   community support for the offender and willingness to be involved
        in the process on behalf of the accused;

(vii)   victim has had meaningful input; or

(viii) the accused has demonstrated sincere intention to be rehabilitated and to participate meaningfully in rehabilitation.[79]

In Saskatchewan, the sentencing circle is generally opened by a prayer, and the defense and Crown agree on the facts. People speak one at a time until a proposal is finally agreed upon. The end of the sentencing circle discussion is typically declared by the circle and not the judge.[80] Practice over the years has found pre-charge diversion useful, but post-charge sentencing circles are very time consuming and less embraced by the community. Many First Nation community-based justice programs exist in Saskatchewan in order to facilitate the usage of these circles of justice.[81]

It is in this context, then, that alternative or restorative justice initiatives can be introduced into the system. The concept of alternative and restorative measures in justice[82] is beginning to emerge strongly and is fundamentally linked to options and choices associated with Aboriginal self-government. While there is much dialogue as to what form self-governance should take (and consensus is fleeting), the constitutional framework does not offer barriers to its creation. There are many innovative cultural and justice initiatives underway, some associated or focussed on healing the individual and community, and some on rehabilitative strategies and spiritual support. One initiative adopts a holistic approach to deviance, and it views crime as "a violation of people and relation-ships. It creates obligations to make things right. Justice involves the victim, the offender, and the community in a search for solutions which promote repair, reconciliation, and reassurance."[83] What is restorative justice, then? Marshall defines restorative justice as, "a process whereby all the parties with a stake in a particular offence come together to resolve collectively how to deal with the aftermath of the offence and its implications for the future."[84] Bazemore and Walgrave define restorative justice as "every action that is primarily oriented toward doing justice by repairing the harm that has been caused by a crime."[85]

Healing approaches can occur through traditional or western approaches focussed on the community, family, or the individual. While often not spe-cifically targeted at the criminal justice system, most healing approaches have focussed on the historical legacy and education, combined with participant discussion and counselling. Community leaders and elders[86] supported by professionals have embraced this concept, making very significant contribu-tions to the well-being of their communities. The healing process is viewed as a journey, and the implications as they relate to criminal justice may seem ancillary, but in terms of bringing communities closer together, the successes have been impressive.

A leading theme in this approach is that communities want to engage strong informal internal community controls,[87] and while this can be very effective for certain types of crime, there is a persistent belief that the mainstream criminal justice system should deal with certain or major criminal problems. The previously discussed band council resolution that banned drug dealers from a reserve is consistent with both traditional Aboriginal practices of banishing and with deferring major criminal problems like drug trafficking to the mainstream criminal justice system.

Another example of community control or empowerment is a recent undertaking strongly supported by the Prince Albert Grand Council Justice Directorate: the Lancombe Log House initiative, a community healing and diversion project, is designed around the concept that many offenders (youth, in particular) suffer from being unemployed, under-employed, and lacking in hope and opportunity.[88] In the process of building a log home, Aboriginal participants target the exploration of their Indian identity, the need for self-determination, and a true sense of ownership.

Community sentencing and mediation[89] has been examined in Aboriginal communities in Saskatchewan and Manitoba, and, while there were many challenges, the idea of circle sentencing providing opinions to sentencing judges has been seen as having significant potential to facilitate strong Aboriginal cultural and community participation. These types of engagement show great promise, but they suffer because of the amount of time required by elders and others to effectively participate in each individual case.

Does restorative justice work, then? Statistical evaluation is showing that these initiatives significantly improve victim and offender satisfaction, reduce recidivism, and seem to have a particular impact on youth.[90]

VI. CONCLUSION

It has been noted that the "nostalgic" character of some alternative programs (sentencing circles, healing circles, and Aboriginal traditions), including the programs' utilization of community involvement and cultural homogeneity, take on an appendage aspect that does not adequately deal with the current complexities of Aboriginal society.[91] The result is that the alternative mechanisms exist on a plane of informality, essentially making them less relevant, as they are only secondary and peripheral mechanisms to the traditional criminal justice system. The alternative mechanisms, however, allow Aboriginal people in the criminal justice system to view the community differently, and the mechanisms enhance the community's "ability to reproduce themselves as a 'community of relatives and friends' rather than 'communities of strangers'."[92] There is substantial agreement that Aboriginal people will benefit from a justice system more in tune with Aboriginal realities, where people can claim some ownership and exercise a degree of control. Victims are less satisfied with "traditional culture" approaches, however, as there is a perception that imbalances exist which defend offender behaviour and that real community involvement has yet to become a reality.

Although the current trend toward restorative principles within the dominant justice system is beneficial in that it permits greater accommodation between our system and Aboriginal systems, it is felt by some to not be a sufficient legal pathway to justice for Aboriginal peoples. Aboriginal peoples must find the pathway in their initiatives.[93] At the very least, consultation and negotiation with the Aboriginal communities must occur in all phases of the development of various justice approaches.

Aboriginal peoples' issues and needs from a criminal justice perspective have been recognized by the various justice commissions; however, despite community, government, and justice efforts, changes are only beginning to take place.[94] What is generally recognized is that the current framework is not sufficient to resolve the complex social and criminal issues facing the Aboriginal peoples. Whether an Aboriginal person, a community leader, a police officer, or a justice system participant, there are gaps in trust, reach, capability, and cultural understanding. As well, the groups struggling to manage this reality face an isolation and accountability that cannot be avoided.

Follow-up on the various commissions has resulted in major advances in education within communities and with justice system participants (the police, judiciary, and legal and support groups), as has community involvement, community policing, alternative justice models, and the establishment of specific courts, such as the Cree Court in northern Saskatchewan. However, despite the inspiring success stories and evidence of the effectiveness of many of these initiatives,[95] the high offender and incarceration rates continue.

The evolution of the criminal justice system in response to its failure toward Aboriginal people evidences that change and adaptation are occurring. These changes are important and useful, however, the transformative, rapid, and significant structural change desired by some, such as the recognition of Aboriginal sovereignty over justice issues, has not yet occurred. It is the authors' conclusion that the changes so far have preserved the fundamental features of the Canadian criminal justice system. In this way, these positive changes evidence Canada's embracing of a liberal pluralist culture.

9

R. V. GLADUE

SENTENCING AND THE GENDERED IMPACTS OF COLONIALISM

Angela Cameron*

I. INTRODUCTION

Various models and practices of restorative justice have been in place in Canada for over a decade.[1] During this time, much feminist commentary on restorative justice practice has focussed on cases where women have been victims of crime, in particular, domestic violence and sexual assault.[2] There has been less attention paid to cases where women themselves come into conflict with the criminal law,[3] and the circumstances under which they may be the focus of a restorative intervention. This chapter will argue that "restorative"[4] sentencing goals and factors, as outlined by the Supreme Court of Canada in *R. v. Gladue*[5] and when applied to Aboriginal women, should include a gender analysis. For many Aboriginal women, systemic gender inequality is inextricably linked to racial inequality in their experiences of colonialism, and it should be similarly taken into account in sentencing. Some of the markers of colonialism set out by the Supreme Court of Canada in the *Gladue* case are experienced disproportionately by Aboriginal women,[6] or they are experienced in particular ways by women.

This chapter will discuss the legislative and jurisprudential framework for sentencing Aboriginal offenders in Canada. It will argue that this framework should be applied to Aboriginal women offenders in ways that account for gendered experiences of colonialism and later will apply this gendered

* I would like to thank Susan Sharpe, Andrea Kennedy, Patricia Cochran, and David Sealy for their insightful comments on earlier versions of this chapter.

sentencing framework to three cases: *R. v. Gladue*,[7] *R. v. Moyan*,[8] and *R. v. Norris*.[9] These cases fall short of systemically accounting for the ways in which race and gender interlock in the lives of Aboriginal women. In particular, they represent incident-based, individual approaches to sentencing, rather than a broad, systemic approach. These cases also provide exemplars of the broader theoretical and practical aspects of sentencing discussed in this chapter.

II. *R. v. GLADUE*: SENTENCING STANDARDS AND CONSIDERATIONS FOR ABORIGINAL OFFENDERS

The Supreme Court of Canada in *Gladue* has laid out criteria by which sentencing judges must make their decisions in individual cases. Judges must seriously consider the goal of reducing the use of incarceration,[10] and, in doing so, they must actively solicit and consider the "circumstances of Aboriginal offenders,"[11] which the Court defines in some detail.

In 1996, major changes were introduced to the sentencing provisions of the *Criminal Code*. An element of these changes was an attempt to introduce restorative justice principles into the Canadian criminal justice system at the sentencing level: "One of the roles of s. 718.2(e) and the various other provisions in Part XXIII [of the sentencing provisions] is to encourage sentencing judges to apply principles of restorative justice alongside or in the place of other, more traditional sentencing principles when making sentencing determinations."[12] In particular, the sentencing provisions link the circumstances of Aboriginal offenders to the use of restorative justice. The resulting provisions read, in part, as follows:

> 718.2 A court that imposes a sentence shall also take into consideration the following principles:
>
> (*a*) a sentence should be increased or reduced to account for any relevant aggravating or mitigating circumstances relating to the offence or the offender, and, without limiting the generality of the foregoing,
>
> (i) evidence that the offence was motivated by bias, prejudice or hate based on race, national or ethnic origin, language, colour, religion, sex, age, mental or physical disability, sexual orientation, or any other similar factor,
>
> (ii) evidence that the offender, in committing the offence, abused the offender's spouse or common-law partner,

(ii.1) evidence that the offender, in committing the offence, abused a person under the age of eighteen years,

(iii) evidence that the offender, in committing the offence, abused a position of trust or authority in relation to the victim,

(iv) evidence that the offence was committed for the benefit of, at the direction of, or in association with a criminal organization, or

(v) evidence that the offence was a terrorism offence shall be deemed to be aggravating circumstances;

(*b*) a sentence should be similar to sentences imposed on similar offenders for similar offences committed in similar circumstances;

(*c*) where consecutive sentences are imposed, the combined sentence should not be unduly long or harsh;

(*d*) an offender should not be deprived of liberty, if less restrictive sanctions may be appropriate in the circumstances; and

(*e*) *all available sanctions other than imprisonment that are reasonable in the circumstances should be considered for all offenders, with particular attention to the circumstances of aboriginal offenders* (emphasis added).[13]

The 1999 *Gladue* case provided the first Supreme Court of Canada interpretation of section 712.2 (e) of these sentencing provisions. It marked a significant change in the way Aboriginal offenders are sentenced in Canadian courts, allowing for more flexibility and de-emphasizing incarceration. The Court has interpreted section 718.2(e) of the *Criminal Code* so as to "sensitize the judiciary to the unique situation of Aboriginals and . . . end the alienation of Aboriginals from the criminal justice system."[14]

In interpreting section 718.2(e) of the *Criminal Code*, the Supreme Court found that the provision is remedial, mandating sentencing judges to take a proactive sentencing approach by paying "particular attention to the circumstances of aboriginal offenders." This case clearly found that judges must actively and consciously consider the effects of colonization on Aboriginal offenders and apply restorative justice principles in deciding on a sentence.[15]

In particular, *Gladue* outlines sentencing goals and factors that are intended to assist a sentencing judge in ascertaining "the types of sentencing procedures and sanctions that may be appropriate for the offender because of his or her particular aboriginal heritage or connection."[16] Writing for the majority, Cory and Iacobucci J.J. note two broad categories of factors that must be taken into account when examining the circumstances of Aboriginal offenders:

(A) The unique systemic or background factors which may have played a part in bringing the particular aboriginal offender before the courts; and

(B) The types of sentencing procedures and sanctions which may be appropriate in the circumstances for the offender because of his or her particular aboriginal heritage or connection.[17]

The Supreme Court of Canada goes on to elaborate on these criteria, dividing them into the background causes of crime and the symptoms of having experienced colonialism, and adds an extra emphasis on avoiding incarceration. The Court notes "low incomes, high unemployment, lack of opportunities and options, lack or irrelevance of education, substance abuse, loneliness, and community fragmentation"[18] as systemic and background factors that figure most prominently among the causes of crime. Further, due to colonialism, Aboriginal people are disproportionately "victims of systemic and direct discrimination, many suffer the legacy of dislocation, and many are substantially affected by poor social and economic conditions."[19] Finally, the Court also notes that appropriate sentencing procedures and sanctions for Aboriginal people will "emphasize community-based sanctions [as they] coincide with the Aboriginal concept of sentencing and the needs of Aboriginal people and communities."[20]

Canadian Courts of Appeal have since further elaborated on these categories, outlining other specific factors that sentencing judges must consider.[21] These factors include: "the occupation and educational status of the offender, together with particulars of his alcohol abuse, the availability of any Aboriginal alcohol and drug aftercare program and the particulars of its method of operation;"[22] "the offender's experiences of racism, substance abuse, family dysfunction;"[23] and "poverty, and alcohol use in the community where the offender lives."[24]

The practical effect of the *Gladue* decision is that Aboriginal offenders may be more likely to receive a non-custodial sentence than they were before this decision was handed down. Judges will frequently employ conditional sentences,[25] diversions into Alternative Measures Programs,[26] or probation in cases where they would likely have previously ordered the offender to be incarcerated. Judges may also request and receive information from defence counsel and/or local social programs regarding the availability of Aboriginal-specific programming for offenders, and they may order attendance at such programs as a condition of the sentence. These practical outcomes may be of substantial benefit to the offender: keeping a person in his or her home and often allowing the offender to continue parenting and working, and thus, avoiding having any children in the family apprehended by the state, as well as providing structured access to available treatment and other social programs.

In *Gladue*, the Supreme Court of Canada grapples with some of the complex effects of historical and ongoing colonialism for Aboriginal people; however, the Court goes on to place particular and persistent emphasis on over-incarceration as one specific impact of colonialism which should be remedied through sentencing practices.

The legacy of colonialism[27] for Aboriginal peoples in Canada is complex and difficult to quantify. In the recent past, Canadian governments actively engaged in a program of cultural, social, and economic destruction of Aboriginal peoples. This campaign included land and resource theft, removal of children to often abusive residential schools, the prohibition of language and cultural practices, the imposition of hierarchical Western governance and gender structures through the *Indian Act*,[28] and the creation of poorly resourced reserve lands. While specific impacts, such as over-representation in prisons, poverty, and racism are clearly discernable, the less quantifiable concept of "colonialism" captures the complex and devastating effects of these attempts to wipe out Aboriginal peoples.[29] The Royal Commission on Aboriginal Peoples' Report, *Bridging the Cultural Divide: A Report on Aboriginal People and Criminal Justice in Canada*[30] points out that it is the cumulative effects of colonization, not merely a culture clash or poverty that increases the presence of Aboriginal peoples in Canadian prisons.[31]

Overrepresentation of Aboriginal people generally in Canada's prisons is a well-recognized and much-studied aspect of colonialism.[32] The Supreme Court draws on legislative and social history, as well as the submissions of both parties and interveners, to explain the connection between addressing over-incarceration and the use of section 718.2(e). It is clear from *Gladue*,[33] and from debates in the House of Commons during the passage of Bill C-41,[34] that reducing the use of incarceration, particularly in relation to Aboriginal peoples, was one of the main goals of section 718.2(e):

A general principle that runs through Bill C-41 is that jails should be reserved for those who should be there. Alternatives should be put in place for those who commit offences but who do not need or merit incarceration. . . .

This bill creates an environment which encourages community sanctions and the rehabilitating of offenders together with reparation to the victims and promoting in criminals a sense of accountability for what they have done.[35]

The criteria outlined above apply to all Aboriginal people, regardless of their gender. In cases involving Aboriginal women, these criteria must be applied in ways that account for gender as it interlocks with race, ethnicity, or culture.

III. ABORIGINAL WOMEN: WHAT IS DISTINCTIVE ABOUT THEIR EXPERIENCES OF COLONIALISM?

In *Gladue*, the Supreme Court embraces a novel, systemic approach to sentencing Aboriginal offenders, acknowledging that, alongside notions of individual responsibility and agency, judges must account for the ways that colonialism has narrowed the choices of Aboriginal offenders and increased their chances of coming into conflict with the law. The Court lays out the kinds of problems that many Aboriginal people face, and it instructs judges to look for these systemic issues in the evidence placed before them.

According to *Gladue*, sentencing judges must go beyond the decontextualized, individual, incident-based approach embedded in the principles of *mens rea* and *actus reus*, and they must seriously consider aspects of offenders' lives that reflect larger social forces at work. According to feminist evidence scholars Christine Boyle and Marilyn McRimmon, *Gladue* "reflects a commitment to egalitarian values by its recognition of constraints imposed upon Aboriginal peoples by history, poverty and racism."[36] In other words, individual Aboriginal offenders are no longer understood to be completely and individually responsible for the ways in which colonialism has narrowed their life choices. In the case of Aboriginal women in conflict with the law, their life choices have been constrained by colonialism that has been experienced *as women*, which may mean that these constraints and barriers take particular forms that are less visible or comprehensible to some judges.

In order to fully and fairly take into account the impact of colonialism in the lives of Aboriginal women in conflict with the law, the gendered aspects of judicially considered circumstances must be actively and consciously considered as interlocking with racial or cultural circumstances. Colonization has depended upon the ways in which gender- and race-based discrimination support and perpetuate one another. This chapter adopts the term "interlocking" from critical race feminist Sherene Razack. She describes the concept of interlocking oppressions as an "attempt to theorize how racial subjects come into existence through gender hierarchies and vice versa" and as language that "captures the simultaneity of systems of domination and the many ways in which they mutually constitute one another."[37]

While the *Criminal Code* explicitly considers "Aboriginality" in sentencing, it is impossible to neatly separate being a woman from being Aboriginal, in the daily lives of Aboriginal women. According to Razack "each system of oppression relie[s] on the other to give it meaning."[38] Considering gender in sentencing is not about "adding" gender discrimination to racial discrimination to arrive at "double discrimination," nor is it an exercise in bare comparison between Aboriginal men and women. This is what feminist legal scholar Rebecca Johnson would call merely "documenting difference."[39] Rather, it is an attempt to understand the ways in which systems of sexism and racism reinforce and maintain each other in the lives of Aboriginal women,[40] with a view to how these insights can serve as a tool of anti-subordination for both Aboriginal men and women in conflict with the law.[41]

Understanding the complex ways that race and gender interlock in the lives of Aboriginal women in conflict with the law helps to shed light on the complex ways that colonialism has undermined, and continues to oppress, Aboriginal peoples generally. For example, it points to the ways in which colonizers used law to attack Aboriginal laws and legal orders governing gender relations that did not neatly align with Western understandings of women's and men's roles, and to enforce an understanding of women as subordinate to men.[42] Understanding race and gender as interlocking also points to possible paths toward emancipation, where Aboriginal laws and legal orders may offer Aboriginal people more satisfying understandings of gender relations than those created and perpetuated under the *Indian Act* regime.

The following section will discuss some of the most prevalent, systemic aspects of (gendered) colonialism by providing practical exemplars illustrating how race and gender interlock inextricably in the lives of Aboriginal women. These patterns of discrimination have *particular* relevance to the *Gladue* factors. They map onto the Supreme Court's sentencing considerations in such a way that they should be considered as a matter of course by sentencing judges, when faced with sentencing Aboriginal women.

IV. The *Gladue* Factors through the Lenses of Gender and Race

A. Reducing the Use of Incarceration

The Court in *Gladue* strongly emphasized a reduction in the use of incarceration as a specific tool with which to remedy the ongoing effects of colonialism on individual offenders. Women generally, and Aboriginal women specifically, make up a tiny proportion of the actual prison population, often making them an "add-on" in prison policy and practice.[43] While both Aboriginal men and women are over-represented in Canadian jails, over-incarceration has been consistently more prevalent, per capita, for Aboriginal women. For example, recent statistics show that Aboriginal women represent one third of all women incarcerated, while Aboriginal men represent one fifth of all men incarcerated.[44] Despite their relatively small numbers, the mandated goal of decreasing the use of incarceration is extremely important for Aboriginal women offenders.

B. Parenting

The reduction of incarceration for Aboriginal women offenders takes on particular relevance when considered alongside the prevalence of lone-parent families headed by Aboriginal women. Many Aboriginal women are the primary or sole caregiver for their children,[45] making them disproportionately responsible for supporting the economic and social success of the next generation. In fact, Aboriginal women are much more likely (19 per cent) than their non-Aboriginal counterparts (8 per cent) to be lone parents.[46] At a practical level, keeping lone Aboriginal mothers out of prison means that they can continue to live in their homes, parent their children, and attend school or work. At a systemic level, very high rates of child apprehension from Aboriginal families[47] and the legacy of family separation due to residential schools[48] makes it especially important to provide Aboriginal mothers with the supports required to parent their children.

C. Systemic and Direct Discrimination

Courts have noted "systemic and direct discrimination"[49] and "the offender's experience of racism"[50] as two particular factors to be counted among the relevant circumstances of Aboriginal offenders. Aboriginal women have been subjected to systemic discrimination based on their race *and* their gender from both the Canadian state and from inside their own communities.[51] In the first instance, the Canadian state imposed the *Indian Act*, undermining and, in some cases, removing Aboriginal laws and legal orders which, in many cases, afforded women positions of power, decision-making opportunities, and access to resources.[52] The *Indian Act* replaced Aboriginal laws and legal orders with real property regimes, and governance structures which, like the colonizers', almost uniformly devalued women and placed men in positions of power and control.[53] The impacts and sexist features of this legislative regime are ongoing, with consequences, for instance, on some Aboriginal women's ability to access matrimonial property on-reserve.[54]

Among the most egregious aspects of the *Indian Act* regime were sexist provisions that caused Aboriginal women who married non-Aboriginal men to lose their status as "Indians" under the Act,[55] thus losing the resources distributed by this legislation, including on-reserve housing. In many instances, the effect was that women were banished from their home reserve communities.[56]

These provisions were changed in 1985, when the federal government passed Bill C-31,[57] allowing for the partial[58] recovery of status for these women and their children. The Act provides for a second generation cut-off, meaning that grandmothers cannot pass on their re-instated status to their grandchildren, although grandfathers under the same regime can do so. The federal government continues to battle against these grandmothers, their children, and their grandchildren in the courts.

Today, *Indian Act* band councils actively resist the re-extension of status and membership benefits to "Bill C-31 women," perpetuating state-sanctioned gender discrimination within reserve communities. Bands have engaged in extensive litigation against women seeking to rejoin their communities.[59] Status and membership benefits can include on-reserve housing, access to cultural, spiritual, and linguistic resources, interaction with elders, subsidized housing, school or post-secondary education funds, and land claim settlement resources.[60] Many Aboriginal women and their children and grandchildren continue to live in off-reserve and/or urban settings because of this discrimination.

In relation to sentencing, the Court in *Gladue* looked to "the legacy of dislocation"[61] as a sentencing consideration. For a large group of Aboriginal women, living in off-reserve and/or urban areas is clear manifestation of this legacy, as well as a symptom of systemic discrimination. There are more urban Aboriginal women than men,[62] and, in fact, the majority of Aboriginal women (72 per cent) live off-reserve, with more than half in urban areas.[63] Despite making up a majority of the overall Aboriginal population women are outnumbered by men on-reserve,[64] comprising less than half of reserve populations.[65] While living in urban areas presents all urban Aboriginal people with risks, including poverty, systemic and direct racism, and sexual exploitation,[66] Aboriginal women and their children are disproportionately affected due to their numbers in urban areas.[67] Housing is a particularly important urban issue, with studies showing an overall housing shortage for urban Aboriginal people,[68] and an even worse situation for urban Aboriginal women and their children.[69] Recent statistics also show that urban Aboriginal women are a highly mobile population, moving residences within urban centres almost twice as often than their on-reserve counterparts. Between 1996 and 2001, 66 per cent of urban Aboriginal women moved residence at least once.[70] Clearly, dislocation is a factor to be considered in the lives of many urban Aboriginal women.

Many urban Aboriginal people are closely tied to their culture.[71] Living off-reserve does not indicate a disconnection from Aboriginal community and culture, nor does living on-reserve guarantee a vibrant cultural or community life. It is clear, however, that two factors[72] associated with living off-reserve have been shown to create specific barriers for some urban Aboriginal people. The first is the lack of a land base:[73]

> Cultural identity for urban Aboriginal people is also tied to a land base or ancestral territory. For many, the two concepts are inseparable. . . . Identification with an ancestral place is important to urban people because of the associated ritual, ceremony and traditions, as well as the people who remain there, the sense of belonging, the bond to an ancestral community, and the accessibility of family, community and elders.[74]

Second, some urban Aboriginal women have specified that being *forced* to live off-reserve creates specific social and community issues for them within their reserve communities. They are reluctant to access (cultural) resources which may exist on-reserve, for fear that they will not be welcomed. In the words of one woman, "You really don't consider yourself an Indian. . . . It is easier to live in urban areas, because on reserve you are discriminated from those that live there."[75]

The Supreme Court of Canada has made it abundantly clear that living off-reserve (either in or outside of urban areas), and therefore, possibly being disconnected from the positive aspects of one's cultural heritage available on-reserve, does not exclude Aboriginal offenders from the application of the *Gladue* principles.[76]

D. Violence

Violence against women is a form of systemic, gendered discrimination,[77] and it interlocks with other forms of colonial oppression in the lives of Aboriginal women.[78] According to feminist legal scholar Elizabeth Sheehy, "Women's vulnerability to male violence and our ability to harness law are inextricably linked to women's social, economic and political position in Canada, in relation to those who hold power."[79] Violence, intimate or otherwise, against Aboriginal women is one of the gendered legacies of colonialism.[80] There are also well-documented connections between women's experiences of violence and their vulnerability to poverty and homelessness, two factors to be considered according to the *Gladue* case.[81]

Aboriginal women are frequently survivors of violence. They experience a disproportionately high level of physical and sexual abuse, both on and off-reserve.[82] Aboriginal women experience three times the rate of intimate violence as other Canadian women[83] and are more likely than their non-Aboriginal counterparts to experience serious forms of intimate violence. Over half (54 per cent) of Aboriginal women who reported being victims of spousal violence reported experiencing severe and potentially life-threatening violence, including being beaten or choked, threatened with or having a gun or knife used against them, or having been sexually assaulted.[84] Aboriginal women living in urban areas are routinely exposed to extremely high levels of violence from a number of sources.[85]

Judges have (at least) two possible avenues for taking this form of systemic discrimination against Aboriginal women into account. The first avenue is to take special care during a trial when considering legal defences, such as self-defence and provocation in cases where battered women have killed or injured their intimate partners. Second, in sentencing, judges could take into account the ways that violence (or the threat of violence) may have been used to coerce or manipulate women into participating in criminal activity or survival strategies (see the *Norris* case, below).

In cases where women are accused of killing or assaulting their intimate partners (as in *Gladue* itself), intimate violence against those women within that relationship should also be taken into account as a matter of course. Most women who come into conflict with the law are incarcerated for non-violent crimes.[86] Many women who commit crimes of intimate violence against partners or spouses do so in self-defence, following episodes of intimate abuse against them.[87] Existing legal mechanisms, such as applying the principles of the "battered woman syndrome,"[88] the argument of self-defence,[89] or the principles of provocation,[90] should be rigorously applied by judges. Each of these defences has been routinely deployed in gendered and racialized ways, subverting their utility in cases involving (racialized) women accused.[91]

E. Poverty

In *Gladue*, the Supreme Court of Canada notes that being "substantially affected by poor social and economic conditions"[92] and "low incomes (or) high unemployment"[93] are systemic or background factors that must be considered among the circumstances of Aboriginal offenders. Also, in *Cappo*, the Saskatchewan Court of Appeal cites poverty as a consideration.[94]

Poverty, lack of education, and under-employment are a reality in the lives of many Aboriginal women, and these factors play key roles in all three cases discussed below. Despite being better educated than their Aboriginal male counterparts, Aboriginal women are disproportionately unemployed and poor.[95] Aboriginal women who find employment suffer a pay equity gap in relation to employed Aboriginal men.[96] Four in 10 Aboriginal women have not completed high school; "In 2001, 40 per cent of Aboriginal women aged 25 and over had not graduated from high school, whereas the figure was 29 per cent among non-Aboriginal women."[97] Urban Aboriginal women are also better educated than their on-reserve counterparts, yet they maintain a higher unemployment rate.[98] Eighty to ninety percent of female-headed Aboriginal households fall below the poverty line.[99] According to the Supreme Court in *Gladue*, poverty plays a major role in the causation of crime, and must be considered in sentencing.[100] For Aboriginal women disproportionate levels of poverty and under-employment can function to limit their survival strategies, forcing them to resort to illegal work, such as dealing drugs or being sexually exploited, to feed and house themselves and their children.

F. Alcohol and Drug Addiction

"Substance abuse,"[101] "the availability of drug and alcohol rehabilitation resources," and "efforts by the offender to fight substance addictions"[102] are all counted as mitigating sentencing factors. Substance abuse is a problem among Aboriginal peoples generally,[103] and the negative health, family, and economic results have been well documented.[104] On average, men use drugs more than women; however, there is a connection between experiences of violence and trauma and an increase in substance use among women.[105]

The role of drugs, alcohol, and addiction in sentencing Aboriginal offenders has a lengthy, complex, racialized, and gendered history in Canadian jurisprudence.

Empirical research by Theresa Nahanee[106] and Margo Nightingale,[107] two Aboriginal women, shows that in cases involving sexual or physical violence against Aboriginal women by Aboriginal men, alcohol abuse or intoxication by the offender is treated by judges as a powerful mitigating factor in sentencing. Sherene Razack, a feminist critical race scholar, argues that in these cases "the stereotype of the drunken Indian operates to ensure that alcohol abuse is viewed as more significant for Aboriginal than for white offenders."[108] In these cases, male Aboriginal offenders had their sentences greatly reduced, relative to similar offences by non-Aboriginal men.

In the three cases below, however, the drug and/or alcohol addictions of the women being sentenced were mentioned, but they were given little mitigating weight. Successful or ongoing efforts to quit drugs were noted with approval; however, these efforts, alongside the availability of (in some cases, residential) drug and alcohol treatment did not mitigate against a sentence of incarceration for any of the women.

v. Sentencing Aboriginal Women: Three Cases

The three cases below represent judicial applications of the sentencing principles found in section 718.2 (e) of the *Criminal Code*, as well as those elaborated in *Gladue*. In their own ways, each of these cases fails to take into account the ways that race and gender interlock in the lives of Aboriginal women. In *Gladue*, the Supreme Court lays down the criteria by which to sentence all Aboriginal offenders, embracing a systemic understanding of the impacts of colonialism; yet, the Court failed to take a broad, systemic approach to sentencing Ms. Tanis Gladue herself.

These cases were selected from a relatively small number of reported cases involving Aboriginal women offenders where these sentencing principles were applied. They were chosen, first, because there were similar cases available for comparison involving similar kinds of criminal activity committed by Aboriginal men. Second, they include biographical information on the defendant which corresponds with demographic information on Aboriginal women across Canada, making a link to the systemic issues outlined in this chapter.

In *Norris*[109] and *Moyan*,[110] two cases which follow *Gladue*, many of the sentencing factors laid down by the Supreme Court are not visible in the judgments, as judges failed to apprehend their gendered manifestations in the lives of the Aboriginal women who came before them.

VI. *R. v. GLADUE:* THE GENDER-NEUTRAL APPROACH OF THE SUPREME COURT

Gladue set the standard for a broad, remedial, and purposive interpretation of section 718.2 (e), in relation to Aboriginal offenders. However, despite the fact that the offender in this case was a woman (19-year-old Jamie Tanis Gladue), the Court failed to direct sentencing judges to consider the unique circumstances of Aboriginal women, missing an important opportunity to recognize the gendered impacts of colonialism.[111]

This case involved a serious crime. Jamie Gladue pleaded guilty to manslaughter in the stabbing death of Reuben Beaver, her common-law partner and the father of her two children. This case, and those which have followed its reasoning, have made it quite clear that the reasoning in *Gladue* applies to such serious offences.[112] Ms. Gladue appealed the sentence of three years of incarceration to the Supreme Court of Canada, where it was found that this sentence was appropriate in the circumstances. Several commentators speculate that this may have been because Ms. Gladue was released on an electronic monitoring program only months after going to jail, and she was, in a sense, really serving her time in the community without the application of an actual conditional sentence.[113]

At the time of the offence, Ms. Gladue was pregnant with her second child, and she had completed a grade nine education.[114] She was also suffering from alcohol addiction (she was intoxicated during the offence), a hyperthyroid condition that effected her emotional reactions, and she was a victim of prior and ongoing domestic abuse at the hands of Mr. Beaver. On the night in question, she was provoked by Mr. Beaver, a mitigating factor under Canadian law: Ms. Gladue had good reason to believe that Mr. Beaver was having an affair with her sister, and he told her she was unattractive and "not as good as the others."[115] During her time on release, awaiting trial, Ms. Gladue completed grade 10, began grade 11 and completed a drug and alcohol counselling program. She also expressed remorse and sadness at Mr. Beaver's death, and she apologized to his family in court during her initial sentencing.[116] Ms. Gladue did not have the benefit of a pre-sentence report,[117] one of the primary methods for delivering evidence of the impacts of colonialism in cases involving Aboriginal offenders. No new trial was ordered, despite the fact that the Supreme Court discussed evidence of "battered woman's syndrome," provocation, and a medical condition (hypothyroid condition) which would likely have altered her sentence.

In fact, the Court overlooked several important mitigating factors in its gender-neutral assessment of Ms. Gladue's circumstances. The first oversight is intimate violence. By discounting evidence of Ms. Gladue's past and ongoing intimate abuse at the hands of Mr. Beaver,[118] the Court failed to contextualize this crime within her life experience and the lives of other Aboriginal women:

> Excluding the issue of spousal abuse made it possible for the Supreme Court to look at Gladue's violence in a gender-neutral way. It made it possible to isolate Gladue's offence from the context in which it occurred and accept the trial judge's decision that she was not afraid of the deceased, that she was 'indeed' the aggressor. . . . Having decontextualised the violence, the Court reverted to . . . traditional sentencing jurisprudence.[119]

In the broader context, this case fails to account for the prevalence and severity of intimate violence against women in Aboriginal communities. The case also fails to take into account the difficulties faced by Aboriginal women, due to poverty and racism, of launching a case of self-defence based on the "battered woman syndrome" or provocation[120] or the pressure to plead guilty to manslaughter when facing a charge of second-degree murder.

The lack of a pre-sentence report is noted by the Court in determining the role of geographic dislocation as a background factor in this case.[121] Originally, Ms. Gladue lived in a small, non-Aboriginal community in Alberta, where she met Mr. Beaver and where she had her first child.[122] During their relationship, Mr. Beaver and Ms. Gladue moved to Nanaimo, a mid-sized urban area, with Ms. Gladue's father and two of her sisters. It was in Nanaimo that Ms. Gladue became pregnant with her second child and also where Mr. Beaver was killed.[123] It is unclear why Ms. Gladue lived in off-reserve and urban areas, and it is equally unclear whether this negatively effected her connection to her Aboriginal heritage or community: "When asked by the trial judge whether the town of McLennan, Alberta, where the appellant grew up, was an aboriginal community, defense counsel responded: 'It's just a regular community.' No other submissions were made at the sentencing hearing on the issue of the appellant's aboriginal heritage."[124]

While the Court does not go on to analyze the relevance of dislocation to Ms. Gladue's specific circumstances, it does later specify that in subsequent cases section 718.2 (e) will be applied regardless of where the offender lives:

> For all purposes, the term "community" must be defined broadly so as to include any network of support and interaction that might be available in an urban centre. At the same time, the residence of the aboriginal

offender in an urban centre that lacks any network of support does not relieve the sentencing judge of the obligation to try to find an alternative to imprisonment.[125]

Another factor the Court fails to account for is child rearing. Jamie Tanis Gladue's status as an Aboriginal mother is steeped in historical and contemporary colonialism. Ms. Gladue was the lone remaining parent of her two children. The Court failed to recognize the high rates of child apprehension in Aboriginal communities, the legacy of residential schools in separating parents and children, and other parenting obstacles faced by Aboriginal women due to poverty and racism.[126] Ms. Gladue's desire to improve her education and employment prospects and end her alcohol addiction were closely related to a desire to continue parenting her children, which the imposition of a conditional sentence would have likely allowed.[127] When applying *Gladue* principles, other courts have accounted for the importance of parenting for Aboriginal offenders in sentencing.[128]

Ms. Gladue being primarily responsible for her children following the death of her partner, may have played an important role in her accepting a guilty plea on the charge of manslaughter. A second degree murder conviction carries with it a mandatory sentence of incarceration. Jamie Gladue was pregnant with her second child, and she was only 19 years old herself. She was poor, suffering from the effects of spousal abuse and from the emotional distress of having killed her common-law partner. The Court failed to discuss or even acknowledge that Ms. Gladue may have taken the quickest way out, even if *bona fide* defences existed which may have mitigated her sentence. These defences(particularly, the battered woman defence and provocation) would have served to introduce evidence which could speak to the particular impacts of colonialism on the life of Ms. Gladue, as an urban Aboriginal woman.

VII. *R. v. Moyan* and *R. v. Norris*: A Comparison of Drug Trafficking Cases

In both of these cases, an urban Aboriginal woman was convicted of trafficking drugs, and sentenced to a period of time in prison. In the *Norris* case, the accused was found guilty of two counts of possession of cocaine for the purposes of trafficking, failing to appear, and breaching a bail condition. She was arrested in the downtown east side of Vancouver on both occasions with "substantial amounts"[129] of cocaine, and she had a previous record of convictions for drug trafficking. She was initially sentenced to eight months incarceration and one year of probation, a sentence which was upheld by the British Columbia Court of Appeal. In the *Moyan* case, the accused pleaded guilty to one count of trafficking methamphetamine. She was arrested for selling a single "flap" of the drug, in co-operation with her sister, while working in a pub in small-town Alberta, and she was sentenced to eight months of incarceration. Each of these cases was decided following the Supreme Court of Canada's decision in *Gladue*, and each case purports to apply the principles of sentencing laid out in that case.

The trafficking of drugs is considered a very serious offence, and courts have struggled with whether applying the principles found in *Gladue* to such cases is appropriate. Supreme Court of Canada jurisprudence has made it clear that any crime, regardless of seriousness, can be a candidate for a conditional sentence under the principles in *Gladue*. The decision in *Wells* further explains the *Gladue* decision in relation to conditional sentences, and the decision clarifies that the seriousness of a crime, while a factor to consider, does not automatically eliminate a case. While a conditional sentence may be lengthy (up to two years), the freedom to parent, work, participate in education and treatment programs, and maintain other positive aspects of life make it a preferable option for many urban Aboriginal women.[130] These sentencing parameters have also been extended to cover other serious crimes, including cases of serious violence against Aboriginal women.[131] There are many examples of drug trafficking cases involving much more serious quantities and circumstances than the cases discussed here, which have resulted in a conditional sentence.[132]

A. Moyan

Moyan is a trial-level case involving a young Aboriginal woman, who was on probation at the time of the offence. She had nine previous criminal convictions, for undisclosed offences, and it is unclear if they were drug related. Her sister, who was also charged for the same drug transaction, received a conditional sentence, although the sentencing judge emphasized that she had no previous criminal record. The court acknowledged that the accused is a "treaty Indian," and that she was teased about being "Indian" during her upbringing. However, the court refused to apply *Gladue* for two reasons.

First, Judge Norheim generally advised: "I do not consider the *Gladue* case to endorse special treatment of aboriginals based on their race. Rather it attempts to address problems arising because of cultural differences and background factors specific to aboriginal society."[133] He then asserted that this means an assessment of "the extent that this accused's aboriginal lifestyle or culture has contributed to her offending"[134] Judge Norheim began with a problematic understanding of the *Gladue* decision, linking it directly to the extent that an accused was seen as participating in Aboriginal lifestyle or culture, as opposed to the accused's experiences of colonialism.

Secondly, Judge Norheim defined Aboriginal lifestyle or culture in an extremely narrow way, effectively eliminating this urban Aboriginal woman from his definition, based on her urban upbringing by her non-Aboriginal parent and her lack of involvement in her "aboriginal heritage." This analysis is problematic for a number of reasons: First, generally it mistakes the experience of being Aboriginal with participating in (what the judge perceives as) a traditional cultural lifestyle. Canadian courts have been rightly criticized for understanding Aboriginal tradition as both primitive and backward-looking.[135] This definition undermines the impact of colonialism on many urban Aboriginal people who, for numerous reasons well beyond their control, have not been able to freely access these aspects of their heritage. It also ignores urban Aboriginal people's experience of race-based oppression and the impacts of colonialism, whether or not they have been exposed to Aboriginal culture and tradition.

More specifically, this analysis ignores the multiple barriers that young urban Aboriginal women face in their lives, including those which impact their connections with their Aboriginal heritage. Many Aboriginal women are effectively prevented from participating in the cultural or traditional lifestyle that may be offered by on-reserve life, because they are unable to live on-reserve. They may also have to remain in an urban area in order to actively pursue employment (or other financial survival strategies, such as dealing drugs) to support their children and meet basic needs as primary caregivers. The accused was a lone parent at the time of sentencing, struggling with poverty and under-employment, and she was making attempts to achieve a high school education.[136] Her lack of exposure to Aboriginal culture did not reduce her exposure to poverty and under-employment, or other forms of race- and gender-based oppression.

The accused committed a relatively minor offence, she had recently made serious efforts at upgrading her education, she was attending counselling, and she had quit her own drug use. She was gainfully employed as wait staff (or "bar maid," to use the sexist term employed by the court), and had been working in the same place for a substantial period of time. The court found, however, that due to the problem with "speed" in the community where she lived, she should be incarcerated. Judge Norheim also points to general and specific deterrence and notes that she had breached her probation on other occasions.

B. Norris

The *Norris* case involves another young, urban Aboriginal woman. The 27-year-old accused in this case was arrested in urban Vancouver, at Main and Hastings Streets, selling substantial amounts of cocaine, in part, to sustain her own drug habit. The accused had five previous drug convictions. She was also HIV and Hepatitis C positive, and she was the mother of a young child. She was sentenced to two concurrent four-month sentences and one year of probation. The Crown appealed on the grounds that it was a lenient sentence given her offences, as well as because of her previous record.

At several important levels, the British Columbia Court of Appeal in *Norris* apprehends the individual circumstances of the accused in ways which were badly missed in *Moyan*. In a gender-neutral (and in most aspects, a highly-individualized) approach the court considers a number of the particular ways in which this Aboriginal woman experienced colonialism. Although the Court of Appeal refused to reduce the period of incarceration or impose a conditional sentence instead, the court did refuse to grant the Crown's appeal to increase the sentence to 18 months incarceration.

First, the court recognized that she was "under the control of her former boyfriend who was taking the profit from her trafficking activity."[137] However, the court fails to note how her own drug addiction and her dependence on (or fear of) her male ex-partner made her particularly vulnerable to criminal survival strategies, such as dealing drugs, nor how her individual experience reflects systemic patterns of Aboriginal women's experiences of colonialism.

Second, the Court recognized her willingness to attend, and the availability of, drug rehabilitation at the time scheduled for her release, and the Court emphasized the importance of taking advantage of this rare resource. Her desire to control her drug addiction was motivated in part by her health, but also by a desire to be reunited with her child, who was, at that time, in the custody of her father, the child's grandfather. The Court of Appeal notes with approval that "the sentencing judge identified two incentives motivating the respondent towards rehabilitation: her health and re-establishing a relationship with her four-year-old daughter."[138] The court fails to explore the option of a conditional sentence, which may have allowed her to begin rehabilitation immediately, while rebuilding her relationship with her child.

In gender-neutral terms, the court discusses the systemic nature of the barriers faced by urban Aboriginal people such as the accused, ironically underlining the futility of incarceration in such circumstances:

It is a notorious fact that there are many aboriginal faces in the population of street addicts in the Downtown East Side of Vancouver . . . as far as deterrence is concerned there seems to be no shortage of desperate addicts to sell on the street. The lifestyle of the street addict should itself be enough to deter others, where it is necessary to steal, engage in prostitution and sell drugs to maintain the habit.[139]

Overall, the court continues to take an individual, incident-based approach to sentencing, rather than the broader, systemic approach mandated by the Supreme Court of Canada in *Gladue*. In *Norris*, the Court of Appeal speaks to gendered aspects of colonialism in the experience of this woman, such as male violence and coercion in her life, her substance abuse problem, and her severed relationship with her child, but the court fails to understand these as anything more than facts in an individual case. According to *Gladue*, these should be understood and constructed both as systemic barriers and as mitigating circumstances, and alternatives to incarceration, such as a conditional sentence, should be actively considered. The British Columbia Court of Appeal missed the opportunity to set provincial precedent and to address these factors as aspects of colonialism experienced by many Aboriginal women that should routinely be considered and seriously taken into account.

While the *Norris* case does note, in oblique ways, gendered aspects of colonial oppression, such as her relationship with her former partner and her role as a lone parent, the approach is neither systematic, nor is it explicitly gendered. In essence, the court stumbles onto an analysis which partially apprehends the gendered manifestations of colonialism, but it does not arrive there by craft.

VIII. CONCLUSION

To exclude or inconsistently apply gendered aspects of the impact of colonialism leads to unfair decisions that are unreflective of the lived experiences of Aboriginal women. They also fail to fulfill the sentencing requirements in the *Criminal Code*, and the requirements laid out in *Gladue*. First, these cases resulted in outcomes that were inappropriately harsh. While the application of the *Gladue* principles to serious offences, such as sexual abuse of children or several counts of trafficking in heroin or cocaine, result in conditional sentences for Aboriginal men,[140] the Aboriginal women in these cases faced time in prison, despite many gender-specific mitigating factors, and being the primary caregivers for their children.

Secondly, through these sentences, these women have been re-oppressed by colonialism. Despite the Supreme Court of Canada's stance in *Gladue* that judges must take into account the ways that colonialism has narrowed the choices of Aboriginal offenders, these women are forced to take full personal responsibility for circumstances that are clearly related to their experiences of colonialism, and the punishment for those actions *strengthens those colonial consequences* (*e.g.*, by further separating them from their children).

Those working in the criminal justice system have a responsibility to accused Aboriginal people to present sufficient and pertinent information at sentencing. While the primary responsibility lies with defence counsel, it is well within the accepted parameters of judicial practice for sentencing judges to request information they feel is lacking in order to comply with the requirements of *Gladue* and the *Criminal Code*.[141] In cases involving Aboriginal women, this must include gender-specific facts, not only about the particular accused, but also more generally about the position of Aboriginal women in Canadian society. Many sentencing judges have come a long way since the *Gladue* decision in understanding the plight of Aboriginal people in Canada, and the next step is to add important information on gender inequality to the array of tools consistently provided to and wielded by judicial decision-makers.

10

THE IMPACT OF REPORTING REQUIREMENTS ON RESTORATIVE JUSTICE AGENCIES

IMPLICATIONS FOR SELF-DETERMINATION

Barbara Tomporowski[*]

The involvement of Aboriginal governments and organizations in restorative justice is linked to concerns about the over-representation of Aboriginal peoples in the criminal justice system, concerns that the justice system has not met the needs or interests of Aboriginal peoples, and Aboriginal peoples' desire to address social issues in their communities while exercising greater autonomy and self-determination or self-government.[1] As such, the community justice programs operated by First Nations, tribal councils, and Métis organizations in Saskatchewan provide an important opportunity for Aboriginal communities to develop justice services. These programs support a restorative justice philosophy, which the Commission on First Nations and Métis Peoples and Justice Reform viewed as "the basis for working toward a healthy, just, prosperous and safe Saskatchewan," which would "return justice to the community."[2]

Restorative agencies in Saskatchewan resolve large numbers of adult and youth criminal cases, and agency workers are very committed to implementing the philosophy of restorative justice. Yet, many agencies struggle with implementing important aspects of this philosophy, such as working with victims and involving community members.[3] Many factors contribute to these issues, such as challenging social and economic conditions, large caseloads,

---

[*] Although the author is employed as a Senior Policy Analyst with the Ministry of Justice and Attorney General in the Government of Saskatchewan, the opinions in this chapter are wholly her own and do not represent the position of the Ministry of Justice and Attorney General or the Government of Saskatchewan.

differing conceptions of restorative justice, and the impact of government reporting requirements on program operations.

This chapter considers how reporting requirements and conceptions of accountability affect the work that occurs in Saskatchewan's restorative agencies. It begins with an overview of restorative justice, a description of the types of restorative agencies in Saskatchewan, and a discussion about the link between reporting requirements and accountability. After a brief discussion of methodology, I outline my findings and consider how accountability relates to the self-determination of Aboriginal peoples.

I. Restorative Justice and Community Justice Programs in Saskatchewan

Brevity precludes a complete discussion of restorative concepts and practices, but for the purpose of this chapter restorative justice will be defined as a philosophy that emphasizes the involvement of victims, offenders, and community members in responding to crime and conflict. This philosophy is deeply concerned with values such as "inclusion, democracy, responsibility, reparation, safety, healing, and reintegration."[4] It is based on the assumption that a crime is more than an offence against the state; it is an act that causes real harms to victims and communities, and it creates an obligation "to make things right."[5] The inclusion of victims, offenders, and community members is a central tenet, as the process of responding to the crime or conflict occurs through an encounter in which the victim, offender, family, friends, and others discuss what happened, how it affected those involved, and what the offender can do to make amends. There is also a problem-solving aspect to restorative justice, as discussions about why an offence occurred have the potential to foster awareness of underlying social and economic conditions that contribute to offending, and they provide an opportunity to clarify and strengthen community norms.[6] Although restorative justice is often used as a way of handling criminal cases, it is also being applied in a wide range of fields, including conflict resolution in schools, child welfare cases, and addressing issues of community disorder, such as public drunkenness.[7]

Programs in Saskatchewan tend to use three models for the restorative encounter: victim-offender mediation, justice conferences, and circles. The first involves the victim, the offender, and a trained facilitator who assesses the case, meets with the victim and offender, and follows up with them after the restorative process. "Justice conferences," which are often called "family group conferences" in youth cases and "community justice forums" with adults, can involve friends, family, community members, and professionals, as well as the victim, the offender, and a facilitator. The third model, referred to as "circles," can take many forms.[8] Sentencing circles are a process in which victims, families, community members, and professionals provide advice to the judge about crafting an appropriate sentence. Circles can also be held to provide emotional support to victims or offenders and to resolve workplace conflict and other issues.

Saskatchewan has been called a leader in the development of restorative justice.[9] Information provided by the provincial Ministry of Justice and Attorney General indicates that academic institutions, faith organizations, and community groups are involved in restorative initiatives, and restorative programs have been operating in the province since 1983.[10] Moreover, restorative justice is strongly supported by the federal and provincial governments. Saskatchewan implemented a Restorative Justice Strategy in 1995, which emphasizes developing community-based restorative projects and provides information and education about restorative justice, as well as coordinating activities between the justice system, government, and communities.[11] By the 1998–1999 fiscal year, the Ministry of Justice and Attorney General was funding 14 community justice and alternative measures programs that emphasized a restorative justice approach.[12] By 2006–2007, the ministry supported 35 programs that provide services to adults, with funding of approximately $2.5 million dollars.[13] Many programs also receive funding from the Aboriginal Justice Directorate of Justice Canada, which contributed approximately $1.7 million dollars in 2006–2007, as well as from Saskatchewan Corrections, Public Safety and Policing, which provided approximately $1.7 million dollars to agencies that handled youth cases in 2006–2007. In addition to providing funding, these ministries also support training, policy development, conferences, and other forms of assistance to restorative agencies.

There are four service delivery models for the agencies funded by the Ministry of Justice and Attorney General that handle cases involving adults: alternative measures programs, community justice programs, community justice committees, and fee-for-service arrangements. Alternative measures programs focus primarily on resolving adult alternative measures cases and youth extrajudicial sanctions cases that are referred by police and authorized by the Crown prosecutor. Alternative measures cases are referred to community-based agencies under the authority of the Canadian *Criminal Code* and the Saskatchewan Justice Alternative Measures Policy, which provides criteria regarding the types of adult cases that are appropriate and how cases are resolved.[14] Youth extrajudicial sanctions cases are referred under the authority of the *Youth Criminal Justice Act* and the Saskatchewan Corrections and Public Safety Youth Extrajudicial Sanctions Policy.[15] While the majority of youth and adult cases are referred after charges are laid, police may make pre-charge referrals as well.

Community justice programs are operated by First Nations, tribal councils, and Métis organizations. These programs provide public education, crime prevention, and support for victims and offenders, in addition to handling alternative measures and extrajudicial sanctions cases. There is a great deal of activity with respect to restorative justice in First Nations across the province. Unpublished information provided by Community Services Branch of the Ministry of Justice and Attorney General indicates that 69 of the 74 First Nations in Saskatchewan had access to community justice programs in 2006–2007. While Aboriginal justice programs do not necessarily involve restorative justice, the interviewed individuals who worked in community justice programs described their agencies as following the philosophy of restorative justice.

There are two types of community justice committees. In First Nations communities, these committees involve elders, youth, and others who provide advice to the staff of the community justice program. In other communities, the committees may provide public education and crime prevention, as well as assess alternative measures cases and refer them to facilitators who conduct the restorative intervention. Finally, in some areas of the province with a low volume of cases, the Ministry of Justice and Attorney General contracts individuals on a fee-for-service basis to handle alternative measures.

There is a small body of graduate research regarding restorative justice in Saskatchewan, as well as three program evaluations and an evaluation on alternative measures and extrajudicial sanctions cases in the province.[16] The existing evaluations tend to use alternative measures data, interviews with stakeholders, and client surveys, rather than empirical research with control groups. The empirical data is therefore limited, although there is a growing body of empirical research from other parts of the world. For example, a New Zealand study that compared the results of cases handled in courts to cases handled with restorative justice found that victims were more satisfied with restorative processes, and offenders could be more involved in dealing with the causes and consequences of their offending.[17] Moreover, there was a small but statistically significant reduction in re-offending among offenders who participated in restorative processes, including offenders involved in violent crimes. Similar results have been demonstrated by a meta-analysis of 22 programs, mostly located in Canada and the United States of America. This research found that restorative programs were more effective at improving victim and offender satisfaction, increasing offender compliance with paying restitution, and decreasing recidivism than traditional criminal justice responses, such as incarceration, probation, and court-ordered restitution.[18]

Unpublished information provided by the Ministry of Justice and Attorney General indicates that there were 7,179 adult alternative measures and youth extrajudicial sanctions referrals in Saskatchewan in 2003–2004.[19] This includes 3,512 adult cases and 3,667 youth cases. In 2000–2001, which is the latest year for which the data analysis has been published, at least 2,778 adult alternative measures cases were referred.[20] It is estimated that this represented 24 per cent of theft cases and 12 per cent of assault cases involving adults in 2000–2001.[21] Forty-eight per cent of the referred youth and adults in 2000–2001 whose ethnicity was known were Aboriginal,[22] and slightly less than two-thirds of the referred offenders were male.[23] Sixty-two per cent of the offences involved property matters, while 23 per cent involved offences against the person, and the rest of the cases involved other matters such as drug offences and administration of justice offences.[24] The three most common charges referred in 2000–2001 were theft under $5,000 (31 per cent), assault (17 per cent), and mischief under $5,000 (10 per cent).[25]

Cases were dealt with using victim-offender mediation in 77 per cent of cases in 2000–2001, while 9 per cent resulted in circles and justice conferences.[26] In 10 per cent of cases, the facilitator met with the offender alone to caution them about the effects of their behavior. In the remaining cases the offender was referred for counselling and other services or the method used was unknown.

An agreement on how to resolve the matter was reached with the offender in 83 per cent of the closed cases in 2000–2001.[27] Offenders were required to apologize, complete community service hours, attend education sessions, make restitution to the victim, attend counselling, write an essay, or make charitable donations. The vast majority of agreements (87 per cent) were completed successfully[28] resulting in charges stayed in post-charge referrals.

Unpublished data collected by Saskatchewan Justice indicates that a high percentage of adult cases have continued reaching agreement in the fiscal years between 2001–2002 and 2004–2005.[29] Approximately 80 per cent of the cases closed during 2001–2002 and 2002–2003 reached an agreement, and almost 90 per cent of the agreements were completed successfully. Preliminary data from 2003–2004 and 2004–2005 suggests that the results will be similar.

Data from a 2006 Saskatchewan Justice evaluation of the Prince Albert Alternative Measures Program are fairly consistent with these results.[30] The program includes several agencies that provide adult alternative measures, youth extrajudicial sanctions, a program for offenders who shoplift, and a school mediation program. While length precludes a thorough discussion of all areas considered in the evaluation, stakeholders were generally satisfied with how the program was administered and delivered.[31] Most of the offenders were satisfied with the process, and they indicated that they "had a better understanding of victimization and how a victim of crime feels."[32] The evaluation revealed some issues regarding victim participation,[33] which will be discussed shortly.

The Prince Albert Alternative Measures Program received 2,855 adult and youth cases between April 1, 1999 and March 31, 2005.[34] Data on ethnicity was not consistently recorded during these years, though it was in 2003–2004, when 64 per cent of adult cases involved Aboriginal offenders.[35] The majority of cases involved property offences, and theft under $5,000 was the most commonly referred offence for adults between 2001–2002 and 2004–2005.[36] An agreement was reached in approximately eight out of ten adult cases during that time.[37] An inability to contact the offender was the most common reason for being unable to reach an agreement, although the refusal of the victim to participate or issues such as inappropriate referrals also occurred in some cases.[38]

II. Accountability and Reporting Requirements

"Accountability" is an important concept in the discourse of issues surrounding criminal justice, restorative justice, and government organizations. In the criminal justice field, the discourse tends to focus on holding offenders responsible for their crimes. Braithwaite & Roche suggest that the retributive model of criminal justice has generally been concerned with a passive conception of responsibility, which focusses on holding an offender accountable for a wrong that occurred in the past.[39] In contrast, restorative justice emphasizes an active conception of responsibility in which offenders are expected to take action to right the situation in the present. Restorative justice also tends to view accountability as a multi-dimensional concept in which offenders are accountable to their victims and their communities, while communities are responsible for the safety and well-being of their members.[40]

Within government organizations, accountability is concerned with ensuring that organizations are operating within their mandates and that public funding is spent appropriately. The Auditor General of Canada has suggested that accountability is necessary to ensure that power is not misused, that

activities are fair, appropriate, and demonstrate good stewardship, and to assist organizations with improving their programs and policies.[41] Respondents
in an evaluation of the Saskatchewan Aboriginal Justice Strategy tended to
discuss accountability in terms of fiscal and program matters, although one
commented that accountability "is not the exclusive domain of any sector or
institution . . . . [Accountability involves a] common understanding of goals,
objectives, purposes and willingness to be open to scrutiny for one's conduct"
in relationships between First Nations and Métis governments and federal
and provincial ministries.[42]

This tendency to focus on fiscal and program accountability is linked to the
development of a new regime of public sector management that emphasizes
rationalization and efficiency.[43] Governments in Canada and other Western
nations implemented fiscal and administrative reforms in the wake of rising
national debt during the 1980s, as well as declining public trust and confidence
in government.[44] These reforms resulted in a funding regime characterized by
the increased use of partnerships and service provision through private and
non-profit organizations. Within this funding regime governments tend to
provide short-term, targeted funding that emphasizes government priorities,
while monitoring contracts to ensure that organizations use the funds for the
purposes they were provided. Requiring agencies to provide frequent written
and financial reports and undergo evaluations are two of the ways in which
this monitoring occurs.

David Garland describes how this new regime has affected the criminal
justice system, which is "saturated with technologies of audit, fiscal control,
measured performance, and cost-benefit evaluation."[45] He suggests that the use
of managerial practices in public policy issues can result in a tendency to "skew
practice to fit performance indicators . . . and diminish an agency's real effectiveness in order to maximize the practices that are most easily measurable."[46]

Monitoring, measuring, and evaluating can have positive results, such as
enabling the organization to improve the efficiency of its services and increase
partnerships and innovation.[47] At the same time, Scott and Torjman both
argue that this emphasis on accountability has worked against non-profit
organizations that are particularly affected by these practices because they are
primarily dependent on government funding.[48] Scott indicates that many non-
profit organizations have been forced to shut down, due to the sudden loss or
unpredictability of long-term funding, and it has become more difficult to
develop stable non-profit organizations because governments are reluctant to
provide core funding for costs that are not directly related to service delivery.[49]
Moreover, the increased requirement for reports and the limited amounts and

terms of funding have required administrators to spend more time looking for funding and providing reports to multiple funding organizations. This can contribute to "mission drift" because the agency spends time writing reports and proposals that conform to changing funding criteria rather than focussing on its core work.

It is important for governments to ensure that public funds are spent appropriately, and accountability is vital in restorative justice because well-meaning but poorly-implemented processes could harm victims, offenders, and communities. As Dickson-Gilmore & La Prairie suggest, it is reasonable to have checks and balances to ensure that restorative agencies are operating appropriately.[50] However, they are skeptical of whether restorative projects will be socially accountable in Aboriginal communities fractured by asymmetrical power relations between community members, and they question whether federal and provincial governments are willing to support formal account-ability.[51] While Dickson-Gilmore & La Prairie raise a number of important questions about the potential for using restorative justice in Aboriginal com-munities, there are formal accountability requirements for restorative agencies in Saskatchewan. These requirements have significant consequences for the agencies' daily work.

III. METHODOLOGY

Research the author conducted has explored the extent to which Saskatch-ewan agencies are able to implement restorative justice, and the factors that affect their ability to do so. A method called institutional ethnography enables researchers to explore an aspect of daily life from the standpoint of the people who work and live within it.[52] This standpoint is a unique location in the world that is based on a person's class, gender, ethnicity, occupation, and many other factors.[53] This method attempts to understand how an aspect of the daily, lived experience is affected by extra-local factors outside the individual's control and often outside their awareness.[54]

My research involved exploring the work performed in restorative agencies from the standpoint of agency workers. I conducted open-ended interviews with 15 individuals who worked in 14 restorative agencies.[55] This included six community justice programs, six alternative measures programs, and two com-munity justice committees. The interviewees included seven program coordi-nators, four caseworkers, two members of community justice committees, and two fee-for-service agents. I also interviewed two police officers, two Crown prosecutors, and one government employee, in order to clarify my findings.

Justice coordinators and caseworkers were enthusiastic about their work, providing many anecdotal examples of the positive impact of restorative justice on victims, offenders, and communities.[56] The agencies developed strategies to handle large volumes of cases[57] while coping with expectations to provide services that were often outside their job descriptions.[58] As the research progressed, however, I noticed that agencies had difficulty implementing some of the major tenets of restorative justice, even though they were deeply committed to these principles.[59] For example, the involvement of victims and community members are crucial to restorative justice, yet there seemed to be a low level of victim involvement in some programs, and most of the restorative agencies did not have community volunteers. I began to understand that these issues were linked to reporting requirements that shaped their work in subtle but significant ways.[60] The reporting requirements affected the amount of time that staff worked with clients, and some caseworkers resisted reporting because they did not understand why the information was collected or how it was used.[61] More importantly, the requirements tend to focus agencies on working with alternative measures cases, rather than performing other tasks that would support a restorative approach.[62]

IV. How Reporting Requirements Shape the Work of Restorative Agencies

Many of the caseworkers and coordinators who participated in the research viewed reporting and accountability as important. As one put it, reporting requirements are needed to ensure that the agency is accountable to its clients and funders.[63] At the same time, they view the amount of reporting as an issue because it detracts from the time they can spend working with clients. One coordinator said, the paperwork detracts from working "hands on with the human."[64]

While the amount and type of paperwork depends on the agency's contract, restorative agencies must prepare proposals, mid-year and year-end reports, budgets, and financial reports for each ministry and level of government that provides funding.[65] As well, they must provide alternative measures and extrajudicial sanctions data to provincial ministries, send forms to the police, write letters to victims and Crown prosecutors, and prepare reports and presentations for their own non-profit boards of directors or authorities within First Nations and tribal councils.[66] Some coordinators and caseworkers were surprised when they thought about how much time the paperwork took.

One initially said, "I don't think that it's too much; it's not onerous or difficult to do it, it just takes time."[67] Upon reflection, however, he concluded that he probably spends almost half of his time on paperwork and half on dealing with clients.

The lack of integration between different ministries and levels of government contributes to this issue, as each ministry has its own requirements for proposals and reports. The situation has improved since 1995, when agencies were expected to prepare quarterly reports for each ministry.[68] In 1998, the Ministry of Justice and Attorney General, Justice Canada, and Saskatchewan Social Services (which was responsible for youth cases at the time) agreed to accept biannual reports. While this significantly reduced the requirement to produce reports, the amount of paperwork remains an issue for restorative agencies.[69]

The fact that reporting can be a burden on community-based agencies and First Nations has been documented in other fields. For example, the Royal Commission on Aboriginal Peoples noted that the reporting requirements of federal departments such as Indian and Northern Affairs "are time-consuming and complex, diverting valuable time of service providers."[70] The Auditor General of Canada made similar observations about the impact of government requirements on First Nations economic development programs and concluded that the federal government should develop integrated, horizontal management practices that would meet the needs of First Nations, as well as government.[71]

Some justice workers and coordinators raised the issue of whether the required data meets their needs. Two individuals indicated that they do not want to comply with reporting requirements because they do not know why the information is collected or how it is used. One said that the information "just goes into the big abyss and nobody knows where it goes."[72] He would like government ministries to explain how the information was taken into consideration in developing government policies. Another mused, "I've often thought who's looking at this [the paperwork]? And wonder . . . does it really matter if I'm doing this or not."[73]

As restorative agencies have little input into government expectations about reporting, some caseworkers resist the requirements because they view the paperwork as a burden that is imposed on them.[74] Although most of the individuals I interviewed indicated that they comply with the reporting requirements, two stated that they provide inaccurate or incomplete information. One admitted, "There's lots of information I fail to report." Another said that he writes down "anything [he] feel[s] like" or leaves areas of the forms blank because he does not understand why ministries ask certain questions.[75] This suggests that the data may not be complete or accurate, which would not assist either government ministries or restorative agencies in assessing the extent or impact of restorative justice in the province.

While these responses raise questions about the amount of reporting and why agencies resist reporting requirements, a more significant issue is that the requirements affect the activities of justice workers and coordinators on a daily basis. Rather than simply reflecting and recording the work that occurs within the restorative agency, the requirements for keeping statistics, filling out forms and producing reports, shape their work by making them accountable for handling alternative measures cases, while downplaying other activities that support a restorative philosophy.[76]

The contract between the restorative agency and the Ministry of Justice and Attorney General contains requirements for how often the agency will provide reports, what information must be included, and the types and number of services that the agency will provide.[77] Many of these services are described in a general way, such as conducting public education, working with victims, and networking with officials in the criminal justice system. In contrast, activities involving alternative measures are described with specific targets. For example, the contract might state that the agency will perform "approximately 150 alternative measures referrals" or "between 50 and 75 cases." Providing a number sets a goal, which prioritizes these activities over tasks that are stated in a more general way.

It appears that the lack of victim involvement in some restorative agencies is related to the structure and wording of the reporting forms.[78] It is not clear whether victim involvement occurs regularly in all Saskatchewan restorative programs, as information about how victims participated was missing in 72 per cent of cases from 2000–2001.[79] Excluding cases where this data was unavailable, victims were personally involved in 35 per cent of alternative measures cases in 2000–2001.[80] Victims were represented by someone else in 27 per cent of cases, participated by telephone or letter in 16 per cent and 15 per cent of cases respectively, and did not choose to participate at all in 7 per cent of cases in 2000–2001.[81] It seems positive that 35 per cent of victims chose to participate in person and 27 per cent were represented by someone else, while only 7 per cent did not participate in any way. However, given the large amount of data that is missing, it is possible that the percentage of victims who chose not to participate may be considerably higher. A significant amount of victim participation data was also missing in the evaluation of the Prince Albert Alternative Measures Program, although the percentage of adult cases in which victim participation was unknown dropped from 79 per cent in 2003–2004 to 44 per cent in 2004–2005.[82]

The failure to record this information may indicate that some agencies do not view victim involvement as a central part of their work. Although all of the justice workers and coordinators who participated in this research strongly agreed with the importance of involving victims, there was wide variation in their efforts to ensure that victims have opportunities to participate. Some agencies went to great lengths to meet with the victim to explain how restorative processes work, find out if the victim would like to attend, and determine how the agency could help the victim feel comfortable participating.[83] Other agencies seemed to view working with offenders as the primary goal of their program, with victim needs a secondary goal. For example, one coordinator indicated that she didn't want to "force" her staff to work with victims because they were "stretched pretty thin already."[84] It is troubling that this coordinator did not view working with victims as an integral part of the agency's services.

There are a number of factors that contribute to this issue, such as the need for links between victims services agencies and restorative agencies,[85] as well as the tendency to view working with victims as the responsibility of victims services programs.[86] However, reporting requirements contribute to this because they focus on quantitative data regarding alternative measures rather than data about working with victims.[87] For example, community justice programs provide a written report to the Ministry of Justice and Attorney General midway through the fiscal year and at the end of the fiscal year.[88] The majority of the questions relate to alternative measures, such as: the number of pre-charge and post-charge referrals; how many cases were opened and closed; the type of process used, such as victim-offender mediation; the outcome of the case (for example, whether the offender agreed to perform community service work, and if so, for how many hours); and the number and types of charges. Other questions ask for demographic data about the offender and issues the program encountered in operational areas such as contacting offenders or securing restitution payments. As well, the agency is asked to comment on changes to their program objectives, training provided to staff, and any public education or community awareness activities they conducted. Although the forms are approximately three pages long, they contain only two questions about working with victims. Agencies are asked to describe the difficulties they encounter with contacting victims, but they are not asked whether victims were contacted in every case or what steps the agency took to involve victims.[89] They are also asked to list the number of victims "assisted," but the forms do not ask how victims were helped or how this assistance was measured.[90]

Alternative measures agencies provide more detailed information about each case through a document called a "case management form." Among other things, the case management form includes data about the type of charge, the restorative process used, and the conditions of agreements with the offender.[91] The case management form tracks some information about victim involvement because the caseworker has to indicate whether the victim was contacted and whether they sent a reminder letter to the victim regarding upcoming meetings.[92] However, checking off the boxes on the form does not indicate whether any attempt occurred beyond a single letter or phone call. Indeed, one coordinator who participated in my research indicated that she was unhappy with the reporting forms because they do not provide space to describe the extensive efforts she puts into working with victims.[93] The foci on data relating to offenders and alternative measures, as well as the lack of specific detail about the services victims receive, gloss over the importance of working with victims, which is an issue if agency staff do not view this as a central aspect of their work.[94]

Interviews with caseworkers and victims in the evaluation of the Prince Albert Alternative Measures Program support the contention that there is a great deal of variation in the extent to which victims are contacted and receive follow-up. For example, one caseworker reported that they usually attempt to contact victims two or three times and send the victim a letter after the offender completes the agreement,[95] and two caseworkers indicated that they always send a letter to the victim regarding how the case was resolved and the status of the case.[96] On the other hand, two of the 21 victims who were interviewed reported that they had not been contacted by the program, and approximately half of the victims "indicated that they had had little contact with the Program."[97] Approximately half of the 21 victims reported that they were satisfied with the program, but six victims were not.[98] The lack of follow-up was an issue for those who were not satisfied, as were cases where the offender did not complete parts of the agreement.[99] These findings reinforce the need for restorative agencies to ensure that victims receive high quality services, from the time of initial contact until the point at which the case is closed and follow-up occurs.

The reporting requirements also affect the extent to which restorative agencies involve community members and perform activities beyond alternative measures. While most of the justice workers and coordinators mentioned the importance of involving communities, only two indicated that volunteers were regularly involved in their programs.[100] Instead, the involvement of community tends to occur through making presentations to service clubs, meeting with human service agencies, and meeting with police and Crown prosecutors.[101] While these activities are important, they do not fully meet the ideal of involving community members as volunteers and participants in restorative processes, particularly because the use of family group conferences and other processes involving individuals besides the victim and the offender accounted for only 9 per cent of cases in 2000–2001.[102] The reporting forms do not emphasize working with volunteers and community members, nor do they emphasize a broader range of activities that would support a restorative philosophy, such as crime prevention, providing mediation programs in schools, and mediating workplace conflict.[103] Many restorative agencies are active in these areas, regardless of whether their activities are measured and recorded, but the fact that they have specific targets for alternative measures leads some agencies to prioritize handling criminal cases over other tasks. For example, one participant said that his agency was not involved in other activities because they were "having trouble just getting the alternative measures started."[104] This comment reveals the tendency to focus on alternative measures as the main aspect of the agency's work, with other tasks added on if the employees have adequate time and resources.

Many efforts have been made to address the issues related to reporting requirements. In addition to reducing the number of reports required by government ministries in 1998, information provided by the Ministry of Justice and Attorney General indicates that officials there and in other ministries are continuing to work with restorative agencies to ensure that victims are involved in restorative processes if they wish to participate, provide training on victims issues, clarify reporting requirements, and improve the process for collecting data. As well, the Ministry of Justice and Attorney General has refined its contracts to reflect activities beyond alternative measures. For example, the contracts include more specific expectations regarding training volunteers, involving elders and community members, meeting with agencies in the justice system, and conducting educational sessions with the police.[105] These are positive steps that assist restorative agencies to reflect a broader conception of restorative justice.

v. The Implications of these Findings for Self-Determination

Aboriginal communities often implement restorative justice programs in order to address community issues, reclaim control over aspects of community life that were lost through colonization, and further their self-government aspirations.[106] In Saskatchewan, Aboriginal agencies are strongly involved in offering restorative programs. Of the 35 agencies funded by the Ministry of

Justice and Attorney General that supported restorative justice in 2006–2007, 16 were operated by First Nations, tribal councils, or Métis organizations and many of the programs provided by non-profit corporations had strong links to Aboriginal organizations.[107] While this research did not focus on whether these organizations see their restorative justice projects as furthering self-government or self-determination, anecdotal reports suggest that this is the case. The findings of this research indicate that a fundamentally different perspective on reporting and accountability is necessary if restorative projects are to support these aims. Despite the significant amount of government funding for restorative agencies and efforts to institutionalize restorative justice through strategies and other supports, it will be difficult for First Nations and Métis governments to achieve their aspirations for self-determination within current reporting practices.

Reporting relationships are inherently hierarchal. As Graham suggests, "the traditional notion of accountability – premised on the delegation of authority from one party to another – establishes a hierarchical and therefore an uneven relationship. Control, blame and punishment tend to be natural outcomes of such a relationship."[108] Graham proposes a definition of accountability that emphasizes a consensual relationship based on mutual obligations. He suggests that a new government-to-government approach to accountability should be developed through discussions between federal and provincial governments and First Nations.[109] This new relationship would involve viewing accountability in "a more positive, forward-looking" way by emphasizing how it can help organizations learn and improve.[110]

In the short-term and the period thereafter, it may be helpful to restructure reporting relationships through discussions between federal and provincial governments and First Nations, tribal councils, Métis organizations, and other restorative agencies.[111] This could begin with a discussion about streamlining reporting requirements between different levels of government to reduce the time spent on reporting. Moreover, the type of information that is provided should be reconsidered to ensure that the data is meaningful and useful for First Nations and Métis communities, as well as for government. There is a need to restructure the forms to emphasize working with victims, recruiting volunteers, and developing innovative programs and processes. This could be accomplished by asking First Nations and Métis communities what activities are important to them and developing reports that have specific questions about those tasks.

Currently, the forms emphasize quantitative data regarding alternative measures. There is a lack of the qualitative data and empirical research that would illuminate how restorative programs are affecting Aboriginal and non-Aboriginal communities. It has been suggested that evaluations about restorative justice tend to focus on quantitative measures because the goal is to assess the agency's caseload and competence at delivering services, rather than whether its services are truly restorative.[112] Measuring progress in areas such as healing and community safety will require changes in the type of data collected. As Barsh suggests, if Aboriginal peoples are interested in looking at the "long-term social advantages" of alternative justice approaches, then there may be a need for fundamentally different measures that attempt to determine whether programs empower communities and promote healing at the individual, family, and community levels.[113] Using a broader set of measures would enable justice workers to provide a better view of what they do and their aspirations for their programs.

In the long term, the struggle for self-determination will be furthered as First Nations and Métis governments continue to develop their own culture of professional administration. Programs for Aboriginal peoples are most likely to be successful when they are developed in support of political autonomy, capacity building, accountability, and good governance.[114] Assisting Aboriginal peoples with building capacity in this area will require training in leadership, governance and program administration,[115] professional development and certification in financial management,[116] and investments in data collection systems.[117]

VI. CONCLUSION

Current reporting requirements are developed and implemented in a way that has unintended consequences for restorative agencies, despite a significant amount of government funding and efforts to institutionalize restorative justice. The reporting requirements reduce the time that justice workers and coordinators have for delivering services, lead some to resist reporting, and tend to focus agencies on handling alternative measures cases rather than implementing a broader conception of restorative justice. These issues occur because restorative agencies operate within a new regime that emphasizes formal accountability, in which reporting requirements are used to monitor program operations and service delivery.

While there is a need to change the aspects of the reporting requirements that cause these difficulties, it is possible that First Nations and Métis governments could develop innovative ways of administering their programs that draw on the best aspects of current accountability practices, while still avoiding the issues discussed here. This is a longterm project with many obstacles to overcome, and it will require additional capacity-building and enhanced support from many levels of government. Nonetheless, being mindful of t he difficulties and acknowledging the need to maintain high standards for accountability, we should be open to the possibility that First Nations and Métis peoples could develop new accountability methods that become the best practices for others to follow.

11

FIRST NATIONS AND THE CHARTER OF RIGHTS

Bill Rafoss

I. INTRODUCTION

First Nations' government is re-emerging rapidly in Canada. Since 1993, more than a dozen modern treaties have been ratified[1] and many more self-government agreements have been signed from one end of the country to the other and into the far north.[2] First Nations are recovering control over their own affairs. For many of these First Nations, determination in managing their affairs is becoming a reality. As these Nations "move toward justice" on First Nation territory by establishing their own justice systems and police services, they will be under increasing pressure to protect individual rights from abuse by these systems. This chapter proposes that the *Canadian Charter of Rights and Freedoms*[3] represents a good starting point for a discussion of individual rights on-reserve, a floor of rights that could be expanded to include Aboriginal traditions, laws, and customs.

Many First Nations' leaders have traditionally been opposed to the application of the *Charter* to their jurisdiction. They see the *Charter* as an imposition of European values on their hard-won right to self-government, an imposition that may limit their Aboriginal rights. Yet, times are changing, and not all Aboriginal peoples share this perspective. Adopting the *Charter* would align these new governments with internationally-accepted principles and values, and it would forge a stronger bond with the broader Canadian public who by and large support the *Charter*.

II. WHY IS THIS AN ISSUE?

Why is this even an issue? One might ask, "Does the *Charter* not apply equally to all Canadians?" Well, the answer is – not exactly. Section 32 of the *Charter* states that the *Charter* applies to the federal, provincial, and territorial governments; it makes no mention of applying to Aboriginal governments.[4] First Nations' people may use the *Charter* against the federal and provincial governments; whether the *Charter* applies to their own governments or whether the *Charter* should apply to their own governments, is what is examined in this chapter.

There is considerable scholarship that suggests that the *Charter* does not apply to First Nations' government. James Youngblood (Sákéj) Henderson, for example, suggests that section 25 is "a protective zone from the colonialists' rights paradigm"[5] that creates judicial and legislative immunity for First Nations from actions under the *Charter*. Kent McNeil concurs: he contends that if Canada had intended to include other forms of government like First Nations' governments, they would have broadened this wording to include all forms of governance in Canada.[6] The Supreme Court of Canada has not yet been asked to rule on this specific point. In the 1999 decision of *Corbiere, et al* v. *the Batchewana Indian Band and Her Majesty the Queen*,[7] the Supreme Court came close when it found that elections held pursuant to the *Indian Act*[8] are subject to the provisions of the *Charter*. In spite of this decision, most observers agree that this issue falls within a grey zone in constitutional law.

This chapter does not propose that the *Charter* ought to be imposed on First Nations. The argument here is instead concerned with whether it is in the best interests of First Nations *and their citizens* to accept the application of the *Charter* to First Nations affairs, as well as whether it is in the best interests of First Nations to adopt the *Charter* as having application over their jurisdiction.

III. TRADITIONAL ARGUMENTS AGAINST THE *CHARTER*

A review of the scholarship in this area identifies three central arguments against the application of the *Charter* to First Nations' jurisdiction:

(i)   First Nations leaders see the imposition of the *Charter* as being antithetical to their hard-won recognition of Aboriginal rights in section 35. They believe that if self-government is to mean anything, it must mean the right to adopt their own laws in accordance with their customs and traditions and to not have the *Charter* imposed on them.[9]

(ii) Some have expressed concerns that the *Charter* is steeped in liberal democratic traditions that may not be consistent with Aboriginal traditions, and *Charter* applications will be adjudicated by the

Canadian court system that has Eurocentric biases.[10] Joseph Carens concurs with this view: he says the *Charter* is "embedded in a complex, costly, and alien legal system."[11]

(iii)   Some leaders believe the *Charter* will stifle self-government rather than enhance it. Joseph Carens believes the *Charter* "could greatly limit the capacity of Aboriginal people to develop their own distinctive arrangements for self-governance."[12] This argument is similar to that of some of the premiers prior to the inclusion of the *Charter* in the patriation package in 1982.[13]

IV. COUNTER-POINT

Do these concerns hold up under scrutiny, then?

It is worth noting that not all Aboriginal people believe the *Charter* has no application, and to be fair, some have no opinion on the subject at all, as they struggle to meet the demands of day-to-day living and governance.

To reiterate, this chapter is not proposing that the *Charter* be imposed on First Nations, although the courts may enter into this debate at some point. Gone are the days when the federal government can impose legislation on First Nations without their consent. First Nations must agree to the application of the *Charter* to their jurisdiction, and, as will be noted later in this chapter, some have already agreed.

With respect to cultural appropriateness of the *Charter*, urbanization and globalization are changing traditional views that the rights of the individual are somehow subordinate to the rights of the community in Aboriginal societies. Aboriginal scholar John Borrows, for instance, suggests that *Charter* values may not be entirely inconsistent with Aboriginal values of harmony and gender symmetry.[14] Borrows further suggests that the *Charter* may actually assist Aboriginal people to disentangle themselves from the shackles of colonialism.[15] The Royal Commission on Aboriginal Peoples (RCAP), which is seen as a blueprint by many for issues surrounding Aboriginal self-determination, traces the history of respect for individual freedoms back to Aboriginal traditions, and the RCAP argues that Aboriginal peoples are no strangers to the doctrines of freedom and equality that animate the *Charter*:[16] these values were recorded as early as 1744 by French historians. In other words, the roots of the *Charter* are found in both Aboriginal and non-Aboriginal traditions. The RCAP recommended that the *Charter* apply to First Nations, with full access to section 33, the notwithstanding clause.[17]

Finally, in rebuttal to those who argue that the *Charter* might limit rather than enhance First Nations government, this point may have some validity. Is that not the purpose of rights instruments, and if so, why should Aboriginal governments not be held to the same standards as other governments? As Pierre Trudeau admonished recalcitrant premiers in the lead-up to patriation in 1982,

> [W]hen we get to protect fundamental rights and freedoms, you say "don't put them in the constitution, the words are too hard to find." Well I say, what is wrong with going to the courts . . . or why shouldn't a minority which is adversely affected be able to call us to account in front of the courts?[18]

v. The Argument in Favour of the *Charter* Application

And so, some of the arguments against the application of the *Charter* may not stand up to close scrutiny. However, there are positive reasons why the *Charter* ought to be accepted by First Nations. For example, the *Charter* offers important rights to all citizens of Canada. It allows for the right to freedom of expression and of peaceable assembly, it guarantees the right to vote in elections, it allows for mobility – the right to live and work anywhere in Canada, it offers important legal rights upon arrest, and it offers the right to a fair trial. It guarantees equality. First Nations' people possess the right to make *Charter*-based claims against the federal and provincial governments on these grounds. It would be ironic if they did not possess these rights against their own governments.

Having the *Charter* apply to First Nations' jurisdiction as a minimum set of rights would guarantee dissidents the right to freely express themselves against band decisions, it would allow for the right to elect their leadership, and it would allow for the right to move on- and off-reserve as resources allow. It would offer important legal rights if arrested by band police, and it would guarantee the right to a fair trial by an Aboriginal justice system. This is not to suggest that a First Nations' justice system would not respect rights; rather, the *Charter* and other rights would act as a check against arbitrary government authority, and it would hold these governments to account at an international standard. As Emilio Mignone observes, "The defence of human dignity knows no boundaries."[19]

Of course, these rights are subject to the limitations of section 25, the "non-abrogation, non-derogation clause,"[20] and it is worth noting that both the failed Charlottetown Accord[21] and the RCAP Final Report[22] recommend a flexible and expansive interpretation of section 25. So, if, for example, a First Nation's elector wishes to challenge the process for electing the leadership of a band, the band government would have access to section 25 to defend their system against erosion by the *Charter*. To date, very few, if any, section 25 arguments have been made before the courts. It is ironic that section 25 of the *Charter* itself offers perhaps the best defence for those who would oppose the application of the *Charter* to First Nations' jurisdiction.

Finally, there is the social cohesion argument. There is no doubt that Canada's federal system can and should accommodate sub-national interests. More than twenty years ago, Kayyam Zev Paltiel suggested that Canada is concerned with accommodating minority interests.[23] Canada accommodates Quebec's nationalism in many ways, and so can it accommodate Aboriginal self-determination. At the same time, there must be some elements of commonality and some national institutions that we accept as having legitimacy over all Canadians. The *Charter* is one such instrument. Some have argued that it is the centrepiece of our liberal democratic traditions, and it enjoys broad public support.[24] Roy Romanow, Attorney-General of Saskatchewan at the time of the constitutional talks in 1981, said the proposed *Charter* has a dual purpose. The *Charter*, he said, "[is] designed to articulate those ideas and goals which are common to nationhood and to serve as a protective shield for all Canadian citizens against arbitrary legislative and executive actions of all governments."[25] It has been variously described as a "statement of nationhood"[26] and a "crucial symbol of citizenship."[27]

Many observers, including supporters of First Nations self-determination, believe that the support of non-Aboriginal Canadians is important for self-government to proceed. This task will be much easier if First Nations strategically adopt some instruments of common nationhood, such as the *Charter*.

VI. THE SITUATION IN CANADA TODAY

In 1995, the federal government adopted an administrative policy known as the "inherent right policy" to facilitate the movement toward self-government and to find jurisdictional space for Aboriginal governments.[28] This policy accepts that First Nations' have an inherent right to self-government; however, there was a catch: The *Canadian Charter of Rights and Freedoms* must apply as a condition of Canada agreeing to self-government. The adoption of this position by the federal government has forced some First Nations to reconsider their traditional opposition to the *Charter*.

The policy has accelerated the pace of self-government negotiations. As indicated earlier, many modern treaties have been ratified in the past decade and many more administrative agreements that devolve self-governing authority to First Nations have been agreed upon. The *Nisga'a Final Agreement* and others in British Columbia stand out in this regard,[29] as does the creation of Nunavut, the *Umbrella Final Agreement Between The Government of Canada, The Council For Yukon Indians And The Government Of The Yukon,*[30] and the recent *Labrador Inuit Land Claims Agreement.*[31] In each of these jurisdictions, there is evidence of some discussion of individual rights. The *Nisga'a Final Agreement* of 1999, for instance, agrees that the Nisga'a people continue to be entitled to all the rights and benefits of other Canadian citizens; it also stipulates that the *Charter* applies "in respect of all matters within [Nisga'a] authority."[32]

In the Yukon, modern treaties have been signed with some 14 First Nations under the auspices of an *Umbrella Agreement* that protects the rights of Yukon First Nations' people as Canadians.[33] One agreement is with the Ta'an Kwäch'än Council (TKC) of Yukon, a band that has a number of interesting human rights provisions within its own Constitution.[34] Their Constitution declares that residents of that First Nation shall have the right to "equal protection and equal benefit of the law . . . without any discrimination, including discrimination based on status, religion, sex or disability."[35] Their Constitution also guarantees freedom of expression, freedom of religion, freedom from unreasonable search and seizure, and the right to peaceable assembly.

There are also critical developments in Nunavut, where Inuit culture is prevalent. Nunavut is a territorial-based, provincial-style government, distinct from other Aboriginal governments in Canada, and by virtue of the *Nunavut Act*[36] and section 32 of the *Charter*, the *Charter* applies to Nunavut. In November of 2003, the legislature of Nunavut adopted a new *Human Rights Act*[37] that contains some innovative provisions. The Preamble ensures that Inuit culture and values remain intact, while at the same time, the Act prohibits discrimination based on race, disability, sexual orientation, and other prohibited grounds.[38]

In Labrador, Inuit peoples have recently ratified a land claims settlement and self-government agreement that will result in the creation of the Inuit territory of Nunatsiavut. The agreement is very comprehensive, and it states that "The *Canadian Charter of Rights and Freedoms* applies to Inuit Government in respect of all matters within its authority."[39] The agreement has an additional provision, however, respecting rights within that Inuit territory. The agreement states:

17.3.4 The Labrador Inuit Constitution may provide for the following matters:

(e) the recognition of Inuit customary law and the application of Inuit customary law to Inuit with respect to any matter within the jurisdiction and authority of the Nunatsiavut Government, as set out in the agreement, on condition that any recognition or application of Inuit customary law shall be proclaimed, published and registered in accordance with part 17.5; and

(f) an Inuit charter of human rights.[40]

This provision opens the door for an Aboriginal or Inuit charter of rights, and it could establish a precedent for future negotiations in the western Arctic or elsewhere. It may also signal a shift in federal government policy away from the *Charter of Rights* and toward something that First Nations find more in keeping with their own traditions and laws.

VII. The Role of the Courts

While the Supreme Court of Canada has not been specifically asked to rule on the application of the *Charter* to First Nations' jurisdiction, as indicated earlier, they came close in the decision of *Corbiere*.[41] The Court was asked to review the Batchewana band's decision to deny voting rights to band members who lived off-reserve. The criteria for electors within the band had been established pursuant to section 77(1) of the *Indian Act*, which requires electors to be "ordinarily resident of the band."[42] The Court determined that this provision discriminated against non-residents of the Batchewana band under section 15 of the *Charter*, the equality rights section, and the Court ordered the Government of Canada to rectify this disadvantage by amending the *Indian Act*. The Batchewana band did not present arguments in this case to the effect that the provision that had disenfranchised non-residents was saved by virtue of sections 35 and 25 of the *Charter*; therefore, the Court did not have to rule specifically on whether the *Charter* applied to First Nations. It did find that the *Indian Act* must comply with section 15, and one could extrapolate that, by implication, Indian bands which operate under the auspices of the *Indian Act* are subject to the *Charter*.[43]

Two other lower-level court decisions made similar findings. In *Scrimbitt v. Sakimay Indian Band Council*,[44] Scrimbitt was denied the right to vote in the band election because her name had been added to the band list by virtue of Bill C-31, which restored Indian status to some previously disenfranchised

Aboriginal people. A Federal Court Justice found that the actions of the Sakimay Band violated section 15 of the *Charter*, the equality rights section. In *Horse Lake First Nation* v. *Horseman*,[45] a group of women occupied the local Horse Lake band office, and the band applied to the courts for an order to evict them. An Alberta Queen's Bench Justice held that the *Charter* should apply to any decision of the band.[46] These are lower-level decisions, and the Indian bands did not argue in these cases that their Aboriginal rights under section 35 or 25 superseded the *Charter* rights being claimed by the plaintiffs. The courts, therefore, did not directly address the intersection of Aboriginal rights and *Charter* rights. Some theorists have suggested however, that the Canadian court system will be looking to First Nations for some rights protection under First Nations' jurisdiction. The argument that individual rights are subordinate on-reserve is not likely to be well received.

Until the Supreme Court of Canada is specifically asked to make a ruling on whether *Charter* rights apply to First Nations residents, this issue remains a grey area in law, particularly given the lack of reference to First Nations' governments in section 32 of the *Constitution Act, 1982*. One possible outcome, based on an interpretation of the *Corbiere* decision, is that while First Nations' governments that are established pursuant to the *Indian Act* may be subject to the rigors of the *Charter*, inherency governments may well be exempted.[47] Kent McNeil, who argues that the *Charter* does not apply to First Nations, has discouraged "judicial activism" from making such a finding.[48] He believes this issue should be left to further investigation and negotiation.

VIII. SUMMARY AND CONCLUSIONS

The *Charter* is not a perfect document, nor has it always been interpreted as *Charter* supporters might like. It remains, however, a cornerstone of the Canadian Constitution, and it enjoys broad popular and judicial support. First Nations seeking greater self-determination could adopt the *Charter* as having authority over their affairs, while at the same time building upon it by re-establishing their own customs and traditions to form a unique blend of individual rights alongside Aboriginal traditions, which would comprise a truly unique set of rights for Indigenous Canadians. Some First Nations have embarked on this course of action already, as witnessed in the Yukon and Labrador Inuit Nations and in Nunavut. Aboriginal governments that develop human rights regimes under their jurisdiction are more likely to enjoy the support of their citizens, the broader Canadian community, the international community, and the Canadian court system.

12

INDIGENOUS AND STATE JUSTICE SYSTEMS IN KENYA

TOWARD A REALIZATION OF JUSTICE

Winifred Kamau

I. INTRODUCTION

As a consequence of Western colonialism, most Africans currently live in legal pluralistic societies where Indigenous justice systems coexist with their state justice system. The question has therefore been raised, particularly in the last four decades, about "what to do with African law"[1] and how it should stand in relation to Western-based state law in the context of politically independent African states. The approach of the Kenyan state has focussed on subsuming Indigenous law within the state legal structures, through a policy of integration or harmonization of African customary law with the received state law. However, these efforts have largely been unsuccessful and Indigenous norms operating outside of the framework of the state are still vibrant and continue to govern the lives of the Kenyan people. The Kenyan approach is based on an erroneous conception of Indigenous law, and it has failed to give adequate weight to the question of what constitutes justice for the African people. This chapter re-examines the question of the relation of Indigenous law to state law, and it proposes an alternative approach that focusses on justice rather than on the incorporation of rules or institutions of Indigenous law within state law. The chapter starts with a historical background that outlines the policy of the Kenyan state on the issue of Indigenous law. It then discusses the forms and characteristics of Indigenous justice systems and proceeds to query why Indigenous justice systems have persisted despite the presence of the state justice system. Finally, should Indigenous justice systems be incorporated into formal state systems, and if they should not, what alternative approach should be adopted? There is a need to change the terms of the debate from focussing on incorporating Indigenous systems into the state system, to addressing the issue of people's realization of justice. This task entails engagement with Indigenous justice systems, in their own right, as offering a viable avenue for the democratization of the Kenyan legal system.

ii. Concepts

A. Indigenous Justice Systems

The conventional understanding of African Indigenous justice systems is that they are merely a continuation or "survival" of traditional systems that existed prior to European contact and penetration, albeit operating in altered socio-economic contexts. Customary law was therefore seen as timeless, static, and unchanging. Hence, the colonial courts applied rigid and often archaic customary rules that were detached from the evolving lived realities of the people, and these rules gradually ossified through the medium of judicial precedent and reliance on restatements or quasi-codifications of customary law. This has led some scholars to make a distinction between judicial (or state) customary law and people's customary law.[2] However, it is increasingly being recognized that, far from being immutable, Indigenous law is flexible and dynamic in nature and its content constantly being negotiated, thus resulting in a continuous process of production of new norms or permutations of older norms.[3] Traditional forms of normative ordering in Africa have undergone major transformation, due to social, political and economic changes in African society, and it is therefore virtually impossible to find "pure" traditional systems. This chapter's conception of Indigenous justice systems is therefore not confined to traditional (*i.e.* pre-colonial or pre-industrialization) legal systems, but it instead includes the full gamut of contemporary normative ordering that draws on local norms and values currently formulated or applied by the community. Indigenous justice in this chapter is taken to include a blend of traditional norms, local norms, and varied localized understandings of official law.[4]

B. The Formal *vs.* Informal Dichotomy

Conventional legal scholarship tends to propose a dichotomy between informal (Indigenous) and formal (state) justice systems, and the two concepts are viewed as discrete and closed systems that operate independently of one another and often in conflict with each other.[5] However, it should be noted that the boundaries between the formal and the informal are by no means as clear as they seem and are very often blurred. In the African context, people simultaneously inhabit the two worlds, and their actions cannot be neatly categorized as either customary or legal. In her concept of the semi-autonomous social field, Sally Falk Moore argues that local norms and practices are in a relationship of semi-autonomy with the larger social matrix of formal laws.[6] The local social field generates and enforces norms governing the conduct of people living within its sphere, but it is at the same time permeable to norms emanating from the larger surrounding social context. Local normative systems are therefore not autonomous entities but have a symbiotic relationship with formal legal norms, influencing and complementing each other and being in tension with each other.[7] In cognizance of this complex interrelationship, more recent scholars use the terms "non-formal" or "non-state" justice systems to mean any system that applies norms or rules whose source is (or purports to be) primarily non-state in origin and which occurs outside the state's immediate control, whether complementary to or in opposition to the state. Such justice systems fall along a continuum, which ranges between community-based forums that have little direct contact with formal state structures and forums created or endorsed by the state and sanctioned to apply community norms or customs.[8]

III. Historical Background

The development of justice systems in Kenya is inextricably linked with the colonial experience and, in particular, the encounter between Indigenous systems of justice and colonial state law. The establishment of British colonial rule in Kenya in the late nineteenth century was accompanied by the superimposition of English law over the territory.[9] Under the policy of indirect rule,[10] a dual legal system was established, with one system of justice for non-Africans and another for the Africans. Thus, English-style courts were established and run by British magistrates and judges who administered English law to govern non-Africans, while native tribunals (courts) were established to be run by ostensibly traditional authorities and apply "native law and custom"[11] to Africans. However, the paternalism implicit in the indirect rule policy was evident in the requirement that African traditional institutions, though allowed to coexist with colonial ones, were to do so in a manner consistent with British standards and subject to supervision by the colonial administrative officials. Underlying this policy were evolutionary legal theories that considered customary law inferior to Western law and as being in an earlier state of development, which would, with time, develop toward Western law.[12] Hence, the so-called repugnancy clause provided that in order for customary law to be applied, it must not be "repugnant to justice and morality."[13] The standards of justice and morality referred to have been judicially interpreted in colonial courts to mean British standards.[14]

Although the native tribunals were mandated to apply customary law without "undue regard to technicalities of procedure,"[15] they became increasingly anglicized and formalistic, introducing unfamiliar norms, procedures, and offences and penalties, thereby losing much of their supposed traditional character. Moreover, the ostensibly "traditional" chiefs were in most cases creations of the colonial officials, as the majority of Kenyan peoples did not have centralized governance structures. The version of "native law and custom" that these tribunals applied was based on abstracted and rigid rules of custom that did not always accord with the lived realities of the African people. Further, the tribunals were closely linked to the executive arm of government and were primarily instruments for the maintenance of law and order, and the African court holders often used their powers to harass their opponents.[16] All this led to the gradual loss of legitimacy and relevance of the native tribunals in the eyes of the Africans, and Indigenous systems of dispute settlement continued to operate unofficially, even though they had been rendered illegal or outside of the law.[17]

Upon independence in 1963, the colonial legal structures and the English basis of state law were largely left intact, and there was no serious attempt to create a legal system based on African concepts of justice. Hence the reception clause and the repugnancy clause were retained in the Kenyan statute law.[18] Customary law was accorded a subservient position in the new hierarchy of laws and would henceforth "guide" the courts, whereas in colonial times, the native courts were at least obligated to apply native law and custom.

In the period immediately after independence in the 1960s, the overriding goal of African governments was national unity in the face of ethnic, racial, and religious plurality. The multiplicity of Indigenous justice systems was perceived as a hindrance to social and economic development, and a uniform legal system was desired.[19] The Kenyan government therefore sought to integrate the dual structure of the legal system. Shortly after independence, the parallel courts system was dismantled, the native courts abolished, and the existing English-style magistrates' courts vested were with both general and customary jurisdiction. However, this integration really amounted to mere Africanization of judicial personnel without any attempt to make structural changes.[20] At the same time, there was an attempt to harmonize or unify the customary laws of the various ethnic groups with the state law. The first step toward harmonization was taken through written restatements of customary law, which were efforts to ascertain the rules of customary law among the ethnic groups of Kenya, with a view to codifying them for easier application by the state courts.[21] These restatements had a rather rigid view of customary law as a system of rules rather than a dynamic process. Although the codification did not materialize, the continued reliance on these restatements by post-independence courts, has elevated them to quasi-codes and has perpetuated the process of ossification of customary law.[22]

The next step comprised the introduction of statutes that attempted to abolish or diminish the application of customary law and entrench Western law, particularly in the areas of marriage, succession, and land tenure.[23] However, these legislative attempts have largely been unsuccessful, owing to popular resistance to some of the proposed legislation. Even where legislation has been passed, it has not been effectively operationalized, largely due to the resilience of custom in the areas sought to be reformed. The expectation in official circles was that over time Indigenous legal systems would become irrelevant and ultimately disappear.[24] However, this prediction has proven untrue, and to this day, Indigenous justice systems remain strong, though not static due to far-reaching socio-economic and political change. In some instances, the state has appropriated the symbols of culture through its sponsorship of institutions ostensibly applying norms of Indigenous justice.[25] An example is the Land Disputes Tribunals that were created in the early 1990s to resolve simple land matters by local elders. However, these Tribunals were instituted hurriedly and for purposes of political expediency, and they suffer from problems of legitimacy due to their perceived partisanship, bureaucracy, and lack of accountability.[26]

Overall, the Kenyan state has not displayed a serious interest in the development of Indigenous legal processes. For instance, in the recent Expanded Legal Sector Reform Strategy Paper (ELSRSP), non-formal justice systems did not feature beyond rhetorical acknowledgement of their importance.[27] Similarly, there has been an absence of serious consideration of Indigenous legal systems in the formal law curriculum or in academic discussions. As Shivji remarks:

> [W]ithin the official academic and political discourse customary law has had very little presence except as a nuisance which ought to be modernized at the earliest convenience.... Academic research on customary law generally, and in particular on customary law as a terrain of alternative perspectives on rights and justice, is scanty.[28]

IV. FORMS AND CHARACTERISTICS OF INDIGENOUS JUSTICE SYSTEMS

Indigenous or informal justice systems in the East African region take a variety of forms, including family-based forums, community-based forums, and, more recently, initiatives assisted by non-government organizations (NGOs). Family-based forums include inter/intra-family and clan mediation, which derive their legitimacy from kinship ties and traditional authority. The clan's authority to make conclusive statements on custom is widely recognized, and it plays an important role in shaping day-to-day interaction, particularly in the rural areas.[29] For instance, in the famous Kenyan burial dispute known as the *S.M. Otieno Case*,[30] the Umira Kager clan of the deceased featured prominently as a party to the suit. Family-based forums generally intervene in matters involving disputes between spouses, co-wives or in-laws, disputes about inheritance of property, and issues relating to witchcraft. However, it should be noted that although the clan is considered a traditional institution, it also exhibits certain traits of modernity. For instance, many clans in Kenya are formally registered under statute and have written rules.[31] Clans also have an interactive relationship with the formal courts, and courts may sometimes refer a matter for resolution by the clan. Further, the decisions of some clans are sometimes recorded in court and form the basis of court orders.[32]

Community-based forums include arrangements involving neighbours or village elders as mediators in interpersonal disputes, "community courts" set up in the urban areas, urban "vigilante" or community policing groups established for the maintenance of neighbourhood security, and adjudication arrangements set up by associations of traders, artisans, and self-help groups.[33]

Disputes may also be referred to chiefs and assistant chiefs who are local administrators, constituting the lowest rungs of the state administrative machinery. These have a broad statutory mandate to maintain law and order at the local level, and although dispute settlement is not explicitly provided for, they frequently adjudicate disputes referred to them by families, clan elders, and village elders, particularly involving family members, neighbours, landlords, and tenants. Although this kind of dispute settlement is informal, chiefs, in fact, have an array of coercive state powers, such as the power to summon and to make orders, which they routinely utilize. Disputes decided by chiefs may be referred to the more senior administrative officials: the district officers and district commissioners. Rarely do matters proceed to the formal courts, and usually, they do so only as a last resort. There is an intricate interrelation between the clan and local administrators, who work closely together and rely on each other's support to boost their respective authority at the grassroots level, and this further obscures the divide between the official/formal and the unofficial or informal systems.[34]

In addition, a number of NGOs have recently established justice forums, usually with the support of community activists and mostly for the amicable settlement of disputes in areas affected by armed conflict. These forums draw on community norms with some adaptations, such as requiring the representation of women and youth in decision-making. In some cases, these forums have revitalized existing traditional systems, while in others, they have supported the emergence of alternative community-based systems.[35] These forums generally aim at providing financial and logistical support, as well as capacity-building geared toward strengthening community-based dispute settlement. One example is the Centre for Conflict Research that facilitated the "peace elders' initiative" in the Laikipia District, a district which has experienced inter-ethnic hostilities.[36] In other cases, NGOs in conjunction with bilateral agencies deal with issues of sustainable and secure livelihoods, particularly in the pastoralist regions. These forums support the use of community-based systems for resolving conflicts over resources such as water and cattle theft.[37]

Indigenous justice systems in Africa share similar attributes with informal justice systems in general. One of the advantages of non-state justice systems in Africa is their affordability and accessibility. In rural areas that are not well served by formal institutions such as courts, these informal structures, employing a blend of customary norms and varying localized understandings of official law, offer a forum of first resort for the vindication of rights claims.[38] Indigenous justice systems do not suffer from many of the difficulties of the formal system. The proceedings are quick and take place within walking distance of the involved. They are conducted in the local language in a manner understandable by everyone involved and by people known to the disputants, as opposed to impersonal state officials. The procedure is informal with no technical procedural or evidentiary rules.[39]

Another feature of Indigenous justice systems is their flexibility, both procedural and normative. In terms of procedure, the flexibility allows disputants to simply tell their stories as they consider relevant, without limitations imposed by strict evidentiary or procedural rules. Apart from providing a complete exposition of the circumstances of the case, this also allows for a "sanctioned purge of anger and emotions."[40] In normative terms, local norms and values are constantly changing through practice and adaptation to new situations. This flexibility allows for responsiveness to specific situations, rather than a mechanical or rigid application of "custom" (as defined by written codes) or of technical legal rules.[41] The flexibility in the application of customary norms facilitates solutions based on compromise rather than precedent. In reaching a solution, the informal forum considers a broad range of issues focussing on the underlying reasons for the conflict, with a view to preventing recurrence in the future. This therefore means that similar cases need not be treated alike. Non-state justice systems also have the advantage of innovation in that local norms and processes may grant recognition to claims that the formal legal system may not entertain or to moral claims that are not acknowledged as "rights" in the formal legal system.[42]

Indigenous justice forums are also characterized by non-professionalization. No special training or skills are required for mediators or adjudicators, and ordinary or lay people are involved in decision-making. Further, these forums generally involve a high degree of public participation, including that of people not directly affected by the dispute, as the conflict is seen as belonging to the community because of the intricate kinship, economic, and social ties between members of the community.[43] A related feature of non-state justice forums is the emphasis laid on reaching consensus and compromise. The dispute is not isolated from its overall context, and these forums therefore seek solutions that maximize social harmony and abate group conflict or tension. This is exhibited by the restorative nature of solutions emanating from these forums, which generally focus on restitution and apology, rather than on the punishment of the offender.[44] In the absence of penal state sanctions like imprisonment, social pressure plays a powerful role in achieving compliance with decisions of non-state justice forums. Due to the high degree of public participation in reaching a solution, disobeying a ruling is tantamount to disobeying the entire community and may result in social ostracism, which involves the withdrawal by members of the community of both social contact and economic co-operation. Fear of supernatural sanctions also serves as a powerful incentive to restoring amicable relations.[45]

Further, dispute settlement processes in Africa are not seen in the abstract but are integrated into the socio-economic fabric. For instance, it was noted during field research the author recently carried out in Huruma, a poor urban settlement in Nairobi, that the mandate of village elders and chiefs extends beyond dispute settlement to other important aspects of community development. Hence, they were concerned with issues of security, environmental issues (*e.g.*, garbage disposal), health matters (*e.g.*, relating to HIV prevention and management), and civic education issues (*e.g.*, the recent constitutional referendum and the campaign against corruption). This may be contrasted with state courts, which are established primarily for the resolution of disputes and whose role is not perceived as embracing socio-economic development.

v. Criticisms Leveled Against Indigenous Justice Systems

Despite the strengths outlined above, Indigenous justice systems in East Africa are characterized by a number of weaknesses. First, a person's ability to access certain non-state justice forums, such as clans and the local administrators is dependent on their position within the social network. Hence, socio-economic status and gender are relevant factors, and the poor and less powerful, as well as youth and women, are disadvantaged in this regard.[46] To a large extent, these factors also determine the power and knowledge required for a person to participate effectively in defining the local norms and in making use of both local fora and formal legal institutions to his/her advantage.[47] This accords with Merry's observation that in small-scale communities, mediated settlements usually reflect the status inequalities between disputants, and a mutually acceptable solution tends to be one where the less powerful party gives up more.[48]

Further, with regard to intra-family disputes, it has been observed that in non-state justice forums, certain engrained ideas about authority and gender roles seem to constrain open deliberation on the facts in a dispute, and they dictate a resort to idealized statements of custom that necessitate particular outcomes. These tacitly-defined boundaries of authority operate to the disadvantage of women. For example, men, rather than women, are perceived as having authority to deal with issues relating to negotiating and financing the purchase of land.[49]

In addition, in local non-state justice forums, women and youth are marginalized as far as decision-making is concerned. With few exceptions, membership and leadership positions in important social forums are held by men. Since African societies generally venerate age, such men generally tend to be of the older generation.[50] Participation in decision-making is important, as it has consequences on whose voice is heard in the process of shaping custom through local practice. Therefore, it is not just a question of women occupying visible positions of leadership, but it is also a question of changing the public perception of women's membership and leadership status in important social institutions.[51]

Local justice forums have also been criticized as being subject to manipulation, prejudice, and subjectivity in their operation, which sometimes results in abuses of the system of community justice. Traditional structures are also prone to politicization, corruption, and abuse, and this has delegitimized these systems in the eyes of some citizens.[52]

Certain forms of non-state justice forums present problems in terms of compliance with human rights standards. Some vigilante groups tend to utilize excessive physical sanctions for dealing with reputed criminals where it is perceived that the state justice system is too lenient on them. For example, in Tanzania, *sungusungu* operatives have been accused of excessive force in their dealings against criminal activity.[53] In Kenya, the *Mungiki* group, which claims to derive its source from traditional norms, is known for its brutality which includes violence against women.[54] One scholar has termed such forms of popular justice, which assume the sovereignty and powers of the state, as "irresponsible," as opposed to "responsible" forms that recognize the authority of the state, such as community courts derived from traditional authority.[55] Other criticisms leveled against non-state forms of justice are the lack of harmonization, owing to the fact that they are as varied as the local communities and ethnic groups concerned, and they are therefore subject to varied interpretations and applications. It is also contended that the localized nature of these conflict management strategies fosters the continuation of ethnic hegemony.[56] Notwithstanding some of the negative aspects of Indigenous justice systems, these systems continue to be regularly used, which begs the question of why this is so.

VI. REASONS FOR THE PERSISTENCE OF INDIGENOUS JUSTICE SYSTEMS

There are two main factors that may explain the persistence of Indigenous justice systems. The first relates to access to state justice systems, while the other concerns the legitimacy of state justice systems. The issue of legitimacy raises fundamental concerns that must be addressed in any serious attempt to deal with the question of Indigenous law. The access issue is secondary and can only be properly addressed in a context where the underlying issue of legitimacy of state justice is given serious attention.

A. Access to State Justice Systems

Despite the imposition of Western-based state law, one of the main explanations for the persistence of non-state justice systems in African countries is the incomplete reach of the state's legal structures. This is due to the weak nature of most African states. Schärf defines a "weak state" or "troubled state" as one that is unable to provide basic services to its citizens.[57] This is even so when such a state uses its armed forces to ensure regime security rather than citizen security. In the areas the state fails to serve the needs of its citizens, citizens tend to create their own structures and processes to provide goods and services such as security, schools, hospitals, and dispute resolution mechanisms.[58] In the administration of justice, the state justice systems in Africa are few, inefficient, and barely penetrate the day-to-day lives of the populace, particularly in the rural areas.[59] Lack of access to formal institutions due to the sparse distribution of courts, lack of access to lawyers and legal aid, and the high financial cost of litigation are therefore major factors in the persistence of non-state justice systems in Africa. Further, the long delays, cumbersome procedures, and technicality of legal proceedings, coupled with legal illiteracy, add to the alienation of the population from the court process.[60]

These are the most cited reasons, and there is an underlying assumption that if only the issue of access to the state courts were resolved, then these courts would be the main arena for justice. Legal aid and legal literacy are therefore seen to be the answer. However, even if the African state were to obtain sufficient resources to create greater access to the formal court system, it is questionable whether this would necessarily result in substantive justice.

B. Legitimacy of State Justice Systems

There is a deeper issue of the legitimacy of the state court system and its ability to meet the people's aspirations of justice, which has roots in the African peoples' general disenchantment with the state's structures. Mutua contends that the development of the state in Africa differs so radically from its European counterpart that the traditional Western liberal conception of the relationship between the individual and the state is of limited applicability to the African legal realm.[61] This is because the modern African state was an artifice imposed by European colonial powers on African ethnopolitical societies, and it was thus not the result of organic growth of those societies. According to Mutua, the failure of the post-colonial state points to the inability of the state to inspire loyalty and a sense of national identity. This disconnection between the people and the state amounts to "a crisis of cultural and philosophical identity: the delegitimation of [African] values, notions, and philosophies about the individual, society, politics, and nature developed over centuries."[62]

In the context of the administration of justice, Africans are generally disenchanted with the colonial-based system, which they perceive as alien, prone to abuse and corruption, and antithetical to the African concept and practice of justice.[63] Indigenous institutions of social control therefore remain relevant in the affairs of the people, particularly in the rural areas where the majority of Africans reside. The above observation points to differences in legal consciousness and legal culture. Legal consciousness has been defined to mean how people make sense of law and legal institutions, as well as how people give meaning to their law-related experiences and actions.[64] Legal consciousness provides people with important interpretive frameworks, even outside legal institutions such as courts.[65] African scholars in recent times have argued that the failure of the Western model of justice arises from its incompatibility with African notions of justice.[66] It has been argued that despite the great diversity of African societies, it is possible to identify common aspects in the normative ordering of Africans consistent with the notion of African law.[67] Notwithstanding the profound socio-economic and political changes arising from the colonial encounter, African societies are still based on kinship structures and reciprocal obligations, with emphasis on the solidarity of the community and harmonious relations between individuals. The African justice system and dispute resolution process has always been a collective enterprise, with the involvement in various ways of the whole community.[68] Legal rights and duties are primarily attached to a group rather than to individuals, and the individual plays a relatively subordinate part. While this does not mean that the individual has no place, it does to a large extent subordinate the individual's interests to those of the group, and certainly it differs from, and may be contrasted with, the Western notion of rights and liberties that is constructed around the concept of the abstract individual.[69]

Thus, the state structures of justice, based as they are (if only notionally) on Western ideas of justice, are not seen as meeting the aspirations of the people. For example, in the area of criminal justice, the formal court system lays emphasis on the punishment of the individual, whereas the African notion of justice emphasizes the restorative aspect that compensates the victim and his or her family for the wrong done.[70] It may also be questioned whether the formal court system is appropriate for the resolution of disputes between people living in rural villages or urban informal settlements that are dominated by multi-stranded relationships, where the breaking of individual social relationships can affect the social and economic co-operation on which the community depends.[71]

VII. INCORPORATION OF INDIGENOUS JUSTICE SYSTEMS INTO FORMAL STATE STRUCTURES

For purposes of clarity, it should be noted that incorporation may be understood in two senses. In post-independence Kenya, discussions of integration or unification of the legal system have related specifically to institutions of state customary law: this is related to the native courts and the body of customary rules constructed and interpreted by the state's judicial and administrative functionaries. Thus, integration of the court system primarily meant the accommodation of the native courts within the post-colonial legal systems through the abolition of the native courts and the vesting of customary jurisdiction in the magistrates' courts.[72] This is the first sense of incorporation. As already seen, the main objective for this exercise was to dismantle the dual legal system in the interests of national unity. Hence, integration was not conceived as relating to traditional or Indigenous systems that operate outside the framework of state structures.

The second sense of incorporation relates to the accommodation of existing Indigenous justice systems within the state's legal system, with the intent that the norms and values of Indigenous systems will continue to thrive in the new arrangement. This type of incorporation has been attempted in a number of post-colonial states, and it has involved either the creation of new institutions ostensibly enforcing Indigenous norms or the co-option of existing Indigenous structures into the formal state system.[73] Examples include the Nyaya Panchayat in India, the Primary Courts in Tanzania, and the Chiefs' Courts in Zimbabwe. Kenya has not attempted this type of incorporation. The main rationale for incorporating Indigenous into the formal state system is:

> to combine the virtues of traditional legal systems (accessibility, informality, economy of time and money, and familiarity of legal norms) with those of the state legal system (impartiality, uniformity of law and procedures, and legitimacy).[74]

However, the experience of a number of countries shows that these attempts are generally unsuccessful. Linking the two systems tends to undermine the positive attributes of the informal system. First, the process loses its voluntary character, and its reliance on social sanctions is drastically reduced as public participation in the process is curtailed, while at the same time there is an emphasis on greater technicality and more procedural rules.[75] For example, the Primary Courts in Tanzania, although originally intended to resemble informal traditional courts, ended up attempting to operate like formal higher courts by insisting on formal procedural requirements, thus reducing accessibility.[76] The paradox of attempting to maintain informality of procedure, and yet applying statutory rules of law, is that the informal courts end up doing neither task well, and the tendency is for the informal model to give way to dictates of the state system.[77]

Another danger of incorporation is that the decisions of the informal courts are liable to be appealed in the higher courts, on the ground of procedural error, when they decide in disregard of the law or on a basis other than law; this defeats the purpose of establishing informal courts in the first place. This situation happened in the Nyaya Panchayats in India, which were created by the state to operate as traditional courts.[78] The usual "solution" to this problem is to severely restrict the jurisdiction of the informal or traditional courts, with these courts being relegated to the lowest tier of the state formal system, as happened in Tanzania and Zimbabwe. The effect of this is to remove all but the most trivial of cases from their jurisdiction.[79]

A further problem of incorporating informal justice systems into the state system is that it has the effect of hardening the informal systems, thus making them unable to adapt to changing conditions and community needs. This is similar to the ossification of customary law in the colonial native courts, owing to the courts' reliance on versions of customary law (usually based on written restatements) that were often archaic and out of touch with the evolving realities in the community.[80] Incorporation can also lead to a vacuum in the community, as Indigenous systems serve community purposes other than merely resolving disputes.

VIII. CHANGING THE TERMS OF DEBATE: JUSTICE AS THE GOAL OF REFORM

There is a need to move the debate beyond the question of incorporation of Indigenous justice systems into the state system to asking what best serves the needs of justice for ordinary citizens, particularly the poor. This task requires a serious engagement with Indigenous systems, in their own right, as systems that offer an alternative perspective of rights and justice, and there needs to be a consideration of what role they can play in ensuring access to substantive justice. This is being done in South Africa by the South African Law Commission in respect of traditional and community-based courts.[81] There are no easy answers, but there is certainly a need for a fundamental rethinking of justice systems and a shift from an approach that has centred on the state to one that focusses on people's perspectives of fairness, rights and justice.[82] Such an approach avoids the two extremes of, on the one hand, ignoring Indigenous justice systems or trying to stamp them out, or on the other hand, romanticizing them and glossing over their weaknesses.

Administration of justice should be viewed in a holistic manner as part of the overall context of community development and not as detached from it. Any reform efforts should also be multi-faceted and should involve not just the state but all stakeholders, including civil society, elders, religious leaders, women, youth, and NGOs.[83] In this context, process should have a more important place than rules.[84] Community structures have the most potential for realizing a people-centred justice, as there is more scope for community participation and consensus building. While the initiatives of some NGOs in conflict resolution are holistic, in that they are linked to a response to tangible needs, there arises the question of who drives the NGOs' agenda, which is linked to the question of funding and long-term sustainability.

Bearing in mind the semi-autonomous relationship between Indigenous and state justice systems, a focus on community-based structures should not mean insulation from the formal legal system. Paralegals working in communities can help bridge the gap between formal and informal systems, for instance through the promotion of rights awareness, referrals, and mediation. There is also a need to forge partnerships with civil society groups, and it may be necessary to strengthen the capacity of the Indigenous justice system (*e.g.*, through training in mediation, problem-solving skills, and referrals). Evidence from the field suggests that community justice forums tend to welcome this type of input.[85] Some of the weaknesses of Indigenous justice systems, such as poor accountability and the marginalization of women and youth, would also need to be addressed. However, we should guard against the assumption that it is always Indigenous systems that need training and acknowledge that the functionaries of the formal state systems also need to learn about democratization of justice.

For instance, reform in the formal system should include a change of attitudes, decentralization, and simplification of procedure. The formal courts and the police should also be made more aware of existing informal justice mechanisms and should be encouraged to refer appropriate cases by agreement of the parties, as this would enable people to have more real choices. All of these potential changes emphasize the importance of consultation, participation, and downward accountability, among other aspects, so that people can have a sense of ownership of the process. The above are tentative suggestions for change. In order to have a well-planned scheme of reform, there is a need for more research into the actual operation of Indigenous justice systems in Kenya and their relationship with the state system. Currently, there is a paucity of such research.

IX. CONCLUSION

The Kenyan state needs to wake up from its lethargy in dealing with Indigenous justice systems as viable avenues for the delivery of justice. As Indigenous systems often offer the kind of justice most accessible and meaningful to the populace, there is a need to engage with these systems in their own right and move from a state-centric vision of justice to one that is centred on people's needs. However, Indigenous and state justice systems should not be viewed as being in competition with each other; rather, the concern ought to be about how to support and improve each system in such a way that its capacity for delivering justice is enhanced. This endeavour calls for meaningful partnerships between Indigenous and state justice systems as well as all concerned stakeholders. Ultimately, the aim should be to develop structures of justice in which broader African cultural values can become a part of the context in which the law, as a whole, operates.

NOTES

NOTE TO FOREWORD

1   Chad Skelton, "When should the police shoot?" *Vancouver Sun*, 18 Aug. 2007, A4.

NOTE TO INTRODUCTION

1   Thomas Gordon, *Leader Effectiveness Training* (New York: Wyden Books, 1977), 244.

NOTES TO CHAPTER ONE

1   Being Schedule B to the *Canada Act 1982* (UK), 1982, c. 11.

2   The full provision states: "The existing aboriginal and treaty rights of the aboriginal peoples of Canada are hereby recognized and affirmed."

3   *R. v. Van der Peet* [1996] S.C.J. No. 77 [1996] 2 S.C.R. 507.

4   *Ibid.*, at paras. 26-43.

5   *Ibid.*, at paras. 30, 32.

6   *Ibid.*, at para. 42, quoting Mark D. Walters, "British Imperial Constitutional Law and Aboriginal Rights: A Comment on *Delgamuukw* v. *British Columbia*" (1992) 17 Queen's L.J. 350, at 412-13; and Brian Slattery, "The Legal Basis of Aboriginal Title," in *Aboriginal Title in British Columbia: Delgamuukw v. The Queen*, ed., F. Cassidy (Lantzville, BC: Oolichan Books, 1992), at 120-21.

7   *Van der Peet, supra* note 3, at paras. 44-46, 55-56, 60-62.

8   *Ibid.*, at paras. 63-64, 73.

9   *Ibid.*, at paras. 76-91.

10   *Ibid.*, at para. 69.

11   This would be true of the portions of Eastern Canada encountered by early English and French explorers and adventurers. See, *e.g.*, Brian Slattery, "French Claims in North America, 1500-59," *Canadian Historical Review* 59 (1978): 139.

12   The following sections draw on Brian Slattery, "Making Sense of Aboriginal and Treaty Rights" (2000) 79 Can. Bar Rev. 196, at 211-15; and Brian Slattery, "A Taxonomy of Aboriginal Rights," in *Let Right Be Done: Calder, Aboriginal Title, and the Future of Indigenous Rights*, eds., Hamar Foster, Heather Raven & Jeremy Webber (Vancouver: University of British Columbia Press, 2007), 111-28.

13   *Supra* note 3, at para. 69.

14   *Delgamuukw* v. *British Columbia* [1997] S.C.J. No. 108 [1997] 3 S.C.R. 1010.

15   *Ibid.*, at paras. 116-32.

16 For discussion of the right of cultural integrity in international law, see S. James Anaya, *Indigenous Peoples in International Law* (New York: Oxford University Press, 1996), 98-104.

17 For fuller discussion, see Slattery, "A Taxonomy of Aboriginal Rights," *supra* note 12, which the following account summarizes.

18 The treaty-making power is reviewed in *R.* v. *Sioui* [1990] S.C.J. No. 48 [1990] 1 S.C.R. 1025, at 1037-43.

19 See *Connolly* v. *Woolrich* (1867), 17 R.J.R.Q. 75 (Que. S.C.); *Casimel* v. *Insurance Corp. of British Columbia* [1993] B.C.J. No. 1834, 106 D.L.R. (4th) 720 (C.A.); *Van der Peet, supra* note 3, at paras. 38-40; *Delgamuukw, supra* note 14, at paras. 146-48; *Campbell* v. *British Columbia (Attorney General)* [2000] B.C.J. No. 1524, 189 D.L.R. (4th) 333, at paras. 83-136 (S.C.); *Mitchell* v. *Canada (Minister of National Revenue)* [2001] S.C.J. No. 33 [2001] 1 S.C.R. 911, at paras. 9-10, 61-64, 141-54.

20 *Van der Peet, supra* note 3, at para. 263. Justice McLachlin was dissenting, but not on this point.

21 *R.* v. *Sparrow* [1990] S.C.J. No. 49 [1990] 1 S.C.R. 1075, at 1108, para. 59. See also *Guerin* v. *Canada* [1984] S.C.J. No. 45 [1984] 2 S.C.R. 335; *Van der Peet, supra* note 3, at paras. 24-25; *Wewaykum Indian Band* v. *Canada* [2002] S.C.J. No. 79 [2002] 4 S.C.R. 245.

22 *Mitchell* v. *Canada (Minister of National Revenue)* [2001] S.C.J. No. 33, 1 S.C.R. 911, at para. 9; *Wewaykum Indian Band, ibid.*, at paras. 79-80.

23 *Haida Nation* v. *British Columbia (Minister of Forests)* [2004] S.C.J. No. 70 [2004] 3 S.C.R. 511, at paras. 16-25.

24 *Ibid.*, at para. 18. See also *Wewaykum Indian Band, supra* note 21, at paras. 72-85.

25 Royal Commission on Aboriginal Peoples, *Report of the Royal Commission on Aboriginal Peoples*, vol. 2 (Ottawa: Minister of Supply and Services Canada, 1996), 163-244; *Campbell, supra* note 19; Brian Slattery, "First Nations and the Constitution: A Question of Trust" (1992) 71 Can. Bar Rev. 261, at 278-87.

26 *Sioui, supra* note 18, at 1054-55.

27 *Ibid.*, para. 74.

28 See s. 92, *Constitution Act, 1867* (UK), 30 & 31 Vict., c. 3, reprinted in R.S.C. 1985, App. II, No. 5; and s. 45 of the *Constitution Act, 1982, supra* note 1.

29 The following discussion draws on Slattery, "Making Sense of Aboriginal and Treaty Rights," *supra* note 12, at 213-14.

30 *R.* v. *Pamajewon* [1996] S.C.J. No. 20 [1996] 2 S.C.R. 821, at paras. 23-30.

31 See *R.* v. *Côté* [1996] S.C.J. No. 93 [1996] 3 S.C.R. 139, at paras. 42-54; *R.* v. *Adams* [1996] S.C.J. No. 87 [1996] 3 S.C.R. 101, at paras. 31-33; Brian Slattery, "Understanding Aboriginal Rights" (1987) Can. Bar Rev. 727 at 736-41.

32 See *Adams, ibid.*, at paras. 27-28; *R.* v. *Marshall*; *R.* v. *Bernard* [2005] S.C.J. No. 44 [2005] 2 S.C.R. 220, at paras. 58-59, 66.

33 Reproduced in *Sioui, supra* note 18, at 1031, para. 5.

34 *Ibid.*, esp. at 1060, 1070.

35 Oren Lyons, "Spirituality, Equality, and Natural Law," in *Pathways to Self-Determination: Canadian Indians and the Canadian State*, eds., Leroy Little Bear, Menno Boldt & J. Anthony Long (Toronto: University of Toronto Press, 1984), 5-6.

36 Assembly of First Nations, *Towards Rebirth of First Nations Languages* (Ottawa: AFN, 1992), 14; quoted in Canada, Task Force on Aboriginal Languages and Cultures, *Towards a New Beginning: A Foundational Report for a Strategy to Revitalize Indian, Inuit and Métis Languages and Cultures* (Ottawa: Department of Canadian Heritage, 2005), 21. (Available online at www.aboriginallanguagestaskforce.ca.)

37 *Supra* note 3.

38 R.S.C. 1985, App. II, No. 1. The most accurate printed text is found in Clarence S. Brigham, ed., *British Royal Proclamations Relating to America* (Worcester, Mass.: American Antiquarian Society, 1911), 212.

39 *Van der Peet, supra* note 3, at para. 272 (italics in original).

40 *R. v. Marshall* [1999] S.C.J. No. 55 [1999] 3 S.C.R. 456.

41 *Ibid.*, at para. 3.

42 *Ibid.*, at para. 25.

43 *Ibid.*, at paras. 56-59.

44 See McLachlin J.'s apt remarks in *Van der Peet, supra* note 3, at para. 242.

45 *Ibid.*, at para. 56.

46 *Ibid.*, at para. 72.

47 For the sources of this law, see Brian Slattery, "Making Sense of Aboriginal and Treaty Rights," *supra* note 12, at 198-206.

48 *Supra* note 3, at para. 227.

49 *Ibid.*, at para. 278.

50 *Ibid.*, at para. 279.

51 *Ibid.*, at para. 280.

52 *R. v. Sappier; R. v. Gray* [2006] S.C.J. No. 54 [2006] 2 S.C.R. 686.

53 *Ibid.*, at paras. 37-40, 45. Justice Binnie dissented on the precise scope of the Aboriginal right in question; otherwise, however, he agreed with the majority reasons.

54 *Ibid.*, at para. 40.

55 *Ibid.*, at para. 37.

56 *Ibid.*, at para. 24.

57 *Ibid.*, at para. 25.

58 *Ibid.*, at para. 48; quoting McLachlin C.J. in *Marshall/Bernard, supra* note 32, at para. 25.

59 *Ibid.*, at para. 49; quoting Dickson C.J. in *Sparrow, supra* note 21, at 1093, and Slattery, "Understanding Aboriginal Rights," *supra* note 31, at 782.

60 *Sappier/Gray, ibid.*

61 For the status of Indigenous rights in international law, see Anaya, *supra* note 16.

62 *Supra* note 23, at para. 17; the quotation is from *Delgamuukw, supra* note 14, at para. 186, which quotes, in turn, *Van der Peet, supra* note 3, at para. 31.

63 For a good survey, see Colin G. Calloway, *New Worlds for All: Indians, Europeans, and the Remaking of Early America* (Baltimore: Johns Hopkins University Press, 1997).

64 See Bruce G. Trigger & William R. Swagerty, "Entertaining Strangers: North America in the Sixteenth Century," in *The Cambridge History of the Native Peoples of the Americas,* vol. 1, eds., Bruce G. Trigger & Wilcomb E. Washburn (Cambridge: Cambridge University Press, 1996), 363. Syphilis was probably carried back to Europe as early as 1493.

65 *Supra* note 3.

66 *Delgamuukw, supra* note 14, at para. 144.

67 *Ibid.*, at para. 145.

68 *Ibid.*

69 *Ibid.*

70 *R. v. Powley* [2003] S.C.J. No. 43 [2003] 2 S.C.R. 207.

71 Section 35(2) of the *Constitution Act, 1982,* provides: "In this Act, 'aboriginal peoples of Canada' includes the Indian, Inuit and Métis peoples of Canada."

72 *Van der Peet, supra* note 3, at para. 67.

73 *Powley, supra* note 70, at paras. 15-18, 36-38.

74 See *Sparrow, supra* note 21, at 1101-19.

75 See Brian Slattery, "The Metamorphosis of Aboriginal Title" (2006) 85 Can. Bar Rev. 255 at 281-86, from which the following discussion draws.

76 *Mikisew Cree First Nation* v. *Canada (Minister of Canadian Heritage)* [2005] S.C.J. No. 71 [2005] 3 S.C.R. 388, at para. 1.

77 For the distinction between an inner core and a negotiated penumbra as applied to Aboriginal governmental rights, see Royal Commission on Aboriginal Peoples, *Partners in Confederation: Aboriginal Peoples, Self-Government, and the Constitution* (Ottawa: Minister of Supply and Services Canada, 1993), 36-48; *Report of the Royal Commission on Aboriginal Peoples, supra* note 25, vol. 2, 213-24.

78 For helpful discussion, see Sonia Lawrence and Patrick Macklem, "From Consultation to Reconciliation: Aboriginal Rights and the Crown's Duty to Consult" (2000) 79 Can. Bar Rev. 252, esp. at 270-72; Shin Imai, "Sound Science, Careful Policy Analysis, and Ongoing Relationships: Integrating Litigation and

Negotiation in Aboriginal Lands and Resources Disputes" (2003) 41 Osgoode Hall L.J. 587; Shin Imai, "Creating Disincentives to Negotiate: *Mitchell* v. *M.N.R.*'s Potential Effect on Dispute Resolution" (2003) 22 Windsor Y.B. Access Just. 309.

79 *Haida Nation, supra* note 23; *Taku River Tlingit First Nation* v. *British Columbia (Project Assessment Director)* [2004] S.C.J. No. 69 [2004] 3 S.C.R. 550. For fuller discussion, see Brian Slattery, "Aboriginal Rights and the Honour of the Crown" (2005) 29 S.C.L.R. (2d) 433.

80 *Haida Nation, ibid.*, at para. 32; *Taku River, ibid.*, at para. 24.

81 *Haida Nation, ibid.*, at para. 25.

82 *Ibid.*, at para. 32 (emphasis added).

83 *Van der Peet, supra* note 3, at para. 262.

NOTES TO CHAPTER TWO

1 See information and publications of the Harvard Project on American Indian Economic Development [online] www.ksg.harvard.edu/hpaied/.

2 See *e.g.*, Melvin H. Smith, QC, *Our Home Or Native Land?* (Toronto: Stoddart Co, Limited, 1996); *Campbell v. British Columbia (Attorney General)* [2000] 4 C.N.L.R. 1.

3 *R. v. Van der Peet* [1996] 2 S.C.R. 507.

4 Brian Slattery, "The Generative Structure of Aboriginal Rights," Chapter 1 herein, at 20.

5 *Ibid.*

6 *Haida Nation* v. *British Columbia (Minister of Forests)* [2004] 3 S.C.R. 511, at para. 38.

7 Slattery, *supra* note 4 at 46.

8 See especially *Constitution Act, 1867* (UK), 30 & 31 Victoria, c. 3, s. 91, 92, reprinted in R.S.C. 1985, App. II, No. 5.

9 *Constitution Act, 1982*, being Schedule B to the *Canada Act 1982* (UK), 1982, c. 11.

10 *R. v. Sparrow* [1990] 1 S.C.R. 1075.

11 *Restructuring the Relationship: Report of the Royal Commission on Aboriginal Peoples*, vol. 2 (Ottawa: Supply and Services Canada, 1996). According to the Royal Commission on Aboriginal Peoples (RCAP), the core of Aboriginal jurisdiction includes the following matters: 1) all matters that are vital to the life and welfare of a particular Aboriginal people, their culture, and their identity; 2) matters that do not have a major impact on adjacent jurisdictions; and 3) matters that are not otherwise the object of transcendent federal or provincial concern. Jurisdiction relating to the "core" can be exercised by Aboriginal peoples unilaterally, without the necessity of concluding self-government agreements with other governments.

12 R.S.C. 1985, c. I-5, s. 88.

13 These exceptions are subject to the terms of any treaty and subject to federal laws.

14 [1980] 1 S.C.R. 1031, per Beetz, J.

15 Being Schedule B to the *Canada Act 1982* (UK), 1982, c. 11, s. 35.

16 Peter W. Hogg, *Constitutional Law of Canada*, looseleaf (Scarborough: Carswell, 1997), at 27-4.

17 Slattery, *supra* note 4 at 29.

18 Alexander Morris, "The Qu'Appelle Treaty, Number 4," in *The Treaties of Canada with the Indians of Manitoba and the North-West Territories including The Negotiations on which they were based* (Toronto: Belfords, Clarke & Co., 1880), 333.

19 The country was created by what is now known as the *Constitution Act, 1867* (*supra* note 8), but was originally the *British North America Act, 1867*, an Act of the Parliament at Westminster. Patriation of the Canadian constitution was obtained through the enactment of another piece of British legislation, the *Canada Act 1982* ((UK), 1982, c. 11). Saskatchewan was created by an Act of the federal Parliament that was enacted in 1905 (*Saskatchewan Act*, S.S. 1905, 4-5 Edw. VII, c. 42).

20 David E. Smith, "Saskatchewan: Approximating the Ideal," *Provincial and Territorial Legislatures in Canada*, eds., Gary Levy & Graham White (Toronto: University of Toronto Press, 1989), 49.

21 *Copyright Act*, R.S.C. 1985, c. C-42. This Act has since been rewritten to explicitly refer to computer software programs as literary works, but the courts arrived at this conclusion first.

22 Some statutes, such as the *Contributory Negligence Act*, R.S.S. 1978, c. C-31, regulate areas of the law of negligence where the common law consequences have been considered inappropriate.

23 See, *e.g.*, *An Act to incorporate The House of Jacob (Beth Yakov) of the City of Regina*, S.S., 1915, c. 44; *An Act to incorporate the Western Canadian Bible Institute of the Christian and Missionary Alliance*, S.S. 1949, c. 129.

24 See *e.g.*, *An Act to incorporate The Yorkton Agricultural and Industrial Exhibition Association, Limited*, S.S. 1909, c. 48.

25 See *e.g.*, *An Act to incorporate St. Peter's College, Muenster*, S.S. 1968, c. 96.

26 See *e.g.*, *An Act to incorporate Saskatchewan Hospital Association*, S.S. 1959, c. 117.

27 R.S.S. 1978, c. B-10.

28 S.S. 1945, c. 17.

29 See additional information about the Conference and about its Commercial Law Strategy [online] www.ulcc.ca.

30 R.S.S. 1978, c. C-29.

31 Part I of the *Constitution Act, 1982*, being Schedule B to the *Canada Act 1982* (UK), 1982, c. 11.

32 [1888] C.J.C. No. 1, 14 App. Cas. 46.

1 A work to begin with would be Duncan Ivison, Paul Patton & Will Sanders, eds., *Political Theory and the Rights of Indigenous Peoples* (Cambridge, UK: Cambridge University Press, 2000).

2 A similar definition can be found in Charles Sanders Peirce, "'Pragmatism' Defined," in *Peirce on Signs: Writings on Semiotic by Charles Sanders Peirce*, ed. James Hoopes (Chapel Hill: University of North Carolina Press, 1991), 246. For an excellent introduction to pragmatic ethics, see John Dewey, *Theory of the Moral Life* (New York: Holt, 1932).

3 These questions are treated fairly well in Mike Sandbothe & William Egginton, eds., *The Pragmatic Turn in Philosophy: Contemporary Engagements between Analytic and Continental Thought* (Albany: SUNY Press, 2004).

4 For a good analysis of this problem in environmental matters, see Andrew Light, "Environmental Pragmatism as Philosophy or Metaphilosophy?" in *Environmental Pragmatism*, eds., A. Light & E. Katz (London: Routledge, 1996), 325.

5 One can read the many reports of the Human Rights Commission of the United Nations that blame Canada for the situation of its Aboriginal peoples. For a very thorough analysis, see Royal Commission on Aboriginal Peoples, *Final Report*, vol. 5 (Ottawa: Minister of Supply and Services Canada, 1996).

6 For a thorough argument on the ascendancy of pragmatism over other political philosophies in producing common goals, see Joseph Heath, "A Pragmatist Theory of Convergence," 24 *Canadian Journal of Philosophy*, 24 (1998): 149.

7 John Rawls, *A Theory of Justice* (Cambridge, MA: Belknap Press of Harvard University Press, 1971).

8 *Ibid.*, 3.

9 *Ibid.*, 13ff.

10 *R. v. Gladstone* [1996] 2 S.C.R. 774 at 61.

11 *Calder v. AG (BC)* [1973] S.C.R. 313.

12 This policy is often referred to as the "White Paper of 1969," Department of Indian Affairs and Northern Development, *Statement of the Government of Canada on Indian Policy* (Ottawa: Queen's Printer, 1969).

13 *Agreement Concerning A New Relationship between le Gouvernement du Québec and the Crees Of Québec*, www.autochtones.gouv.qc.ca/relations_autochtones/ententes/cris/entente-020207_en.pdf (accessed 10 July 2007).

14 *James Bay and Northern Quebec Agreement* (11 Nov. 1975), www.gcc.ca/pdf/LEG000000006.pdf.

15 *Paix des Braves, supra* note 13, s. 2.3.

16 The recognition paradigm was famously developed by Georg Wilhelm Friedrich Hegel in *Phenomenology of the Spirit*, trans. by A.V. Miller (Oxford: Oxford University Press, 1977), 111-19. Alexandre Kojève commented the master-slave

dialectic in a well-known and influential text, *Introduction à la lecture de Hegel* (Paris: Gallimard, 1947), 11-34. The last few decades have been rich with the development of recognition theories. The names of Charles Taylor and Axel Honneth come readily to mind. For a complete and thorough introduction, see Simon Thompson, *The Political Theory of Recognition: A Critical Introduction* (Cambridge, UK: Polity Press, 2006). For a postmodern approach to recognition, the author strongly recommends Patchen Markell, *Bound by Recognition* (Princeton: Princeton University Press, 2003).

17 Marc-Urbain Proulx & Josée Gauthier, "Renaissance Autochtone" in *L'Annuaire du Québec 2006*, eds., Antoine Robitaille & Michel Venne (Saint-Laurent: Fides, 2006), 521.

18 The treaty with the Innu nations was due to be signed in the course of 2005, but owing to the provincial government's procrastination and, to a lesser extent, quarrels between the Innu First Nations of Quebec, it has been postponed to an unknown date.

19 *Entente de principe d'ordre général entre les premières nations de Mamuitun et de Nutashkuan et les gouvernements du Québec et du Canada* (31 Mar. 2004), www.versuntraite.com/documentation/publications/EntentePrincipeInnus.pdf.

20 *Ibid.*, ss. 3.3.1.

21 *Ibid.*, s. 3.3.

22 *Ibid.*, ss. 13.1.5 [translated by author].

23 To be precise, the second "Whereas" clause of the preamble states: "WHEREAS this Agreement, concerning a global approach in favour of greater autonomy and greater responsibility on the part of the Crees for their development, will make possible an active and ongoing participation by the Crees in economic development activities on the James Bay Territory." *Paix des Braves, supra* note 13 at 1.

24 The notion of *Innu tshishe utshimau* is defined in the definition section of the AIP (*supra* note 19 at 2). There are 72 occurrences of *Innu tshishe utshimau* in the agreement, but the most interesting discussion is in the chapter on self-government (AIP, *supra* note 19, c. 8).

25 *Ibid.*, ss. 8.4.4.1 [translated by author].

26 In the same vein, see also the recognition of juridical status of First Nations (*ibid.*, s. 8.2) and interpreting ancestral rights as development capacities (*ibid.*, s. 2.1).

27 *Ibid.*, ss. 8.4.4.1.

28 *Ibid.*, ss. 8.3.1.2.

29 *Constitution Act*, 1867 (UK), 30 & 31 Vict., c. 3, s. 91, reprinted in R.S.C. 1985, App. II, No. 5 (Power of the Parliament).

30 AIP, *supra* note 19, ss. 8.4.2.1.

31 *Ibid.*, ss. 8.4.2.2. One may wonder what would constitute an Innu interpretative principle of the law. Although the literature is not abundant on this matter, John Borrows has developed a very compelling view of Aboriginal jurisprudence. See

e.g., John Borrows, *Recovering Canada: The Resurgence of Indigenous Law* (Toronto: University of Toronto, 2002).

32 AIP, *supra* note 19, s. 8.1; *Canadian Charter of Rights and Freedoms*, Part I of the *Constitution Act*, 1982, being Schedule B to the *Canada Act* 1982 (UK), 1982, c.11.

33 AIP, *supra* note 19 at 1 (Preamble), c. 2. 5 (Preamble), ss. 8.4.1.

34 *Ibid.* Chapter 9 of the AIP is devoted to the implementation of Innu tribunals and more generally, of an Innu system of law.

35 Assemblée Nationale du Québec, *Consultation générale sur le document intitulé Entente de principe d'ordre général entre les premières nations de Mamuitun et de Nutashkuan et le gouvernement du Québec et le gouvernement du Canada*, 36th Leg., 2nd Sess. (21 Jan. – 7 Mar. 2003), www.assnat.qc.ca/fra/Publications/debats/ci.htm.

36 Proulx & Gauthier, *supra* note 17.

37 The AIP distributes 300,000 square km. of shared territories called *Nitassinan* to Innu First Nations. The co-management extends not only to resource management but also to political powers (see the preceding discussion in subsection «C. Self-Government,» section III, at note 25). The *Paix des Braves* restates the JBQNA's distribution of roughly 1,000,000 square kilometers of land in shared management with Cree and other First Nations.

38 For an overview of his position concerning what he calls "Indigenous rights," see Will Kymlicka, "Theorizing Indigenous Rights" and "Indigenous Rights and Environmental Justice" in *Politics in the Vernacular* (Oxford: Oxford University Press, 2001). Also see Will Kymlicka, *Multicultural Citizenship* (Oxford: Clarendon Press, 1995).

39 This argument is elegantly deployed by Joseph Heath, "Culture: Choice or Circumstance?" 5:2 *Constellations* (1998): 183 at 193.

40 Patrick Macklem, *Indigenous Difference and the Constitution of Canada* (Toronto: University of Toronto Press, 2001).

41 *Ibid.*, 287.

42 A peaceful and long-lasting containment of self-determination conflicts is almost always directly related to autonomy agreements that provide "some combination of political recognition, greater rights and regional autonomy to the populations represented by [separatist] movements." Monty Marshall & Ted Robert Gurr, *Peace and Conflict, 2003: A Global Survey of Armed Conflicts, Self-Determination Movements, and Democracy* (College Park, MD: CIDCM, University of Maryland Press, 2003), 23.

43 Will Kymlicka, *Contemporary Political Philosophy: An Introduction* (Oxford: Clarendon Press, 1990), 209.

44 A very good outlook on pragmatism as an inquiry of public policies can be found in Andrew Light, "What is Pragmatic Philosophy?" *Journal of Philosophical Research*, Special Supplement (2005): 341.

45 Avigail Eisenberg, *Reconstructing Political Pluralism* (Albany: SUNY Press, 1995), 61-62.

46 Michel Seymour, "Rethinking Political Recognition" in *The Conditions of Diversity in Multinational Democracies*, eds., Alain-G Gagnon, Montserrat Guibernau & François Rocher (Montréal: McGill-Queen's University Press, 2003), 62.

NOTES TO CHAPTER FOUR

1 *Constitution Act, 1982*, being Schedule B to the *Canada Act 1982* (UK), 1982, c. 11. Note that my discussion of "reconciliation" is limited to the positive concept, described as being the purpose of section 35. There is a semantically similar notion to which my chapter is not referring, this being the portion of the "Aboriginal title" test that limits the content of modern Aboriginal title to a set of rights over the land that are not "irreconcilable with the nature of the attachment to the land which forms the basis of the particular group's aboriginal title." *Delgamuukw* v. *British Columbia* [1997] 3 S.C.R. 1010 at para. 111. A full explanation of the possible legal connections that goes beyond semantic linkages is a task to be completed elsewhere.

2 For a similar claim in the Australian context, Neva Collings & Rhonda Jacobsen, "Reconciliation with Australia's Young Indigenous People" (1999) 22 Univ. New South Wales Law J. 647; *cf.* Patricia Monture, *Community Governance and Nation (Re)Building: Centering Indigenous Learning and Research*, National Centre for First Nations Governance, www.fngovernance.org/pdf/MontureNationReBuilding.pdf, 34: "Although reconciliation is an admirable goal, judicial process may not be the best forum for finding the pathway toward a true reconciliation between First Nations and the Crown."

3 *Cf.* Roderick A. Macdonald, "Critical Legal Pluralism as a Construction of Normativity and the Emergence of Law," in *Théories et émergence du droit: pluralisme, surdétermination et effectivité*, eds., Andrée Lajoie et al. (Montréal: Les Éditions Thémis, 1998), 15. "Explicitly made legal rules . . . are not the only vehicles of normativity, but compete with a variety of indigenous and customary rules, practices and purely implicit interactional expectancies. Normativity cannot be equated with institutional organization."

4 *R.* v. *Sparrow* [1990] 1 S.C.R. 1075.

5 See *ibid.*, at 1081 (list of authors cited in judgment). The judgment cites seven different authors who had commented on dimensions of section 35. See *ibid.*, at 1092 (citing Brian Slattery, Kent McNeil, William Pentney), 1105 (citing Douglas Sanders, Noel Lyon), 1108 (citing Bryan Schwartz), 1112 (citing Leroy Little Bear).

6 Noel Lyon, "An Essay on Constitutional Interpretation" (1988) 26 Osgoode Hall L.J. 95 at 100, cited in *Sparrow, supra* note 4 at 1105-06.

7 Brian Slattery, "Understanding Aboriginal Rights" (1987) 66 Can. Bar Rev. 727.

8 *Canadian Charter of Rights and Freedoms*, Part 1 of the *Constitution Act, 1982, supra* note 1. It provides that the *Charter* "guarantees the rights and freedoms set out in it subject only to such reasonable limits prescribed by law as can be demonstrably

justified in a free and democratic society" (s. 1) thereby containing an explicit internal limit within the text. For a comparison between the Court's interpretation of this clause and the internal limits it has read into section 35, see Dwight Newman, "The Limitation of Rights: A Comparative Evolution and Ideology of the *Oakes* and *Sparrow* Tests" (1999) 62 Sask. L. Rev. 543.

9   Slattery, *supra* note 7 at 782, cited in *Sparrow, supra* note 4 at 1109-10.

10 Slattery does imply the appropriateness of a middle path between the extremes of recognizing and guaranteeing Aboriginal rights in their original form and Aboriginal rights, simply as modified by later law; *supra* note 7 at 781-82.

11 *Sparrow, supra* note 4 at 1109.

12 *R. v. Van der Peet* [1996] 2 S.C.R. 507.

13 *Delgamuukw, supra* note 1.

14 *Van der Peet, supra* note 12 at para. 31.

15 *Ibid.*, at paras. 230-31.

16 *Delgamuukw, supra* note 1 at para. 81.

17 *Ibid.*, Justice McLachlin concurred with Lamer C.J., while also agreeing with the reasons of LaForest J.; Justice LaForest's judgment, however, said nothing on the meaning of reconciliation.

18 *Ibid.*, at para. 81.

19 *Ibid.*, *Van der Peet, supra* note 12 at para. 50.

20 See generally Dwight G. Newman, *"Tsilhqot'in Nation* v. *British Columbia* and Civil Justice: Analayzing the Procedural Interaction of Evidentiary Principles and Aboriginal Oral History" (2005) 43 Alta. L. Rev. 433.

21 Monture, *supra* note 2 at 28; *cf.* Russell Lawrence Barsh & James (Sákéj) Youngblood Henderson, who describe the *Van der Peet* concept of reconciliation as a distortion from a limit on federal power to a limit on Aboriginal rights. "The Supreme Court's *Van der Peet* Trilogy: Naive Imperialism and Ropes of Sand (1997) 42 McGill L.J. 993 at 998-99.

22 Barsh & Henderson, *ibid.*, at 999. But see *Mitchell* v. *M.N.R*, where Binnie J. argues that the Royal Commission on Aboriginal Peoples conceptualized Aboriginal peoples as partners in a shared Canadian sovereignty and that this made a concept of reconciliation necessary. [2001] 1 S.C.R. 911 at paras. 133-35.

23 Barsh & Henderson, *ibid.*

24 See generally Michelle Grattan, ed., *Reconciliation: Essays on Australian Reconciliation* (Melbourne: Bookman Press, 2000).

25 See *e.g.* André Émond, « Le sable dans l'engenage du droit inhérent des autochtones à l'autonomie gouvernementale » (1996) 30 R.J.T. 89, cited in *Van der Peet, supra* note 12 at 111. Although *Van der Peet* incorrectly cites the article to the wrong page of the volume and wrongly pinpoints to a page of the article that does not exist, the intellectual connection is clear.

26 See also: Michel Morin, « Quelques réflexions sur le rôle de l'histoire dans la détermination des droits ancestraux et issues de traités » (2000) 34 R.J.T. 329; Ghislain Otis, « Le titre aborigène: émergence d'une figure nouvelle et durable du foncier autochtone? » (2005) 46 C. de D. 795. Both works explain the central role of negotiations in the resolution of Aboriginal title claims, with a manner that differs significantly from typical explanations in English-language writing on the issue.

27 *Mitchell, supra* note 22.

28 *Ibid.*, at para. 164.

29 *R. v. Marshall and Bernard*, 2005 S.C.C. 43 [2005] 2 S.C.R. 220 at paras. 51-52.

30 *Reference Re Secession of Quebec* [1998] 2 S.C.R. 217.

31 *Ibid.*, at para. 43.

32 *Ibid.*, at paras. 93, 101, 152-53.

33 *Reference Re Remuneration of Judges of the Provincial Court of Prince Edward Island; Reference Re Independence and Impartiality of Judges of the Provincial Court of Prince Edward Island* [1997] 3 S.C.R. 3. On the shift in interpretive methodology, see generally Robert G. Richards, "Provincial Court Judges Decision Case Comment (1998) 61 Sask. L. Rev. 575.

34 *Cf.* Dwight G. Newman, *Community and Collective Rights* (D.Phil. thesis, Oxford University Faculty of Law, 2005), 6.

35 Reflect on John Rawls' turn in his later writings: John Rawls, *Political Liberalism*, rev. ed. (New York: Columbia University Press, 2005); John Rawls, *The Law of Peoples* (Cambridge: Harvard University Press, 2005).

36 *Mikisew Cree First Nation v. Canada*, 2005 S.C.C. 69 at para. 1.

37 *Haida Nation v. British Columbia (Minister of Forests)*, 2004 S.C.C. 73 [2004] 3 S.C.R. 511.

38 *Taku River Tlingit First Nation v. British Columbia (Project Assessment Director)*, 2004 S.C.C. 74 [2004] 3 S.C.R. 550.

39 *Cf.* Brian Slattery, "Aboriginal Rights and the Honour of the Crown" (2005) 29 Sup. Ct. L. Rev. (2d) 433 at 433-34, 442-43.

40 *Cf.* E. Ria Tzimas, "*Haida Nation* and *Taku River*: A Commentary on Aboriginal Consultation and Reconciliation" (2005) 29 Sup. Ct. L. Rev. (2d) 461 at 477.

41 *Haida Nation, supra* note 37 at para. 32; *cf. Taku River Tlingit First Nation, supra* note 38 at para. 25.

42 *Haida Nation, ibid.*, at para. 50; *cf. Taku River, ibid.*, at para. 42.

43 See *e.g., Campbell v. British Columbia (Attorney General)*, 2000 B.C.S.C. 1123, 189 D.L.R. (4th) 333 at paras. 167-68; *Cheslatta Carrier Nation v. British Columbia*, 2000 B.C.C.A. 539, 193 D.L.R. (4th) 344 at para. 18; *Davis v. Canada (Attorney General)*, 2004 NLSCTD 153, 240 Nfld. & P.E.I.R. 21 at para. 90; *Makivik Corp. v. Canada (Minister of Canadian Heritage)* [1999] 1 F.C. 38 at para. 119 (F.C.T.D.). Note that, in this endnote and the seven subsequent endnotes, I do not necessarily indicate

higher court decisions that have sometimes overturned the lower judgments; even a lower court judgment that is overturned is nonetheless relevant to demonstrating the diversity of ways in which lower courts have been understanding the concept of reconciliation.

44 See *e.g., Chippewas of Sarnia Band* v. *Canada (Attorney General)* (1999), 101 O.T.C. 1 at para. 743 (Ont. S.C.); *Tsilhqot'in Nation* v. *Canada (Attorney General)*, 2002 B.C.C.A. 434, 3 B.C.L.R. (4th) 231 at para. 92.

45 See *e.g., Chippewas, ibid.*, at para. 306; *Skeetchestn Indian Band* v. *British Columbia (Registrar of Land Titles)*, 2000 B.C.C.A. 525 [2000] B.C.J. No. 1916 at para. 78.

46 See *e.g., Skeetchestn Indian Band, ibid.*, at paras. 45-46 (B.C.S.C.).

47 See *e.g., R.* v. *Bernard* [2000] 2 C.N.L.R. 97 at para. 66 (N.S. Prov. Ct.); *R.* v. *Jacobs* [1999] 3 C.N.L.R. 239 at paras. 104-105 (B.C.S.C.); *R.* v. *Morris*, 2004 B.C.C.A. 121, 237 D.L.R. (4th) 693 at paras. 85, 218.

48 See *e.g., Chippewas, supra* note 44 at paras. 745-47; *Halfway River First Nation* v. *British Columbia (Minister of Forests)*, 1999 B.C.C.A. 470, 178 D.L.R. (4th) 666.

49 See *e.g., Campbell, supra* note 43 at para. 168; *Huu-Ay-Aht First Nation* v. *British Columbia (Minister of Forests)*, 2005 BCSC 697 [2005] 3 C.N.L.R. 74 at para. 94; *Musqueam Indian Band v. British Columbia (Minister of Sustainable Resources Management)*, 2005 B.C.C.A. 128, 251 D.L.R. (4th) 717 at para. 92; *R.* v. *Blais*, 2001 MBCA 55, 198 D.L.R. (4th) 220 at para. 91.

50 See *e.g., Mohawk Council of Akwesasne* v. *Canada (M.N.R.)* [1997] 4 C.N.L.R. 103, 134 F.T.R. 1 at para. 17; *R.* v. *Francis*, 2003 N.S.P.C. 20, 216 N.S.R. (2d) 211; *R.* v. *Stump* [1998] B.C.J. No. 1890 at para. 31 (BC Prov. Ct.).

51 We could be puzzled as well by undeveloped discussions of reconciliation in academic literature. Consider the following less-than-straightforward analogy in the recently-published *First Nations Governance Law*: "[T]he reconciliation of original Aboriginal sovereignty with the power structure under the *Indian Act* is central to an understanding of Aboriginal governance, just as the need to reconcile the original Aboriginal occupation of the land with the assertion of Crown sovereignty is the foundation of Aboriginal title and rights under our legal and political system." Brian A. Crane, Robert Mainville & Martin W. Mason, *First Nations Governance Law* (Markham: LexisNexis Butterworths, 2006), 1-2.

52 *Mitchell, supra* note 22 at para. 164. Again, part of the citation on this paragraph in the Court's judgment is incomplete (see my discussion of other errors in Supreme Court citation at note 25, above), once again compounding difficulties in probing the intellectual influences of the Court.

53 Dwight G. Newman, "Toward a Cross-Cultural Moral Theorizing of Aboriginal Rights" (paper presented at the University of Edinburgh Centre for Canadian Studies, "First Nations, First Thoughts" 30th anniversary conference, 6 May 2005) McGill L.J. [forthcoming in 2008].

54 See Dwight G. Newman, "Negotiated Rights Enforcement" (2005) 68 Sask. L. Rev. 119 at 120-24.

55 See *e.g.*, Newman, *Collective Rights, supra* note 34; Dwight G. Newman, "Collective Interests and Collective Rights" (2004) 49 Am. J. Juris. 127; Newman, "Evidentiary Principles and Aboriginal Oral History," *supra* note 20.

NOTES TO CHAPTER FIVE

1 *Mitchell* v. *Minister of National Revenue* [2001] 1 S.C.R. 911 at para. 115.

2 *Constitution Act, 1982,* being Schedule B to the *Canada Act 1982* (UK), 1982, c.11, as am. by the *Constitution Amendment Proclamation, 1983,* R.S.C. 1985, App. II, No. 46 (am. ss. 25(b) and add. ss. 35(3), 35(4), 35.1, 37.1 and 54.1).

3 *R.* v. *Sparrow* [1990] 1 S.C.R. 1075. See Thomas Isaac, "Balancing Rights: The Supreme Court of Canada, *R.* v. *Sparrow,* and the Future of Aboriginal Rights," *Canadian Journal of Native Studies* XIII (1993): 199.

4 *Reference Re: Amendment of Canadian Constitution* [1982] 2 S.C.R. 793 at 805.

5 *Re: Manitoba Language Rights* [1985] 1 S.C.R. 721 at para. 59-60.

6 Peter Hogg, *Constitutional Law of Canada,* looseleaf (Toronto: Carswell, 2005), 1-2. See also Albert Venn Dicey, *Introduction to the Study of the Law of the Constitution,* 8th ed. (London: Macmillan, 1915), reprinted in *Introduction to the Study of the Law of the Constitution* (Indianapolis: Liberty Classics, 1982), 24-25: "Parliamentary sovereignty is therefore an undoubted legal fact. . . . This doctrine of the legislative supremacy of Parliament is the very keystone of the law of the constitution."

7 *Re: Manitoba, supra* note 5 at para. 64.

8 Nicholas Kasirer, "Bijuralism in Law's Empire and in Law's Cosmos" (2002), 52 J. Legal Educ. 29 at 34.

9 *Mitchell, supra note 1* at para. 10; for commentary, see Thomas Isaac, "The Meaning of Subsection 35(1) of the *Constitution Act, 1982*: A Commentary on *Mitchell* v. *Minister of National Revenue," The Advocate* 60 (2002), 853.

10 *Mitchell, ibid.,* at para. 70.

11 The Supreme Court has taken a similar approach to plurality, in regard to international human rights law and the interpretation of the *Canadian Charter of Rights and Freedoms* (Part I of the *Constitution Act, 1982,* being Schedule B to the *Canada Act 1982* (UK), 1982, c. 11, ss. 1-34). As noted by Ruth Sullivan, "the legislature is presumed to respect the values and principles enshrined in international law, both customary and conventional. These constitute a part of the legal context in which legislation is enacted and read. In so far as possible, therefore, interpretations that reflect these values and principles are preferred," in *Driedger on the Construction of Statutes,* 3d ed. (Toronto: Butterworths, 1994), 330. Similarly, in *R.* v. *Keegsta* [1990] 3 S.C.R. 697 at para. 259, the Supreme Court stated: "Canada's international obligations, and the accords negotiated between international governments, may well be helpful in placing Charter interpretation in a larger context. Principles agreed upon by free and democratic societies may inform the reading given to certain of its guarantees. It would be wrong, however, to consider these obligations

as determinative of or limiting the scope of those guarantees. The provisions of the Charter, though drawing on a political and social philosophy shared with other democratic societies, are uniquely Canadian. As a result, considerations may point, as they do in this case, to a conclusion regarding a rights violation which is not necessarily in accord with those international covenants." As in the case of Aboriginal law, the Supreme Court affirms the rule of law based on the Canadian legal framework, yet it allows space for plurality in the context of international human rights law to exist.

12 See *e.g.*, John Borrows, "Sovereignty's Alchemy: An Analysys of *Delgamuukw* v. *British Columbia*" (1999) 37 Osgoode Hall L.J. 537 at 556-57: "However, the Court's progressive instruction to adapt the laws of evidence to incorporate Aboriginal factual perspectives does not scrutinize Crown assertions of sovereignty. Aboriginal title and sovereignty are still diminished despite the Court's extraordinarily fair and generous approach. For Indigenous peoples, the language and culture of law is not their own; legal interpretation of Aboriginal traditions and history is centralized and administered by non-Aboriginal people. Aboriginal peoples barely participate in the administration of this system, and they are certainly not in positions of control. Furthermore, the evidence they present to establish their case must not 'strain the Canadian legal and constitutional structure'." The justification for this approach is that Aboriginal rights must be reconciled with the Crown's assertion of sovereignty over Canadian territory. Once again, Crown sovereignty is the standard against which Aboriginal rights must be measured. Sovereignty disciplines and defines the terrain on which Aboriginal peoples must operate if they are going to dispute the actions of Canadian governments in Canadian courts. Thus, even though the Court has made great efforts to ensure that the 'laws of evidence [are] adapted in order that [oral histories and tradition] can be accommodated and placed on an equal footing with the types of historical evidence that courts are familiar with,' the fact that they must be reconciled with assertions of Crown sovereignty means that, in the end, this new standard risks 'perpetuating the historical injustice suffered by aboriginal peoples at the hands of colonizers who failed to respect the distinctive cultures of pre-existing aboriginal societies'."

13 This section of the chapter is based on an article by Thomas Isaac and Anthony Knox, "Canadian Aboriginal Law: Creating Certainty in Resource Development" (2005) 23:4 *Journal of Energy and Natural Resources Law*, 427-64.

14 *R.* v. *Moosehunter* [1981] 1 S.C.R. 282 at 293, 123 D.L.R. (3d) 95, Dickson J.

15 George R., Proclamation, 7 Oct. 1763 (3 Geo. III), reprinted in R.S.C. 1985, App. II, No. 1.

16 The *Constitution Act, 1982*, states that "the existing aboriginal and treaty rights of the aboriginal peoples of Canada are hereby recognized and affirmed," *supra* note 2, ss. 35(1).

17 *R.* v. *Van der Peet* [1996] 2 S.C.R. 507.

18 *Delgamuukw* v. *British Columbia* [1997] 3 S.C.R. 1010: see generally Thomas Isaac, *Aboriginal Title* (Saskatoon: University of Saskatchewan Native Law Centre, 2006).

19 *R.* v. *Badger* [1996] 1 S.C.R. 771.

20 Thomas Isaac, *Aboriginal and Treaty Rights in the Maritimes: The Marshall Decision and Beyond* (Saskatoon: Purich Publishing Ltd., 2001).

21 *Sparrow, supra* note 3.

22 *Badger, supra* note 19.

23 *Delgamuukw, supra* note 18.

24 *Sparrow, supra* note 3 at 1112; see also *R.* v. *Gladstone* [1996] 2 S.C.R. 723, Lamer C.J.

25 *Sparrow, ibid.,* at 1111, Dickson C.J. and La Forest J. See also *Delgamuukw, supra* note 18 at para. 160, Lamer C.J.

26 *Sparrow, ibid.,* at 1112, Dickson C.J. and La Forest J.

27 *Ibid.,* at 1113, Dickson C.J. and La Forest J.; *Badger, supra* note 19 at paras. 82-96, Cory J.; and *Delgamuukw, supra* note 18 at para. 161, Lamer C.J.

28 *Delgamuukw, ibid.,* at para. 165, Lamer C.J.

29 *Badger, supra* note 19 at para. 80, Cory J.

30 *Sparrow, supra* note 3 at 1113, Dickson C.J. and La Forest J.; *Delgamuukw, supra* note 18 at para. 161, Lamer C.J.

31 *Gladstone, supra* note 24 at para. 73, Lamer C.J.

32 *Sparrow, supra* note 3 at 1113, Dickson C.J. and La Forest J.; *Gladstone, ibid.* at para. 74, Lamer C.J.; *Delgamuukw, supra* note 18 at para. 161, Lamer C.J.

33 *Delgamuukw, ibid.,* at para. 165, Lamer C.J.

34 For example, the objectives of "conservation or other purposes" (*R.* v. *Marshall* [1999] 3 S.C.R. 533, recon'd 179 D.L.R. (4th) 193 at para. 21 ["*Marshall* (reconsideration)"] cited to S.C.R.]) and "conservation or other public purposes" (at para. 26) are included.

35 *Sparrow, supra* note 3 at 1114, Dickson C.J. and La Forest J.; *Gladstone, supra* note 24 at para. 54, Lamer C.J.; *Delgamuukw, supra* note 18 at para. 162, Lamer C.J.

36 *Sparrow, ibid.*

37 *Sparrow, ibid.,* at 1119, Dickson C.J. and La Forest J.

38 Through a series of decisions, the Supreme Court of Canada has attempted to provide an understanding of the meaning of Aboriginal and treaty rights, as recognized and affirmed in section 35(1), including *Sparrow* (*supra* note 3), *Badger* (*supra* note 19), *Van der Peet* (*supra* note 17), *Delgamuukw* (*supra* note 18), *R.* v. *Marshall* ([1999] 3 S.C.R. 456, 177 D.L.R. (4th) 513 ["*Marshall*" cited to S.C.R.]), and *Marshall* (reconsideration) (*supra* note 34).

39 *Haida Nation* v. *British Columbia (Minister of Forests)* [2004] 3 S.C.R. 511. For commentary, see Thomas Isaac, "The Crown's Duty to Consult and Accommodate Aboriginal Peoples: The Supreme Court of Canada Decision in *Haida*," *The Advocate* 63 (2005) 671.

40 *Reference Re Secession of Quebec* [1998] 2 S.C.R. 217 at para. 32, citing *Reference Re Remuneration of Judges of the Provincial Court of Prince Edward Island* [1997] 3 S.C.R. 3, 150 D.L.R. (4th) 577 and *Reference Re: Amendment of the Constitution of Canada* [1981] 1 S.C.R. 753, 125 D.L.R. (3d) 1, *sub nom. Reference Re Resolution to Amend the Constitution* [1981] 6 W.W.R. 1, 39 N.R. 1.

41 *Secession Reference, ibid.,* at para. 33.

42 *Delgamuukw, supra* note 18 at paras. 84-87.

43 *Mitchell, supra* note 1 at paras. 31- 32.

44 *Van der Peet, supra* note 17 at para. 49.

45 See *Mitchell, supra* note 1 at para. 32, where McLachlin C.J. stated: "Aboriginal oral histories may meet the test of usefulness on two grounds. First, they may offer evidence of ancestral practices and their significance that would not otherwise be available. No other means of obtaining the same evidence may exist, given the absence of contemporaneous records. Second, oral histories may provide the aboriginal perspective on the right claimed. Without such evidence, it might be impossible to gain a true picture of the aboriginal practice relied on or its significance to the society in question. Determining what practices existed, and distinguishing central, defining features of a culture from traits that are marginal or peripheral, is no easy task at a remove of 400 years. Cultural identity is a subjective matter and not easily discerned: see R. L. Barsh and J. Y. Henderson, 'The Supreme Court's *Van der Peet* Trilogy: Naive Imperialism and Ropes of Sand' (1997), 42 McGill L.J. 993, at 1000. Also see *Sparrow, supra* note 3 at 1103; *Delgamuukw, supra* note 18 at paras. 82-87; and J. Borrows, 'The Trickster: Integral to a Distinctive Culture' (1997), 8 Constitutional Forum 27."

46 *Secession Reference, supra* note 40 at para. 33.

47 *Canada* v. *Benoit* (2003), 228 D.L.R. (4th) 1 (Fed. C.A.).

48 *Ibid.,* at para. 113.

49 *Mitchell, supra* note 1 at para. 34.

50 *Ibid.,* at para. 29.

51 *Ibid.*

52 *Ibid.*

53 *Ibid.,* at para. 30.

54 *Ibid.*

55 *Ibid.,* at para. 31.

56 *Ibid.,* at para. 38 [emphasis added in *Mitchell*].

57 *Ibid.,* at para. 39.

58 John Sopinka, Sidney N. Lederman & Alan W. Bryant, *The Law of Evidence in Canada*, 2d ed. (Toronto: Butterworths, 1999), 609.

59 *Ibid.*, at 616.

60 *Tsilhqot'in* v. *British Columbia*, 2004 B.C.S.C. 1022.

61 *Secession Reference, supra* note 40 at paras. 142, 144.

62 Patrick Macklem, "Normative Dimensions of an Aboriginal Right of Self-Government" (1995) 21 Queen's L.J. 173 at 193.

63 *Mitchell, supra* note 9 at paras. 112-13.

64 Macklem, *supra* note 62 at 194, states: "A similar pragmatic stance marks international law's reluctance to second-guess the legitimacy of state borders. In the words of James Anaya there exists 'a normative trend within international legal process toward stability through pragmatism over instability, even at the expense of traditional principle. Sociologists estimate that today there are around 5,000 discrete ethnic or national groupings in the world, and each of these groups is defined – and defines itself – in significant part by reference to history. This figure dwarfs the number of the independent states in the world today, approximately 176. Further, of the numerous stateless cultural groupings that have been deprived of something like sovereignty at some point in their history, many have likewise deprived other groups of autonomy at some point in time. If international law were to fully embrace ethnic national autonomy claims on the basis of the historical sovereignty approach, the number of potential challenges to existing state boundaries, along with the likely uncertainties of having to assess competing sovereignty claims over time, could bring the international system into a condition of legal flux and make international law an agent of instability rather than stability.' [J. S. Anaya, "The Capacity of International Law to Advance Ethnic or Nationality Rights Claims" (1990) 75 Iowa L. Rev. 837 at 840]."

65 *Mitchell, supra* note 1 at para. 61.

66 *Ibid.*, at para. 68.

67 *bid.*, at para. 118.

68 *Ibid.*, at para. 129.

69 *Ibid.*

70 *Ibid.*, at para. 130.

71 *Ibid.*, at para. 135.

72 *R.* v. *Blais* (2001), 156 Man. R. (2d) 53 (Man. C.A.), aff'd [2003] 2 S.C.R. 236 at para. 91.

73 *Haida, supra* note 39 at para. 50.

74 *Delgamuukw, supra* note 18 at para. 207.

75 Aileen Kavanagh, "The Idea of a Living Constitution" (2003) 16 Can. J.L. & Jur. 55 at para. 97.

76 *Mitchell, supra* note 1 at para. 115.

77 *Van der Peet, supra* note 17 at para. 31.

78 *R. v. Marshall; R. v. Bernard* [2005] 2 S.C.R. 220.

79 *Mikisew Cree First Nation* v. *Canada (Minister of Canadian Heritage)* [2005] 3 S.C.R. 388.

NOTES TO CHAPTER SIX

1 See *An Act to Prevent the Employment of Female Labour in Certain Capacities,* S.S. 1912, c. 17. The language of section 1 is more explicit: "No person shall employ in any capacity any white woman or girl or permit any white woman or girl to reside or lodge in or to work in . . . any restaurant, laundry or other place of business or amusement owned, kept or managed by any Japanese, Chinaman or other Oriental person" (s. 1). For a discussion of this legislation, see Constance Backhouse, *Colour-Coded: A Legal History of Racism in Canada, 1900-1950* (Toronto: The Osgoode Society, U. of T. Press, 1999), 132-72.

2 This is not to suggest that the practices of intercommunity respect are not shaped by governmental multiculturalism policies. Likewise, intersocietal disrespect can be produced through public administration practices and policies, such as police racial profiling. Hence, social practices can be shaped by race- and ethnicity-sensitive public policies. Furthermore, in Canada, the Constitution contains positive recognition of multiculturalism policy (*Constitution Act, 1982,* s. 27).

3 To be sure, this condition of a weak common citizenship has been lamented. See, *e.g.,* Alan Cairns, *Citizens Plus: Aboriginal Peoples and the Canadian State* (Vancouver: UBC Press, 2000), 188-200.

4 See Stephen Slemon, "The Scramble for Post-colonialism" in *De-scribing Empire: Post-colonialism and Textuality,* eds., Alan Lawson and Chris Tiffin (London: Routledge, 1994). Slemon states: "I believe that post-colonial studies needs always to remember that its referent in the real world is a form of political, economic and discursive oppression whose name, first and last, is *colonialism*" (at xx). See, also, James Youngblood Henderson, *First Nations Jurisprudence and Aboriginal Rights: Defining the Just Society* (Saskatoon: Native Law Centre, 2006), 8-16; and Robert Williams, *The American Indian in Western Legal Thought: The Discourses of Conquest* (New York: Oxford University Press, 1990), 325-20.

5 For an exploration of the relationship between political stability and justice as aims of constitutionalism, see Bruce Ackerman, *We The People: Foundations* (Cambridge: Belknap Press, 1991), 165-99.

6 Resilience of Indigenous identity in the face of global Europeanization, both economic and cultural, is discussed in Brian Goehring, *Indigenous Peoples of the World* (Saskatoon: Purich Publishing, 1993), 1-8.

7 See *e.g.,* Constance Backhouse, "'Bedecked in Gaudy Feathers': The Legal Prohibition of Aboriginal Dance: Wanduta's Trial, Manitoba, 1903," *supra* note 1 at 56.

8   See, for example, discussion of federal governance initiatives for First Nations in Kent McNeil, "Challenging Legislative Infringements of the Inherent Aboriginal Right to Self-Government" (2003) 22 Windsor Y.B. Access Just. 329 at 330-31 and 354-60.

9   A usufruct is a right – common in Indigenous societies – to use and take benefit from the property of another when needed for survival or for sustaining one's self, family, or community, so long as the use does not harm the property or make it less valuable.

10 A similar narrative with a similar description of its consequences appears in John Borrows, "Uncertain Citizens: Aboriginal Peoples and the Supreme Court" (2001) 80 Can. Bar Rev. 15 at 16-17.

11 See David Ingram, "Liberalism and the Right of Indigenous Peoples to Self-government," in *Group Rights: Reconciling Equality and Difference* (Lawrence, Kansas: University Press of Kansas, 2000), 97.

12 See *Aboriginal Peoples in Canada* (Ottawa: Statistics Canada, 2001) (Canadian Centre for Justice Statistics Profile Series).

13 Carol La Prairie, "Aboriginal Over-representation in the Criminal Justice System: A Tale of Nine Cities," *Canadian Journal of Criminology and Criminal Justice* 44: 2 (2002), xx; Carol La Prairie, "Aboriginal Governance and Criminal Justice: No Single Problem, No Simple Solution" (Nov. 2002) (unpublished paper prepared for the federal Department of Justice).

14 La Prairie, "Aboriginal Governance and Criminal Justice," *ibid.*, at 4.

15 *Ibid.*, at 7. La Prairie adds: "For visible minorities the rates were similar to those of the general population; for the immigrant group, the rates were lower than for the general population. Aboriginal people, and particularly aboriginal women, were found to be at much grater risk for spousal violence."

16 *Ibid.*, at 5-8. La Prairie states that there is growing evidence that the same factors that cause non-Aboriginal people to offend cause members of Indigenous populations to offend – unemployment, low income, low educational attainment – and that the age structure of Indigenous populations (high proportions of young people) is also a factor (at 5). These conditions are clearly relevant to offending rates, but they should not blind us to deeper causes embedded in the colonization of Indigenous populations and on-going practices of social exclusion. See, also, Loïc Wacquant, "From Slavery to Mass Incarceration: Rethinking the 'race question' in the US," 13 *New Left Review* (Jan-Feb, 2002): 41, in which he argues that incarceration is a follow-on phenomenon in oppressive interracial relations that occurs when other mechanisms, such as slavery and separation, are exhausted. For Wacquant these are all stages of "civic death."

17 La Prairie, "Aboriginal Governance and Criminal Justice," *supra* note 13 at 6. The data police forces record as reported crime is highly variable. Also variable is which interpersonal conducts are brought to the attention of police in the form of complaints of criminal conduct.

18 RCMP reports, based on detachment reports, generate geographic information. However, in light of strong ethnicity-based patterns of residential location (both prescribed by law and driven by socio-economic factors), this probably does not significantly distort conclusions based on ethnicity. More significantly, police reporting practices vary with respect to crime incidents that come to their attention.

19 In Canada, there are broad regulations against discrimination in both private and public arrangements, a series of public measures designed to create an equal opportunity environment have been adopted, and instruments of human and social development are treated as public goods. It is not surprising therefore that entry to the middle class has been achieved across a wide range of social classes and ethnic identities. Nevertheless, there is an actual continuing condition of social and economic deprivation broadly experienced in Aboriginal communities: see John Richards, *Neighbours Matter: Poor Neighbours and Urban Aboriginal Policy*, C.D. Howe Institute Commentary 156 (Toronto: C.D.Howe Institute, 2001) at 1.

20 The relationship between culture and development is discussed in Goehring (*supra* note 6, at 59-60).

21 See Richards, *supra* note 19. Some commentators have claimed that while urbanization imposes social costs such as high levels of mobility, detachment from family support and cultural bearings, more acutely experienced social exclusion and racism, and loss of control over children's and young persons' peer group influences, it nevertheless has a beneficial impact on social well-being. The ready access to specialist schools, stronger child protection, more extensive health services (including mental health services), family support services, and police services means that social distress can be more effectively dealt with.

22 The connection between poverty and offending suggests that the social policy response should be increased public support of persons seeking to escape poverty, rather than focussing on politico-economic challenges of Aboriginal communities *qua* communities. See, Rick August, *Social Assistance and the Perpetuation of Poverty* (Regina: Department of Social Services, Government of Saskatchewan, 2000) [unpublished]. August states: "The argument rests on a key assumption that, in general, the path to future prosperity for those on the margins of society is essentially the same as for those in the mainstream – that is to say, education, training, good health and productive employment" (at 2). This depoliticized, de-racialized view of social development is countered by the theory that improvement in the social condition of Aboriginal people requires specific and general political policies of decolonization.

23 See Elliot Liebow, *Tally's Corner: A Study of Negro Streetcorner Men* (Boston: Little, Brown, 1967), 212-13. Liebow writes of men who, from an employment perspective, are expendable: "He carries this failure home where his family is undergoing a parallel deterioration. His wife's adult male models also failed as husbands and fathers and she expects no less from him. . . . Her demands mirror the man both as society says he should be and as he really is, enlarging the failure in both their eyes. Sometimes he sits down and cries at the humiliation of it all."

24 The problem of underscoring the close linkages between social pathology and race is evident. It is explored more fully and critically in Linda Tuhiwai Smith, *Decolonizing Methodologies: Research and Indigenous Peoples* (London: Zed Books, 1999), 153: "One of the reasons why so many of the social problems that beset indigenous communities are never solved is that the issues have been framed in a particular way.... [Governments] have framed indigenous issues in 'the indigenous problem' basket, to be handled in the usual cynical and paternalistic manner."

25 Judith Rich Harris, *The Nurture Assumption: Why Children Turn Out the Way They Do* (New York: Free Press, 1998). Harris argues that in the struggle of adolescents to become individuals, they do not seek to become like the adults they need to differentiate themselves from, but seek to become like those adolescents who have already formed distinct identities.

26 But see *Criminal Code*, which states that in imposing a sentence, "all available sanctions other than imprisonment that are reasonable in the circumstances should be considered for all offenders, with particular attention to the circumstances of aboriginal offenders," R.S.C. 1985, c. C-46, s. 718.2(e), as amended. This section was considered in *R. v. Gladue* [1999] 1 S.C.R. 688.

27 Police-Aboriginal community relations in Saskatchewan are problematic, notwithstanding attempts by the Royal Canadian Mounted Police and other forces to engage First Nations and Métis communities in policing goals and strategies. The problems may be more attributable to resources (small detachments handle high volumes of offending and high demands for assistance) and the visibility of police services (in many Aboriginal communities, police services are the most visible public service, and community complaints about services tend to focus on police) than to racism.

28 Claims to this effect were made by witnesses to the Commission of Inquiry into Matters relating to the Death of Neil Stonechild at hearings held in Saskatoon, Saskatchewan, Sept.-Oct., 2003.

29 The Saskatchewan Indian Justice Review Committee and the Saskatchewan Métis Justice Review Committee (Chair: Patricia Linn) were established by the Saskatchewan Department of Justice with the Government of Canada and the Federation of Saskatchewan Indian Nations in 1991, and reported in 1992.

30 Commission on First Nations and Metis Peoples and Justice Reform (Saskatchewan), *A Dialogue in Progress: Focus on Youth*, Interim Report (2003), 49.

31 *Ibid.*

32 *Ibid.*

33 Commission of Inquiry into Matters Relating to the Death of Neil Stonechild, *Report* (Oct., 2004) at 208. For further discussion of racism in the administration of justice in Saskatchewan, see Commission on First Nations and Métis People and Justice Reform, "Eliminating Racism: Creating Healthy Relationship in Saskatchewan" in *Legacy of Hope: An Agenda for Change*, Final Report, vol. 1 (June 21, 2004) 7-1.

34 These connections have been explored in a vast literature on development theory. See *e.g.*, Amartya Sen, *Development as Freedom* (New York: Anchor Books, 2000); David Apter, *Rethinking Development: Modernization, Dependency, and Postmodern Politics* (Newbury Park, CA: Sage, 1987); Mancur Olson, *Power and Prosperity: Outgrowing Communist and Capitalist Dictatorships* (New York: Basic Books, 2000); especially Albert O. Hirschman, "The Case Against 'One Thing at a Time'," and "The On-and-Off Connection Between Political and Economic Progress," *A Propensity to Self-Subversion* (Cambridge: Harvard University Press, 1995), 69, 221.

35 Hirschman, *ibid.*, at 225-229.

36 Hirschman, *ibid.*, at 221-22. Hirschman rejects any simple relational thesis such that "economic progress necessarily exacts a cost in the political domain or . . . political advances are bound to jeopardize economic progress," and he also rejects the view that political progress must be held back or reversed or "sacrificed for the sake of the growing economy [and] during a second period a reward is reaped for the temporary sacrifice as political progress catches up."

37 Sen, *supra* note 34. The connection between meeting economic needs and active democratic practices is also explored (at 146-59). He states: "Expansion of freedom is viewed . . . both as the primary end and as the principal means of development. . . . If the point of departure of the approach lies in the identification of freedom as the main object of development, the reach of the policy analysis lies in establishing the empirical linkages that make the viewpoint of freedom coherent and cogent as the guiding perspective of the process of development" (at xii).

38 Olson, *supra* note 34.

39 Stephen Cornell and Joseph P. Kalt, *Sovereignty and Nation-Building: The Development Challenge in Indian Country Today* (Cambridge: Harvard Project on American Indian Economic Development, John F. Kennedy School of Government (Malcolm Weiner Center for Social Policy), Harvard University, 1998), 32-33 [unpublished]. See, also, Stephen Cornell and Joseph P. Kalt, eds., *What Can Tribes Do? Strategies and Institutions in American Indian Economic Development* (Los Angeles: American Indian Studies Centre, 1992).

40 *Ibid.*, Harvard Project.

41 See John D. Whyte, "Identity, Community and the *Charter*," *Canadian Issues/ Thèmes canadiens* (Fall, 2007): 127. But see Thomas Flanagan, *First Nations? Second Thoughts* (Kingston: McGill-Queens University Press, 2000), 9.

42 For an exploration of the connection between multiculturalism and stronger theories of group rights, see Charles Taylor, "The Politics of Recognition," in *Multiculturalism and "The Politics of Recognition*," ed. Amy Gutmann (Princeton: Princeton University Press, 1992), 61; Ayelet Shachar, *Multicultural Jurisdictions: Cultural Differences and Women's Rights* (Cambridge: Cambridge University Press, 2001), 17-44.

43 *Constitution Act, 1982*, *supra* note 2, s. 35(1).

44 One obvious limit is that Aboriginal self-government that derives from section 35(1) of the *Constitution Act, 1982,* must be exercised within Canada and under a regime of recognition that is an exercise of Canadian sovereignty. In other words, recognition of Aboriginal communities' self-governance structures will not create warring sovereignties: see *Mitchell* v. *M. N. R.* [2001] S.C.R. 911, Binnie, J. While acknowledging the constitutional reality of an Aboriginal right to self-government, Binnie, J. makes it clear that the exercise of that right must occur within Canadian national sovereignty (at para. 134).

45 The general groundwork for reflecting multiple allegiances and diverse cultural factors in asymmetrical constitutional structures has been explored by Jeremy Webber, *Reimagining Canada: Language, Culture, Community, and the Canadian Constitution* (Kingston: McGill-Queen's University Press, 1994).

46 Brian Slattery, "Varieties of Aboriginal Rights," *Canada Watch* 6 (1988): 71.

47 Samuel LaSelva, *The Moral Foundations of Canadian Federalism: Paradoxes, Achievements, and Tragedies of Nationhood* (Kingston: McGill-Queen's University Press, 1996), 150-51. Cairns, *supra* note 3 at 202-3: Cairns recruits LaSelva's commentary to his view of the dangers of political apartness created by Aboriginal self-government.

48 For a brief history of how state development and state stability, which were originally dependent on notions of all-or-nothing sovereignty, have come to be based on a more mediated and pluralist form of sovereignty, see Jonathon Schell, "No More Unto the Breach, Part Two: The unconquerable world," *Harper's Magazine* 306: 1835 (Apr. 2003): 41 at 52.

49 Ingram, *supra* note 11 at 105.

50 See Bruce Ackerman, "Discovering The Constitution" (1991) 93 Yale L. J. 1013 at 1072 ; Ulrich Preuss, "The Politics of Constitution Making: Transforming Politics Into Constitutions" (1991) 13 *Law and Policy* 107.

51 See Roderick Macdonald, "Metaphors of Multiplicity: Civil Society, Regimes and Legal Pluralism" (1998) 15 *Arizona Journal of International and Comparative Law* 69. Professor Macdonald states: "We know that this language [of nineteenth century forms of democratic governance] is inadequate to capture the richness, complexity and social diversity of the contemporary world" (at 91).

52 It is misleading to think that religion, language, colour, or ethnicity necessarily divide people or that enmity is a natural consequence of difference. There are too many examples of positive intersocietal relations to accept a theory of innate disrespect for difference. However, if the experience of the members of a distinct community – however identified – includes systematic denigration and social exclusion (or, even, a consistently expressed non-recognition of distinctiveness), that community is likely to adopt the politics of fervent "nationalism" in order to effect cultural survival.

53 Sen, *supra* note 34 at 8.

54 GA Res. 217 (III), UN GAOR, 3d Sess., Supp. No. 13, UN Doc. A/810 (1948) 71.

55 19 Dec. 1966, 999 U.N.T.S. 171, arts. 9-14, Can. T.S. 1976 No. 47, 6 I.L.M. 368 (entered into force 23 Mar. 1976, accession by Canada 19 May 1976).

56 For a strong argument in favour of justice-based international relations and particularly the case for penetrating state sovereignty in order to create a just system of recognition and protection of minority communities, see Allen Buchanan, *Justice, Legitimacy and Self-Determination: Moral Foundations for International Law* (Oxford, Oxford U.P., 2004).

57 See, Amy Gutmann, "Introduction" in Michael Ignatieff, *Human Rights as Politics and Idolatry* (Princeton: Princeton University Press, 2001). Gutmann argues that human rights "must be consistent with a plurality of comprehensive belief systems" (at xxii) and that human rights regimes depend on deliberation by everyone over what should be included within the system of rights and that this process depends on respect between people and the communities that they are in (at xxvi-xxvii).

58 The accommodation within liberalism of a communitarian understanding of powers within the state is always a conceptual challenge: see Joyce Appleby, *Liberalism and Republicanism in the Historical Imagination* (Cambridge: Harvard University Press, 1992), 17-20.

59 [1996] 2 S.C.R. 821.

60 [2000] 4 C.L.N.R. 1 (B.C.S.R.).

61 *Nisga'a Final Agreement* (4 May 1999), www.ainc-inac.gc.ca/pr/agr/nsga/nisdex12_e.pdf.

62 [1997] 3 S.C.R. 1010.

63 *Campbell, supra* note 60 at para. 137.

64 The "Canada Clause" of the *Consensus Report of the Constitution*, otherwise known as the Charlottetown Accord, states that the Canadian Constitution was to be interpreted in a manner consistent with the following "fundamental characteristic" of Canada: ". . . the Aboriginal peoples of Canada, being the first people to govern this land, have the right to promote their languages, cultures and traditions and to ensure the integrity of their societies, and their governments constitute one of the three orders of government in Canada." (*Consensus Report on the Constitution* (Charlottetown: Government of Canada, 1992 ["Charlottetown Accord"]). Although the constitutional amendments contained in the Charlottetown Accord did not receive popular approval in a national referendum and, hence, were not incorporated in the Constitution, it is significant that in Aug., 1992, all of the thirteen federal, provincial, and territorial governments of Canada agreed to place this concept in the Canadian Constitution.

65 See, *e.g.* Kent McNeil, *supra* note 8 at 331-33, who notes that although the inherent right of self-government has been recognized politically in Canada, it has not received definitive approval from the Supreme Court of Canada. He also notes, however, that it has been recognized, as a matter of legal expression, by section 35(1) of the *Constitution Act, 1982*. For a similar position, see Patrick Macklem, *Indigenous*

Difference and the Constitution of Canada (Toronto: University of Toronto Press, 2000), 107-19; Brian Slattery, "Making Sense of Aboriginal and Treaty Rights" (2000) 97 *Can. Bar Rev.* 196 at 213-15; and Brian Slattery, "Aboriginal Sovereignty and Imperial Claims" (1991) 29 Osgoode Hall L.J. 681.

66 *R. v. Sioui* [1990] 1 S.C.R. 1035 at para. 69.

67 *Benoit* v. *Canada* [2002] 2 C.N.L.R. 1 (F.C.T.D.).

68 *Treaty No. 8* (21 June 1899), www.ainc-inac.gc.ca/pr/trts/trty8/trty_e.html.

69 *Benoit, supra* note 67 at para. 22.

70 *Ibid.*, at para. 23.

71 *Ibid.*, at paras. 22-23. The Commissioners reported that they were asked to deal with at least three First Nations – the Wood Cree, the Chipewyan, and the Beaver, as well as with the Métis. They conducted their negotiations on the basis that they were negotiating with a large number of distinct self-governing communities.

72 This, of course, is exactly what occurs in every instance of nation-to-nation treaty-making – the signatory nations give up some degree of autonomy over the matter dealt with in the treaty, but their political systems remain intact.

73 *Benoit* v. *Canada* [2003] 3 C.N.L.R. 20 (F.C.A.). Although the applicants in *Benoit* succeeded in the Federal Court Trial Division, the Government of Canada appealed to the Federal Court of Appeal and that Court reversed the Trial Division decision. The Court of Appeal held that, looking at the whole of the historical record, the applicants were not able to establish that the understanding of the First Nations signatories to Treaty 8 was that the Commissioners had promised that members of the Treaty 8 First Nations would be exempt from taxation at all times in the future, regardless of the type of tax or the reasons for it.

74 See Ackerman *supra* note 5 at 1-33: for an examination of different levels of political decision-making, based on the distinction between ordinary choices of everyday politics and moments of high politics in which basic state structures and commitments are constituted.

75 Macklem, *supra* note 65 at 159.

76 For a thoughtful examination of bases for recognition of Aboriginal self-government and an argument for a developmental justification for Aboriginal governance powers rather than a justification based on preserving cultural integrity, see Tim Schouls, *Shifting Boundaries: Aboriginal Identity, Pluralist Theory, and the Politics of Self-Government* (Vancouver: UBC Press, 2003).

77 See Alan C. Cairns, *First Nations and the Canadian State: In Search of Coexistence* (Kingston, Institute of Intergovernmental Relations, Queen's University, 2005), for an analysis of challenges in implementing Aboriginal self-government. See, in particular, "Small Populations and Other Practical Considerations," 16. Professor Cairns' concerns seem not to reflect the possibilities arising from political and structural innovation.

1   *Inuvialuit and Gwich'in Self-Government Agreement-in-Principle* (16 Apr. 2003) (Ottawa: Public Works and Government Services Canada, 2003), c. 18, online: Inuvialuit/Gwich'in Self-Government Agreement-in-Principle Backgrounder, www.gov.nt.ca/MAA/negotiations/backgrounder_bdaip.pdf. This AIP was a joint agreement negotiated by the Inuvialuit (Inuit) and their Gwich'in (First Nation) neighbours. During 2006, the Gwich'in decided to pursue a separate agreement. Subsequent Inuvialuit negotiations were based substantively on the text of the 2003 *Inuvialuit and Gwich'in AIP*.

2   In discussions with self-government negotiators, it was confirmed that generally this and other factors heightened awareness of the importance of "workability" of self-government arrangements, which would be determined in large by how they were implemented.

3   Raymond Geuss, *History and Illusion in Politics* (Cambridge: Cambridge University Press, 2001), 147–52.

4   James Tully, "The Unfreedom of the Moderns in Comparison to Their Ideals of Constitutional Democracy" (2002) 65:2 Modern Law Review, 227.

5   *Gwich'in Comprehensive Land Claim Agreement* (22 Apr. 1992), App. B, c. 5, www.gwichin.nt.ca/documents/GCLCA.pdf. See also Nunavut Tungavik Inc., *Statement of Claim in the Nunavut Court of Justice* (5 Dec. 2006), www.tunngavik.ca/english/pdfs-english/NTI%20Statement%20of%20Claim%20Dec%202006.pdf.

6   Auditor General of Canada, "Chapter 8: Indian and Northern Affairs Canada – Transferring Federal Responsibilities to the North," *Report of the Auditor General: Nov. 2003* (Ottawa: Public Works and Government Services, 2003), online: www.oag-bvg.gc.ca/domino/reports.nsf/html/20031108ce.html, c. 8.10.

7   Tully, *supra* note 4 at 227.

8   For a discussion of breaches of numbered treaties, see Royal Commission on Aboriginal Peoples, "Part 1," *Final Report*, vol. 2 (Ottawa: Libraxus Inc, 1996), s.3; in the case of "modern-day" treaties, also known as land claims, see Land Claim Agreement Coalition, *Redefining Relationships: Learning From a Decade of Land Claim Implementation* (report of the LCAC conference held in Ottawa, Ontario, 27–30 Nov. 2003), www.consilium.ca/alcc/main.html.

9   This chapter focusses on these two areas for the sake of brevity and detail; a list of *all* conditions is beyond the scope of the current discussion. Most notably, I do not analyze the issue of financing which is possibly the most important condition of all.

10 In this case, financing arrangements have not been negotiated.

11 The Canada-Aboriginal Peoples' Roundtable held during 2004 provided an oppor- tunity for discussion among federal Cabinet ministers and leaders of national rep- resentative organizations of Indigenous peoples, including Indigenous women: see *Strengthening the Relationship: Canada–Aboriginal Peoples' Roundtable* (report of the

Canada-Aboriginal Peoples' Roundtable held in Ottawa, Ontario, 19 Apr. 2004), www.aboriginalroundtable.ca.

12 *Agreement concerning a New Relationship between the Government of Canada and the Crees of Eeyou Istchee* (10 July 2007), www.gcc.ca/pdf/LEG000000017.pdf, s. 2.

13 A discussion of implementation disputes is included in Auditor General of Canada, "Federal Responsibilities" (*supra* note 6); See also Nunavut Tungavik Inc., *Nunavut Land Claims Agreement, supra* note 5. The Nunavut agreement has also run into serious implementation disputes with Indian and Northern Affairs Canada (INAC). According to John Bainbridge, policy advisor with Nunavut Tungavik Inc., "There have been no referrals to arbitration from any claim signed since 1992 because Canada has a veto. Without any process of settling disputes other than recourse to the courts the implementation process is effectively carried through according to Canada's agenda. Not only that, but INAC claims that the lack of any reference to arbitration is proof that there are no issues in dispute" (Interview of John Bainbridge, former Gwich'in Tribal Council Implementation Coordinator and NTI advisor (17 Feb. 2006).

14 *Supra* note 6, s. 8.1-8.3.

15 See LCAC, *supra* note 8.

16 Interview of John Bainbridge, *supra* note 13.

17 Land Claim Agreement Coalition, *Achieving Objectives: A New Approach to Land Claims Agreements in Canada* (report of the LCAC conference held in Gatineau, Quebec, 27-30 June 2006), www.consilium.ca/alcc2006.

18 Auditor General of Canada, "Chapter 6: Indian and Northern Affairs Canada – Development of Non-Renewable Resources in the Northwest Territories," *Report of the Auditor General: Apr. 2005* (Ottawa: Public Works and Government Services, 2005).

19 Thomas Berger, *The Nunavut Project: Nunavut Land Claims Agreement Implementation Contract Negotiations for the Second Planning Period, 2003-2013,* Conciliator's Final Report: 1 Mar. 2006 (Ottawa: Public Works and Government Services Canada, 2006).

20 Nunavut Tungavik Inc., *supra* note 5.

21 These specifically stem from the obligations to negotiate self-government found in *Gwich'in Comprehensive LCA* (*supra* note 5); *Sahtu Dene and Metis Comprehensive Land Claim Agreement* (6 Sept. 1993), App. B, c.5, www.ainc-inac.gc.ca/pr/agr/sahtu/sahmet_e.pdf; *Inuvialuit Final Agreement* (1 Jan. 1984), s. 4.1, www.taiga.net/wmac/ifa/inuvialuitfinalagreement.pdf>.

22 Interviews with self-government negotiators and the author's fieldnotes (1 July -1 Aug. 2001).

23 Originally, this chapter was to focus on the *Inuvialuit and Gwich'in AIP* (*supra* note 1). During Feb. of 2006, the Gwich'in discontinued joint negotiations. The Inuvialuit negotiations are continuing, based on the *Inuvialuit and Gwich'in AIP*, as the contents pertain to the Inuvialuit. Thus, the analysis in this chapter applies to Inuvialuit governments recognized under the *Inuvialuit and Gwich'in AIP*.

24 *Gwich'in Comprehensive LCA, supra* note 5, App. B, s.1.3.

25 *Constitution Act, 1982*, being Schedule B to the *Canada Act 1982* (UK), 1982, c. 11, s.35.1

26 Indian and Northern Affairs Canada, "Part 1," *Federal Policy Guide: Aboriginal Self Government* (Ottawa: Public Works and Services Canada, 1995), 2.

27 Interview of Bob Simpson, Chief Negotiator of self-government for the Inuvialuit Regional Corporation (15 Mar. 2004).

28 *Inuvialuit and Gwich'in AIP , supra* note 1, c. 18.

29 Public Safety Canada, *First Nations Policing Policy* (Ottawa: Public Works and Government Services Canada, 2002), s.18.6.

30 During Inuvialuit and Gwich'in Self-Government Negotiations (held at Inuvik, NWT, 23 Apr. 1998), the author witnessed the Government of NWT Department of Justice claim they were "working on" policing legislation to facilitate policing powers under self-government. As of Feb. 2006, no policing legislation had materialized.

31 INAC, "inherent right policy," *supra* note 26.

32 *Inuvialuit and Gwich'in AIP , supra* note 1, ss. 18.2.3-18.2.5.

33 *Ibid.*, ss. 18.2.6.

34 *Ibid.*, ss. 18.2.7.

35 *Ibid.*, ss. 18.2.3, 18.2.6.

36 *Indian Act,* R.S.C. 1985, c. I-5

37 *Supra* note 26.

38 *Ibid.*, ss.18.2.3-18.2.12.

39 *Supra* note 26 at 2.

NOTES TO CHAPTER EIGHT

1 Law Reform Commission of Canada, *Aboriginal Peoples and Criminal Justice* (Ottawa: Law Reform Commission of Canada, 1991), 5. Carol La Prairie, "Aboriginal Over-Representation in the Criminal Justice System: A Tale of Nine Cities," *Canadian Journal of Criminology* 44:2 (2002): 181; Valerie Pottie Bunge, Holly Johnson & Thiema Balde, *Exploring Crime Patterns in Canada* (Ottawa: Statistics Canada, 2005).

2 A plethora of research questions the utility of incarceration. See Curt T. Griffiths & Alison Hatch Cunningham, *Canadian Criminal Justice: A Primer*, 2d ed. (Scarborough: Thomson Nelson, 2002), 215.

3 Canadian Corrections Association, *Indians and the Law* (Ottawa: Canadian Corrections Association, 1967), quoted in *ibid.*, at 215.

4   Jim Harding, "Policing and Aboriginal Justice," in *Criminal Injustice: Racism in the Criminal Justice System*, ed., Robynne Neugebauer (Toronto: Canadian Scholars' Press Inc., 2000), 209.

5   Royal Commission on Aboriginal Peoples, *Bridging the Cultural Divide: A Report on Aboriginal People and Criminal Justice in Canada* (Ottawa: Canada Communication Group, 1995), in Saskatchewan Justice Reform Commission, "Aboriginal Justice Inquiries: An Overview of Findings," www.justicereformcomm.sk.ca/docs/interm/Abor_Justice_Inquiry.pdf, 25.

6   Royal Commission on Aboriginal Peoples, *Partners in Confederation: Aboriginal Peoples, Self Government and the Constitution*. vol. 2, part 1 (Ottawa: Royal Commission on Aboriginal Peoples, 1993), 223. Academic authors have also argued that for successful restorative justice programs in Indigenous communities, the foundation of dialogue and justice initiatives must be a recognition of the inherent right of Indigenous peoples to self-determination and self-government. See Evelyn Zellerer & Chris Cunneen, "Restorative Justice, Indigenous Justice, and Human Rights," in *Restorative Community Justice* (Cincinnati: Anderson Co., 2001), 245.

7   Associate Chief Justice A.C. Hamilton, Commissioner & Associate Chief Judge C.M. Sinclair, Commissioner, *The Justice System and Aboriginal People: Report of the Aboriginal Justice Inquiry of Manitoba*, vol. 1 (Winnipeg: Queen's Printer of Manitoba, 1991), www.ajic.mb.ca/volumel/toc.html.

8   Mr. Justice Robert Allan Cawsey, *Report of the Task Force on the Criminal Justice System and its Impact on the Indian and Metis People of Alberta*, Mar. 1991, vol. 1 (Edmonton: Alberta Government Publications, 1991), www.justice.gov.ab.ca/publications/default.aspx?id=2679.

9   Patricia Linn, *Report of the Saskatchewan Métis Justice Review Committee* (Regina: Saskatchewan Justice, 1992); Patricia Linn, *Report of the Saskatchewan Indian Justice Review Committee* (Regina: Saskatchewan Justice, 1992).

10 Saskatchewan Commission on First Nation and Métis Peoples and Justice Reform, *Legacy of Hope: An Agenda for Change*, Final Report from the Commission on First Nations and Métis Peoples and Justice Reform, www.justicereformcomm.sk.ca.

11 Law Reform Commission of Canada, *supra* note 1.

12 Ontario Commission on Systemic Racism in the Criminal Justice System, *Report of the Ontario Commission on Systemic Racism in the Criminal Justice System* (Toronto: Queen's Printer for Ontario, 1995).

13 *Supra* note 7, "Chapter 4: Aboriginal Over-Representation," 85; Ontario Commission on Systemic Racism in the Criminal Justice System, *ibid*; Law Reform Commission of Canada, *supra* note 1 at 5.

14 Law Reform Commission of Canada, *ibid.*

15 Michael R. Peterson, "Developing a Restorative Justice Programme" (2000) 5:3 *Justice as Healing* 1 (as published by the Native Law Centre of Canada).

16 *Supra* note 7, Aboriginal Justice Inquiry of Manitoba, "Chapter 17: A Strategy for Action," 639.

17 Paul L.A.H. Chartrand & Wendy Whitecloud, *Aboriginal Justice Implementation Commission Final Report* (Winnipeg: Manitoba Statutory Publications, 2001).

18 *Supra* note 9.

19 *Ibid.*

20 *Treaty of peace and friendship between Sir William Johnson and the Hurons of the Detroit* (18 July 1764), archived in Ottawa: Library and Archives Canada (file: Mg19:F31), mikan3.archives.ca/pam/public_mikan/index.php?fuseaction=genitem .displayItem&lang=eng&rec_nbr=106678&rec_nbr_list=106678,3675772.

21 John Borrows, "Constitutional Law from a First Nation Perspective: Self-Government and the Royal Proclamation," 28 U.B.C. L. Rev. 1.

22 R.A. Williams, Jr., "The Algebra of Federal Indian Law: The Hard Trail of Decolonizing and Americanizing the White Man's Indian Jurisprudence" (1986) Wis. L. Rev. 219 at 291.

23 These policies were even termed as "cultural genocide" in Dean Neu & Richard Therrien, *Accounting for Genocide: Canada's Bureaucratic Assault on Aboriginal People* (Black Point, NS: Fernwood, 2003), 23.

24 Cecil Foster, *Where Race Does Not Matter: The New Sprit of Modernity* (Toronto: Penguin Canada, 2005), 81.

25 Neu & Therrien, *supra* note 23 at 102-8.

26 *R. v. Van der Peet* [1996] 2 S.C.R. 507 at paras. 27-42.

27 Colin Yerbury & Curt T. Griffiths, "Minorities, Crime and the Law," in *Diversity and Justice in Canada*, eds., John A. Winterdyk & Douglas E. King (Toronto: Canadian Scholars Press Inc., 1999), 36.

28 See Figure 1, "Zones of Conflict in the Justice Arena" in Catharine Crow, "Patterns of Discrimination: Aboriginal Justice in Canada" in *The Canadian Criminal Justice System: An Issues Approach to the Administration of Justice*, ed. Nick Larsen (Toronto: Canadian Scholars' Press Inc., 1995), 429 at 438.

29 *R. v. Sioui* [1990] 3 C.N.L.R. 127 (S.C.C.).

30 Schedule B to the *Canada Act 1982* (UK), 1982, c.11, s. 35.

31 See *R. v. Sparrow* [1990] 3 C.N.L.R. 160 (S.C.C.), where it is concluded: "[T]here was from the outset never any doubt that sovereignty and legislative power . . . to such lands vested in the Crown." Also see *Mitchell* v. *Peguis Indian Band* [1990] 3 C.N.L.R. (S.C.C.), 46 at 50.

32 Although the cases deal with sovereignty and underlying title, arguments could be advanced respecting a lesser or different jurisdiction, such as resolution of criminal offences or Aboriginal justice on-reserve. See Lambert's dissent in *Delgamuukw* v. *British Columbia* [1993] 5 C.N.L.R. (B.C.C.A.).

33 Mathias R.J. Leonardy, *First Nations Criminal Jurisdiction in Canada: The Aboriginal Right to Peacemaking under Public International Law* (Saskatoon: Native Law Centre, 1998).

34 *Ibid.*, 182.

35 Pasqua First Nation in Saskatchewan has passed a Band Council Resolution, which is generally an expression of will, and the Grand Rapids First Nation in Manitoba banished gang members after passing a drug bylaw. "Pasqua First Nation, Drug Dealers to be banished," *The Leader Post* (27 Jan. 2006) B1.

36 *Canadian Charter of Rights and Freedoms*, being Part I of the *Constitution Act, 1982*, being Schedule B to the *Canada Act 1982* (UK), 1982, c. 11, s. 7.9, s. 15.

37 See *Delgamuukw* v. *British Columbia* [1998] 1 C.N.L.R. 14 (S.C.C.).

38 See *Van der Peet, supra* note 26.

39 *Charter of Rights, supra* note 36.

40 *Van der Peet, supra* note 26 at paras. 27-42; *Mikisew Cree First Nation* v. *Canada (Minister of Canadian Heritage)*, 2005 S.C.C. 69, Binnie J. at para. 1.

41 John Giokas, "Accommodating the Concerns of Aboriginal People Within the Existing Justice System," in *Diversity and Justice in Canada*, eds., John A. Winterdyk & Douglas E. King (Toronto: Canadian Scholars Press Inc., 1999) 45 at 48.

42 Colin Goff, *Criminal Justice in Canada,* 3d ed. (Scarborough: Thomson Nelson, 2004), 120.

43 Giokas, *supra* note 41 at 48.

44 *Ibid.,* 49.

45 Zellerer & Cunneen, *supra* note 6 at 249.

46 Adapted from a list found in Zellerer & Cunneen (*ibid.,* at 259).

47 *Constitution Act, 1982, supra* note 30, s. 35. See conclusions of Law Reform Commission of Canada (*supra* note 1 at 5).

48 David R. Newhouse & Yale D. Belanger, *Aboriginal Self-Government in Canada: A Review of the Literature Since 1960* (2001), 38 [unpublished]; First Nations Chiefs of Police Association in partnership with Human Resources Development Canada, *Setting the Context: The Policing of First Nations Communities, Module One,* www.fncpa.ca/Publications/Moduleone.doc, at 126; Peter Jull, "Building Nunavut: A Story of Inuit Self-Government," *Northern Review* 1 (1988), 69.

49 This agreement has proceeded through a *Meadow Lake First Nations Tripartite Agreement-In-Principle*, www.ainc-inac.gc.ca/pr/agr/ml/mltaip_e.html; *Meadow Lake First Nations Comprehensive Agreement-in-Principle*, www.ainc-inac.gc.ca/pr/agr/ml/mlcaip_e.html.

50 Federation of Saskatchewan Indian Nations, "Vision," www.fsin.com/justice/vision.html.

51 Griffiths & Cunningham, *supra* note 2 at 75.

52 Public Safety and Emergency Preparedness Canada, "First Nations Policing Policy Handbook," ww2.ps-sp.gc.ca/publications/abor_policing/fnpp_handbook_e.asp.

53 The Louis Bull Police Service in Alberta was established in 1987, and the Six Nations Police Service in Ontario was established in 1989. See Donald Clairmont & Christopher Murphy, *Self-Administered First Nations Policing: An Overview of Organizational and Managerial Issues* (Ottawa: Ministry of the Solicitor General Canada, 2000), 14. Harding points out the existence of the Dakota Ojibway Tribal Council (DOTC) in Manitoba, the Amerindian Police Force in Quebec, the Aboriginal Peace Keeper Force in BC, and the Mohawk Police keeper Force in Ontario (*supra* note 4 at 217).

54 Email from Luc Major of the Aboriginal Policing Directorate of Public Safety and Emergency Preparedness Canada to Rick Linden (6 July 2005), cited in Rick Linden, "Policing First Nations and Metis People: Progress and Prospects" (2005) 68:2 University of Saskatchewan Law Review, 303 at 305.

55 *Ibid.*, 306.

56 Saskatchewan Commission on First Nation and Métis Peoples and Justice Reform, "Chapter 2: Creating Healthy, Just, Prosperous and Safe Saskatchewan," in *Legacy of Hope: An Agenda for Change, supra* note 10, www.justicereformcomm.sk.ca/volumeone/07ChapterTwo.pdf.

57 *Ibid.*

58 See information on the First Nations Chiefs of Police Association and Human Resources Development Canada's *Human Resource Study of First Nations Policing in Canada*, www.fncpa.ca/hrstudies.htm.

59 Bryan D. Cummins & John L. Steckley, *Aboriginal Policing: A Canadian Perspective* (Toronto: Pearson Education Canada Inc., 2003), 175.

60 Canadian Criminal Justice Association, "Part V: Changes within the Present System," in *Aboriginal People and the Criminal Justice System* (Ottawa: Canadian Criminal Justice Association, 2000),www.ccja-acjp.ca/en/abori5.html.

61 *Ibid.*

62 An argument can be made that an Aboriginal right to criminal jurisdiction exists: see Leonardy, *supra* note 33 at 209.

63 The first initiative was the appointment of Aboriginal lay persons as Justices of the Peace or Lay Assessors under the *Indian Act* (R.S.C. 1985, c. I-5, s. 107) or the Lieutenant Governor under provincial legislation. The government has promised to appoint a Cree-speaking Justice of the Peace to a Cree community and a Dene Justice of the Peace to a Dene community: Betty Ann Adam, "Aboriginal Provincial Court Party - Translation services to be expanded," *Leader-Post* (19 Nov. 2005) D12.

64 Honourable M. E. Turpel-Lafond, "Some Thoughts on Inclusion and Innovation in the Saskatchewan Justice System" (2005) 68 University of Saskatchewan Law Review, 293 at 302.

65 "Sask to hire more aboriginal cops, court workers," Canadian Broadcasting Corporation (13 May 2005), CBC News, www.cbc.ca/canada/story/2005/05/13/sask-aboriginal050513.html.

66 Canadian Plains Research Center, "Northern Cree Court Initiative," in *Encyclopedia of Saskatchewan* (Regina: Canadian Plains Research Center, 2006), esask.uregina.ca/entry/northern_cree_court_initiative.html.

67 A.J. Ehman, "A People's Justice" (June/July 2002) 11:4 *The National* (as published by the Canadian Bar Association), 12 at 12.

68 Honourable L.S. Tony Mandamin, Judge of the Provincial Court of Alberta, "Peacemaking and the Tsuu T'ina Court" (2003) 8:1 *Justice as Healing* 1 (as published by the Native Law Centre of Canada).

69 *Ibid.*; M.E. Bryant, "Tsuu T'ina First Nation Peacemaker Justice System" (2002) 26:4 LawNow 16.

70 M. Mildon, "First Native Court Set up in Alberta" (2001) 25:5 LawNow 6.

71 *Ibid.*, 3.

72 For more information on the Gladue Court, see "Gladue (Aboriginal Persons) Court, Ontario Court of Justice: Old City Hall Fact Sheet," www.aboriginallegal.ca/docs/apc_factsheet.htm.

73 R.S.C. 1985, c. C-46.

74 *R. v. Gladue* [1999] 1 S.C.R. 688.

75 See Aboriginal Legal Services of Toronto, www.aboriginallegal.ca.

76 One of the first recorded cases using this approach was *R. v. Moses* [1992] 3 C.N.L.R. 116, 11 C.R. (4th) 357 (Y. Terr. Ct.).

77 The provision for diversion, prior to plea, exists in the *Criminal Code* (*supra* note 73, s. 717) and the *Youth Criminal Justice Act* (S.C. 2002, c.1, s. 10). The power for a court to hold a sentencing circle flows from *R. v. Gardiner* [1982] 2 S.C.R. 368 (S.C.C.) and *R. v. Morrissette* (1970), 1 C.C.C. (2d) 307 (Sask. C.A.).

78 Chris Andersen, "Governing Aboriginal Justice in Canada: Constructing Responsible Individuals and Communities through Tradition" (1999) 31:4 *Crime, L. & Soc. Change*, 303 at 310. See also R.G. Green, *Justice in Aboriginal Communities: Sentencing Alternatives* (Saskatoon: Purich, 1998).

79 *R. v. Joseyounen* [1995] 6 W.W.R. 438 (Sask. Prov. Ct.); *R. v. Alaku* (1992), 112 D.L.R. (4th) 732 (Que. Ct.); *Moses, supra* note 76.

80 Michael R. Peterson, "Developing a Restorative Justice Programme" (2000) 5:4 *Justice as Healing* 1 at 1 (as published by the Native Law Centre of Canada).

81 Twenty-three of these programs are listed on the Department of Justice Canada website: canada.justice.gc.ca/en/ps/ajs/programs/Saskatchewan.html. Saskatchewan Justice states that the work of the community-based justice programs and committees is to be expanded; no mention is made of funding of these programs which has not increased in several years: Saskatchewan Justice, *2005-2006 Annual Report*, www.justice.gov.sk.ca/JUO2005-2006AR.

82 Don Clairmont & Linden Rick, *Developing & Evaluating Justice Projects in Aboriginal Communities: A Review of the Literature* (Ottawa: Aboriginal Corrections Policy Unit, 1998) (part of the Aboriginal Peoples Collection).

83 *Ibid.*

84 Tony F. Marshall, "The Evolution of Restorative Justice in Britain" (1996) 4:4 *Eur. J. Crim. Pol'y & Research* 21.

85 Gordon Bazemore & Lode Walgrave, "Restorative Juvenile Justice: In Search of Fundamentals and an Outline for Systemic Reform," in *Restorative Juvenile Justice: Repairing the Harm of Youth Crime*, eds., Gordon Bazemore & Lode Walgrave (Monsey, NY: Criminal Justice Press, 1999), 45 at 48.

86 Kishk Anaquot Health Research, *Journey and Balance: Second Interim Evaluation Report of Aboriginal Healing Foundation Program Activity* (Ottawa: Aboriginal Healing Foundation, 2002).

87 Donald Auger, Anthony Doob & Paul Driben, "Crime and Control in Three Nishnawbe Communities: An Exploratory Investigation" (1992) 34 *Can. J. Crim.* 317.

88 Information on the Lancombe Log House Initiative provided by Gloria Lee (paper presented at "Moving Towards Justice" conference hosted by the Saskatchewan Institute of Public Policy held in Regina, Saskatchewan (1-3 Mar. 2006)).

89 Gordon Green, "Aboriginal Community Sentencing and Mediation: Within and Without the Circle" (1997) 25:1 M.L.J. 77.

90 Jeff Latimer, Craig Dowden & Danielle Muise, *The Effectiveness of Restorative Justice Practices: A Meta-Analysis* (Ottawa: Department of Justice Canada, 2001).

91 Robert Depew, "Popular Justice and Aboriginal Communities" (1996) 36 *Journal of Legal Pluralism and Unofficial Law* 21.

92 *Ibid,.* 57-58.

93 Zellerer & Cunneen, *supra* note 6 at 251.

94 Saskatchewan's *Department of Justice Budget, 2005-2006* (*supra* note 81) details efforts to meet the recommendations of the Saskatchewan Commission on First Nation and Metis Peoples and Justice Reform report (*supra* note 10). Goals and measurement indicia are set for increasing the participation of Aboriginal people in the administration of justice by increasing the hiring of Aboriginal people for policing and justice administration, increasing involvement in community justice committees, increasing cultural awareness, partnering to reform the justice system, increasing Community Tripartite Agreements, and reducing the number of Aboriginal offenders and victims by increasing therapeutic approaches to justice with Aboriginal involvement.

95 Latimer, Dowden & Muise, *supra* note 90.

1   Kent Roach, "Changing Punishment at the Turn of the Century: Restorative Justice on the Rise," *Canadian Journal of Criminology* 42 (2000): 249.

2   See, *e.g.*, Angela Cameron, "Stopping the Violence: Canadian Feminist Debates on Restorative Justice and Intimate Violence," *Theoretical Criminology* 10 (2006): 49; Emma LaRoque, "Re-Examining Culturally Appropriate Models of Criminal Justice Applications," in *Aboriginal and Treaty Rights in Canada: Essays on Law, Equality and Respect of Difference*, ed. Michael Asch (Vancouver: UBC Press, 1997), 73; Kelly MacDonald, *Literature Review: Implications of Restorative Justice in Cases of Violence Against Aboriginal Women and Children* (Vancouver: Aboriginal Women's Action Network, 2001).

3   Existing commentary includes: Josephine Savarese, "Gladue was a Woman," in *Restorative Justice: New Directions*. eds., Elizabeth Elliot & Robert Gordon (Portland: Willan Press, 2005), 134; Jean Lash, "Case Comment: *R* v. *Gladue*," *Canadian Woman Studies* 20 (2000): 85.

4   I argue elsewhere that the sentencing practices outlined in this chapter cannot by themselves be considered a full form of "restorative justice," as envisioned by restorative justice advocates and practitioners: see Angela Cameron, "Sentencing Circles and Intimate Violence: a Canadian Feminist Perspective" (2007) 18 C.J.W.L. 1019 at 1027. For the purposes of this chapter, "restorative justice" is limited to the Supreme Court of Canada's understanding and definition of the concept in *R. v. Gladue* (see, *e.g.* [1999] 1 S.C.R. 688 at paras. 31, 43).

5   *Gladue, ibid.*

6   For instance, over-incarceration and geographical displacement are experienced disproportionately by Aboriginal women, when compared to Aboriginal men.

7   *Gladue, supra* note 4.

8   [1999] A.J. No. 1458 (Alta. Prov. Ct.) (QL).

9   2000 B.C.C.A. 374 [2000] B.C.J. No. 1442 (B.C.C.A.) (QL).

10 In the subsequent case of *R. v. Wells* [2000] 1 S.C.R. 207: the Supreme Court elaborated a sentencing methodology to be used in applying these factors. In particular, the Court lays out the order in which non-incarceral sentencing options must be considered and the stage at which to emphasize an offender's Aboriginal cultural heritage (at para. 27).

11 *Criminal Code*, R.S.C. 1985, c. C-34, s.718.2(e) .

12 *Gladue, supra* note 4 at 387.

13 *Supra* note 11, s. 718.2 (emphasis added).

14 David Stack, "The Impact of RCAP on the Judiciary: Bringing Aboriginal Perspectives into the Courtroom" (1999) 62 Sask. L. Rev. 472 at 481.

15 Kent Roach & Jonathan Rudin, "*Gladue*: The Judicial and Political Reception of a Promising Decision" (2000) 42 Can. J. Crim. 335 at 344-45; Judge Mary Ellen

Turpel-Lafonde, "Sentencing within a Restorative Justice Paradigm: Procedural Implications of *R. v. Gladue*" (1999) 43 Crim. L. Q. 34. See also: *Gladue, supra* note 4 at para. 33.

16 *Gladue, supra* note 4 at para. 65.

17 *Ibid.*, at para. 66.

18 *Ibid.*, at para. 67.

19 *Ibid.*

20 *Ibid.*, at para. 74.

21 In a recent decision, the Ontario Court of Appeal ruled that a failure to adequately consider the *Gladue* factors is an error of law: *R. v. Brizard* [2006] O.J. No. 729 at para. 2 (QL).

22 *R. v. Kakekagamick* [2006] O.J. No. 3346 at para. 49 (Ont. C.A.) (QL).

23 *R. v. Gopher (Moccasin and Night Appeals)* [2006] S.J. No. 12 at para. 42 (Sask. C.A.) (QL).

24 *R. v. Cappo*, 2005 SKCA 134 at para. 7.

25 *Criminal Code, supra* note 11, s. 742. See *e.g., Norris, supra* note 9; *R. v. A.J.*, 2000 YTTC 68; *R. v. Belrose* [2001] B.C.J. No. 1310 (B.C.C.A.) (QL).

26 *Criminal Code, supra* note 11, s. 717. Because of the extra-judicial nature of Alternative Measures Programs, there are no reported cases available.

27 While the concept of colonialism is frequently poorly defined, understood, and applied by courts, it is used with some specificity in the *Gladue* decision. The Court provides a list of what it considers to be legitimate markers of colonial impact that can, and should, be addressed in sentencing. Whether this constitutes a satisfactory understanding of colonialism is beyond the scope of this chapter.

28 *Indian Act*, R.S.C., 1985, c. I-5, s. 1.

29 Jonathan Rudin, "Aboriginal Justice and Restorative Justice," in *New Directions in Restorative Justice: Issues, Practice, Research*, eds., Elizabeth Elliot & Robert Gordon (Portland: Willan Press, 2005), 94.

30 Canada, Royal Commission on Aboriginal Peoples, *Bridging the Cultural Divide: A Report on Aboriginal People and Criminal Justice in Canada* (Ottawa: Canada Communication Group, 1996).

31 Rudin, *supra* note 29 at 94.

32 See *e.g.*, Canadian Bar Association, *Locking Up Natives in Canada* (Ottawa: Canadian Bar Association, 1989); Manitoba, *Report of the Aboriginal Justice Inquiry of Manitoba: The Justice System and Aboriginal People*, vol. 1 (Winnipeg: Queen's Printer, 1991) (Commissioners: Alvin C. Hamilton & C. Murray Sinclair); Canada, *Bridging the Cultural Divide, supra* note 30; Canada, *Creating Choices: The Report of the Task Force on Federally Sentenced Women* (Ottawa: Correctional Services Canada, 1990).

33 *Gladue, supra* note 4 at paras. 35-38, 52-57, 58-65.

34 The Bill introduced section 718.2(e) and other sentencing provisions in 1996: *An Act to Amend the Criminal Code (Sentencing)*, S.C. 1995, c. 22 (passed into law Sept. 1996).

35 Allan Rock, Minister of Justice, *House of Commons Debates*, vol. IV (20 Sept. 1994) at 5873.

36 Christine Boyle and Marilyn McRimmon, "To Serve the Cause of Justice: Disciplining Fact Determination" (2001) 20 Windsor Y.B. Access Just. 55 at 71.

37 Sherene Razack, *Looking White People in the Eye: Gender, Race and Culture in Courtrooms and Classrooms* (Toronto: University of Toronto Press, 1999), 12.

38 *Ibid.*

39 Rebecca Johnson, *Taxing Choices: The Intersection of Gender, Parenthood and the Law* (Vancouver: UBC Press, 2003), 7.

40 Razack, *supra* note 37 at 11, 12.

41 *Ibid.*, 158.

42 Jo-Anne Fiske & Evelyn George, *Seeking Alternatives to Bill C-31: From Cultural Trauma to Cultural Revitalization through Customary Law* (Ottawa: Status of Women Canada, 2006), 25.

43 Holly Johnson & Karen Rodgers, "A Statistical Overview of Woman and Crime in Canada," in *In Conflict with the Law: Women and the Canadian Justice System*, eds., E. Adelburg & C. Currie (Vancouver: Press Gang, 1993), 95.

44 Statistics Canada, "Adult Correctional Services" *The Daily* (16 Dec. 2005). See also, Statistics Canada, *Women in Canada: A Gender-Based Statistical Report*, 5th ed. (Ottawa: Statistics Canada, 2006), 171.

45 Statistics Canada, *Women in Canada*, *ibid.*, 189; Susan Boyd, *Child Custody, Law and Women's Work* (Toronto: Oxford University Press, 2002), 180.

46 Statistics Canada, *Women in Canada*, *ibid.*, 191.

47 Marlee Kline, "Child Welfare Law, 'Best Interests of the Child' Ideology, and First Nations" (1992) 30 Osgoode Hall L.J. 375.

48 The Aboriginal Healing Foundation, "Residential Schools and the Intergenerational Legacy of Abuse," in *Justice as Healing*, ed., Wanda D. McAslin (Minnesota: Living Justice Press, 2005), 25.

49 *Gladue, supra* note 4 at para. 68. While the cases discussed below may reveal incidences of direct discrimination, the primary focus of this section will be systemic discrimination.

50 *Gopher, supra* note 23 at para. 43.

51 Sharon McIvor, "Aboriginal Women Unmasked: Using Equality Litigation to Advance Women's Rights" (2004) 16 C.J.W.L. 107; Emma LaRocque, "Re-examining Culturally Appropriate Models in Criminal Justice Applications," in

Aboriginal and Treaty Rights in Canada: Essays on Law, Equality and Respect of Difference, ed., Michael Asch (Vancouver: UBC Press, 1997), 75.

52 Mary Ellen Turpel-Lafond, "Patriarchy and Paternalism: The Legacy of the Canadian State for First Nations Women," in *Women and the Canadian State*, eds., Caroline Andrew and Sanda Rogers (Montreal: McGill-Queen's University Press, 1997), 64; Fiske & George, *supra* note 42 at 8, 25.

53 McIvor, *supra* note 51; Turpel-Lafond, *ibid.*

54 Mary Ellen Turpel, "Home/Land" (1991) 1 C.J.F.L. 17.

55 The same provisions did not apply to Aboriginal men who married non-Aboriginal women; in fact, non-Aboriginal women who married Aboriginal men gained full status as "Indians" under the Act. See Fiske & George, *supra* note 42 at 4-12).

56 See *e.g.*, Audrey Huntley, Fay Blaney, *et al.*, "Bill C-31: Its Impact, Implications and Recommendations for Change in British Columbia – Final Report" (Vancouver: Aboriginal Women's Action Network, 1999); Thomas Isaac & Mary Sue Maloughney, "Dually Disadvantaged and Historically Forgotten?: Aboriginal Women and the Inherent Right to Self Government" (1992) 21 Man. L.J. 453.

57 *An Act to Amend the Indian Act*, S.C. 1985, c. 27.

58 See *McIvor v. Canada (Registrar Indian and Northern Affairs)*, 2006 BCSC 96. Sharon McIvor won this gender discrimination case against the federal government. In Nov., 2007, the federal government began an appeal against McIvor's legal victory.

59 See *e.g.*, *Sawridge Band v. Canada*, 2003 FCT 347; *Mousseau v. Canada* [1991] 121 N.S.R. (2d) 403 (N.S.C.A.). For litigation involving housing benefits, see also: *Poitras v. Sawridge* [2001] F.C.J. No. 1031 (F.C.T.D.) (QL); *Tuplin v. Canada (Registrar)* [2001] P.E.I.J. No. 113 (P.E.I.S.C.T.D.) (QL).

60 Fiske & George, *supra* note 42 at 12, 13.

61 *Gladue, supra* note 4 at para. 68.

62 Statistics Canada, *Women in Canada, supra* note 44 at 182.

63 *Ibid.*

64 Royal Commission on Aboriginal Peoples, *Perspectives and Realities*, vol. 4 (Ottawa: Minister of Supply and Services, 1996), 9.

65 Statistics Canada, *Women in Canada, supra* note 44 at 183.

66 Carol La Prairie, "Victimization and Family Violence," *Seen but Not Heard: Native People in the Inner City,* Report 3 (Ottawa: Department of Justice, 1994).

67 Canada, *Report to the United Nations Conference on Human Settlement* (Ottawa: Government of Canada, 1996).

68 RCAP, *Perspectives and Realities, supra* note 64 at 553.

69 Centre for Equality Rights in Accommodation, Women's Housing Program, *Women and Housing in Canada: Barriers to Equality* (Toronto: CERA, 2002), 33-45; Pauktuutit Inuit Women's Association of Canada, *Inuit Women: The Housing Crisis and Violence* (Toronto: Pauktuutit, 1986), 9.

70 Statistics Canada, *Women in Canada, supra* note 45 at 185.

71 RCAP, *Perspectives and Realities, supra* note 64 at 521.

72 The first factor is noted in *Gladue*, in relation to urban Aboriginal people generally.

73 RCAP, *Perspectives and Realities, supra* note 64 at 525.

74 *Gladue, supra* note 4 at para. 91.

75 Fiske & George, *supra* note 42 at 45.

76 *Gladue, supra* note 4 at para. 92.

77 Ann Duffy & Julianne Momirov, *Family Violence: A Canadian Introduction* (Toronto: Lorimer, 1997), 128-64; Lee Lakeman, *Ninety-Nine Federal Steps Toward an End to Violence Against Women* (Toronto: National Action Committee on the Status of Women, 1993); Bertha Wilson, "Family Violence" (1992) 5 C.J.W.L. 137.

78 While the argument here outlines the systemic effects of violence, the Saskatchewan Court of Appeal also names "family dysfunction" as a *Gladue* sentencing consideration. See *Gopher, supra* note 23 at para. 42.

79 Elizabeth Sheehy, "Legal Responses to Violence Against Women in Canada," *Canadian Woman Studies* 19:1 & 2 (1999): 62.

80 See *e.g.*, Sharon McIvor & Teressa A. Nahanee, "Aboriginal Women: Invisible Survivors of Violence," in *Unsettling Truths: Battered Women, Policy, Politics and Contemporary Research in Canada*, eds., Kevin D. Bonnycastle & George Rigakos (Vancouver: Collective Press, 1998), 63; Huntley, Blaney *et al, supra* note 56.

81 Suzanne Lenon, "Living on the Edge: Women, Poverty and Homelessness in Canada," in *Violence Against Women, New Canadian Perspectives*, eds., Katherine McKenna & June Larkin (Toronto: Innana Press, 2002), 403; Karen-Lee Miller & Janice Dumont, "Countless Abused Women: Homeless and Inadequately Housed," *Canadian Woman Studies* 20:3 (2000): 115.

82 RCAP, *Perspectives and Realities, supra* note 64 at 573; Isaac & Maloughney, *supra* note 56 at para. 7, n. 14; Jocelyn Proulx & Sharon Perrault, *No Place for Violence: Canadian Aboriginal Alternatives* (Halifax: Fernwood, 2000), 102.

83 Statistics Canada, *Women in Canada, supra* note 44 at 163; Anne McGillivray & Brenda Comaskey, *Black Eyes All of the Time: Intimate Violence, Aboriginal Women and the Justice System* (Toronto: University of Toronto Press, 1999), 13.

84 Statistics Canada, *Women in Canada, supra* note 44 at 195.

85 La Prairie, *Seen But Not Heard, supra* note 66.

86 Statistics Canada, *Women in Canada, supra* note 44 at 169.

87 Angela Browne, Brenda Miller & Eugene Maguin, "Prevalence and Severity of Lifetime Physical and Sexual Victimization Among Incarcerated Women," *International Journal of Law and Psychiatry* 22 (1999): 301 ; Elizabeth Comack, *Women Offenders: Experiences with Physical and Sexual Abuse* (Winnipeg: Criminology Research Centre, 1993); Elizabeth Sheehy, "Review of the Self-Defense Review" (2000) 12 C.J.W.L. 197.

88 Kimberley White-Mair, "Experts and Ordinary Men: Locating *R*. v. *Lavallée*, Battered Woman Syndrome, and the "New" Psychiatric Expertise on Women Within Canadian Legal History" (2000) 12 C.J.W.L. 406-38; Elizabeth Sheehy, "Battered Women and Mandatory Minimum Sentences" (2001) 39 Osgoode Hall L.J. 529-54.

89 Christine Boyle, "The Battered Wife Syndrome and Self-Defense: *Lavalee* v. *R*." (1990) 9 Can. J. Fam. L. 171 at 171-79; Sheehy, *supra* note 79.

90 Christine Boyle, "A Feminist Approach to Criminal Defenses," in *Canadian Perspectives on Legal Theory*, ed., Richard Devlin (Toronto: Edmond Montgomery, 1991), 273; Dennis Klimchuk, "Outrage, Self-Control and Culpability" (1994) 44 U.T.L.J. 441.

91 Additionally, as in the *Gladue* case, poverty on the part of the accused restricts the kinds of defences that can be fully mounted by defence counsel.

92 *Gladue*, *supra* note 4 at para. 68.

93 *Ibid.* at para. 67.

94 *Cappo*, *supra* note 24 at para. 7.

95 Statistics Canada, *Women in Canada*, *supra* note 44 at 199; RCAP, *Perspectives and Realities*, *supra* note 64 at 9.

96 Pay Equity Task Force, *Pay Equity: A New Approach to a Fundamental Right* (Ottawa: Pay Equity Task Force, 2004), 40.

97 Statistics Canada, *Women in Canada*, *supra* note 44 at 196.

98 RCAP, *Perspectives and Realities*, *supra* note 64 at 570.

99 *Taking Responsibility for Homelessness: An Action Plan for Toronto*, Report of the Mayor's Homelessness Action Task Force (Toronto: City of Toronto, 1999).

100 *Gladue*, *supra* note 4 at para. 67.

101 *Ibid.*, at para. 69.

102 *Kakekagamick*, *supra* note 22 at para. 49.

103 This statement is also true of many non-Aboriginal Canadians.

104 Jodi-Anne Brzozowski, Andrea Taylor-Butts & Sara Johnson, *Victimization and Offending among the Aboriginal Population in Canada* (Ottawa: Statistics Canada, 2006), 8; Assembly of First Nations, *First Nations Regional Longitudinal Health Survey: The People's Report* (Ottawa: Assembly of First Nations, 2007), 68.

105 Nancy Poole & Colleen Anne Dell, *Girls, Women and Substance Abuse* (Ottawa: Canadian Centre on Substance Abuse, 2005), 7.

106 Teressa Anne Nahanee, "Sexual Assault of Inuit Females: A Comment on 'Cultural Bias'" in *Confronting Sexual Assault: A Decade of Legal and Social Change*, eds., Julian Roberts & Renate Mohr (Toronto: University of Toronto Press, 1994), 192.

107 Margo Nightingale, "Judicial Attitudes and Differential Treatment: Native Women in Sexual Assault Cases" (1991) 23 Ottawa L. Rev. 71.

108 Razack, *supra* note 37 at 69-70.

109 *Norris, supra* note 9.

110 *Moyan, supra* note 8.

111 In the context of off-reserve voting rights, the Supreme Court *has* noted the unique effects of colonialism on Aboriginal women: *Corbiere* v. *Canada (Minister of Indian and Northern Affairs)* [1999] 2 S.C.R. 203 at para. 72.

112 See Jonathan Rudin & Kent Roach, "Broken Promises: A Response to Stenning and Roberts' 'Empty Promises'" (2002) 65 Sask. L. Rev. 1 at 7.

113 Rudin & Roach, *ibid.*, 6; Lash, *supra* note 3 at 87.

114 *Gladue, supra* note 4 at para. 10.

115 *Ibid.*, at para. 5. For commentary on provocation in the *Gladue* case, see Lash, *supra* note 3; Rudin & Roach, *supra* note 113 at 6.

116 Lash, *ibid.*, *at* 87.

117 *Ibid.*, *at* 85.

118 Despite accepting evidence of Mr. Beaver's past physical abuse toward Ms. Gladue (*Gladue, supra* note 4 at para. 9), the Court accepts the trial judge's assertion that Ms. Gladue was not a "battered or fearful wife [sic]" (at para. 10). The Court goes on to say: "further, the appellant was not afraid of the deceased; indeed, she was the aggressor . . ." (*Gladue, supra* note 4 at para. 160).

119 Lash, *supra* note 3 at 87.

120 See Elizabeth Sheehy, "Battered Woman Syndrome: Developments in Canadian Law after *R.* v. *Lavalee*," in *Women, Male Violence and the Law*, ed., J. Stubbs (Sydney: Institute of Criminology, 1995), 175.

121 *Gladue, supra* note 4 at para. 12.

122 *Ibid.*, at para. 2.

123 *Ibid.*

124 *Ibid.*, at para. 12.

125 *Ibid.*, at para. 92.

126 British Columbia, *Strategic Plan for Aboriginal Services* (Victoria: BC Ministry for Children and Families, 2000); Tracey Renee Fleck, "Aboriginal Child Welfare: Solutions to the Crisis," *Aboriginal Women's Law Journal* 1 (1994): 13.

127 Lash, *supra* note 3.

128 See discussion of *Norris*, below.

129 *Norris, supra* note 9 at para. 4.

130 *Wells, supra* note 10 at para. 50-51.

131 See *supra* note 25.

132 See *e.g.*, *R.* v. *Pankewian* (2002), 161 C.C.C. (3d) 534 (Sask. C.A.), which states that a conditional sentence is available even for commercial quantities of drugs; *R.* v. *Luff* (2002), 170 C.C.C. (3d) 339 (Man. C.A.) is a case of possession for purposes of trafficking where the defendant was found in possession of over 40 grams of cocaine; *R.* v. *Shahnavaz* (2000), 149 C.C.C. (3d) 97 (Ont. C.A.) is a case of four counts trafficking heroine; *R.* v. *Ploumis* (2000), 150 C.C.C. (3d) 427 (Ont. C.A.) is a case of possession for the purposes of trafficking commercial quantities of cocaine.

133 *Moyan, supra* note 8 at para. 2.

134 *Ibid.*, at para. 2.

135 Dara Culhane, *The Pleasure of the Crown: Anthropology, Law and First Nations* (Burnaby: Talon Books, 1998); Patricia Monture-Angus, *Thunder in My Soul: A Mohawk Woman Speaks* (Halifax: Fernwood Press, 1995), 217, n. 4.

136 *Moyan, supra* note 8 at para. 7.

137 *Norris, supra* note 9 at para. 5.

138 *Ibid.*, at para. 7.

139 *Ibid.*, at para. 10.

140 See *supra*, notes 131, 132.

141 Kent Roach & Jonathan Rudin, "*Gladue*: The Judicial and Political Reception of a Promising Decision" (2000) 42 Can. J. Crim. 335 at 344-45; Judge Mary Ellen Turpel-Lafond, "Sentencing within a Restorative Justice Paradigm: Procedural Implications of *R.* v. *Gladue*" (1999) 43 *Criminal Law Quarterly* 34.

NOTES TO CHAPTER TEN

1 See Don Clairmont & Rick Linden, *Developing and Evaluating Justice Projects in Aboriginal Communities: A Review of the Literature* (Ottawa: Public Safety Canada, 1998); Jane Dickson-Gilmore & Carol La Prairie, *Will the Circle be Unbroken? Aboriginal Communities, Restorative Justice, and the Challenges of Conflict and Change* (Toronto: University of Toronto Press, 2005).

2 Commission on First Nations and Métis Peoples and Justice Reform, "Restorative Justice: Restoring Justice in Saskatchewan" in *Legacy of Hope: An Agenda for Change*, vol. 1 (Regina: Government of Saskatchewan, 2004) at 4-1.

3 The author has discussed these topics in Barbara Tomporowski, "The Involvement of Victims in Saskatchewan's Restorative Justice Agencies" (paper presented to the Building Relationships and Restorative Justice Provincial Conference held in Regina, Saskatchewan, 23 Feb. 2005) [unpublished]; Barbara Tomporowski, "Community Involvement in Saskatchewan's Restorative Justice Agencies" (paper presented to the 10th Annual International Society for Justice Research Social Justice Conference held in Regina, Saskatchewan, 30 June – 3 July 2004) [unpublished].

4 Susan Sharpe, "How Large Should the Restorative Justice 'Tent' Be?" in *Critical Issues in Restorative Justice*, eds., Howard Zehr & Barb Toews (Monsey, NY: Criminal Justice Press, 2004), 19.

5 Howard Zehr, *Changing Lenses* (Scottdale, PA: Herald Press, 1990), 181.

6 See Dennis Sullivan & Larry Tifft, *Restorative Justice: Healing the Foundations of Our Everyday Lives* (Monsey, NY: Willow Tress Press, 2001); Ted Wachtel & Paul McCold, "Restorative Justice in Everyday Life" in *Restorative Justice and Civil Society*, eds., Heather Strang & John Braithwaite (Cambridge, UK: Cambridge University Press, 2001).

7 Laura Mirsky discusses these applications of restorative justice in a number of articles available through the International Institute for Restorative Practices. See *e.g.*, Laura Mirsky, *Community Conferencing: An Interview with Gena Gerard*, Real Justice, International Institute for Restorative Practices, www.realjustice.org/library/ccgerard.html.

8 Federal-Provincial-Territorial Working Group on Restorative Justice, *Restorative Justice: A Consultation Paper*, Justice Canada, www.justice.gc.ca/en/ps/voc/rjpap.html.

9 Kris Vanspauwen, *Working Apart and Together: Restorative Justice in Saskatchewan – Opinions and Attitudes of a Growing Movement* (M.A. thesis, the Faculteit Rechtsgeleerdheid Criminologische Wetenschnappen, Katholieke Universiteit Leuven, Belgium, 2001) [unpublished], 38.

10 Saskatchewan Justice, *Saskatchewan Adult Diversion Program* (Regina: Saskatchewan Justice, 1995).

11 Community Services Branch, *Alternative Measures Policies* (Regina: Saskatchewan Justice, 2005), 2.

12 Les Samuelson, *Saskatchewan Aboriginal Justice Strategy, the Origins, Rationale and Implementation Process: An Evaluation Report* (Regina: Policing, Planning and Evaluation Branch, Saskatchewan Justice, 2000), 14.

13 This information on finances and the number of programs has been provided by Community Services Branch, Ministry of Justice and Attorney General, which maintains a list of the community justice and alternative measures programs and community justice committees supported by the ministry. The program list is available on the ministry website, www.justice.gov.sk.ca/Default.aspx?DN=da73dfe1-6653-4a17-8449-07be71aff4e2. As the number of funded programs changes frequently, the current list may not correspond to the figures provided for 2006-2007.

14 *Criminal Code*, R.S.C., 1996, s. 717; information on the Saskatchewan Justice Alternative Measures Policy can be found in Community Services Branch (*supra* note 11 at 4-6).

15 *Youth Criminal Justice Act*, R.S.C., 2002, s.10; information on the Saskatchewan Corrections and Public Safety Youth Extrajudicial Sanctions Policy can be found in Community Services Branch (*ibid*).

16 In addition to Kris Vanspauwen's work (*supra* note 9), graduate studies include: Marc Craddock, *Family Group Conferences and Restorative Justice: Challenging the Existing Reactive Police Wisdom?* (M.A. thesis, Law & Criminology Program, University of Sheffield, UK and the International Exchange Program on Victimology and Restorative Justice, 1998) [unpublished]); and Miriam Handel, *Pushing the Boundaries: Restorative Justice Practice in a First Nations Community* (M.A. thesis, Faculty of Graduate Studies and Research, University of Regina, 2003) [unpublished]. Evaluations conducted by the Ministry of Justice and Attorney General include *Prince Albert Alternative Measures Program: Program Evaluation Report* (Regina: Saskatchewan Justice, 2006); and *Use of Adult Alternative Measures in Saskatchewan 1999-2000 and 2000-2001* (Regina: Saskatchewan Justice, 2003). Other evaluations include Carol La Prairie, *Seeking Change: Justice Development in La Loche* (Regina: Saskatchewan Justice, 1997); and Joan Nuffield, *Evaluation of the Adult Victim-Offender Mediation Program - Saskatoon Community Mediation Services* (Regina: Saskatchewan Justice, 1997).

17 Crime and Justice Research Centre, Victoria University of Wellington with Sue Triggs, *New Zealand Court-Referred Restorative Justice Pilot* (Wellington, New Zealand: New Zealand Ministry of Justice, 2005).

18 Jeff Latimer, Craig Donden & Danielle Muise, *The Effectiveness of Restorative Justice Practices: A Meta-Analysis* (Ottawa: Research and Statistics Division, Department of Justice Canada, 2001), 12-20.

19 Saskatchewan Justice maintains a database that collects statistical information about alternative measures referrals. Information for alternative measures cases in 1999-2000 and 2000-2001 is publicly available (see Saskatchewan Justice, *Alternative Measures in Saskatchewan, supra* note 16). At the time of writing, the database analysis of alternative measures statistics for more recent years had not been finalized.

20 Saskatchewan Justice, *Alternative Measures in Saskatchewan, ibid.,* at 6. This figure includes 2,226 adult alternative measures referrals recorded in the provincial database, as well as 552 adult alternative measures referrals that were not included in the provincial database because some adult alternative measures programs do not report the data.

21 *Ibid.*, 14.

22 *Ibid.*, 11.

23 *Ibid.*, 10.

24 *Ibid.*, 12.

25 *Ibid.*, 13.

26 *Ibid.*, 18.

27 *Ibid.*, 17.

28 *Ibid.*, 19.

29 These statistics were provided by the Policy, Planning and Evaluation Branch, Ministry of Justice and Attorney General. The provincial alternative measures database is continuing to collect statistical information regarding alternative measures referrals. The data for 2001–2002 and more recent years have not been published.

30 Saskatchewan Justice, *PA Alternative Measures Program*, *supra* note 16.

31 *Ibid.*, 10, 50.

32 *Ibid.*, 56.

33 *Ibid.*, 61.

34 *Ibid.*, 21.

35 *Ibid.*, 25.

36 *Ibid.*, 28.

37 *Ibid.*, 32.

38 *Ibid.*, 36-37.

39 John Braithwaite & Declan Roche, "Responsibility and Restorative Justice" in *Restorative Community Justice: Repairing Harm and Transforming Communities*, eds., Gordon Bazemore & Mara Schiff (Cincinnati: Anderson Co, 2001), 64.

40 Daniel Van Ness & Karen Heetderks Strong, *Restoring Justice* (Cincinnati: Anderson Co., 1997), 35-36.

41 Auditor General of Canada, *Modernizing Accountability in the Public Sector: 2002 Report of the Auditor General of Canada* (Ottawa: Minister of Public Works and Government Services Canada, 2002).

42 Samuelson, *supra* note 12 at 32.

43 Katherine Scott, *Funding Matters: The Impact of Canada's New Funding Regime on Nonprofit and Voluntary Organizations Summary Report* (Ottawa: Canadian Council on Social Development, 2003) 1, www.ccsd.ca/pubs/2003/fm/; Sherri Torjman, *Are Outcomes the Best Outcomes?* (Ottawa: Caledon Institute of Social Policy, 1999).

44 John Graham, *Building Trust: Capturing the Promise of Accountability in an Aboriginal Context*, Policy Brief No. 4, The Institute on Governance, www.iog.ca/publications/policybrief4.pdf; Richard Mulgan, *Accountability in a Contemporary Public Sector* (Canberra, Australia: Asia Pacific School of Economics and Government, Australian National University, 2005); Torjman, *ibid.*

45 David Garland, *The Culture of Control* (Chicago: University of Chicago Press, 2001), 189.

46 *Ibid.*

47 Scott, *supra* note 43 at 11.

48 Scott, *ibid.*, 7-8; Torjman, *supra* note 43 at 3.

49 Scott, *ibid.*, 11-16.

50 Dickson-Gilmore & La Prairie, *supra* note 1 at 223.

51 *Ibid.*, 225.

52 Barbara Tomporowski, *Exploring Restorative Justice in Saskatchewan* (M.A thesis for the Social Studies Program, University of Regina, 2004) [unpublished] at 35-51. The method of institutional ethnography has been developed by Canadian sociologist Dorothy Smith: see Dorothy Smith, *The Everyday World as Problematic* (Toronto: University of Toronto Press, 1987); Dorothy Smith, *Writing the Social: Exploring the Relations of Ruling* (Toronto: University of Toronto Press, 1999).

53 Tomporowski, *Exploring Restorative Justice, ibid.*, 2-3.

54 *Ibid.*, 36-37.

55 *Ibid.*, 46-47.

56 *Ibid.*, 80.

57 *Ibid.*, 81-82.

58 *Ibid.*, 103-4.

59 *Ibid.*, 72.

60 *Ibid.*, 58.

61 *Ibid.*, 55-57.

62 *Ibid.*, 59-60.

63 *Ibid.*, 83.

64 *Ibid.*, 55.

65 *Ibid.*, 53-54.

66 *Ibid.*, 55.

67 *Ibid.*, 55-56.

68 *Ibid.*, 54.

69 *Ibid.*, 55.

70 Institute on Governance, *Developing Capacity for Program Management: Summary of the Major Conclusions of the Royal Commission on Aboriginal Peoples* (Ottawa: Institute on Governance, 1997), Institute on Governance, www.iog.ca/publications/devcapeng.pdf, 13.

71 Auditor General of Canada, *Economic Development of First Nations Communities: Institutional Arrangements – Report of the Auditor General of Canada to the House of Commons* (Ottawa: Auditor General of Canada, 2003), Office of the Auditor General of Canada, www.oag-bvg.gc.ca/domino/reports.nsf/html/20031109ce.html, s. 9.39, 9.85, 9.90. 9.94.

72 Tomporowski, *Exploring Restorative Justice, supra* note 52 at 56.

73 *Ibid.*, 56-57.

74 *Ibid.*, 56.

75 *Ibid.*

76 *Ibid.*, 59.

77 *Ibid.*

78 *Ibid.*, 74.

79 Saskatchewan Justice, *Alternative Measures in Saskatchewan*, *supra* note 16 at 16.

80 *Ibid.*

81 *Ibid.*

82 Saskatchewan Justice, *PA Alternative Measures Program*, *supra* note 16 at 30-31.

83 Tomporowski, *Exploring Restorative Justice*, *supra* note 52 at 75.

84 *Ibid.*, 73.

85 *Ibid.*, 76-77, 110-12.

86 *Ibid.*, 110.

87 *Ibid.*, 74.

88 *Ibid.* The requirement to provide midyear and year-end reports are outlined in contracts between the Ministry of Justice and Attorney General and the community-based agency.

89 *Ibid.*

90 *Ibid.*

91 Saskatchewan Justice, *PA Alternative Measures Program*, *supra* note 16 at 3.

92 Tomporowski, *Exploring Restorative Justice*, *supra* note 52 at 74.

93 *Ibid.*

94 *Ibid.*, 73-74.

95 Saskatchewan Justice, *PA Alternative Measures Program*, *supra* note 16 at 48.

96 *Ibid.*, 49.

97 *Ibid.*, 61-62.

98 *Ibid.*, 61.

99 *Ibid.*

100 Tomporowski, *Exploring Restorative Justice*, *supra* note 52 at 94.

101 As discussed in Tomporowski, "Community Involvement," *supra* note 3 at 4.

102 Saskatchewan Justice, *Alternative Measures in Saskatchewan*, *supra* note 16 at 18.

103 Tomporowski, *Exploring Restorative Justice*, *supra* note 52 at 59-60.

104 *Ibid.*

105 Information provided by Community Services Branch, Saskatchewan Justice.

106 See Dickson-Gilmore & La Prairie, *supra* note 1 at 87, 181; Maxine Hodgson & John Whyte, "Developing Community Justice in Saskatchewan" (paper presented to the Symposium on Understanding Change: Justice Issues and Public Policy in

Saskatchewan hosted by the Saskatchewan Institute of Public Policy in Regina, Saskatchewan, 10 Apr. 2003) [unpublished].

107 Information provided by Community Services Branch, Saskatchewan Justice, *supra* note 13.

108 Graham, *supra* note 44, 3-4.

109 *Ibid.*, 4.

110 *Ibid.*, 3.

111 Tomporowski, *Exploring Restorative Justice, supra* note 52 at 113-15.

112 Vanspauwen, *supra* note 9 at 64.

113 Russel Barsh, "Evaluating the Quality of Justice" in *Justice as Healing: Indigenous Ways - Writings on Community Peacemaking and Restorative Justice from the Native Law Centre*, ed, Wanda McCaslin (St. Paul, Minnesota: Living Justice Press, 2005), 169. See also Curt Taylor Griffiths & Ray Corrado, "Implementing Restorative Youth Justice: A Case Study in Community Justice and the Dynamics of Reform," in *Restorative Juvenile Justice: Repairing the Harm of Youth Crime*, eds., Gordon Bazemore & Lode Walgrave (Monsey, NY: Criminal Justice Press, 2002), 252.

114 Martin Papillon & Gina Consentino, *Lessons from Abroad: Towards a New Social Model for Canada's Aboriginal Peoples*, CPRN Social Architecture Research Papers, Research Report F/40, Canadian Policy Research Networks, www.cprn.org/ doc.cfm?doc=565&l=en; Hodgson & Whyte, *supra* note 106; John Graham & Jake Wilson, *Toward Sound Government-to-Government Relationships with First Nations: A Proposed Analytical Tool*, Policy Brief No. 21, The Institute on Governance, www.iog.ca/publications/policybrief21.pdf; David Hawkes, "Rebuilding the Relationship: The 'Made in Saskatchewan' Approach to First Nations Governance" (paper presented at the Conference on Reconfiguring Aboriginal-State Relations, Queen's University, Kingston, Ontario, 1-2 Nov., 2002) [unpublished].

115 Commission on First Nations and Métis Peoples and Justice Reform, "Empowering First Nations and Metis Leadership" in *Legacy of Hope: An Agenda for Change*, vol. 1 (Regina: Government of Saskatchewan, 2004), 14-15.

116 Graham & Wilson, *supra* note 114 at 28.

117 Institute on Governance, *supra* note 70 at 14.

NOTES ON CHAPTER ELEVEN

1 Frances Abele & Michael J. Prince, "Constructing Political Space for Aboriginal Communities in Canada" (paper given at "Constructing Tomorrow's Federalism" conference held by the Saskatchewan Institute of Public Policy in Regina, SK, 24-26 Mar. 2004).

2 For a list of recent agreements, see Indian and Northern Affairs Canada, www.ainc-inac.gc.ca/pr/agr/index_e.html.

3 *Canadian Charter of Rights and Freedoms*, Part I of the *Constitution Act, 1982*, being Schedule B to the *Canada Act 1982* (UK), 1982, c. 11 (which came into force 17 Apr. 1982).

4 *Constitution Act, 1982*, being Schedule B to the *Canada Act 1982* (UK), 1982, c. 11, s. 32: "This Charter applies (*a*) to the Parliament and government of Canada in respect of all matters within the authority of Parliament including all matters relating to the Yukon Territory and Northwest Territories; and (*b*) to the legislatures and governments of each province in respect of all matters within the authority of the legislature of each province."

5 James Y. Henderson, "Empowering Treaty Federalism" (1994) 58:2 Sask. L. Rev. 286.

6 Kent McNeil, "Aboriginal Governments and the *Canadian Charter of Rights and Freedoms*" (1996) 34:1 Osgoode Hall L.J. 61 at 69.

7 *Corbiere* v. *Canada (Minister of Indian and Northern Affairs)* [1999] 2 S.C.R. 203, 173 D.L.R. (4th) (S.C.C.).

8 *Indian Act*, R.S.C., 1985, c. I-5.

9 See Ovide Mercredi & Mary Ellen Turpel, *Into the Rapids: Navigating the Future of First Nations* (Toronto: Penguin Books, 1993), 104.

10 Mary-Ellen Turpel, "Aboriginal Peoples and the *Canadian Charter*: Interpretive Monopolies, Cultural Differences" (1989-90) 6:3 Can. Hum. Rts. Y.B. 503 at 512-13.

11 Joseph H. Carens, *Culture, Citizenship and Community: A Contextual Exploration of Justice as Evenhandedness* (Oxford: Oxford University Press, 2000), 193.

12 *Ibid.*, at 192. See Dan Russell, *A People's Dream: Aboriginal Self-Government in Canada* (Vancouver: UBC Press, 2000), 96-145. Russell articulated similar concerns and identified a number of potential challenges that could proceed if the Charter were to apply to First Nations.

13 See Alan C. Cairns, *First Nations and the Canadian State: In Search of Coexistence* (Kingston, ON: Institute of Intergovernmental Relations, 2005), 30. Cairns refers to the negative reaction from the "gang of eight" to P.E. Trudeau's proposed *Charter*.

14 John Borrows, "Contemporary Traditional Equality: The Effect of the Charter on First Nations Politics," in *Charting the Consequences: The Impact of the Charter of Rights on Canadian Law and Politics*, eds., David Schneiderman & Kate Sutherland (Toronto: University of Toronto Press, 1997), 184.

15 *Ibid.*, at 172.

16 Royal Commission on Aboriginal Peoples, *Partners in Confederation: Aboriginal Peoples, Self-Government, and the Constitution* (Ottawa: Supply and Services Canada, 1993), 40.

17 Royal Commission on Aboriginal Peoples, "Chapter 3: Governance" in *Restructuring the Relationship: Report of the Royal Commission on Aboriginal Peoples*, vol. II (Ottawa: Supply and Services Canada, 1996), www.ainc-inac.gc.ca/ch/rcap/sg/sgmm_e.html.

18 Roy Romanow, "Re-working the Miracle: The Constitutional Accord 1981" (1982) 8 Queen's L.J. 74, at 92.

19 Emilio Mignore, cited in Andrew G. McGrew, "Human Rights in the Global Age: Coming to Terms with Globalization," in *Human Rights Fifty Years on: A Reappraisal*, ed., Tony Evans (Manchester: Manchester University Press, 1998), 197.

20 *Charter of Rights, supra* note 3, s. 25. See also *Consensus Report on the Constitution* (Charlottetown: Government of Canada, 1992), www.solon.org/Constitutions/Canada/English/Proposals/CharlottetownConsensus.html#apccrf, s. 43.

21 Charlottetown Accord, *ibid.*

22 *Supra* note 17, App. A, s. 2.3.12.

23 Khayyam Zev Paltiel, "Group Rights in the Canadian Constitution and Aboriginal Claims to Self-determination," in *Contemporary Canadian Politics*, eds., Robert J. Jackson, Doreen Jackson & Nicolas Baxter-Moore (Scarborough: Prentice-Hall Canada Inc., 1987), 26.

24 See Jack Jedwab, *Canada's Charter of Rights and Freedoms seen as having positive impact on rights and is growing symbol of Canadian identity*, www.acs-aec.ca/oldsite/Polls/Poll1.pdf: an analysis of a 2001-02 Environics Research Group poll on the impact of the *Charter*.

25 Romonow, *supra* note 18 at 90.

26 Roy Romanow, John Whyte & Howard Leeson, *Canada Notwithstanding: The Making of the Constitution, 1976-1982* (Toronto: Carswell/Methuen, 1984), 200.

27 Alan C. Cairns, *Citizens Plus: Aboriginal Peoples and the Canadian State* (Vancouver: UBC Press, 2000), 83.

28 Indian and Northern Affairs Canada, "Part 1," *Federal Policy Guide: Aboriginal Self Government* (Ottawa: Public Works and Services Canada, 1995) 2.

29 *Nisga'a Final Agreement* (4 May 1999), www.ainc-inac.gc.ca/pr/agr/nsga/nisdex_e.html.

30 *Umbrella Final Agreement Between The Government of Canada, The Council For Yukon Indians And The Government Of The Yukon* (29 May 1993), www.ainc-inac.gc.ca/pr/agr/umb/index_e.html.

31 *Labrador Inuit Land Claims Agreement* (22 Jan. 2005), www.laa.gov.nl.ca/laa/liaclaims/default.htm, c. 2, s. 2.18.1.

32 *Supra* note 29, c. 2, s. 2.9.

33 *Supra* note 30, c. 2.

34 *Constitution of the Ta'an Kwäch'än Council*, www.taan.ca/constitution.html (esp. s. 4.1, s. 4.2).

35 *Ibid.*, s. 4.1.

36 S.C., 1993, c. 28.

37 *Human Rights Act*, S.Nu., 2003, c. 12 (assented 5 Nov. 2003).

38 *Ibid.*, Preamble.

39 *Supra* note 31, s. 2.18.1.

40 *Ibid.*, s. 17.3.4 (e), s. 17.3.4 (f).

41 *Supra* note 7.

42 *Supra* note 8, s. 77(1).

43 *Corbiere, supra* note 7. Also see analysis by Beverley O'Neil of the Ktunaxa Nation, "274 First Nations still operate under the *Indian Act* Election Process," in *Off-Reserve Gain Right to Vote*, www.designingnations.com/pdf_s/Corbiere.PDF. Additionally, Ian Peach suggests that off-reserve First Nations people could utilize the *Charter* against the federal government if they are denied services by the federal government because they are no longer residents on the reserve. By extrapolation again, such an argument could be made against a band government that similarly denies services to its members living off-reserve. See Ian Peach, "The *Charter of Rights* and Off-Reserve First Nations People: A Way to Fill the Public Policy Vacuum," *Public Policy Paper 24* (Regina: Saskatchewan Institute of Public Policy, University of Regina, 2004).

44 [2000] 1 C.N.L.R. 205.

45 [2003] 2 C.N.L.R. 193 at para. 29.

46 *Ibid.*, at para. 29.

47 Patrica Monture-Angus, *Journeying Forward: Dreaming of First Nations Independence* (Halifax: Fernwood Publishing, 1999), 150: "It would be an odd conclusion if government whose independent authority originates outside of any Crown action were forced to submit to the discipline of the *Charter*, itself a Crown Act."

48 McNeil, *supra* note 6 at 98.

NOTES TO CHAPTER TWELVE

1 Antony N. Allott, "What is To Be Done with African Customary Law?: The Experience of Problems and Reforms in Anglophone Africa from 1950" (1984) 28 J. Afr. L. 56.

2 Gordon R. Woodman, "How State Courts Created Customary Law in Ghana and Nigeria," in *Indigenous Law and the State*, eds., B. Morse & Gordon R. Woodman (Dordrecht: Foris, 1988), 181; Julie E. Stewart, "Why I Can't Teach Customary Law," in *The Changing Family: International Perspectives on the Family and Family Law*, eds., John Eekelaar & Thadabantu Nhlapo (Oxford: Hart, 1998), 217.

3 Martin Chanock, *Law, Custom and Social Order: The Colonial Experience in Malawi and Zambia* (Cambridge: Cambridge University Press, 1985); Terence Ranger, "The Invention of Tradition in Colonial Africa," in *The Invention of Tradition*, eds., Eric Hobsbawn & Terence Ranger (Cambridge & New York: Cambridge University Press, 1983), 211.

4 Celestine Nyamu-Musembi, "Are Local Norms and Practices Fences or Pathways?: The Example of Women's Rights," in *Cultural Transformation and Human Rights*, ed., Abdullahi A. An-Na'im (London: Zed Books Ltd., 2002), 126.

5 Celestine I. Nyamu, "Achieving Gender Equality in a Plural Legal Context: Custom and Women's Access to and Control of Land in Kenya," *Third World Legal Stud.* (1998-99): 21.

6 Sally Falk Moore, "Law and Social Change: The Semi-Autonomous Social Field as an Appropriate Subject of Study," in *Law as Process: An Anthropological Approach* (London: Routledge & Kegan Paul, 1978), 54.

7 *Ibid.*

8 Celestine Nyamu-Musembi, "Review of Experience in Engaging with 'Non-State' Justice Systems in East Africa" (2003) [unpublished], www.gsdrc.org/docs/open/DS37.pdf.

9 For a more detailed account of Kenya's legal history, see Y.P. Ghai & J.P.W.B. McAuslan, *Public Law and Political Change in Kenya* (Nairobi: Oxford University Press: 1970); H.F. Morris & James S. Read, *Indirect Rule and the Search for Justice in East Africa* (Oxford: Clarendon Press, 1972).

10 The essence of the indirect rule doctrine was that colonial officials would rule through traditional authorities, whereby the former would formulate the broad outlines of policy and leave the practical details to be worked out on the ground by traditional leaders, notably, the chiefs. For a more detailed elucidation of the indirect rule policy, see Lord Lugard, *The Dual Mandate in British Tropical Africa* (Hamden, Conn.: Archon Books, 1965). For a critique of the doctrine, see Mahmoud Mamdani, *Citizen and Subject: Contemporary Africa and the Legacy of Late Colonialism* (Princeton, N.J.: Princeton University Press, 1996).

11 This was the term used in British colonial legislation to refer to African customary law. See *East African Protectorate Order in Council*, S.R.O. 661/1902, s. 20.

12 Sally Falk Moore, "Treating Law as Knowledge: Telling Colonial Officers What to Say to Africans about Running 'Their Own' Lives" (1992) 26:1 Law & Soc'y Rev. 11.

13 The *Order in Council* provided *inter alia* that in all civil and criminal cases to which natives were parties, courts would be guided by native law so far as it was applicable and was not repugnant to justice and morality or inconsistent with any order in council, ordinance, or any regulation or rule made thereunder (*Order in Council, supra* note 11, s. 20 (a)). This provision has substantively been retained and is currently contained in the *Judicature Act* No. 16 of 1967, Cap. 8, s. 3 (2).

14 See dictum in *Gwa bi Kilimo* v. *Kirunda bin Ifuti* [1938] 1 T.L.R. 5.

15 *Order in Council, supra* note 11, s. 20 (b):provided *inter alia* that all cases between natives would be decided according to substantial justice and without undue regard to technicalities of procedure and without undue delay. This provision was retained in section 3 (2) the *Judicature Act*, No. 16 of 1967 (Cap. 8).

16 Ghai & McAuslan, *supra* note 9 at 153.

17 *Ibid.*, at 154.

18 See *Judicature Act, supra* note 13, s. 3 (a), 3 (b).

19 Allott, *supra* note 1; Robert A. Bush, "A Pluralistic Understanding of Access to Justice: Development of Systems of Justice in African Nations," in *Emerging Issues and Perspectives*, vol. 3, eds., Mauro Cappelletti & Bryant Garth (Milan: Sijthoff, 1979), 259.

20 H.W.O. Okoth-Ogendo, "Customary Law in the Kenyan Legal System: An Old Debate Revived," in *The S.M. Otieno Case: Death and Burial in Modern Kenya*, eds., J.B. Ojwang & J.N.K. Mugambi (Nairobi: Nairobi University Press, 1989), 135.

21 Eugene Cotran, *The Law of Marriage and Divorce*, vol. 1 (London: Sweet & Maxwell, 1968); *The Law of Succession*, vol. 2 (London, Sweet & Maxwell, 1969).

22 Agnes Weis Bentzon, Anne Hellum & Julie Stewart, *Pursuing Grounded Theory in Law: South-North Experiences in Developing Women's Law* (Harare, Mond Books, 1998).

23 In 1967, the Kenya government established two commissions, one on marriage and divorce, and the other on succession and each with the mandate to recommend legal reforms in marriage, divorce, and succession, respectively. The former commission drafted a marriage bill which sought to unify the diverse marriage law systems but was never passed by Parliament owing to widespread controversy over certain provisions that were seen as contrary to African custom. The recommendations of the latter commission resulted in a unified law of succession, whose provisions overrode customary norms of succession. The *Registered Land Act* effectively extinguished customary land tenure in favour of Western concepts of individual land ownership (No. 25 of 1963, Cap. 300, ss. 27 and 163).

24 J.B. Ojwang, "The Meaning, Content and Significance of Tribal Law in an Emergent Nation: The Kenyan Case," *Law and Anthropology* 4 (1989): 125; Antony N. Allott, "Introduction," in E. Cotran, *Casebook on Kenya Customary Law* (Oxon: Professional Books Ltd, 1987), xi.

25 *Supra* note 8 at 21.

26 *Ibid.*

27 *Ibid.*, at 36.

28 Issa G. Shivji, "Contradictory Perspectives on Rights and Justice in the Context of Land Tenure Reform in Tanzania," in *Beyond Rights Talk and Culture Talk*, ed., Mahmoud Mamdani (New York: St. Martins Press, 2000), 39-40.

29 *Supra* note 4.

30 *Otieno* v. *Ougo & Another* [1987] K.L.R. 407.

31 *Supra* note 4.

32 African Rights, *Kenya Shadow Justice* (London: African Rights, 1996).

33 *Supra* note 8 at 22-23.

34 *Supra* note 4.

35 *Supra* note 8 at 24.

36 *Ibid.*

37 *Ibid.*; Ciru Mwaura & Susan Schmeidl, eds., *Early Warning and Conflict Management in the Horn of Africa* (Lawrenceville, N.J.: The Red Sea Press Inc., 2002).

38 *Supra* note 4.

39 Joanna Stevens, *Access to Justice in Sub-Saharan Africa: The Role of Traditional and Informal Justice Systems* (London: Penal Reform International, 2001), L, www.penalreform.org/resources/rep-2001-access-to-justice-africa-en.pdf.

40 *Ibid.*

41 *Supra* note 4.

42 *Ibid.*

43 *Supra* note 39.

44 *Ibid.*; Oko O. Elechi, "Human Rights and the African Indigenous Justice System" (paper presented at the 18th International Conference of the International Society for the Reform of Criminal Law held in Montreal, Quebec, Canada, 8-12 Aug. 2004) [unpublished], www.isrcl.org/Papers/2004/Elechi.pdf.

45 Sally Engle Merry, "The Social Organization of Mediation in Nonindustrial Societies: Implications for Informal Community Justice in America," in *The Politics of Informal Justice*, vol. 2, ed., R.L. Abel (New York: Academic Press, 1982), 17.

46 Anne Griffiths, "Legal Pluralism in Botswana: Women's Access to Law," *Journal of Legal Pluralism* 40 (1998): 123; Nyamu-Musembi, "Local Norms," *supra* note 4.

47 *Supra* note 4.

48 Merry, *supra* note 45.

49 *Supra* note 4.

50 Griffiths, *supra* note 46; Ronald Thacker, "Traditional Justice Systems," in *Justice for Children: Challenges for Policy and Practice in Sub-Saharan Africa*, eds., Celia Petty & Maggie Brown (London: Save the Children, 1998), 83.

51 *Supra* note 4.

52 Thacker, *supra* note 50; African Rights, *supra* note 32.

53 Ray Abrahams, "Sungusungu: Village Vigilante Groups in Tanzania," *African Affairs* 86 (1987): 179.

54 Gray Phombeah, "Profile: Kenya's Secretive Mungiki Sect," *BBC News Online, Nairobi* (11 Feb. 2003), news.bbc.co.uk/1/hi/world/africa/2745421.stm.

55 J.A. Bidaguren & D.N. Eestrella, "Governability and Forms of Popular Justice in the New South Africa and Mozambique: Community Courts and Vigilantism," *J. Legal Pluralism* 47 (2002): 113.

56 Nyamu-Musembi, *supra* note 8; Leah Wambura Kimathi, "Non-State Institutions as a Basis of State Reconstruction: The Case of Justice Systems in Africa" (paper presented for the Council for the Development of Social Science Research in Africa 11th General Assembly, Maputo, Mozambique, 6-10 Dec. 2005) [unpublished].

57 William Schärf, "Non-State Justice Systems in Southern Africa: How Should Governments Respond?" (Rondebosch: Institute of Criminology, University of Cape Town, South Africa, 2003), www.csvr.org.za/confpaps/scharf.htm.

58 *Ibid.*; Kimathi, *supra* note 56.

59 Stevens, *supra* note 39; D.W. Nabudere, "Towards the Study of Post Traditional Systems of Justice in the Great Lakes Region of Africa," *East African Journal of Peace and Human Rights* 8 (2002): 1.

60 African Rights, *supra* note 32.

61 Makau wa Mutua, "The Banjul Charter and the African Cultural Fingerprint: An Evaluation of the Language of Duties" (1994-95) 35 Va. J. Int'l L. 339.

62 *Ibid.*, 342-43.

63 Elechi, *supra* note 44.

64 Patricia Ewick & Susan S. Silbey, *The Common Place of Law* (Chicago: University of Chicago Press, 1998).

65 E.A. Hoffman, "Legal Consciousness and Dispute Resolution: Different Disputing Behaviour at Two Similar Taxicab Companies" (2003) 28:3 *Law and Soc. Inquiry,* 691.

66 For example, Mutua, *supra* note 61; Shivji, *supra* note 28.

67 Keba M'Mbaye, "The African Conception of Law," in *International Encyclopaedia of Comparative Law*, eds., Rene David, *et al.* (New York: Tubingen, J.C.B. Mohr, 1978), 138.

68 Mutua, *supra* note 61; Nabudere, *supra* note 59; Elisabetta Grande, "Alternative Dispute Resolution, Africa and the Structure of Law and Power: The Horn in Context" (1999) 42 Journal of African Law 63.

69 Mutua, *ibid.*; Shivji, *supra* note 28.

70 Elechi, *supra* note 44.

71 Stevens, *supra* note 39.

72 Nyamu-Musembi, *supra* note 8. This integration was provided for in the *Magistrates' Courts Act*, No. 17 of 1967 (Cap. 10).

73 Joanna Stevens, *Traditional and Informal Justice Systems in Africa, South Asia, and the Caribbean: A Review of the Literature* (London: Penal Reform International, 1999).

74 Catherine Meschievitz & Marc Galanter, "In Search of Nyaya Panchayats: The Politics of a Moribund Institution," in *The Politics of Informal Justice*, vol. 2, ed., Richard L. Abel (New York: Academic Press, 1982), 48.

75 *Supra* note 73.

76 Ulrike Watnizek, "Legally Unrepresented Women Petitioners in the Lower Courts of Tanzania" (1990-91) 30 & 31 J. Legal Pluralism, 255.

77 *Supra* note 73.

78 Upendra Baxi & Marc Galanter, "Panchayat Justice: An Indian Experiment in Legal Access," in *Access to Justice*, vol. 3, *Emerging Issues and Perspectives*, eds., Mauro Cappelletti & Bryant Garth (Milan: Sijthoff, 1979), 343.

79 *Supra* note 73.

80 *Ibid.*

81 See South Africa Law Commission, *Community Dispute Resolution Structures: Discussion Paper 87, Project 94*, www.doj.gov.za/salrc/dpapers/dp87_prj94_dispute_1999oct.pdf.

82 Shivji, *supra* note 28.

83 Mwaura & Schmeidl, *supra* note 37.

84 Martin Chanock, "Law, State and Culture: Thinking About 'Customary Law' After Apartheid" (1991) Acta Juridica, 52.

85 Research conducted by the author on informal justice systems in Huruma, Nairobi (Jan.-Feb. 2006). See Winifred W. Kamau, *Law, Families and Dispute Resolution: Negotiating Justice in a Plural Legal Context* (Ph.D. Dissertation, Osgoode Hall Law School, York University, 2007) [unpublished].

CONTRIBUTORS

MARTIN BLANCHARD is Coordinator and Assistant Director of the Centre for Research on Ethics at the University of Montreal (CREUM). He holds a Ph.D. in Philosophy from the University of Montreal and Paris IV-Sorbonne, where he studied different variants of the politics of recognition, in particular in the work of the German philosopher and sociologist Jürgen Habermas. His area of research includes deliberative democracy, advocacy groups, pragmatic ethics, politics of recognition, Aboriginal claims, philosophy of identity, philosophy of language, and moral and political philosophy.

ANGELA CAMERON is a Ph.D. candidate at the Faculty of Law at the University of Victoria. She is an SSHRC Doctoral Fellow, and a University of Victoria President's Research Scholar. Her doctoral work examines the safety and utility of restorative justice in cases of domestic violence. Her other research areas include criminal law, property law, family law, socio-legal methods, legal theory, and feminist approaches to law. She is a Research Associate at the FREDA Centre for Research on Violence against Women and Children at Simon Fraser University.

MARGOT HURLBERT is an Assistant Professor in the Department of Justice Studies and the Department of Sociology and Social Studies at the University of Regina. Margot graduated from the University of Regina with a B. Admin, and Osgoode Hall Law School with an LL.B. and finally an LL.M. in constitutional law after working for 12 years in private practice and seven years as the Assistant General Counsel for SaskPower.

STEPHANIE IRLBACHER-FOX is a lifelong NWT resident. For the past decade she has worked as a political advisor, researcher, and consultant to Indigenous organizations on self-government negotiations and implementation, NWT devolution, and related community-development processes. Stephanie is the principal of Fox Consulting. She holds a Ph.D. from Cambridge University, and is a Research Associate of the Canadian Circumpolar Institute and the Steffanson Arctic Institute, Iceland. Stephanie lives in Yellowknife with her spouse Andrew and their two sons.

THOMAS ISAAC holds a B.A., M.A., LL.B., and LL.M., and is a Partner at McCarthy Tétrault LLP, Vancouver, BC. Thomas is a nationally recognized authority in Aboriginal law and has published numerous books and many articles in the area, including *Aboriginal Law: Commentary, Cases and Materials* (3rd ed.). His published works have been cited with approval by numerous Canadian courts including the Supreme Court of Canada and the Federal Court of Appeal. He has appeared before the Supreme Court of Canada, the British Columbia Court of Appeal and other courts on Aboriginal legal matters. His practice is solely focussed on providing Aboriginal and constitutional legal advice to businesses and governments across Canada. He is a former Chief Treaty Negotiator for the Government of British Columbia and prior to that was Assistant Deputy Minister for the Government of the Northwest Territories responsible for establishing Nunavut. He has taught Aboriginal, constitutional, and business law at a number of universities across Canada and is a member of the bars of Alberta, British Columbia, Northwest Territories, and Nunavut.

WINIFRED KAMAU holds a Ph.D. from Osgoode Hall Law School, York University, Toronto, as well as LL.B. and LL.M. degrees from the University of Nairobi, Kenya. She is currently a Lecturer at the School of Law, University of Nairobi. She is also an Advocate of the High Court of Kenya and has practiced in various law firms in that country. Her research interests include alternative dispute resolution, cross-cultural conflict resolution, traditional and non-state justice systems, and gender and human rights.

JOHN MCKENZIE, a registered Professional Electrical Engineer, has an MBA in finance, and is a graduate of the Richard Ivey School of Business Executive program. John is also a sessional instructor at the University of Regina, Faculty of Business Administration, in Policy and Strategy, and International Comparative Industrial Relations. John's current position at SaskPower is Manager of Strategic Corporate Development, where he has had the opportunity to explore Aboriginal history, culture, and strategic issues.

DWIGHT NEWMAN is an Assistant Professor in the University of Saskatchewan, College of Law, where he teaches constitutional law, international criminal law, and a seminar course on Theorizing Aboriginal Rights. He completed his undergraduate degree at the University of Regina and his law degree at the University of Saskatchewan. He subsequently served as a law clerk to Chief Justice Lamer and Justice LeBel at the Supreme Court of Canada; he has also worked for the Canadian government and for human rights organizations in China and South Africa. He is a member of the Ontario bar. He most recently completed graduate work and his doctorate in legal theory at Oxford University in 2005, where he studied as a Rhodes Scholar and a SSHRC Doctoral Fellow. In his doctoral thesis, he sought to develop a theoretical account of collective rights. In his ongoing research, Professor Newman has recently commenced a three-year SSHRC Standard Research Grant program on Theorizing Aboriginal Rights.

TONY PENIKETT is the author of *Reconciliation: First Nations Treaty Making in British Columbia*, published by Douglas & McIntyre in 2006. Currently a Vancouver-based mediator and negotiator, Penikett was Deputy Minister of Negotiations and, later, Labour for the BC government. His 20-year political career included 18 years in the Yukon Legislative Assembly.

BILL RAFOSS is the chief investigating officer at the Saskatchewan Human Rights Commission, a position he has held for more than 20 years. Bill's chapter was the subject of his M.A. thesis in Political Studies, which he defended in 2005 at the University of Saskatchewan. He has presented on the topic of the intersection of Aboriginal rights and human rights at numerous conferences including the "First Nations, First Thoughts" conference in Edinburgh, Scotland. Bill worked previously for the Saskatchewan Legal Aid Plan and in the NGO sector. Under Bill's leadership, the Saskatchewan Human Rights Commission began using Aboriginal elders to resolve some human rights complaints.

MERRILEE RASMUSSEN is a lawyer in private practice in Saskatchewan where she has worked for many years, both on behalf of First Nations and on behalf of the Government of Saskatchewan regarding issues of Aboriginal and treaty rights. She has a B.A. and M.A. in political science from the University of Regina. Her M.A. thesis, *Democracy and the Saskatchewan Legislature* (1995) was awarded the Governor General's gold medal. She also has an LL.B. and LL.M. from the University of Saskatchewan. Her LL.M. thesis *Prairie First Nations and Provinces: Is there a Fiduciary Relationship that gives rise to Fiduciary Obligations?* (2001) addresses the fiduciary obligations of the provincial Crown to prairie First Nations. As legislative counsel and law clerk for the Saskatchewan Legislature from 1976 to 1988, the author is also familiar with the legislative process and the management of legislative information. She is chair of the Law Reform Commission of Saskatchewan and is personally involved in the Commission's work with the Uniform Law Conference of Canada in extending its Commercial Law Strategy to Aboriginal jurisdiction.

BRIAN SLATTERY is a Professor of Law at Osgoode Hall Law School, York University, Toronto. He has numerous publications dealing with Aboriginal and treaty rights and the history of Indigenous relations with the Crown. In other scholarly work, he has explored the philosophical foundations of human rights and the continuing vitality of the natural law tradition. He was elected to the Royal Society of Canada in 1995 for his contributions to the development of the law relating to Aboriginal rights.

BARBARA TOMPOROWSKI is a Senior Policy Analyst with the Ministry of Justice. Her work focusses on Aboriginal justice and restorative justice projects. She co-chairs the Federal-Provincial-Territorial Working Group on Restorative Justice, and helped develop the provincial Action Plan responding to the recommendations of the Commission on First Nations and Métis Peoples and Justice Reform. She teaches as a sessional lecturer with the School of Justice Studies at the University of Regina.

JOHN WHYTE is the Law Foundation of Saskatchewan Professor of Law at the University of Saskatchewan. He has held academic appointments at a number of Canadian universities including Queen's University, where he also served as Dean of Law, the University of Toronto, York University, and the University of British Columbia. Until recently he was a Senior Policy Fellow at the Saskatchewan Institute of Public Policy. He has edited and co-edited numerous books and is a co-author of *Canada. . . Notwithstanding*.

INDEX

A

Aboriginal children and youth 114-15, 154, 158, 164, 167-9, 175, 180, 212, 242n21

Aboriginal law 55-7, 59: as a separate source of law arising out of Aboriginal sovereignty 92, 100, 106; Aboriginal perspectives of law 88-9, 90-2, 98-9, 138, 149; subsumed as part of Canadian law 89, 91, 100, 103-4, 106; denied 110-11, 166, 168

Aboriginal peoples 20-1; history of 45, 83-4, 109-12; as prior occupants of Canada 21, 25, 64, 82, 84, 91, 96; experiencing social exclusion 12, 13, 45, 107-8, 112-15, 121, 127, 146; over-representation in criminal justice system 112-18, 144, 159, 163-5, 167; relationships with non-Aboriginal peoples 12-13, 85-6, 54, 108-9; historically 109-12, 121; in urban communities 63-4, 116, 149, 152, 168-9, 170-7, 178, 200, 211. *See also* cultural distinctiveness; cultural integrity; traditional

Aboriginal policy 13, 125, 139

Aboriginal rights 24, 27, 70, 71-2, 106, 148, 198; as generative rights 20-48, 50, 55-6; defined 24, 93; as historical rights 20-5, 27, 31, 33-5, 37, 43-8, 73, 91, 104, 146-7, 205; as intersocietal law 21, 33, 41, 70; policy of extinction of 69, 72, 73; specific versus generic rights 21-9, 122-3, 131, 137-8. *See also* self-government; *Van der Peet* test

Aboriginal sovereignty 86, 120, 123, 159, 234n51; as pre-existing 38, 46, 53, 82, 84, 106, 125-6; "two row wampum" 102-3, 145-6

Aboriginal title (right to ancestral territory) 27, 40-2, 69, 80-7, 96, 104, 169; defined 93, 148; recognized in *Calder* 64; redefined as uniform right (in *Delgamuukw*) 23, 24, 27, 40, 41-2, 125

Aboriginal women: and Bill C-31 168; *Criminal Code* too harsh in sentencing 16, 165-6, 172, 180; gendered experience of colonialism 165-6; as *Gladue* sentencing consideration 160, 163-5, 167-9, 179-80; as victims of crime 160, 170-1, 174

agreements-in-principle 128, 151; "difference" perspective on 73, 75-6, 78; "minority rights" perspective on 73-5, 76, 77, 78. *See also* Innu AIP; *Inuvialuit and Gwich'in* AIP

alcohol/drug abuse and addiction 114, 143, 145, 148, 154, 163, 171-2

alternative justice mechanisms 71, 136, 145, 149-50, 154, 157, 159, 164-5, 183, 190-1, 194; in Kenya 206, 212, 219; in Saskatchewan 182-6, 188-9; for sentencing 131, 158, 163, 174-5, 179; and youth extrajudicial sanctions 183-6. *See also* First Nations courts; restorative justice

assimilation 63, 104, 108-9, 124, 139, 146

Auditor General 132-3, 134, 186, 190

B

Bill C-31 168, 204

Bill C-41 164-5

C

Calder v. *A.G. (BC)* 64

Campbell v. *BC (A.G.)* 125

Canada v. *Benoit* 97, 125

Canadian Charter of Rights and Freedoms 17, 198-205; argument for application to First Nations 201-4, 205; First Nations opposition to application of 198-9, 199-201, 202; and the *Indian Act* 199, 204-5; and the Innu 71; and the Inuit 203-4; as limiting Aboriginal rights 198, 200-1; Supreme Court ruling on applicability to First Nations 199, 204-5; s.15 (equality rights) 204

colonialism 109-12, 117-18, 121, 127-8, 130, 141, 153, 160, 163-4, 194, 200; gendered impact of 16, 160-80; in Kenya 206-9, 216-19

common law: and rights 23, 24-5, 27, 41, 48, 91, 105, 144; absorbing Aboriginal laws 91-2, 95, 96-7

community-based projects 72, 115, 157, 183, 190, 211-12, 219-20

community development 17, 115-16, 118-19, 216, 219; maintenance of distinctive communities 24, 108-9, 121

community justice mechanisms 16, 149, 181, 183-4, 188, 192

Conservative government and health 8

Constitution Act, 1867 27, 50-1, 56, 122; s.91(24) (Indians and lands reserved for Indians) 51-2, 52-3, 71

Constitution Act, 1982 56; s.15 (equality rights) 204-5; s.25 (non-abrogation) 199, 201-2, 204; s.32(1) (application of *Charter*) 198, 203, 205; s.33 (notwithstanding clause) 200; s.35 (Aboriginal rights) 20-2, 24, 25, 34-6, 43-8, 51, 53, 80, 88-93, 96-7, 104-6, 122, 124, 136, 147-8, 151, 199, 204

constitutional law 125, 199: versus administration of justice 12, 16

Constitutional Questions Act 59-60

constitutional reform: and Aboriginal self-government 121, 219-20

constitutional space 83, 124

consultation: Crown obligation to seek Aboriginal 26, 46-7, 50, 70, 85-6, 92, 94-5, 147-8, 159

Corbiere, et al v. *the Batchewana Indian Band and Her Majesty the Queen* 199, 204-5

crime 49, 107, 136, 142, 214-15; and Aboriginal values 131, 147-8, 155-9, 176, 182, 186; causes of 114-119, 163, 164-5, 170-1, 173-4; reduction of 16, 49, 114, 142, 149, 153, 158, 184, 194; as social issue 8, 16, 107, 112-18, 128, 143, 146-7, 150. *See also* Aboriginal women; poverty

Criminal Code 148, 161, 183; too harsh in sentencing Aboriginal women 16, 165-6, 172, 180; and *Gladue* 155-6, 161, 179, 180; s.25 9; s.718.2 155, 161-2, 172

criminal justice system 13-14, 16, 49, 110, 112-18, 142-59; and accountability 186-7, 191; discrimination in 142, 143, 149, 170; over-representation of Aboriginal people in 112-18, 143-4, 147, 159, 163-5, 167; racial biases in 116-17, 143-5, 153, 161; separate Aboriginal justice system [proposed] 144-5, 148, 151, 153, 198; systemic failure to protect and reflect Aboriginal needs 142-5, 149-50, 159, 181. *See also* alternative justice mechanisms; First Nations courts; restorative justice; traditional concepts of justice

critical date 21, 22, 35-43, 45, 48: in *Delgamuukw* 40-2; for Métis (in *Powley*) 42-3; and treaties 38, 45

cultural distinctiveness 13, 21, 63, 75-9, 82, 108-12, 121, 123-4, 127; and identity 15, 70-1, 123-4, 126, 169; right of 15, 29, 70-1, 74, 93. *See also* traditional: practices

cultural integrity, right of 23-4, 28, 29-32, 39, 41, 50, 56, 93, 122-3, 126, 127 customary law 56-7, 124; Inuit 204; African 206, 207-10, 217-19; right to 24, 25, 27, 29, 39, 50, 54, 91

D

Delgamuukw v. *British Columbia* 23, 24, 27, 40-1, 82, 93, 104, 125; effect on rules of evidence 82, 96, 97-8

devolution of power 71, 73, 203

discrimination 199-200, 203; gender-/race-based 101, 108, 116-17, 143-5, 153, 161, 163-4, 165-72, 174-5; systemic 163, 167-9

dislocation 110-11, 112; as sentencing consideration 163, 168-9, 174

diversity, value of 74, 76-8, 79, 84, 87, 108, 121, 124, 217

E

economic development 15, 32-6, 58, 64-5, 69, 118-21, 127-8, 209, 213-14, 217; and good government 120-2, 128, 190, 207; of the Cree in Quebec 67, 68, 72, 73; socio-economic conditions and crime 150, 153-4, 163-4, 170, 181, 182

education 65, 68, 73, 78, 145, 157, 159, 168; Aboriginal control over 30-1, 57, 70, 73; levels of 114, 163, 171, 173, 175-6; public 184, 185, 190-1, 213

effective sovereignty of Crown. *See* sovereignty

equality rights 112, 148, 201, 204-5

evidentiary law 82, 89, 95-100, 173-5, 212-13

exclusion 12, 13, 45, 107-8, 112-13, 121, 127

F

federalism as Aboriginal concept 39, 127

Federation of Saskatchewan Indian Nations (FSIN) 151

fiduciary responsibility of federal government toward Aboriginal peoples 25-6, 28, 38, 52, 92, 94

First Nations courts 150, 153; circles of justice 71, 150, 156-8, 182-3, 185; Cree Court 145, 154, 159; Gladue Court 155-6; Tsuu T'ina (peacemaking) Court 155

First Nations Policing Policy (FNPP) 152, 153

H

Haida Nation v. *BC (Minister of Forests)* 25, 38, 46, 50, 85, 94-5, 104, 106

Harvard Project on American Indian Economic Development 49, 120

healing: Aboriginal perspectives on 14, 65, 155, 157-8, 182, 196

health 151, 171, 181; Aboriginal jurisdiction over 68, 70, 73, 78, 114, 213; social health 107, 109, 111-12, 113, 118, 119-20, 121, 128

honour of the Crown 25-6, 38, 46-7, 92, 94

honourable treatment: Aboriginal right to 24, 25-8, 37-8, 46-7

human rights 17, 112, 123, 124, 138-9, 203-4, 205, 214-15

I

identity 70-1, 74, 107, 108-111, 115, 148, 158, 163, 216; and language 31, 111, 146; preservation of 127. *See also* cultural distinctiveness

incarceration: alternatives sought for over-use 161, 163-5, 167; Aboriginal people over-represented in criminal justice system 112-18, 144, 159, 163-5, 167; as ineffective 143, 149, 159

Indian Act 52; and the *Charter* 199, 204-5; externally imposed 55, 139, 164; as sexist 166, 168, s.88 52

P

Paix des Braves 67-9, 71

police 14, 16, 116-17, 142; Aboriginal control over services 137-8, 141, 151, 152-3, 159, 198; biases of 143, 149; community policing 149; paucity of Aboriginal members on forces 117, 144-5, 149

poverty 114, 165, 169, 170, 174, 175, 177, 214, 219; role in crime 13, 112-16, 150, 153-4, 163-4, 170, 181, 182; and as factor in sentencing 163-64, 171; and self-government 120

Prince Albert Alternative Measures Program 185-6, 191, 193

prior occupation. *See* Aboriginal peoples: as prior occupants

public government 16, 112, 118, 120-2, 124-6, 128, 187

public policy 59, 61-3; model of justice 63-5, 66-7, 78

R

R. v. Blais 104

R. v. Badger 93, 97

R. v. Gladstone 93n24

R. v. Gladue 160-80; details 173-5; court's failure to consider parenting responsibilities 175; sentencing considerations (Aboriginality, addictions, discrimination, dislocation, poverty, victimization) 161-5, 167-9, 172, 179

R. v. Marshall 31-2

R. v. Marshall; R. v. Bernard 84, 106

R. v. Moyan 161, 172, 175, 176-7, 178

R. v. Norris 161, 170, 172, 175; court's failure to consider parenting responsibilities 178-9

R. v. Pamajewon 26-7, 124-5

R. v. Powley 42

R. v. Sioui 26, 28

R. v. Sparrow 25, 52, 81-2, 83, 88, 93, 95, 96, 106

R. v. Van der Peet 50, 82-4, 106. *Van der Peet* test 21-6, 33, 34, 42, 47-8, 96-9; ethnohistorical bias of 33; as ignoring post-contact interactions 21-2, 43; Supreme Court reshaping 22, 23, 42, 47-8, 82-3

racism. *See* discrimination: race-based

recognition of Aboriginal rights 44-6, 50, 68, 71, 91-3, 122, 125-8, 131, 136-9, 144

reconciliation between Aboriginal peoples: and the Crown 15, 21-2, 43-4, 45-6, 81-5, 104-6, 139, 146; and non-Aboriginal peoples 81, 84-5

reconciliation of section 35 and Aboriginal case law 80-7, 81-5, 104-6

religion: freedom to exercise 28-30, 39, 126, 203; prohibition of 146,

residential school 111, 126, 146, 164, 167, 175

restorative justice: definition 182-3; institutional/fiscal accountability of 186-8, 189-94, 195-6; principles of 71, 86, 143, 144, 149-50, 157-9, 161-2, 181, 213, 217; practical considerations of 181-5, 186-97; reporting requirements 186-9, 189-93, 195-6, 196-7; Saskatchewan statistics 183, 185-6, 191-2; service delivery models of (Saskatchewan) 183-4, 194-5; successes of 184-5, 189, 191

Royal Canadian Mounted Police (RCMP) 113, 137-8, 152

Royal Commission on Aboriginal Peoples (RCAP) 83, 144, 190; and the *Charter* 200, 202; on colonization 164; on "merged sovereignty" 103; on the scope of federal jurisdiction 52

Royal Proclamation of 1763 31

Index   287